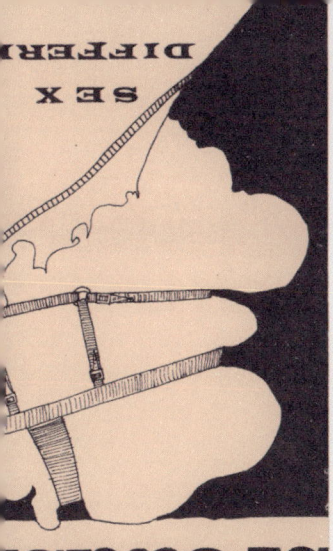

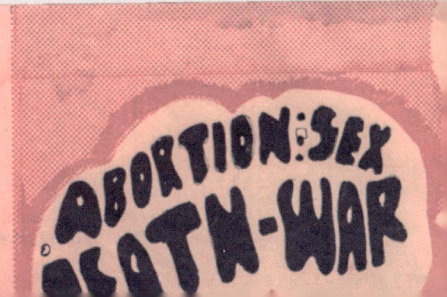

Jumping Sundays

The Rise and Fall of
the Counterculture in
Aotearoa New Zealand

'A compelling and important history of the counterculture in Aotearoa New Zealand. Meticulously researched and full of vivid details and memorable photographs, this book is an immensely readable and absorbing account of an important era in our recent history.'

Sue Kedgley

'Jumping Sundays is a fluent, vivid, coherent and succinct account of a period of turmoil during which major changes took place in New Zealand society, and of the ways we understood what that society was, what it had been, and what it could yet become.'

Martin Edmond

'An absorbing and serious account that is also terrific fun. Deft interviews and personal letters provide rollicking recollections together with many amazing new photographs and images. Bollinger puts a personal and personable stamp on this critical decade with words, sights and sounds that surprise and delight.'

Bronwyn Labrum

Jumping Sundays

The Rise and Fall of
the Counterculture in
Aotearoa New Zealand

NICK BOLLINGER

AUCKLAND
UNIVERSITY
PRESS

First published 2022

Auckland University Press
University of Auckland
Private Bag 92019
Auckland 1142
New Zealand
www.aucklanduniversitypress.co.nz

© Nick Bollinger, 2022

ISBN 978 1 86940 951 7

Published with the assistance
of Creative New Zealand

A catalogue record for this book is
available from the National Library
of New Zealand

This book is copyright. Apart from
fair dealing for the purpose of private
study, research, criticism or review,
as permitted under the Copyright Act,
no part may be reproduced by any
process without prior permission of
the publisher. The moral rights of the
author have been asserted.

Every effort has been made to trace
copyright holders and obtain their
permission. The publisher apologises
in advance for any errors or omissions
and would be grateful to be notified
of any corrections that should
be incorporated in future reprints
or editions.

Book design: areadesign.co.nz

This book was printed
on FSC® certified paper

Printed in Singapore
by C.O.S. Printers Pte Ltd

Cover & Contents page images: Clare Ward at The Great Ngaruawahia Music Festival, 1973. **John Miller photograph, private collection**

P. 4–5: Albert Park, 1969. **Max Oettli photograph, Alexander Turnbull Library, PAColl-1386-1**

In memory
of
Arthur Baysting

CONTENTS

	PROLOGUE	11
1	BACKWATER BOHEMIANS	27
2	RED SKIES AND YOUNG REBELS	47
3	ALTERED STATES	71
4	FREAK FLAGS, FREE LOVE	97
5	FREEING THE WORD	121
6	THE WAR AT HOME	157
7	AQUARIAN EXPOSITIONS	181
8	GIMME SHELTER	219
9	THE NEW SEEKERS	245
10	ROOTS AND BRANCHES	273
11	ROUZE UP!	287
12	BULLSHIT AND GELIGNITE	301
13	CHANGING VALUES	313
14	WHO KILLED THE COUNTERCULTURE?	341
	EPILOGUE	367
	NOTES	372
	SOURCES	385
	ACKNOWLEDGEMENTS	396
	INDEX	398

Albert Park, Auckland, 1969. Geoff Studd photograph, private collection

10 JUMPING SUNDAYS

PROLOGUE

On a Sunday afternoon in the spring of 1969, thousands of people defied Auckland city bylaws and came to party in Albert Park. A rock band played on the rotunda. Some people held hands, some danced alone, some sat under trees with guitars, flutes and bongos and made music of their own. They wore kaftans, ponchos and leather-fringed jerkins, floppy hats, headbands, beads and flowers. Poetry and political diatribes were delivered from a podium, improvised from an upturned tea chest. There were bikies, balloons, bubbles, sack races and a lolly scramble, lots of dogs and a pet possum. Someone brought a canoe and paddled it around the fountain, until it capsized. As the afternoon wore on there were joss sticks, skyrockets and what some will have recognised as the musky smell of marijuana.

It wasn't the first gathering of this kind in New Zealand, but it was, up to this point, easily the biggest. Here, on a seemingly vast scale, people who had been variously labelled as hippies, freaks, weirdies, radicals and dropouts were able to see and celebrate with a great many others who looked and acted a lot like they did. For those watching from the sidelines or looking at newspaper photos in the days that followed, the effect was quite the opposite. The revellers were a strange group whose lives, looks, beliefs and aspirations were evidently not only very different from their own but also a challenge to post-war New Zealand's social norms.[1]

Jumping Sundays, as the weekly Albert Park gatherings became known, had their origins in another park, another Sunday. Just a few blocks away, on the upper slopes of Queen Street, Myers Park was the only public place in Auckland where it was legally permitted to lecture or preach, play musical instruments, dance, or assemble to partake in any of the above. In the late sixties much of the activity in Myers Park had centred on the war in Vietnam. Protesters waved placards. Speakers decried New Zealand's involvement in the war and its powerful American allies. One group staged a hunger strike in support of an imprisoned protester, and stayed in the park for several days. But while opposition to the war was earnest, a distinguishing feature of this new kind of protest was the idea that such causes could, and should, be fought in a spirit of mischief and fun. Along with politics there would be songs, dancing, poetry and theatre. For some of the participants, most of whom were in their teens and early twenties, the politics were almost immaterial. Underlying it all was the idea that the world was on the brink of a momentous change, and this was a way to be part of it.

The Myers Park gatherings had been gaining force through the year. At first just a handful, then hundreds came, and soon the crowd had outgrown the venue. The players and dancers felt constrained by the park's steep narrow slopes. And there was the principle of free speech. Shouldn't you be able to speak your mind whenever and wherever you liked? The limits on gatherings were draconian and had to be challenged. So one Sunday, with little planning and no advance publicity, a group of several hundred left Myers Park and set off down the middle of Queen Street. The musicians carried their instruments, which included an iron-framed upright piano. The small number of police on duty in the city that day were taken by surprise. Assuming the marchers were headed for the United States Consulate in Customs Street, the site of several previous demonstrations, they hastily arranged a cordon at the bottom of Queen Street, but the marchers never reached it. Instead they made a right turn up Vulcan Lane in the direction of the much larger Albert Park, just across from the University of Auckland campus. A taxi driver, picking up the police on his CB radio, heard an agitated official exclaim, 'But sergeant, three hundred people can't just disappear!'

Albert Park was liberated.

Albert Park, Auckland, 1969. Geoff
Studd photographs, private collection

For the rest of that Sunday, and every other Sunday that year, the crowds would gather there. There was no conventional advertising, no notices in the paper or jingles on the radio, just word of mouth and a few Gestetner-printed flyers distributed around the streets. With each weekend the numbers grew, while police stood by with the onlookers. Among the guardians of law and order the consensus seemed to be that youth rebellion would be reluctantly tolerated, as long as it was confined to Sunday afternoons.

In many ways Jumping Sundays were like the local recordings of international songs often heard on New Zealand radio in the sixties: a cover version of something that had already happened in another part of the world and had taken a while to get here.

In California, the challenging of authorities over the use of public space had been going on for much of the decade, spearheaded by a growing alternative culture. A piece of unused land adjacent to

the University of California campus in Berkeley had been occupied by students and activists and declared People's Park, a place for frolicking and free speech—and, eventually, a violent confrontation with police. But the first such gathering to gain widespread attention had been a permitted event: the First Human Be-In, which in January 1967 had drawn forty thousand people to the grounds of the polo field in San Francisco's Golden Gate Park. Rock group the Grateful Dead had played, and poet Allen Ginsberg intoned pacifist chants. Over the following months, similar gatherings of longhaired, brightly clad youths took place in cities across America. To the mainstream media this signalled the arrival of a movement. A 1967 cover story in *Time* magazine attempted to define it:

> Its disciples ... are mostly young and generally thoughtful Americans who are unable to reconcile themselves to the stated values and implicit contradictions of contemporary Western society, and have become internal emigres, seeking individual liberation through means as various as drug use, total withdrawal from the economy and the quest for individual identity ...

Albert Park, Auckland, 1969. Geoff Studd photographs, private collection

They are predominantly white, middle class, educated youths, ranging in age from 17 to 25 (though some as old as 50 can be spotted). They feel 'up tight' (tense and frightened) about many disparate things—from sex to the draft, college grades to thermonuclear war.[2]

With a front-cover image crudely approximating the graphic style of a San Francisco psychedelic rock poster, and the strapline 'The Hippies—Philosophy of a Subculture', the *Time* story may have done more to promote the movement than anything the movement had yet done to promote itself—if it even *was* a movement. Ross Somerville, a student at Kaikorai Valley High School in Dunedin in 1967, tells me: 'I was radicalised by *Time* magazine, in my school library. These big articles and all these pictures with lots of colours. All this interesting-sounding music and all these interesting-sounding drugs.' The world seemed to be changing in new and exciting ways, and all around the world were young people like Ross, dreaming of being a part of it.

At the same time, the Vietnam War was provoking some of the biggest anti-war rallies the world had seen. These started in America and quickly spread to Europe, Australia, New Zealand. While the protesters were not solely young, longhaired, drug-taking, rock-revelling rebels, the prevailing impression was one of youth revolting against its elders. The message was clear: one generation was being enlisted to fight a war that another had started, and it was rising up in substantial numbers to say no—or to chant '1, 2, 3, 4, we don't want your bloody war!' But while Vietnam was the common cause that brought dissenters into the streets, the mood of disruption encompassed other issues as well, and these varied from nation to nation, city to city.

In Britain, students occupied the London School of Economics, bringing classes to a standstill as they protested a roll of injustices, from the racist policies of the Rhodesian and South African governments to the installation of security gates in the university buildings.

In Germany, students rose against authority under the leadership of the charismatic Rudi Dutschke, who drew parallels between the struggles of the Vietnamese people and the working classes of Europe.

In Tokyo, there were demonstrations against visiting American warships, while students occupied university buildings and university administrators summoned riot police to quell protests over misappropriated funds.

In Czechoslovakia, young longhaired Czechs would gather to hear the subversive experimental rock of local band the Plastic People of the Universe, and continued to listen in secret after the government revoked the band's licence to perform.[3]

In Mexico City, the staging of the Olympic Games became a focus for students angry with a repressive and patriarchal system, culminating in a massacre when troops opened fire on protesters, in the wake of which came the proliferation of a native hippie movement, the *jipitecas*.

And in Paris, in May 1968, French students combined with striking workers in acts of civil disobedience, bringing the country's economy to a standstill. Their demands included wage rises for workers and the rights of teenage students to sleep together.

Festivals were the flip side of protests: giant communal get-togethers, for the most part harmonious and conflict-free, where self-expression was central and rules were redundant. The Woodstock Festival of August 1969, which drew almost half a million people to a muddy field in upstate New York for what was promoted as 'three days of peace and music', was the exemplar: a forecast of what the world could be like after the rebellion had triumphed.

And there were attempts to create longer-term utopias which found expression in all kinds of re-imagined living arrangements, from urban crash pads to rural communes. Some people decided the whole Earth was their home, adopting a peripatetic lifestyle that would take them across continents and oceans.

Then there were the more inward pursuits which nevertheless connected the individual to this global movement. Some people explored spiritual disciplines quite different from those with which they were brought up. Eastern belief systems found favour, as seekers adopted practices such as yoga, meditation and non-attachment. Drugs such as LSD and marijuana were employed by some as tools to use in the spiritual search. Others saw drugs simply as a recreational alternative to the alcohol that was the sanctioned stimulant of mainstream society.

What all these different activities had in common was a rejection of things as they were. Young people were demanding to live their lives in ways of their own choosing. They challenged their parents' attitudes to war and peace, sex and traditional gendered roles, art, music and literature, education, the environment, politics, spirituality, work and domestic life. They had their own attitudes to these and would tie them together under one banner. As John Sinclair, the Michigan-based activist and manager of the rock band MC5, declared: 'Our art, the music, newspapers, books, posters, our clothing, our homes, the way our hair grows, the way we smoke dope and fuck and eat and sleep—it is all one message and the message is FREEDOM!'[4]

This call for freedom signified—in a phrase indelibly connected to the period—a change of consciousness. Whether achieved by drugs, meditation or other means, it implied a new way of seeing and experiencing the world: one that rejected a society governed as though human needs were purely technical. 'Science has got a lot going for it,' wrote Auckland-based mathematician and cosmological explorer Chris King in the second edition of *The New Zealand Whole Earth Catalogue*. 'It can make transistor radios, psychedelics and atom bombs. There must be something there, but it's next to useless as a guide to man. It ignores consciousness altogether.'[5]

The change would be defined and fought for in ways that varied from place to place, as groups in different countries experienced different shades of oppression and encountered different forms of resistance from the existing power structures. Yet all employed what American historian Eric Zolov calls 'an emergent globally shared repertoire of imagery, slogans, fashion statements and music that linked youth, psychically if not materially, to each other's struggles'.⁶

✱

New Zealand, too, had its struggles, and a version of this repertoire with its own distinctive character. That version is the one I have set out to record. It is the story of a group with an intense self-belief, acting in ways that often brought it into conflict with mainstream society. Though driven by high ideals, this group could also be blind to its own shortcomings, and the search for a new consciousness was not without its casualties.

Albert Park, Auckland, 1969. Geoff
Studd photograph, private collection

What compels me to tell this story? Born in 1958, I was a late boomer. While others were changing their consciousness I was still learning to read. And yet, as the sixties careened towards the seventies, I became increasingly aware that the adult world I was about to step into was being reshaped by people only a few years older than I was.

It was the music that first told me about it. The Beatles were singing that love could change the world, the Rolling Stones declared the time was right for a palace revolution. Jimi Hendrix's guitar playing just *sounded* revolutionary. There was something in the air, I wasn't sure what, but I wanted to be a part of it. By the time I got there, many revolutions had taken place, and not all of them had turned out as intended. This book is my way of understanding what happened in this country during those turbulent years, and why.

I started by reading what others had already written. I trawled through newspapers, magazines, letters, notebooks, diaries, memoirs, oral histories and Facebook groups. I pored over photographs, some of which appear in this book, met photographers who told me some of the stories behind the images, and tracked down people who had been part of those stories. Of the hundreds of names that appear in these pages, there are some it would be difficult to tell the story without. Political activists Tim Shadbolt and Sue Kedgley, the entrepreneur Alister Taylor, poet James K. Baxter, composer Jenny McLeod, and theatre-makers Sally Rodwell and Alan Brunton are so embedded in the public memory of the period that to ignore them would be to leave an obvious gap. Yet there were literally thousands of others who, in less visible ways, played vital roles. There could never be enough pages to tell the stories of every one of them, but the testimonies of those I spoke to are the heart of this book.

I found my informants by various means. Sometimes it was simply by mentioning in conversation an aspect of the project I was working on. 'My sister could tell you about that' or 'I have a friend who was there', I would hear, and an exchange of phone numbers or email addresses followed. Some people provided vivid accounts of particular moments, while there were others whose lives were so closely enmeshed in a sequence of events that they became recurring characters, popping up at intervals throughout these pages. Each one brought their own point of view. My task was to organise these into a greater whole. Occasionally my own memories and personal history found their way into the story, often in the context of events I had witnessed or heard about but not fully grasped the significance of at the time. It was by re-examining those experiences in the light of my subsequent discoveries that the answers to my questions, and the shape of this book, began to emerge.

I first learned the word 'counterculture' from Lenore Webster, my Sixth Form English teacher at Onslow College in Wellington. It was 1974. I was working on the school magazine, and she had remarked on the striking difference between the sports pages, with their stolid accounts of the First Fifteen's achievements, and the music section I was deliberating over, with its fanciful profiles of the school rock bands and illustrations of longhaired, glazed-eyed figures which my friend Tony Sayle had drawn in the style of American underground cartoonist Robert Crumb. 'It looks like the counterculture is going to be well represented,' she said, and I sensed her quiet approval.

I already knew I belonged with the longhairs, the rock musicians and anti-authoritarians, not the shorthaired rugby players whom my friends and I regarded as dullards at best, bullies at worst. I didn't know there was a name for us. And to be honest, I didn't much like it. Though I wore my hair down to my shoulders and, when I wasn't in school uniform, dressed in the same outfit of jeans, T-shirts and baggy jerseys as the rest of my social group, I fancied myself as a non-conformist. Still, I understood what she meant. If a culture is the beliefs and practices of a dominant group, then a group that opposes or challenges that culture is a *counter*culture. That sounded like us.

American social theorists had begun using the term in the 1950s in studies of delinquent gangs, but it was Theodore Roszak who introduced *counterculture* into the vernacular when he identified the emergence of 'a culture so radically disaffiliated from the mainstream assumptions of our society that it scarcely looks to many as a culture at all, but takes on the alarming appearance of a barbaric intrusion'.[7]

Roszak, an American, had spent part of the sixties in London, editing the magazine *Peace News*. His 1969 book *The Making of a Counter Culture* helped what was in many ways a group of disparate elements to see itself as an entity. The counterculture, as Roszak defined it, encompassed drug-taking, mysticism, rock music, political protest, communitarian experiments and more. His book was widely read, especially among those who thought they might be part of this barbaric intrusion, or liked the sound of it and were keen to know how they could join in.

By the late sixties, *counterculture* was in common use and remained so for much of the following decade, after which, for reasons that will be explored in this book, it began to slip into the past tense. It is a term that every interview subject I approached was familiar with, even readily identified with, though they came from a range of backgrounds and had spent the period engaged in a wide variety of activities. Some had blown up buildings, some had blown their minds; some made loud music, while others meditated in silence. Some had stood up for the rights of women, Māori and Pasifika. Others had generated alternative forms of theatre, music and printed media. The counterculture, when examined, can seem wildly diverse. As Roszak noted, a movement becomes harder to identify 'when one gets down to scrutinising the microscopic phenomena of history. At that level one tends only to see many different people doing many different things and thinking many different thoughts.'[8]

Two particular issues helped to unify this disparate group: nuclear weapons and the Vietnam War. Though both remained active issues throughout the period in question, the nuclear issue dominated the early period, Vietnam the latter. There was a broad agreement that both exemplified the moral bankruptcy of the dominant culture. A world that could devise such an effective means of destroying itself clearly had something wrong with it, and needed some sort of radical challenge, as did a superpower that would wage war against a people who were simply claiming the right of self-determination.

Not that all or even the majority of the counterculture took a close interest in politics. Some saw politics as another institutional straitjacket to be cast off. Yet the very existence of a counterculture could be seen as political, even when it expressed itself in personal ways. To grow your hair, experiment with drugs, explore forms of mysticism, live together without marrying, or leave the city to start a commune became, in their ways, political acts. It is by examining the sometimes surprising ways that such different ideas and actions intersected and influenced each other that the outlines of a movement appear, one made up of many parts.

Other words have been used almost synonymously with counterculture. When people refer to the hippie era, flower power, the underground, or even employ that impossibly sweeping catch-all The Sixties, it is usually as a kind of shorthand for the things Roszak called the counterculture. And there is a popular impression that in the sixties everything went countercultural. The decade is often reduced to a caricature, painted in fluorescent colours and captioned in psychedelic bubble writing, of a longhaired hippie in tie-dye and bellbottoms, smoking dope, listening to mind-bending rock music and protesting against the war. In fact, the counterculture was always a minority, though its impact was ultimately much wider. Nor did everyone who played a role in the counterculture conform to the caricature, though every hippie was, by definition, a part of the counterculture—along with the Beats, freaks, subterraneans, weirdos, revolutionary activists, communards, and other assorted dissenters from mainstream society. I'll mostly stick with Roszak's term because it has enough breadth to include them all.

The counterculture had a large pool from which to recruit. Around the end of the Second World War, as the servicemen returned home, women started having a lot more babies. While this was particularly noted in America, New Zealand's baby boom reached even higher levels per head of population. The boom, often credited to a general surge of post-war optimism, was not confined to the victor countries.[9] There was also an increase of births in Germany and Japan. After the economic hardship of the 1930s and the austerity of the war years, the 1950s were more affluent, and the boomers grew up enjoying the benefits. In America teenagers had their own cars, and around the country there were four thousand drive-in theatres where they could go to watch B-movies, buy junk food and make out. In Britain, the teenage mods who emerged from the middle and working classes in the early sixties could afford to buy high-fashion, tailored clothes. Young people were asserting their own style and a soundtrack to go with it. These developments did not go unnoticed by teenagers in New Zealand who, from the 1950s, were increasingly tuned in to British and, particularly, American teen culture.

The new affluence was still growing as the boomers left school and were stepping into adulthood. Their lives were already different from the lives their parents had led at a similar age. University education was

A pet possum in Albert Park.
Max Oettli photograph, Alexander
Turnbull Library, PAColl-1386-1

more widely available. So was work and money. There had never been such a range of consumer goods on offer. The world was not at war.

To the generation that had spawned them, the boomers seemed to have been blessed with unprecedented opportunities. They could enjoy all the material gains of their parents, and more. 'The lucky generation', more than one commentator would call them. So it came as a surprise when the boomers, or rather a significant group of them, appeared to reject suburban bliss in favour of a life that looked more like a suburbanite's view of poverty. This was the counterculture.

When and where the counterculture actually began is up for debate. Certain seminal events are often named as critical. One is the aforementioned Human Be-In at Golden Gate Park. Another is the International Poetry Incarnation held in June 1965 at the Royal Albert Hall in London—which was, in fact, organised by a New Zealander, John Esam. 'The Albert Hall reading was definitely the catalyst for the whole London underground scene,' asserts Barry Miles, who would start the influential countercultural magazine *International Times* the following year with the patronage of a twenty-four-year-old Paul McCartney. 'That was really the first time that the community got together, recognised each other and saw each other for what they were—some kind of countercultural group.'[10]

While it would be a stretch to conclude therefore that the British counterculture had its roots in New Zealand, Esam's story (one of many told in this book) demonstrates that countercultural energies were exported from here as well as imported. We didn't only do cover versions.

Throughout New Zealand's history there have been figures whose beliefs and actions could be seen as countercultural. There was Ray Hansen who in the early 1930s established the Beeville community in the Waikato, where he studied the teachings of Krishnamurti, and practised vegetarianism and free love. While imprisoned as a conscientious objector during the Second World War, Hansen hung out with Richard Greville Lord, an adherent of American sect the Israelite House of David, who according to Ian Hamilton 'cherished nature and surprised his friends with naked handstands'.[11] With his shoulder-length hair and abundant beard, Lord appears in photographs like a premonition of a 1960s hippie. And there was the British-born, Havelock-based Herbert Sutcliffe, who in the 1930s founded proto-New Age organisation The School of Radiant Living, an early disciple of which was a young Edmund Hillary. But while radically disaffiliated from the mainstream, such figures remained isolated, and it was not until sometime in the 1960s that enough connections between similarly isolated groups existed for them to be seen as a movement.

So if the counterculture has a dawn, however misty, does it have a twilight? As early as 1973 (or 4 A.W.: After Woodstock, as the date was given on the masthead), Dunedin periodical *The Counter Culture Free Press* was declaring 'the counter culture is failing' for allowing 'merciless exploitation from those within and without'.[12] In her history of the counterculture in Britain, published in the late 1980s, Elizabeth Nelson refers to the movement entirely in the past tense, and other studies since have conveyed a similar sense of its having come to an ignominious end. Then again, there are those who insist to me that the counterculture is alive and well, citing in evidence everything from intentional communities that continue after more than four decades to new fringe belief systems that have been able to thrive in the internet era.

For this story, I've focused mainly on a fifteen-year period, from the early 1960s to the mid-1970s. Though it was not until the late sixties that the word counterculture was widely used, and even later before anyone honoured it with the definite article, stirrings of a movement were clearly evident from the start of that decade. Likewise, by 1975 a number of decisive events had made it apparent that an era was coming to an end.

Each of the chapters that follow is broadly focused on a different aspect of the counterculture: protest, drugs, sex, music, religion, community, and so on. But there is a good deal of crossover between the chapters as well, and many of the themes overlap. There are also many connections between the individuals whose stories I tell, partly because New Zealand is a small place but also perhaps because interconnectedness was a part of the countercultural ethos.

When did the counterculture arrive in New Zealand? Even if one could agree on a particular moment—for instance the first Jumping Sunday in Albert Park—the events and individual journeys that led to that moment can still be traced back months, years, decades, perhaps even centuries. There will be a good deal of tracing trails through time in this telling. But to give it a nominal starting point, let's rewind to the dawn of a decade, the decade with which the counterculture is inseparably linked: the sixties.

BACKWATER BOHEMIANS

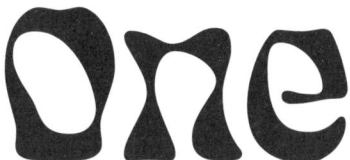

One

My sixties began at sea.

I was eighteen months old and on my way home to New Zealand on the passenger ship *Rangitoto* with my parents Conrad and Marei. They had gone to Britain early in 1959 in search of the cultural and intellectual riches of which they felt starved in their own country, expecting to stay two, three years, maybe longer. In London they attended premiere productions at the Royal Court Theatre, saw the latest Ingmar Bergman films and mime artist Marcel Marceau, marched against the atom bomb, heard philosopher Bertrand Russell speak and visited the progressive educator A. S. Neill at his school, Summerhill.

Suburban street, Porirua, circa 1960.
Duncan Winder photograph, Alexander Turnbull Library, DW1852-F

The pace of cultural life in Britain was overwhelming. Con wrote home: 'In theatre, cinema, politics, literary circles, everywhere events speed by so fast that you have scarcely made up your mind to see or do something than you have lost the opportunity. Massive protest movements well up overnight out of the big heart of the English working class against every dirty move of their overlords.'[1]

But the casual teaching work he was relying on had not been as regular as he had hoped, and their own one-year-old overlord put limits on how much time he and Marei could devote to loftier pursuits. Changing nappies, scrubbing spattered food off the floor of their rented Chelsea flat and rescuing the family wallet from the lavatory (my favourite receptacle) dominated their lives. And though they had been dazzled by the speed and vitality of London's cultural life, Con, a socialist and idealist, was appalled by how entrenched the British class structure seemed to be. In a particularly flamboyant letter he described 'the intolerable arrogance of the rich, the nannies wheeling great fat overfed congenital imperialists in prams as big as stage coaches …'[2]

New Zealand, by comparison, seemed still unformed, full of utopian potential. So after just a year away Con was returning to his former job at the Ministry of Works. He explained in an aerogramme, written from the ship on New Year's Eve and mailed to his in-laws from somewhere in the Caribbean, that he wanted to start a weekly left-wing newspaper. Marei had 'some fruitful looking thoughts about drama'. With the help of the Public Service Investment Society they would buy a house in Wellington. 'We have definite ideas about age and type of house, as well as of locality. Also boundless faith in the future.'[3]

'A GREY, FRIENDLY ENVIRONMENT'

What was this country they had run from, and to which they were now returning with such optimism?

In 1960 there were a little under two and a half million New Zealanders. About 154,000 were Māori. Despite the myth of the country's homogeneity, there were both cultural and economic divisions. The day-to-day life of, say, a rural Māori whānau such as the one Ans Westra would document in her controversial 1964 school bulletin *Washday at the Pa*, bore little resemblance to that of an urban Pākehā family in a suburb like Karori or Fendalton.[4] As the decade unfolded, the kind of life Westra depicts would become less common as Māori moved in unprecedented numbers from the country to the cities, drawn by a boom in manufacturing. In 1960, the Waitangi Day Act was passed, making 6 February 'a national day of thanksgiving in commemoration of the signing of the Treaty of Waitangi'. However, the Act did not provide for a public holiday, which Prime Minister Walter Nash said would be too costly and would only emphasise divisions that society should be trying to eradicate. 'We should not think of ourselves as Maoris or Pakehas, but rather as one people,' he said.[5] Yet the differences between Māori and Pākehā—in cultural values, economic status, health and crime statistics—would become only more pronounced.

Most New Zealanders had a roof over their heads, and the number of families owning their own homes was rising. Though only 403 people were registered as unemployed, almost ten thousand were in psychiatric institutions. The major cities were growing, and the farms were flourishing, with international prices for wool and dairy products at record highs. Incomes, too, were on the up. Families could mostly get by on a single wage, so while the man worked, the married woman usually stayed home, unpaid, to look after children, house and husband. Women were the nominal recipients of the Family Benefit, a weekly universal government grant of 15 shillings per child to assist with household costs. If you were a widow you were eligible for a special benefit, but the same did not apply if you were divorced, separated or a solo mother.

University intakes were also booming. In a couple of years' time a bursary system covering student fees and boarding costs would be introduced. Over the course of the decade, bursaries would increase and the number attending university would more than triple.

But there was also what Sandra Coney, looking back, identified as 'a strong strand of philistinism and anti-intellectualism', with academics and artists 'stereotyped as bearded, sandalled beatniks—failures when it came to the real business of being a New Zealand man'.[6]

And what did the real business of being a man involve? The national heroes were almost all sportsmen: Snell and Halberg with their Olympic medals for running, Hillary 'the bee keeper who climbed mountains'.[7] And, most of all, rugby players. Rugby, which became a game in the 1820s when someone at a posh school in England picked up a football and ran with it, had been played here for almost as long as Pākehā have been in the country. With its national team drawn from the best provincial players, there was a myth that the All Blacks were the embodiment of the country's social unity. This is despite the fact that only men participated in the game, and that when the national team went to play against the other most rugby-possessed nation, South Africa, Māori were not allowed on the field.

If New Zealand had a culture in which practicality and physicality were valued more than words and ideas, when it came to rhetoric men again dominated. In spite of having pioneered women's suffrage, sometimes touted as a measure of the country's egalitarianism, the New Zealand Parliament in 1960 included only four women among its eighty members.

Another mark of manliness was the ability to drink a lot of beer in as little time as possible. Public bars were female-free zones where beer was served by the jugful. Due to an anachronism left over from regulations introduced during the First World War, all pubs had to close at 6p.m. The hour between 5p.m., when men knocked off work, and closing time an hour later, was known as the six o'clock swill, during which pub-goers consumed as much beer as possible before staggering home to their families. To Dutch-born Boyd Klap, who arrived in New Zealand in 1951, the way men spoke to each other in the male-only public bars was strikingly different from the way he heard them speak in their homes. In Holland, socialising was traditionally done as a family unit, which naturally included men, women and children.[8]

The five-day working week was similar. Shops normally closed half an hour before the pubs, though they remained open for a few extra hours one night a week, usually Fridays, so you could buy the things you might need over the weekend: oil for the lawnmower, paint for the shed, white bread for sandwiches after the game. Then they shut their doors and didn't reopen until Monday.

But if few people engaged in paid work on weekends, they found plenty to keep them busy. After a year in New Zealand in the late 1950s, American educational psychologist David Ausubel would observe: 'I have never seen any people tackle sport, gardening or household projects with greater energy or enthusiasm.' As for their diligence as wage-earners, he noted that 'the forty-hour week and morning and afternoon tea are observed with scrupulous religiosity'.

Ausubel saw a people proud of their country's apparent egalitarianism and 'fond of contrasting their conceptions of equality' favourably 'with those of the British'. But he found the society insular, with 'a strong undercurrent of repressed hostility', and noted a 'coolness toward strangers', except in Māori homes where he had 'precisely the opposite feelings', discovering that in those places 'the guest is king'. Among Pākehā he noted an 'authoritarian, moralistic and punitive approach to children' reminiscent of Victorian England, and remarked on 'the apparent paradox of an advanced Welfare State coexisting with an essentially mid-Victorian social ideology'. Male drinking habits he found 'suggestive of prolonged adolescent revolt against the authoritarianism of their secondary school days …'[9]

These were some of the same traits visiting English writer and proto-countercultural figure Anna Kavan had noted more than a decade earlier. 'I don't like the set-up between the sexes,' she wrote, '…the men getting together around the bottles and the women getting on with the chores. The men worrying about the Labour Government and the women worrying about something in the oven.'[10]

'A grey, friendly environment' was how the country appeared to Boyd Klap, 'where the men were very poorly dressed and the women were overdressed. The women with the blue and the pink berets with a pin through it … and the guys—brown shoes with grey trousers, and often pullovers. But I don't think it was grey in terms of grey trousers. It was grey in terms of the buildings and the streets and the six o'clock closing and going home and talking about sport only and not international affairs or politics.'[11]

Though there was not yet a counterculture as it would come to be known, almost any kind of cultural activity might, against this grey backdrop, have seemed countercultural. The country's first National Orchestra had been founded only after the Second World War, and included a number of recent immigrants and refugees from Europe. Classical music was part of a cultural package these new New Zealanders brought with them, along with an appreciation of poetry, painting, architecture and decent coffee.

Modern thinkers such as the Austrian architect Ernst Plischke and Berlin-born town planner Gerhard Rosenberg had brought innovative ideas about society and housing. The Czech immigrant Mirek Smisek was showing for the first time that a New Zealander could be a full-time, independent ceramicist. Dutch-born Eelco Boswijk in Nelson and German Odo Strewe in Auckland had recently opened cafés, Chez Eelco and Babel respectively. In Wellington in 1957, British-born Fabian socialist Roy Parsons had opened Parsons Books in the iconic Massey House on Lambton Quay, designed by his friend Plischke. The shop included a café, run by the Jewish refugee Harry Seresin, where customers were encouraged to pass the time with coffee and conversation. Goulash and apple strudel were on the menu. To these exotic aesthetes the arts were alive. Attuned to innovations, they were natural allies and mentors to the burgeoning local Bohemia, while their baby-boomer offspring would grow up to be bohemians almost by default.

In 1950, John O'Shea and Roger Mirams had launched Pacific Films in Wellington. This would not only confront New Zealand with a somewhat critical representation of itself in the feature films of O'Shea, but also offer both a training ground for creative artists and sanctuary for non-conformists. Earlier still, Denis Glover's Caxton Press and Bob Lowry's Pilgrim Press helped the careers of New Zealand poets and novelists, going on to publish the likes of Janet Frame, Frank Sargeson, Allen Curnow and James K. Baxter. Around the same time a bohemian and predominantly gay scene revolved around the Queen Street studio of Auckland filmmaker Robert Steele, who had arrived from Australia in the late 1920s and, with Rex Harris, operated a lively salon that attracted dancers and theatre performers.[12]

Despite such noble enterprises, Kiwis committed to a life in the arts tended to dwell on the margins, both socially and economically, and were dismissed as dreamers or elitists. When future filmmaker Geoff Murphy finished school at the end of 1956, he wanted to be a jazz trumpet player or abstract artist, but there seemed no way to make a living from either option. His parents insisted he take up a cadetship with the New Zealand Railways. As Ausubel noted: 'Tolerance for non-conformity and unorthodox opinions is relatively low, practically all newspapers tend uniformly to present the same conservative point of view, and vigorous controversy about significant issues is surprisingly sparse.'[13]

The Cold War between the US and Soviet Union that had begun as the superpowers jostled for power and influence after the Second World War entered its second phase with the nuclear arms race — with the space race as its entertainment division. Despite New Zealand's emotional ties to Mother England, it had become evident that Britain, weakened by the war, could no longer be relied on to defend its far-flung empire. Increasingly bound to America, New Zealand's government bought into its anti-communist rhetoric. In 1951, a long and bitter dispute saw waterside workers vilified and branded as communists by the recently elected National government. The watersiders had struck for better pay. The government, arguing that the strikers were putting the country's vital export trade in jeopardy, declared a state of emergency, granted sweeping powers to the police and made it an offence to assist strikers in any way. Even to provide food for the strikers' families was deemed a crime. After the strike was crushed, industrial action and public protest of any kind were scarce for more than a decade.

The New Zealand Security Service (later renamed the New Zealand Security Intelligence Service, and generally referred to as the SIS), modelled on Britain's MI5, was established in 1956 with a brief to combat the perceived growth of Soviet intelligence operations down under.[14] Though its chief role seems to have been snooping on Eastern Bloc representatives in New Zealand at the behest of its powerful American and British allies, it also involved surveilling any citizens with socialist sympathies, one of whom was my father.

Also coming under state scrutiny were teenagers, particularly those growing up in new housing settlements like those in the suburbs of Upper and Lower Hutt, where reports of 'sexual immorality among juveniles' had spurred an urgent government inquiry.[15] The result was *The Report of the Special Committee on Moral Delinquency in Children and Adolescents* (the Mazengarb Report), a copy of which was sent to every family home in the country. Chaired by lawyer and failed National Party candidate Oswald Chettle Mazengarb, and comprised of a health professional, a boys' school headmaster, the chairman of the Junior Chamber of Commerce, and two members of an Inter-Church Council on Public Affairs, the Special Committee on Moral Delinquency applied a conservative moral code to its findings. It reported that 'in many cases girls, by immodest conduct, have become the leaders in sexual misbehaviour and have in many cases corrupted the boys', and that 'nearly one-third of the delinquent children whose cases were considered by the Committee belonged to homes where the mother worked for wages'. 'Fathers are not free from blame,' the report hastened to add. 'As breadwinners they have necessarily to be away from home throughout the day, but they have opportunities in the evenings and at week-ends to identify themselves with their children's interests and activities.'[16]

While the report recommended that the message 'crime must never pay' should be featured more prominently in radio serials, there was also a campaign, waged from high places, against the leisure and entertainment forms many teenagers preferred. Gordon Mirams, chief film censor until 1959 (and brother of Pacific Films' Roger Mirams), made clear his distaste for Hollywood cinema and preference for British movies. He banned the 1953 Marlon Brando film *The Wild One*. (It would remain banned in New Zealand, despite repeated appeals, until 1977.) Historian Gary Whitcher suggests that gatekeepers such as Mirams 'based their objections to American culture on the grounds that they were acting as the nation's moral and cultural guardians', believing that 'a "civilized" middle-class imbued with cultural authority should exercise a hegemonic aesthetic influence within society'.[17]

Then there was music. Since rock'n'roll wiggled its way onto the world stage in the second half of the 1950s, it had been largely absent from the government-monopolised radio stations, just as jazz, the other major African-American-derived popular music style, had been in the preceding decades. The New Zealand Broadcasting Corporation (NZBC) was modelled on the principles of the BBC with, as Whitcher puts it, 'its stern, paternalistic emphasis on "high" culture as the instrument for the moral and cultural improvement of the citizenry'.[18]

Journalist Gordon Campbell, whose first job on leaving school was in the NZBC, remembers the prevailing attitude in the early sixties as being: 'If we have to expose the children to this stuff let's limit it to the *Lever Hit Parade*, and entrust the paternal task of supervision to a respected elder, such as Selwyn Toogood.'[19] Toogood was well known as the genial host of radio game show 'It's In the Bag', which began in 1954 and continued as a television series until Toogood's retirement in the 1980s.

Completing this trinity of unholy influences was the comic book, along with various youth-oriented magazines and 'pulp fiction' of the kind filmmaker Quentin Tarantino would parody in the 1990s. While the Mazengarb Report acknowledged that many of these influences 'cannot be rejected under the law as it at present stands because that law relates only to things which are indecent or obscene', it noted that all the examples the committee had examined were 'objectionable in varying degrees'. [20]

Paradoxically, this view was shared by hard left-wingers like the communist Elsie Locke, whose antipathy for American influence of any kind put the left in a moral alliance with the conservative, right-wing Mazengarb. Not that New Zealand was a welcoming place for communists either, as the activities of the SIS attest. Locke was another who was being spied upon by the state.

Slightly more sympathetic to this 'youth in revolt' was A. E. Manning, author of *The Bodgie: A Study in Abnormal Psychology*. Manning's study, published in 1958, was of a focus group of thirty bodgies and widgies: the Australasian term for what in Britain were called rockers or Teds, in America greasers, and in both juvenile delinquents. Essentially, these are the same kids targeted by the Mazengarb Report. To Manning, the rebels were simply 'expressing the emotional thinking that has been developed by their own experience of life ... in a neurotic world, a world that has lost too many of the eternal verities in an insane scramble in the service of Mammon'.[21]

'THE ICY DAWN OF THE SIXTIES'

In 1960, to mark the start of the new decade, the *New Zealand Listener*, a weekly magazine published by the state-owned broadcasting corporation, and combining radio listings and related content with some social, political and arts coverage, attempted to take the existential temperature of the nation. A twenty-four-year-old actor interviewed for a feature headed 'Our Life and Times' might have been one of Manning's rebels. 'I'd rather be unhappy than bored,' he said. 'I believe people are terribly bored and there's not much I can do about it right now. There's this overwhelming emphasis upon conformity — and I think we could do with some other god than money.'[22]

The notion of the 'angry young man' had recently entered the popular imagination via a new school of disaffected writers from the British working class, and the *Listener* seemed to have caught one, live and local. 'If a person is not upset these days there's something wrong,' the malcontent continued. 'He's either ignoring the facts or he just can't be bothered. In gaining materially we seem to be losing in personal capacity and energy. People who emerge from the chaos of deprivation seem to have more drive and life and personality. We are like the tigers in the zoo, who are well-fed, toothless and lazy. But I don't see what we can do.'

Yet his appeared to be a lone dissenting voice. Other youths interviewed for the article expressed mostly mild contentment and bland resignation. Said a sixteen-year-old: 'I've no real worries; I like everything about life. I don't worry about politics and things like that.'

'There's a threat of war,' shrugged an eighteen-year old, 'but there's always been that.'

'I'm content to be just me,' said a boy of sixteen. 'I just take everything as it comes.'

'Wider things are a bit beyond me,' said a youth of nineteen. 'It's no good worrying about them; they seem so far away.'

One interviewee looked forward to owning a sports car. 'I'd want happiness before success,' said another, 'but I'd want material success a close second.'[23]

Aboard the *Rangitoto*, my parents contemplated their return to New Zealand and the life they wanted for their children. Their own childhoods had been spent on opposite edges of Wellington's Town Belt—Conrad in Khandallah, Marei in Oriental Bay—where bush tracks led to adventures and the beach was just down the road. Even in the cities there was room to roam. The 'quarter-acre section', established in the early days of colonisation as the optimum size for a suburban plot, remained the norm. 'A great place to bring up children' was a coveted national endorsement.

'Bomb Tests Broke Monotony of Life' read a headline in Wellington's *Evening Post* during the first week of 1960, as our family sailed towards home. It was a human interest story of another New Zealand family, recently returned after two bleak years on Fanning Island in the northern Pacific that had been enlivened only by the nuclear tests they could observe taking place on Christmas Island some 300 kilometres away. In New Zealand, the monotony of life would be broken this year with the arrival of television. Initially it started at 7 p.m., and you could watch until 9 p.m. if you were one of the few thousand people with access to a licensed TV set and lived within range of Channel Two's Auckland transmitter. Wellington and Christchurch wouldn't get TV for another year, and Dunedin not until the year after that. Tuning in on the first few nights, you might catch an early episode of the 1950s British series *The Adventures of Robin Hood*, a documentary on salmon farming in Scotland, or a locally taped performance of the Howard Morrison Quartet, all in grainy black and white. Meanwhile, BOAC was advertising 'jet services to all continents— five services weekly from Sydney', and Smith & Brown's was offering trade-in deals on radiograms, refrigerators, washing machines and vacuum cleaners.

With an increasing number of things to distract them from the burdens of domestic life, many New Zealand citizens in 1960 were relatively untroubled, yet there was a muted but persistent air of repression which might have given anyone with an imagination, or a different set of ideals or an aversion to authority something to rebel against. 'The decade of the sixties has opened in such a way that those in New Zealand who write or live close to the current of poetry as a social, spiritual or creative force must view the prospects for the poet and his art with some apprehension,' Louis Johnson worried in his essay 'The Icy Dawn of the Sixties', published later that year.[24]

A CIRCLE OF INTENSE LIGHT

In 1960, pop stars had names like Ricky, Frankie and Connie, and were famous for their hits and their hairstyles, not their insights or intellects. Teenagers cut pictures of their pimple-free faces from magazines and pinned them to bedroom walls; they didn't memorise their idols' lyrics as though these were the wisdom of sages. There was no Bob Dylan, at

John Esam, 1965. John 'Hoppy' Hopkins
photograph © 1965, Estate of J. V. L. Hopkins

least not as far as anyone knew outside of a tiny Minneapolis folk music scene. John Lennon, Joni Mitchell, Mick Jagger and Leonard Cohen were likewise unknown. But there were poets. For the romantic and rebellious, poetry occupied the place that, by the end of the decade, would be largely filled by the music of rock stars.

You could tell just by looking at him that John Esam was a poet. Mark Young saw him for the first time in the late 1950s and never forgot it. 'I was sitting on the bus on my way home from school. Then John appears, escorting a lady friend to this same bus, dressed totally in black, plus shades, black hair, not sure if he had a beard. I had no idea who he was, but what an impression he made on me.'[25]

'He was tall and thin, with thick lustrous black hair which he combed frequently, and had a pleasing voice,' recalled Peggy Garland. 'He liked to think of himself as a dandy, dressing immaculately all in black. He was not handsome, since he was too thin and pale, his lips too narrow, his nose too sharp. But he had wonderfully expressive dark eyes, often demoniacal, always tremendously alive and expressive, sometimes gentle.'[26]

John Esam had come to Wellington from Hawke's Bay with a thirst for experience. His mother, who was French and well read, expected him to become a barrister, and he dutifully enrolled at Victoria University to study law, but he was drawn to more existential questions. Catholic teachers in Hawke's Bay had fed his love of literature. Now, with the capital's libraries and bookshops at his disposal, he immersed himself in the absurdism of Camus and Ionesco, the proto-existentialism of Dostoevsky, and the symbolist poetry of Rimbaud who, more than any nineteenth-century writer, foreshadowed the psychedelic seekers of the 1960s in his pursuit of visions through 'systematic derangement of the senses'.[27]

At occasional arthouse screenings Esam beheld the poetic realism of European cinema. He especially identified with the character of Baptiste Deburau in Marcel Carné's *Les Enfants du Paradis*, played by the mime artist Jean-Luis Barault. When Esam danced, which he did with a double-jointed grace, he incorporated gestures picked up from the mime. He appeared serious, with an element of sadness about him. He had already begun writing what would be his life's work, a cycle of poems which he called *Orpheus, Eurydice*.

He loved jazz, both for its sensory and its cerebral qualities. He listened to Miles Davis on disc, and Dizzy Gillespie and Sarah Vaughan in concert when they played at the St James Theatre, Wellington, in October 1960. He formed a friendship with Ron Polson, a local jazz singer. Polson, more a hedonist than a seeker, introduced him to marijuana. Esam would try numerous other substances too, but unlike the hedonistic Polson he was always in pursuit of visions rather than just stoned kicks.[28]

Years later, after he had left New Zealand, Esam described one such vision, perhaps it was even an epiphany, in a letter to Garland:

> When I was stumbling down the hill below Victoria University long ago, going to sleep from the nembuttal [sic] I had taken, I lent against a fence for a moment and the darkness closed in until there was a circle of intense light about me. I was looking down a tunnel at a field. Then I heard a voice coming through the grass, the tree in the corner of the field — Nature — calling my name, 'John ... John ... Come ... Come ...' beckoning me. The life went out of me into that world; I possessed nothing of mine any more, no talents, no personality, possessions, no life of my own ... but the tree, the grass, the colours I could see became incredibly radiant. I had not lost anything, I had just gone from myself into Nature's world. Well, I considered this for awhile, then straightened up and went down the hill to find a chemist, a florist and a stomach pump, came out of the hospital ward and left for England.[29]

While John Esam was considering the radiance of nature's world, another poet in a nearby suburb was finding his voice. David Mitchell was born in 1940, grew up in Karori and Aro Valley, and went to Wellington College. Shakespeare's sonnets 'made immediate sense, were wise and immediately attractive'.[30] At nights he would tune in to 'Rhythm on Record', the jazz show on 2YA presented by the eccentric, encyclopaedic broadcaster Arthur Pearce, under his radio name,

Turntable. He bought a pair of brushes and played jazz drums on the kitchen table. He read the French poets—Villon, Baudelaire, Rimbaud. By the time he left school in 1957 Mitchell had produced a sheaf of poems which survive in title only but show the influence of jazz and the Beats: 'The Casa Pepe Stomp', 'The Christchurch Ferry Blues', 'Wailin' at the Casa Fontana', 'Tete a Tete Table Talkin' Hand Jive Blues'.

He went to Victoria University in 1958 and graduated from Teachers' College in 1960. He read *On the Road*, Jack Kerouac's definitive novel of the Beats, and like its protagonist Dean Moriarty he was restlessly seeking ... something. Writing to girlfriend Anna Mirams (daughter of chief film censor Gordon Mirams, the man who banned *The Wild One*), he identified his mission: 'I must explore my own inner universe, that strange exciting country beyond the soul, and in some degree attempt its expression.'[31]

In January 1962 he left for Europe. He went to visit Anna in Paris; then on to Spain, France and Germany, arriving in London in the autumn. He moved into a large old house in East Finchley 'with a bunch of Bohemians and eccentrics, all artists or students'.[32] One night someone brought to the house a young, little-known American folk singer on his first visit to London. Perched on the edge of Mitchell's bed, Bob Dylan listened to the New Zealand poet read from his work, then offered a piece of advice: get a harmonica.[33]

By this time John Esam was also in Europe, though whether he and Mitchell ever crossed paths is unclear. In 1963, Mitchell married Elsebeth Nielson, a Danish au pair working in London. By the end of the year, Mitchell had returned to Wellington with Elsebeth.

FOLK, JAZZ AND EXISTENTIALISM

Bohemians didn't listen to pop music, or if they did they didn't take it seriously. The delinquent youths of the Mazengarb Report might have gone on to become fans of Elvis Presley, but to the discerning boho Elvis was just a commercialised product of the capitalist machine. Johnny Devlin, Elvis's real gone local epigone, was of even less interest. There were three types of music they found meaningful: classical, folk and jazz. Though classical music is old music by definition, its audience and practitioners in New Zealand tended to be modern-minded progressives.

Folk music had long been championed in left-wing circles as 'the people's music', and was played in coffee houses such as Wellington's Monde Marie. To the Left it represented authenticity and a stand against mass culture. Though some of the local folk singers sought out material from local history such as the gold rush of the nineteenth century, most drew from British and American songbooks, notwithstanding the fact that local interpreters seldom if ever had any authentic experience of mining, moonshining, murder or any of folk's other quintessential themes.

The Monde Marie was run by Mary Seddon, freethinking granddaughter of former Premier Richard Seddon. Travelling through Europe in the late 1940s, she had been struck by the way folk music seemed an integral part of every community she visited. In Austria and France it rang out of coffee bars. In Portugal, *fadistas* — singers of the traditional fado music — had their own tavernas. Returning to New Zealand in 1950, the contrast between romantic Europe and utilitarian New Zealand weighed down on her even before she had left the ship. 'Out of the porthole … I saw corrugated iron,' she remembered. 'I turned my face to the wall and thought "I can't take it … I can't go back to it." That feeling of despair.'[34]

Though Seddon had no previous experience in hospitality, the coffee bar she opened on the corner of Roxburgh and Majoribanks streets was a successful attempt to fill a cultural gap. With fishing nets draped from the ceiling and wine-bottle candelabra, the Monde Marie evoked the ambience of the fado tavernas, while the menu offered the eclectic exotica of Cona coffee, cheesecake and chilli con carne. Local folk singers played six nights a week. A favourite was Nick Villard, a former ship's bosun from London, whom Seddon recalled as 'incredibly good looking. Nick never really had to look for a place to sleep. Those beautiful, almond-shaped blue eyes …'[35]

The Monde Marie became the go-to place for visiting musicians. Theodore Bikel, Tom Lehrer, Josh White, Judy Collins and Ravi Shankar all passed through. When Shankar, having been offered a choice of coffee or whisky, requested a cup of tea, kitchen staff were sent into the neighbourhood in search of a teapot. The steaming brew eventually placed in front of the sitar star was, he declared, the worst he had ever tasted.[36]

As the sixties got underway, the coffee bars saw traditional balladry supplanted by modern songs in a folk style, often political in content. The leading international suppliers of these were Bob Dylan and his angel-voiced inamorata Joan Baez. Monde Marie regular Max Winnie was one of the first local folk singers to pepper his set with Dylan songs. Wellington trio the Folkestone Three recorded 'Blowin' in the Wind' in 1963, the same year Dylan's own recording was released, and it was played fifteen times by the NZBC.[37]

John Esam, before his departure for Europe, was less likely to be found at the Monde Marie than the Mexicali, an open-late café with a similarly European ambience that sometimes hosted live jazz. Esam and fellow bohos would hold court, dressed in tight black clothes, with goatee beards and dark glasses, providing an exotic sight for more staid locals. 'The old burghers would go in there at night if they had been to the pictures and really felt they had had an adventurous twist to the evening,' recalled Robert Jones.[38]

Jazz, especially in its most advanced form, bebop, was sophisticated and exclusive. Invented and perfected by black Americans, it was like the language of a secret society. It was the music Kerouac's characters fetishised in On the Road. It was the music that drummer Lachie Jamieson had brought back with him from America, along with a heroin habit. Originally from Whanganui, Jamieson had spent time in Chicago in the early 1950s, where he soaked up as much music as he could and jammed on nightclub bandstands with first-generation bebop players, including the superlative saxophonist Sonny Rollins. Eventually deported from the US as an overstayer, Jamieson turned up in Auckland in 1955, 'a loose cannon with a lot of energy', as pianist Mike Nock would describe him.[39] But his first-hand knowledge and feel for the music was an inspiration to anyone who spent time with him.

Weaving a wilful path through the jazz, poetry, art and drug scenes of Auckland and Wellington during this period, usually clutching a violin case, was a small, blonde-haired bohemian calling herself Anna Karina Hoffmann. She was actually Lorna Jenks, a classical music student from Papatoetoe, but she possessed a strong sense of adventure and vivid imagination, and by her mid-teens was living as though Queen Street was a place as exotic and romantic as her concocted name.

'My desires and ambitions were simple enough,' she would write years later. 'I wanted to take music lessons at the Sorbonne, drink absinthe in nightclubs with Apache dancers, and sketch patrons for pocket money. I wanted to starve in a freezing garret in Montmatre [sic] ... I bought Balzac, borrowed A Taste of Honey and bought a second-hand copy of Les Fleurs du Mal in French.'[40]

In the back room of Somervell's Milk Bar, where corduroy and duffel-coat-wearing intellectuals gathered on Friday nights, she rubbed shoulders with painters Colin McCahon and Michael Illingworth, the art curator Peter Webb, writers Kevin Ireland and Frank Sargeson, and printer Bob Lowry. 'This was the first place in Auckland where one could find some kind of genuine bohemian life. The atmosphere was stimulating and the coffee was excellent.'[41]

Sometimes she would accompany the Somervell's crowd to the Golden Dragon in Greys Avenue for a Chinese meal and more talk, or to the Hi Diddle Griddle in Karangahape Road to hear live jazz. She had a propensity for being in the same place as trouble. She was sitting in Somervell's, perusing an issue of Soviet Weekly, the afternoon in 1955 when nineteen-year-old usherette Sharon Skiffington was shot dead in the aisle by her spurned lover Frederick Foster. Not long after, Anna left for Sydney, ostensibly to study music, but while there she was introduced to opium, initiated into a witch's coven and imprisoned for vagrancy. Deported back to New Zealand, she was arrested again, this time for swearing in Wellington Railway Station. 'I am an existentialist,' she told the magistrate, by way of explanation.[42] In 1960 she spent six months in jail for selling marijuana to an undercover police officer. Further arrests followed, one for selling 'sex chocolates': imported sweets supposedly impregnated with an aphrodisiac. Then there was

Anna Hoffmann and Michael Illingworth fail to attract police attention, Vulcan Lane, Auckland, 1961.
Leon Lesnie photograph, private collection

Bruno Lawrence swings, Geoff Murphy takes five, circa 1965. Barry Clothier photograph, Alexander Turnbull Library, PAColl-7031-1-03

the time she and her housemate Billy Farnell, a gay, professional pianist who kept a pet monkey, were apprehended under a full moon in the bush beneath Auckland's Grafton bridge, surrounded by candles and animal skulls, apparently about to make a blood sacrifice of a goat.

If Anna Hoffmann was a partly fictional character of her own creation, she had an unsolicited collaborator in the tabloid *New Zealand Truth*, which reported her exploits in gleeful, lurid headlines such as 'Black Mass Allegations in Sydney', 'She Sold Reefers to a Cop' and 'Gruesome Goings On in Grafton Gully'. When she wasn't explaining herself to the courts, she continued to expand her bohemian circles. In Wellington she hung out at the Mexicali, where her friends included musicians Bruno Lawrence and Geoff Murphy.

Growing up, Geoff Murphy had learned classical piano but switched to trumpet after hearing Louis Armstrong. In 1957 he met music student John Charles — a brilliant pianist and budding composer — and David Lawrence, known to everyone as Bruno, who played drums with a wild intensity that matched his personality. The three became foundation members of the Victoria University Jazz Club. Bruno never actually enrolled as a student but 'attended any lectures that took his interest, and slept under the stage in the campus theatre where the Jazz Club met'. Murphy remembered: 'If, during this period, anyone asked what he was doing, he would say "I'm at university" and who could argue?'[43] The three would work together off and on, in music and film, over the next three decades. They would also become brothers-in-law, each marrying one of the Robins sisters, Pat, Judy and Veronica.

By this time Mark Young had had his beatnik epiphany, seeing John Esam boarding a bus. Young came from a family of readers, and now supplemented his cultural diet with the surrealist poetry of Apollinaire and prose of Genet. On the recommendation of an English jazz drummer, he had read *On the Road*. At the short-lived University Film Society he had seen films by Akira Kurosawa, Ingmar Bergman and François Truffaut. He wrote his own poetry, and played bass in a jazz group that sometimes included Bruno Lawrence.

By the mid-sixties, the Murphy-Charles-Lawrence triumvirate had drifted away from campus, Murphy to primary school teaching, Charles to television production, and Lawrence to a series of jazz, R&B and pop bands that would find him travelling back and forth between New Zealand and Australia for the next few years. But they would often reunite at the Studio Jazz Club, a coffee bar above the Regent Pool Room in Manners Street, which Murphy had helped establish. Murphy's recollection that it doubled as a front for an illegal book-making operation run by Charles's uncle sounds like a plot point from one of the movies he would later make. 'Everybody knew that jazz people were long-haired bearded weirdos in dark glasses, with not the slightest interest in horse racing. A jazz club would be the last place cops would look to find a bookie!'[44] Alan Brunton's description is even more cinematic: 'Hustlers floated from pool hall to jazz club, George the Greek, Arnold the Finn, Billy Goat. Bohemians met the petty crims. Both elements were aware that they were on an edge.'[45]

Murphy's group, which specialised in the music of Charles Mingus, played on Friday nights. The Mark Young Quartet (according to Murphy the most polished of the groups) played on Saturdays. An assortment of characters would pass through the club, including poet James K. Baxter and literary bushman Barry Crump, actors Tim Eliott and Ian Mune, and television director Derek Morton, attracted by the beatnik ambience and the whiff of marijuana as much as the music. But while the volatile mix of personalities would sometimes explode into lively arguments, Murphy recalled that these were more likely to be philosophical than political.[46]

AN INCUBATOR FOR THE COUNTERCULTURE

Where I lived at that time, politics were discussed a great deal, though I was too young to grasp anything much of the conversation.

My parents were born between the First and Second World Wars. Marei, born in Cologne, Germany in 1936, became a Jewish refugee, and arrived in Wellington at age three with her parents, brother and nanny. Conrad was born in Wellington in 1929. Con and Marei had fallen in love at Student Congress, an annual summer school held at Curious Cove in the picturesque Marlborough Sounds, where the political and social issues of the day would be vigorously debated by 120 or so students and lecturers over ten days in an atmosphere of leisure and lust.

Congress had been running since 1949 and was, in many ways, a proto-countercultural event. At nineteen, Con had been at that first Congress, by which time he was already a member of the New Zealand Communist Party. He remained a member until the Soviet invasion of Hungary in 1956, when Marei, to his chagrin, accused him of having accepted when he should have questioned.[47] After that he began attending branch meetings of the Labour Party, though his politics stayed to the left of Labour's. He once recalled how, during a banal and dreary meeting, his friend Hugh Price leaned over to him and whispered ironically, 'Sometimes I feel socialism is very close, don't you?'[48] But more of his political energies went into pressure groups like Socialist Forum, CND and the Wellington Committee on Vietnam.

Along with their commitment to progressive politics, Marei and Con loved drama, music and laughter, and in 1964 and '65, with a group that included Monde Marie folk singer and political activist Jim Delahunty, and a recent emigrant from Britain with theatrical ambitions, Roger Hall, mounted several seasons of satirical theatre in galleries and coffee bars around Wellington. They called themselves the Rubbishers. Marei's puppets, which caricatured political figures such as Prime Minister Keith Holyoake and Wellington Central MP Dan Riddiford, were a notable feature.

My parents were part of the generation that slightly pre-dated the counterculture. While Holyoake's supporters might have viewed them as dangerous radicals, I doubt they ever seriously entertained thoughts of bloody revolution. Con was a lifelong pacifist. He was also an eternal optimist and believed that society would eventually shift to an increasingly egalitarian, worker-driven model—socialism, in a nutshell—through rational persuasion and common sense. Both Con and Marei had rejected their religious upbringings, and did not subscribe to religion of any kind. Nor did they have any interest in drugs, though Con, whose book *Grog's Own Country* was a searing indictment of New Zealand's liquor industry, liked to drink beer. They didn't reject the institution of the family; in fact they maintained a happy one together right up until my father's death, in spite of each having a few extramarital affairs.

Yet, looking back, I realise that our house, which was often filled with guests, sometimes acted as a kind of incubator for the incipient counterculture. I have childhood memories of visits from a parade of unorthodox characters. There was Brian Bell, eventually banned from the premises by my mother on account of his odour, who would turn up to discuss various schemes, literary and subversive, that he thought Con ought to assist him with. Brian was the same age as Con but lacked Con's discipline or sense of responsibility. He had children of his own, but didn't seem to live with them or have anything to offer them in the way of material support. In a time of near-full employment, he carried a letter from his doctor stating that he suffered from a nervous condition that rendered him unsuitable for work. He was hilariously grandiloquent, frequently obscene and usually drunk. As Alan Brunton would note in his introduction to a posthumous collection of Bell's writings: 'His idea of life as an artistic possibility rather than gradual resignation to economic necessity alienated him both in youth and old age.'[49]

Then there was Bill Dwyer, who I recall chiefly for his hat, a battered felt object with a greasy brim, which I found on the floor one morning after a party and which became a costume item in the dress-up games I played with my siblings. The flamboyant, anti-authoritarian Dwyer had immigrated to New Zealand in 1954 from his native Ireland, got a job on the Wellington wharves and become involved in the Waterside Workers' Union. At meetings he would rail theatrically against the union's Communist Party-dominated executive, winning some support from the rank-and-file wharfies who at the very least found him entertaining. He was also popular in those days of six o'clock closing for selling grog on the sly.[50] After being forced out of the union, he became a presence on the Victoria University campus, where he founded the Anarchist Association. Yet even an organisation opposed to authority on principle and commanded by Dwyer himself was apparently too formal a structure to contain his manic energies. He would soon relocate to Auckland where he was prosecuted for neglecting his children, then to Sydney and finally back to the British Isles, where he would continue to play an influential role in the counterculture, of which more later.

Our home also received younger visitors: teenagers in dark duffel coats who would come to meetings and sit in Con's study, drink Nescafé and talk earnestly. I was too young to understand much of it, but they often seemed to be discussing something called The Bomb.

RED SKIES AND YOUNG REBELS

To the British writer Jeff Nuttall, it was The Bomb that created the counterculture. So monstrous was the very notion of the nuclear weapon and its destructive potential, it had obliterated any common ground between the generation that had conceived it and the one that now lived in its perpetual shadow. Nuttall saw an unbridgeable gulf between 'the people who had passed puberty at the time of the bomb', who were incapable of imagining a life without a future, and those who had not yet reached puberty, who were incapable of imagining life *with* a future. In his book *Bomb Culture*, published the year before Roszak's manifesto, he wrote: 'No longer could teacher, magistrate, politician, don or even loving parent, guide the young. Their membership of the H-Bomb society automatically cancelled anything they might have to say on questions of right and wrong.'[1]

Thermonuclear detonation during Pacific tests, 1958. National Nuclear Security Administration, Nevada Site Office

What Nuttall called bomb culture others would come to call counterculture. This mistrust and rejection of the older generation and everything it represented was total. He wrote: 'Dad was a liar. He lied about the war and he lied about sex. He lied about the bomb and he lied about the future ... The so-called "generation gap" started there and has been increasing ever since.'[2] Ken James, a teenager in Auckland when Nuttall's book came out in 1968, saw in this gap the seeds of a movement: 'The movement against nuclear weapons and the totalitarianism of cold war. There was nowhere in the world you could get away from it. So we did the only thing we could. We turned our backs on the antagonists. We said, "No, thank you."'[3]

Nuttall's ideas about the psychological and spiritual impact that the prospect of total annihilation had on the post-war generation were well founded, but The Bomb darkened the horizons of those born before the war as well.

✳

I am looking at a black-and-white picture that was given to me by the New Zealand photographer Gil Hanly. Gil took the photo in London in 1959, when she was living with her husband Pat and young son Ben in Cornwall Mansions, an apartment block on a Chelsea estate known as World's End. My parents and one-year-old self lived on the bottom floor. Con and Marei had known the Hanlys back in New Zealand and the couples were close friends. Gil's photo shows a small section of the second Easter march against nuclear weapons. It had begun in Aldermaston, the site of the Atomic Weapons Research Centre, roughly 80 kilometres from London. Gil took the photo in Kensington High Street as the march headed to its final gathering place in Trafalgar Square, by which time it was sixty thousand strong. It was believed to be the largest protest ever held in Britain thus far.[4] Though the issue was life-and-death, the mood was euphoric. There were students in duffel coats and clergymen in collars. There were skiffle groups, jazz bands and Trinidadian steel drummers. Even the English rain couldn't dampen the marchers' spirits. The idea that protest and social change should be celebratory might have started here.

In the centre of Gil's photo, between banners identifying the Cypriot and Australian contingents, is a small group of New Zealanders. They are joining in the singing. Near the front of the Kiwis is the writer Maurice Shadbolt, whose first collection of short stories, *The New Zealanders*, is about to be published. Beside him walks his wife Gill. Immediately behind them are my parents. My mother is wheeling an empty pushchair. The intended occupant is riding on Con's shoulders. That's me. I'm nine months old and I like the singing.

The Aldermaston marches were the most visible achievement of the Campaign for Nuclear Disarmament, or CND as it came to be known. It had been formed in January 1958, the culmination of

CND march, London, 1959. Gill and Maurice Shadbolt (second and third from left); Conrad Bollinger behind Maurice, with Nick on shoulders; Marei with pushchair.
Gil Hanly photograph, private collection

concerns in left-wing circles about the rapid proliferation of nuclear weapons since the war. Figureheads of the movement were intellectuals of the pre-war era such as the philosopher Bertrand Russell, the writer J. B. Priestley, and politician and pacifist Fenner Brockway.

APOCALYPTIC VISIONS

While my parents were in London, New Zealand's own anti-nuclear movement had begun to take shape. As in Britain, it was led primarily by the left-leaning middle class, with a number of church-based groups trying in various ways to educate the public and influence the government on what they believed to be the greatest ever threat to human survival.

It began as a series of small regional groups with interchangeable and unmemorable names: the Campaign Against Nuclear Warfare (Christchurch), the Committee for the Prevention of Nuclear War (Dunedin), the Movement for Nuclear Disarmament (Wellington), the Movement for International Co-operation and Disarmament (Palmerston North), and — take a breath — the Movement Against Further Testing, Manufacture and Use of Nuclear Weapons (Auckland).

In 1959, a convention in Dunedin saw most of these combine as the New Zealand Council for Nuclear Disarmament, which soon became the New Zealand *Campaign* for Nuclear Disarmament, bringing it into line with its British counterpart.[5]

The new national committee was headed by two Christchurch women, Mary Woodward and Elsie Locke. Woodward, in her mid-thirties, was a teacher and a Quaker. Locke, in her late forties, had been a member of the Communist Party, and founder and editor of the party-produced feminist journal *Woman Today*. Like my father, Locke had resigned in disillusionment in 1956 after the Soviet invasion of Hungary. While responsible for much of CND's organisation, she tried to stay in the background, fearing that her communist associations would compromise the broader acceptance of the movement, which also included church figures such as the Reverend Alan Brash (whose son Don Brash would later emerge as a major proponent of neoliberalism).[6]

It also drew support from what was starting to be referred to as the New Left: a scattering of small socialist and anarchist groups who had emerged since the Communist Party defections of 1956, and who were looking for an alternative to Stalinism and the Cold War blocs of the US and USSR.[7] But CND's lack of formal ideology and party political affiliations was also an attraction to a growing group of young non-conformists, enabling them to focus anti-establishment feelings on a single issue which could be boiled down to a choice between good and evil. For them, the appeal of politics was essentially existential. Although CND strove to be seen by the wider community as respectable and representative of a larger group than just the weird and bearded, it was in these terms that the media and other more conservative voices — the establishment — tended to portray them. Covering a 1961 march in Wellington to mark the sixteenth anniversary of the US bombing of Hiroshima, the *Evening Post* noted 'the usual representation of university students, plus a number of leather jacketed young men in suede shoes, corduroy trousers and a few who sported beards', although the keen-eyed reporter had to concede that the marchers were 'a mixed lot ranging in age from an elderly grandmother … to babies in prams pushed by mothers with a crusading glint in their eyes' and that 'those who one onlooker classed as weirdies were only a small minority and there was a large number of average, well dressed, sensible looking citizens'.[8]

One night in the winter of 1962, Aucklanders witnessed a bright red glow above the northern horizon that spread rapidly across the sky before 'the luminous red band widened, and quivering white shafts of light could be seen within it'.[9] The United States had just exploded a 1.2-megaton hydrogen bomb above Johnson Atoll in the Pacific Ocean, some 6500 kilometres from New Zealand. David Lange was twenty at the time of the explosion. Many years later, when he was Prime Minister, he would recall with his usual rhetorical flair that 'the confusion in the sky that night haunted me as a vision of a man-made apocalypse, a

Youth CND on the beach, 1964.
Hugh Young private collection

terrifying retaliation of natural forces against the evil of unnatural invasion and a warning that a small country at the edge of the world in the South Pacific was no longer far enough away from the quarrels of the great powers to escape their consequences'.[10]

    That year, too, a group of young Aucklanders, mostly from left-leaning artistic backgrounds, formed Youth CND, and other branches quickly sprouted around the country. Over the summer of 1964, Youth CND members from various centres gathered at Tahunanui Beach in Nelson where they endeavoured to spread the anti-nuclear message to holidaymakers through folk singing, films and puppet shows. Hugh Young, one of the young puppeteers, remembers an adaptation of the story of Hansel and Gretel that had the bad witch turning out to be good, to show that appearances are deceptive.[11] Though such activities, matched with the bright smiles evident in the group photograph, evince an almost Bible-class wholesomeness, there was an apocalyptic undertone in the name they gave to the summer event: *On the Beach*, a reference to Nevil Shute's novel of post-nuclear holocaust.

    Then there were the Easter marches. Beginning in 1961, these were the most visible of CND's activities. Modelled on the Aldermaston events, they would set out on Good Friday from north of Wellington

and arrive on Easter Sunday at Parliament Buildings in Thorndon. University and secondary school students were a sizeable part of the inaugural march on its 50-kilometre journey from Featherston. 'Mostly youths and girls', reported the *Evening Post* as the crowd reached Kaiwharawhara.[12] At least some of the young marchers leaned more towards the traditional values of the Labour Party than any beatnik or anarchist agenda. Mark Young recalls sitting in a tent one night of the march, 'listening to two of the Auckland contingent discuss what ministerial roles they would hold in a distant Labour Government. And lo, when Norman Kirk came to power, there they were!'[13]

The 1962 march was met during its ascent of the Remutaka Hill by Prime Minister Keith Holyoake, en route to his electorate of Pahiatua, and they discussed the forthcoming nuclear tests on Christmas Island. The fact that Holyoake chose to intercept the marchers showed he was not entirely deaf to their concerns, yet he remained hopelessly beholden to New Zealand's alliance with the United States. 'I do not pretend to like this situation in the slightest, but if the Russians will not agree to a test ban treaty, what is the alternative?' he pleaded in a statement that month.[14] The daily newspapers tended to echo Holyoake's position: nuclear weapons are terrible but unilateral disarmament is inconceivable. Meanwhile, New Zealand's ally continued its preparations for further poisoning of the Pacific.

Though some of the marchers brought guitars and sang, there was continuing concern among the elders of the movement that the marches should present a dignified face to the public. I was four years old when my parents took me on the 1963 march. I remember striding out in front with my friend Micky Rose, the pair of us singing and shouting with festive enthusiasm though no real idea of what any of it meant, only to be ordered back into line by a stern family friend, an old communist, who mumbled something to my dad about how the public would never take the movement seriously if they saw a bunch of kids having fun. Yet as Sheila Rowbotham noted of the British movement, 'CND was to act as a catalyst for a counter-culture in which many kinds of youthful dissidence assumed visibility.' It 'enlarged the space to be weird'.[15]

The Easter marches reached their peak that year. The previous October had seen the world come perilously close to a nuclear showdown between the United States and Soviet Union over the Soviet placement of missile bases in Cuba, and the close brush with catastrophe intensified the mood. The marchers set out from Paraparaumu and stopped for one night at Takapūwāhia marae in Porirua, with some of the local iwi joining the protesters as they continued towards Wellington the following day. By the time the march reached Parliament it was a thousand strong.

Yet the following year's march, which took the same route, saw numbers more than halved. 'A failure,' declared Murray Rowlands in student newspaper *Salient*. Rowlands noted that a partial test-ban

Students protest against The Bomb, Wellington, 1963. Helmut Einhorn photograph, Alexander Turnbull Library, PA12-7992-11

treaty between the United States, the Soviet Union and Britain, signed in August 1963, and the Labour Party's support of the proposal for a nuclear-free southern hemisphere, meant that at least some of the movement's goals had been achieved. But mostly he blamed the sharp drop in numbers on 'the over-riding demand there seems to be on a "nice" public image'. Arguments about whether marchers should be allowed to sing, and resistance to 'direct and positive action — sit-downs etc.', had alienated younger 'libertarian' members.[16]

Though nuclear weapons would continue to be one focus of protest, generational divisions continued to widen, both inside and outside the anti-nuclear movement, as young New Zealanders pursued an increasingly personal politics.

SCHOOLGIRLS AND STAGE DOORS

In 1964 The Bomb wasn't the only thing that got young New Zealanders out on the streets.

The Beatles flew into Wellington on a Sunday, a day on which the country was usually closed, to find seven thousand young people lining the airport fences. The devotees then followed the Beatles' motorcade from Rongotai into the city, where they jammed the streets around the Hotel St George. During the Beatles' stay, the hotel saw break-ins, bomb threats and a suicide attempt. Similar scenes would be repeated over the days that followed, as the Beatles travelled to play concerts in Auckland, Dunedin and Christchurch.

Media had begun priming New Zealand's teenagers for this moment months earlier. The term Beatlemania that first appeared in British media towards the end of 1963 had spread to the US with the Beatles' first visit in early 1964, and the mass hysteria at their concerts had been heavily reported. At the same time, their records were being played on radio and their pictures were appearing in local teen magazines like *Playdate*. All of this was enough to flick a switch that was ready to be activated.

Rachel Stace, age fifteen, went to three of four Wellington shows (there were two on Monday and two the following night) though she never purchased a ticket. 'They had doormen, these old chaps, standing outside. So I waited until the concert started and then said, "Look I haven't got a ticket, could I just go and stand by those inside doors? I'll just look through the porthole window, I won't go inside", and they said, "Oh, okay then, all right."'

Rachel forgot her promise the moment the old chap shut the doors. Now inside the auditorium, she made her way swiftly up the aisle, shrieking to get John Lennon's attention. He waved back just as the police descended on her. It wasn't her only attempt to gain a more intimate audience with the group. At the St George, she scaled a fire escape, carrying a roll of toilet paper on which she and a couple of friends had written an epic fan letter, but a locked door prevented its delivery. Undeterred, she also tried climbing in a dressing-room window of the Town Hall but was pulled down by a policeman. The latter incident was reported in the *Dominion*, complete with photograph, which got Rachel hauled up in front of the headmistress next day in school. 'That's not the kind of behaviour we expect from an L1 girl!' she was told. (The L stood for Latin, studied only in the school's top stream.)[17]

Auckland's mayor Dove-Myer Robinson turned on a civic welcome for the Beatles, despite grumblings from councillors like Tom Pearce. President of the Auckland Rugby Football Union, Pearce had managed the All Blacks' 1960 tour of South Africa from which Māori players were banned. Now he declared that 'if we are going to pander to the hysteria, antics, adulation, rioting, screaming and roaring and all the things these bewigged musicians engender, then I think we should make a point of honouring any youths with a sporting background who are at least endeavouring to act in the best traditions of the young men of this nation'.[18]

Thousands of school-age fans, defying threats of expulsion, bunked classes to attend, while adult New Zealanders tried to understand the effect the Beatles were having on their children. Tony Taylor, Professor of Psychology at Victoria University, undertook a unique project 'to unravel some of the complex factors that underlie the Beatle

The Beatles arrived at Wellington Airport on 21 June 1964. David Sache photograph, South Pacific Photos, private collection

stimulus and the response of "Beatlemania"'. With special dispensation from the police to access restricted areas, he and ten of his senior psychology students set about recruiting teenage subjects from the crowds around the airports, hotels, concerts and local schools. He then administered a series of psychological tests 'in a search for relationships between their personality factors and social background, and their enthusiasm for the Beatles'.

The kids, he decided, weren't mad. 'There was no evidence from the Hysteria Scale of the Minnesota Multiphasic Personality Inventory to support the popular opinion that the enthusiasts were hysterics,' he wrote in a report that would appear in the *British Journal of Social and Clinical Psychology*. '"Beatlemania" is the passing reaction of predominantly young adolescent females to group pressures of such a kind that meets their special emotional needs.'[19]

Police restrain a fan during a Rolling Stones concert, Wellington Town Hall, 1965. Dominion Post Collection, Alexander Turnbull Library, EP/1965/0521-F

Meanwhile the *Listener*, still several years away from employing a rock critic (in fact, the term did not yet exist), assigned the task of assessing the Beatles and their impact on New Zealand youth to the country's premier playwright Bruce Mason, then aged forty-three. He came away a believer, albeit one with a tendency to see Beatlemania in classical terms: 'The four Evangelists, the four temperaments of medieval philosophy, the four traditional characters of early Italian comedy …' He may have oversold himself when he declared, 'I am now with it. I know every word of their recorded songs, every plangent thrum of their guitars'. Nevertheless, he clearly identified the social need they filled: 'The overwhelming response to The Beatles suggests that our strait-laced society offers little opportunity for passionate and spontaneous feeling.'[20]

Less perceptive pundits aired their prejudices in the letters pages of the local papers. 'Driven into the juvenile brain day and night over the air by radio broadcasts, the unrelenting drivel and sloppy sentiment is bound to tarnish the high ideals and the good grammar instilled in our modern youth and to deteriorate young concepts of what is good and what is bad,' fretted L. C. Smith of Wellington, while Dismayed of Dannevirke simply blamed the amplifiers that enabled 'four ordinary young men with small voices … to create all this unseemly excitement'.[21]

Perhaps the person best qualified to explain this unseemly excitement was a self-confessed screamer. Writing to the *Dominion* as Beatle Fan 6,309,612 of Wadestown, Rachel Stace posited: 'Maybe the deep-down reason is frustrations and tensions but my reason is simply because screaming is enjoyable. The Beatles have all the vital ingredients necessary for good screaming: lots of noise, a loud beat, other screamers, and encouragement so you can let yourself go and scream as much as you like … Anyway where else can you scream and have a wild time?'[22] Their audience may have been dominated by young women, but the Beatles also offered sexual liberation to the New Zealand male. Defying the popular image of masculinity, these were no brooding, musclebound hunks. They were skinny, sexy and longhaired at a time when 'longhair' —a term originally coined for dead classical composers—still meant effete intellectuals. Basically, they were the opposite of rugby players. As US critic Richard Brody puts it, 'the Beatles changed the stereotype: they eroticised their consciously soft and loose masculinity'.[23]

The Beatles were as crucial as CND in the formation of the counterculture; they helped blast a space in which the counter-culture could exist. And yet ultimately they were shaped by the counterculture at least as much as it was shaped by them. Over the next few years they would be early adopters of most significant countercultural trends, including psychedelic drug use and Eastern spirituality, which they would transmit to all corners of the world, New Zealand included, via the massive telegraph system of their music. When they stood on New Zealand stages in 1964 in their matching suits singing 'She loves you, yeah, yeah, yeah', they could hardly have

The Pretty Things' Viv Prince lights up Christchurch, August 1965. Bruce King photograph, private collection

imagined that within two years they would be intoning lines from the *Tibetan Book of the Dead*, studying Indian classical instruments and *musique concrète*. Like surfers on the zeitgeist, they had no notion of how far they would travel and in how short a time.

But even at the time of their only New Zealand visit, when Beatlemania was still in its infancy, the cultural reverberations were inescapable. Unless you were an unreconstructed specimen of Kiwi blokedom like Tom Pearce, it was impossible to deny their charms: the radiant harmonies, the working-class wit. The NZBC had no choice but to play their records, and happily complied. In the end, everybody was a little bit of a Beatles fan.

The same could not be said for other British bands that toured in the Beatles' wake. The Rolling Stones and the Pretty Things, both of which visited in 1965, didn't bother with the melodic and harmonic sweetenings, witty repartee or tidy uniforms of the Beatles. They were hairy and scary, looked like layabouts and drew heavily on black American blues, lending a London leer to the music's inherent sex and swagger. The Stones had begun to augment their blues covers with originals that expressed even more directly their cynical view of modern society, summed up in songs like '(I Can't Get No) Satisfaction' and 'Get Off My Cloud'. On stage they defied social norms in other ways.

Phil Gifford recalled their 1965 show in Auckland. 'When the curtains parted, and there were four Stones, from stage left in my memory — Wyman, Jones, Watts and, way stage right, Keith — playing "Not Fade Away" twice as loud as I'd ever heard a band play before, the fans started screaming. Then they went totally crazy when Jagger appeared rattling maracas, and did that heel toe and back again sideways dance across the stage. When he got to Keith he leaned in and kissed him on the cheek. And for a couple of stunned, weird seconds the girls stopped in astonished mid-scream. It was '65, and in New Zealand we didn't do androgyny. It took a song or two before they, the fans, were back to full volume again.'[24]

The Pretty Things toured as part of an incongruous package that included fading British teen idol Eden Kane and barefoot teenage songstress Sandie Shaw. Though not nearly as famous as the Beatles or Stones, and nowhere near in their league as songwriters, the Things rivalled both groups in terms of the publicity generated during their short stay, thanks mostly to the extra-musical activities of drummer Viv Prince. A little older than the rest of the group, he was a drunk, a surrealist and an outrageous clown. Between shows he would rampage about sleepy New Zealand streets dressed in a bedspread and a leopard-skin pillbox hat, and brandishing a lightbulb. He would disrupt and upstage the other acts. He drank alcohol out of a boot. He lit fires in theatres. To newspaper reporters wishing to scandalise their readers, he was a keen co-conspirator. '"It Keeps Us Warm" say Hairy Things', 'These, Believe It Or Not, Are Men!' and 'Pretty Things Shock Exhibition' screamed the headlines.

Though the establishment had seemed in a hurry to get rid of them, when the time finally came for the Things to depart, circumstances determined that Prince would stay a little longer. Shortly before takeoff, Pan American officials evicted him from the plane for being intoxicated, forcing him to spend a further night in New Zealand. The last images of him in this country show him drunk and dishevelled in an airport lounge, beating a tambourine and waving a large crayfish. After the departure, Minister of Immigration Tom Shand was questioned in Parliament about the scrutiny given by his department to entry applications by such groups as the Pretty Things. Shand gave an assurance that any return visit by this group would be closely scrutinised. As it turned out, they would not return for forty-seven years, by which time Viv Prince had long since been fired from the band.

Earlier in the year there had been two other musical tourists of countercultural significance, though both came under the aegis of orthodox institutions. In February and March, the NZBC sponsored concerts by the Bengali sitar player Ravi Shankar in Auckland, Christchurch, Dunedin and Wellington. While the Beatles would not demonstrate their interest in Indian instruments until their *Rubber Soul* album at the end of the year, a smattering of broadminded aesthetes and young trailblazers would join local Indian communities to hear the master perform.

The following month the classical community opened a door to a burgeoning counterculture when the Chamber Music Society toured bebop pioneer Thelonious Monk and his quartet. Though he had been a doyen in jazz circles for more than twenty years, a February 1964 cover story in *Time* had announced the New York pianist's arrival 'at the summit of serious recognition', and he had suddenly become very much sought after around the world. In fact, the society had been considering bringing a jazz musician to New Zealand for some time and the organisation's manager Joan Kerr had already written to Monk proposing the tour before the *Time* article appeared. Her prospicience impressed Monk's manager George Wein, who green-lit the visit.[25] The society booked the great pianist for concerts in eight centres. Did Monk bestow his benediction of hipness—'These guys are with it!'—upon the people of Hamilton and Tauranga as he had, according to *Time*, in Düsseldorf the year before? Not likely. His inquiries about where he might obtain some 'special cigarettes' during his stay proved fruitless until a reception in Auckland where he encountered local painters and musicians who were able to interpret his request for marijuana.

Though his eccentricities had been well publicised ('every day is a brand-new pharmaceutical event for Monk', the *Time* story had noted), Monk was unlike anything the Chamber Music Society

Programme for Thelonious Monk Quartet's 1965 New Zealand tour, designed by Geoff Nees. Alexander Turnbull Library, Eph-B-MUSIC-WFC-1965/1969-1965-2

had encountered. Joan Kerr shared with Gordon Campbell a memory of Monk's final moments in New Zealand: 'With half an hour to go to flight time she entered the hotel room to find Monk lying naked on the sofa with the floor covered by the contents of "about 40" suitcases. After ordering Monk his requested breakfast—four beers and four whisky chasers—she somehow managed to get Thelonious and his wife Nellie to the airport on time.'[26]

For Phil Dadson, an art student and aspiring jazz musician, seeing Monk in New Zealand was an inspirational lesson in kinetic art: one he would take with him as he went on to form the experimental music and movement group From Scratch in the 1970s. 'I have a memory of Monk getting up from playing and, when Charlie Rouse was taking a solo, he wandered round the stage and started turning round in circles with his eyes closed.' Recounting the memory to me more than fifty years later, Dadson closes his eyes either in imitation of Monk or to better revisit the moment, or both. 'He got his feet all tangled up in the mic lines which he had to unwind and then just got back to the piano in time for his solo. It might have been choreographed, it was so beautifully timed.'[27]

But for most local musicians in 1965 the main influence was the British beat boom, which spawned imitators all over the country. Some of the more polished outfits—Ray Columbus and the Invaders from Christchurch, the Librettos from Wellington—made records for established labels, got airplay on the national commercial stations and appeared on television. Their instant embrace by mainstream media confirmed their lack of subversive intent. These were slick, professional entertainers, even as they rocked.

That couldn't be said for Christchurch's Chants R&B. Too raw for radio, too hairy for television, they held court at the Stage Door, a basement club in Hereford Lane, where their frenzied rearrangements of rhythm and blues songs drew crowds of what Chants' guitarist Mike Rudd would sum up as 'dissolute kids, schoolgirls, the unemployed and the unemployable'.[28] Longhaired and favouring mod-style clothes handmade by local English tailor Les Sherlock, the Chants and their audience were rebelliously stylish.[29] They were also under constant threat of violence from bikies and rockers, who would lurk outside looking for trouble.

The Stage Door was a place where several strands of the counterculture—wild expressive rock music, unorthodox dress and progressive politics—met under one roof. Above the venue was a coffee bar. A teenage Richard Hill frequented both. In the basement he would join his mod friends and revel in the exuberant din of Chants R&B.[30] Upstairs he would encounter his first debates on the Vietnam War.[31]

'WHAT'S VIETNAM?'

Deborah Yates, a founder member of Youth CND in Auckland, first heard about Vietnam on one of the Easter marches. 'We had a meeting with a young Wellington group and they said "Why are you worrying about The Bomb? Why aren't you worrying about Vietnam?" And we said "What's Vietnam?"'[32]

Vietnam is 9000 kilometres from New Zealand, the easternmost country on the Indochina peninsula. Dominated for centuries by China before being colonised by the French, the country had developed a

Beehives and burgundy at the opening of the Stage Door, Christchurch, 1964; Chants R&B at Stage Door, 1965. Gordon Cope-Williams photographs, private collection

strong independence movement, led by the charismatic nationalist Ho Chi Minh. At the end of the Second World War, Ho Chi Minh had set up government in the northern city of Hanoi and, quoting the American declaration of independence, began his attempts to unify the country under communism. The French, who administered an unstable government in the south, called on America to help fight the communist threat from the north.

By the mid-fifties the Americans had replaced the French and soon began signalling to New Zealand and other allies that it could not afford to let Vietnam go communist. President Eisenhower came up with the image of falling dominoes to illustrate the idea that a communist victory in one nation would inevitably lead to communist takeovers in neighbouring states. If the domino theory was right, then a communist Vietnam would quickly see communism spread throughout Southeast Asia, possibly all the way to Australia and New Zealand, which in 1951 had signed the ANZUS Treaty that agreed on military co-operation with the United States to protect the Pacific.

Keith Holyoake had visited South Vietnam on a tour of Asia shortly after he was elected Prime Minister in 1960. Though the forty-page report he wrote on the trip suggests he did not take a close interest in politics, he did speak after of being 'captivated' by the attractive Vietnamese women in their national dress and that he 'longed to pat them on the bottom'.[33]

Holyoake was, in Roberto Rabel's phrase, a 'reluctant Cold Warrior'. In 1962 he had resisted America's request to send a small military force to Vietnam, opting instead to provide a civilian surgical team. By 1963 most New Zealanders still probably couldn't have told you where Vietnam was. Nor could most Americans, though the number of US troops there was rapidly growing. At the end of the 1950s there had been fewer than a thousand; by 1963 there were sixteen thousand. Following John F. Kennedy's assassination that year, incoming President Lyndon Johnson expanded the number even further.

Visits to New Zealand from American dignitaries became more frequent. In 1964 Holyoake was paid a call by General Hamilton Howze, a veteran US commander who had, among other things, helped plan an invasion of Cuba during the missile crisis. During a meeting with Holyoake at Victoria University, members of the campus-based Anarchist Association took the general's cap, which he had left unattended on a hat stand, filled it with a gooey mixture of cooking and cleaning products, and hurled it into the grounds of the nearby US Embassy. The architects of this symbolic act were hunted down and fined by the student executive, and charged by the police.[34]

The escalated bombing of North Vietnam in early 1965 drew widespread protests in the US. Increasingly these were driven and dominated by baby boomers, who had become eligible for the draft and could now be sent to fight. In New Zealand, too, it was the young who would be most directly affected. Though conscripts would not be sent to

Police remove a protester from the corridor outside Prime Minister Holyoake's office. Morrie Hill photograph, Dominion Post Collection, Alexander Turnbull Library, 1/4-071875-F

fight in Vietnam, the law required all New Zealand males at age twenty to register for military service. Ballots were then conducted based on date of birth. If your birthday was picked, you had to undergo three months' compulsory military training, plus an annual commitment of three weeks' part-time training for the next three years.

In March that year, Youth CND members picketed the American Embassy in Wellington, while in Auckland several dozen bedded in for a week-long fast on the steps of the Methodist Mission in Queen Street. In April, President Johnson's special envoy Henry Cabot Lodge paid a visit to New Zealand and CND marched on Parliament in protest. There were still no New Zealand soldiers in Vietnam, to the consternation of some of the government's more hawkish officials. In early May, Alister McIntosh, head of External Affairs, wrote to George Laking, New Zealand's ambassador to the US, that he was 'positively sick with frustration' over Holyoake's hesitance. The Prime Minister had apparently been 'greatly upset by a crowd of idiot boys and girls keeping an all-night vigil and by a deputation of churchmen'.[35]

In the wake of Cabot Lodge's visit, a number of organisations opposing the war were formed, the most prominent being the Wellington Committee on Vietnam. Though the organisations were led by some of the same middle-class, middle-aged liberals who had steered CND, they also attracted younger people who were angry, impatient and didn't care about a polite public image. There were internal debates as to whether the movement was against war per se, or whether it favoured victory for Ho Chi Minh.

On 27 May, Holyoake announced New Zealand would be sending an artillery battery consisting of approximately 120 men. Within hours of the announcement, the Committee on Vietnam had staged a vigil outside Parliament. A few days later, a group of young activists began a sit-in outside the Prime Minister's office. 'They look a bit odd but I think that's their objective,' Holyoake remarked. He had heard of this form of demonstration overseas. 'They seem to be a pure carbon copy. I thought we would have had some originality from New Zealanders.'[36] Original or not, this was the first time in the twentieth century that a large-scale protest movement had arisen in New Zealand as the result of dissent over a specific diplomatic decision.[37] Opposition would continue to come in a variety of new and challenging forms.

*

Teach-ins, like sit-ins, were an American innovation—participatory seminars directed towards action. The prototype had taken place in March 1965 at the University of Michigan. The first New Zealand teach-in was held just four months later. It was instigated by twenty-one-year-old Alister Taylor, secretary of the New Zealand Students' Association, who was just back from a world trip as a New Zealand representative of the International Student Conference. He would later learn that the ISC was principally funded and controlled by CIA front organisations, and he would call the trip a 'round-the-world witch-hunt' in which he was manipulated 'to vote against this radical and to reveal secrets about that student organisation'.[38] One thing his hosts would not have engineered, though, was that his arrival in Washington would coincide with the National Teach-In on Vietnam, which he attended. 'Those speeches,' he would write, 'had an incalculable effect on me.'[39]

On his way back to New Zealand, Taylor's flight stopped in the American territory of Guam, where he was shocked to see more than a hundred B-52s lined up for bombing missions. He arrived home on the day Holyoake announced his commitment of New Zealand troops to Vietnam. As his plane flew low over Wellington, he could see the protesters rallying around the Cenotaph, just below Parliament Buildings. Galvanised, Taylor and his girlfriend Helen Sutch set about organising the first local teach-in. It was held at Victoria University, drew a thousand attendees, lasted fourteen hours and was considered an unqualified success. Over the next few months, teach-ins sprang up on campuses all over the country. It would not be the last time Taylor carried off with entrepreneurial panache a local version of an imported idea.

Nor was it the first. As a high school student in Palmerston North he had organised church dances, providing a rare opportunity for teenagers to get close to members of the opposite sex. His band of choice were a local group, the Senators, who would tour the region in a 1928 Dodge hearse. Taylor usually followed in his father's yellow Volkswagen. But after one such event a girl reported that she had been raped in a vehicle parked outside the hall—the yellow Volkswagen, which Taylor had left there, unlocked. Though Taylor was not accused of the rape, the school principal held him responsible as organiser of the dance and owner of the vehicle, and sentenced him to six strokes of the cane. Taylor refused the punishment. 'And that,' he said, 'started my antagonism with authority.'[40]

Paradoxically for a professed anti-authoritarian, Taylor had been leader of the school cadet battalion, and still had ambitions to become a military officer. A few months after the Volkswagen incident, he requested a reference from the principal to accompany his application to the Royal Military College in Duntroon, Australia. The principal, at last finding the opportunity to punish Taylor, wrote that as the student's only interest was in social activities he would be unsuitable military material. Unsurprisingly, the application was declined. Rejected by the military, Taylor instead took his mobilising skills to Victoria University, where he became secretary of the Students' Association.

By 1964, reports were filtering through from America of unrest at universities such as Berkeley, where a ban on political activity had resulted in protests and altercations between students and police. Out of this came the Free Speech movement, which maintained a programme of student civil disobedience that continued through 1965 with sit-ins, seminars and demonstrations. Inspired by reports from Berkley, Taylor and Tony Ashenden launched Forum, a regular series of talks in the university quadrangle on a range of topics, of which Vietnam was one.

Though Taylor's transformation from aspirant military officer to student radical was underway, he remained interested in the mechanisms of the establishment. While still at high school he had joined the National Party. At Victoria he formed the National Club. This didn't stop him from targeting the National government with what would be the largest student protest march the country had seen. The issue was one in which students could be said to have a selfish interest: a demand for increased bursaries. It may have helped that as founder of the National Club, Taylor was already on speaking terms with Holyoake and his deputy Jack Marshall. The protest yielded results: in the mid-year Budget, government raised bursaries by up to one-third. As Taylor said later, 'I became intoxicated with the idea that with research, useful argument and public protest one could achieve anything.'[41]

As opposition to the war grew, visits from American envoys became more frequent. In February 1966, just hours before the arrival of Johnson's Vice-President Hubert Humphrey, four young protesters chained themselves to pillars in Parliament grounds. 'Ordinary middle-class ways of demonstrating are just no use any more,' one of the tethered quartet told the *Evening Post*.[42] It was nothing British suffragettes hadn't done half a century earlier, and meek compared to the kinds of protest that would follow, but it marked a step away from the polite, acceptable marches of the Old Left. Later, outside the American ambassador's residence, there were scuffles between protesters, police and security guards. 'Misguided youths and their calamitous looking female associates' were to blame, according to the *National Observer*, the National Party's monthly publication.

In October, Lyndon Johnson himself paid a visit, the first American President to do so. Though protesters gathered outside the American consul's office in Auckland and Government House in Wellington, they were heavily outnumbered by thousands of supporters who turned up for a glimpse of the tall Texan statesman. But it was predominantly protesters who gathered at Parliament for the arrival of South Vietnamese Prime Minister Air Vice-Marshal Ky in January 1967. Ky had risen to leadership after participating in the 1963 coup that saw former leader President Diem assassinated. He had been involved in numerous subsequent coups in the unstable South, and his professed admiration for Hitler provided those protesting his visits with damning material. In Auckland, two thousand demonstrators assembled outside the Town Hall where Ky was to speak, and later a smaller but more unruly group marched on the Star Hotel where Ky was staying, and where there were violent scenes and nine arrests.

In his 1979 thesis on the Auckland opposition to the Vietnam War, Paul Jackman noted this as a watershed moment. 'The police violence outside the Star Hotel was for most of the demonstrators a new experience. Being roughed-up by an employee of the New Zealand Government did not teach anything new about the war in Vietnam but it still had the effect of creating a measurable and immediate opponent so that the demonstrator felt less that he or she was just protesting alone without being heard, but rather was involved in a radical struggle.'[43] All the younger people he interviewed 'said that the violence against what they considered legitimate non-violent political activity caused them to have much less faith in New Zealand as a free democratic society'.[44] The Ky demonstrations were notable also for the involvement of the newly formed Progressive Youth Movement, whose confrontational stunts [of which more in Chapter 6] would add to the tension.

In August, a visit from US presidential advisers Clark Clifford (soon to become Secretary of Defense) and General Maxwell Taylor drew two thousand protesters to Parliament grounds. Though it could be safely assumed the American visitors were here to seek an increase in New Zealand troops, for Clifford the Wellington visit sowed the seeds of his own doubt. Two years later, after he had left office, he recalled that while meeting with Holyoake and his Cabinet:

> [H]undreds of students picketed the Parliament Building carrying signs bearing peace slogans ... New Zealand at one time had 70,000 troops overseas in the various theatres of World War II. They had 500 men in Viet Nam. I naturally wondered if this was their evaluation of the respective dangers of the two conflicts. I returned home puzzled, troubled, concerned. Was it possible that our assessment of the danger to the stability of Southeast Asia and the Western Pacific was exaggerated? Was it possible that those nations which were neighbours of Viet Nam had a clearer perception of the tides of world events in 1967 than we?[45]

ALTERED STATES

Three

When John Roy Hayward, a twenty-seven-year-old barman, was convicted in February 1960 of selling marijuana, the magistrate remarked: 'It is the first occasion in ten years on the bench that I have heard anything to do with charges concerning marijuana.'[1]

Hayward had been tending bar at the Criterion Hotel in Ōtāhuhu when he was approached by a man he had previously met while working on trawlers in Wellington. Unknown to Hayward, the man was a detective in the police special duties branch. He said he had heard Hayward could get 'reefer'—an American term for marijuana cigarettes, popularised by *Reefer Madness*, a lurid 1936 movie masquerading as moral guidance, in which a group of high school students smoke marijuana and descend into manslaughter and madness. Could Hayward get him some?

René Wilson, Herne Bay, Auckland, circa 1970.
Max Oettli photograph, Alexander Turnbull Library, PAColl-1386-1

In court Hayward wouldn't say how he had come by the drug, but testified to its benefits. 'I had a bit of wife trouble. Someone offered me one and it gave me a bit of a boost. Every time I felt a bit downhearted I'd have one.'[2]

JAZZ CIGARETTES AND SMOKING GUNS

During the sixties, smoking marijuana became a shared act that linked members of an evolving counterculture. But at the start of the decade, unless you moved in the kind of circles Hayward did—in bars, on boats, among transients and itinerants—you were unlikely to come across so much as a whiff of it. Few smoked it, even fewer grew it, and those who did kept it on the down-low.

It went by a variety of names: reefer, pot, grass, Indian hemp, jazz cigarettes, *special* cigarettes. In Mexico they called it marijuana, and this was the word picked up by American prohibitionists, probably because it made it sound foreign and dangerous. In *On the Road* it was referred to as tea. Jazz icon Louis Armstrong called it muggles, a word that would much later be appropriated, ironically, by children's author J. K. Rowling to refer to those lacking magical powers: the straight world, in Harry Potter terms.

During the Second World War, members of American Artie Shaw's jazz band, in New Zealand on a morale-boosting tour of US marine stations, had asked local musicians where they might find some, to no avail.[3] The marines, however, had their own supply, likely brought in on a banana boat acquired by the US Navy to ferry troops and supplies from the Pacific Islands.[4] By the fifties the local jazzers had begun to smoke it. For anyone with an interest in African-American music, Beat literature or the dark underside of popular culture, marijuana held a romantic allure. It featured in Billie Holiday's ghostwritten *Lady Sings the Blues* and in the autobiography of jazz clarinetist, proto-hipster and self-described 'voluntary Negro' Mezz Mezzrow. Film-noir star Robert Mitchum's cool had snowballed after he spent six weeks in prison in 1949 for possession.

Pot-smokers developed their own vocabulary. They *turned on* and *got high*. *Weird*, *strange*, *bizarre*, *far-out* ... they would mutter to each other or themselves as they contemplated some aspect of the world with their freshly rearranged synapses, or registered some small, curious coincidence, the significance of which had been magnified by their stoned state. They identified fellow users as potheads, or simply heads.

The use of marijuana amplified the sense of otherness that already existed among the bohemian crowd. Added to their questioning of such beliefs as the necessity of war or the sanctity of the nuclear family, it removed them even further from the rugby-beer-and-home-improvement society from which they felt estranged. Its effects were so markedly different from those of alcohol, the country's legally sanctioned intoxicant, that drinkers became an object of derision. 'Pissheads', pot-smokers would scoff.

Nonetheless, the covert nature of recreational drug-taking meant that marijuana inevitably brought bohemians into contact with a criminal world they might otherwise have had little reason to engage with. Ever since the introduction of six o'clock closing in 1917, beerhouses had operated where people could drink after hours. The beerhouse was usually a nondescript dwelling in the suburbs, its location advertised by word of mouth, where someone who had procured a supply of alcohol would dispense it for an inflated price. The beerhouses were illegal and police often shut them down, only for them to pop up again somewhere else. But little serious effort was put into patrolling them when many police officers tacitly disapproved of the licensing laws and were known to frequent such premises when off duty.

Beerhouses, often run by criminals or their associates, provided cover for other illicit activities such as gambling, prostitution and drug dealing. They could be a safe haven for crims to meet, share knowledge and plan jobs.[5] But they also attracted general defectors from the straight world, including musicians and poets. For a period in the early sixties the poet and short-story writer John Yelash ran his own beerhouse. Other beerhouse habitués included Gordon Esam (half-brother of the poet John Esam) and Bryce Peterson, a former borstal boy and petty criminal-turned folk singer and drug dealer to the bohemian set.

A couple of weeks before Christmas 1963, bad blood between two groups of operators resulted in two men being shot dead in a beerhouse in the upscale Auckland suburb of Remuera. The fact that a machine-gun was used in the murders—common in depictions of gangland USA but exotic in 1960s New Zealand—gave an extra-sensational slant to the headlines. A favourite on NZBC's recently launched national television was American crime show *The Untouchables*, set in Chicago during the prohibition era. Suddenly 1920s Chicago seemed to have come to Auckland.

Ronald Jorgensen and John Gillies, sometime seamen and full-time criminals, were found guilty of the slayings. Prominent in reports of their trial was the fact that the pair had smoked marijuana before committing the crime. The weapon, a .45-calibre Reising submachine-gun, had been procured for Gillies by Bryce Peterson, who had got to know Jorgenson and Gillies while all three were in borstal in the early 1950s. After the killings, Gillies had laid low for several days at the home of Gordon Esam.[6]

The Bassett Road machine-gun murders hastened the end of the beerhouse era, which would be finished off a few years later with the introduction of ten o'clock closing. Though the incident remained an outlier, the link between marijuana and psychotic violence was perpetuated by the press, the police and particular Members of Parliament.

In the months following the Bassett Road convictions, musicians and bohemians increasingly became the focus of police attention. Undercover detectives in Auckland infiltrated a jazz-listening session above a Cook Street panelbeaters' shop, where reefers were being passed around while bebop was played. Attempting unconvincingly to depict a scene of debauchery, a detective told the court: 'Some go into hysterical laughter and can't stop—others give the general impression of being drunk while some go into a trance when music is played.'[7] In separate incidents, two of the country's top professional jazz musicians, singer Marlene Tong and pianist/saxophonist Claude Papesch, were charged with cannabis possession.

Meanwhile, jazz trumpeter Geoff Murphy, now a primary school teacher, had 120 cannabis plants growing on the nature table in his Wellington classroom, ostensibly part of a science project. He had asked all the children in his class to bring seeds from home—birdseed would do, he told them—thus providing himself with an alibi should he ever be questioned. He never was, and once the plants had reached a foot or so in height they were transplanted, and eventually harvested and disseminated through the local jazz scene.

RITUAL AND RETRIBUTION

An amendment to the Dangerous Drugs Act in 1960 had increased the penalties for possession to up to seven years in prison. A new Narcotics Act, introduced in 1965, classified marijuana as a narcotic, which was pharmacologically incorrect, placing it in the same category as opiates such as opium and heroin. That year Bob Walton, who had led the Bassett Road case and subsequently been promoted to Chief Detective Inspector, visited the United States, where he was taken on 'a tour of American drug hotspots'.[8] He returned an anti-drug zealot and would go on to oversee the establishment of vice squads around the country.

Local surfers were meantime being introduced to marijuana on surfing trips abroad or by visiting wave-chasers from the United States and Australia. A student at high school in Christchurch in 1967 had a classmate who was a champion junior surfer. One night at a party he realised that what the surfer friend was smoking with a couple of older surfers in the back yard was marijuana. He encountered it again a year or two later in Wairoa on the East Coast, where its use seemed to be rife among the boardriders. It transpired that entrepreneurial Aussies had smuggled quantities of high-grade marijuana into the country encased in their fibreglass surfboards.[9]

Local pop groups, responding to pot references in the songs of the Beatles, Bob Dylan and other social influencers, were early adopters. In 1968 the Underdogs were invited to perform the Beatles' song 'The Inner Light' on *C'mon*: a rare sighting of an underground band on the normally strait-laced New Zealand television pop show. Their appearance, hairy and inordinately amused by some apparently private joke, led *Truth* to ask in a headline: 'Underdogs Gone to Pot?'[10] In Wellington, Rick Bryant, setting out on a singing career with bands Gutbucket and the Original Sin, was simultaneously discovering the attractions of marijuana. 'It is as if the music you are hugely enjoying visualises itself as substantial, in the sense that you think you can reach out and touch it,' he would write.[11]

In 1969, Ricky Ball, who would go on to play drums with psychedelic rockers Ticket and later Hello Sailor, was in chart-scaling pop group the Challenge on a national package tour, sandwiched between pop star Larry Morris (recently departed from Larry's Rebels and embarking on a solo career) and middle-New Zealand favourites the Hamilton County Bluegrass Band. Travelling between shows, the Challenge occupied the centre of the bus, both literally and figuratively. The country pickers sat up front breathing the clean air, while Morris and his band occupied the rear. Ball remembers: 'We used to smell this stuff coming from the back of the bus, and it wasn't bluegrass!'[12]

Though his band had been the Rebels, Morris's public image had hardly been rebellious. His hits were heard on radio; he was a regular on *C'mon*; he had even stood in a pulpit and read extracts from the Bible in a television programme about religion in New Zealand. He had left the band and was being groomed for a post-rock career in cabaret when, in early 1971, he was busted for cannabis possession. The papers gloated over his fall from grace. The breweries, by this time running most of the licensed music venues, cancelled his contracts. By the end of the year, Morris was in even more serious trouble: charged and convicted with supplying LSD, for which he was sentenced to seven years in prison.

In Britain and North America marijuana was often mixed with tobacco and smoked more like a cigarette, but New Zealanders preferred their grass uncut. They would roll it into small but generous cigars from which they inhaled deeply. They also developed a ritual of sharing. Flatmates would form a small ceremonial circle around which a lighted joint was passed. At a party, several joints might burn at once, while at bigger occasions such as festivals, rock shows or protest marches, strangers might be invited to join a circle of smokers in recognition of a common cause. Clandestine as pot-smoking was, it was easy enough to detect by its sweet loamy smell—but it wasn't always easy to see where. In public, smokers developed a way of passing joints almost by sleight of hand, and those in possession were always ready to throw away their stash (often carried in a matchbox) if detected. Penalties for possession were high. Nonetheless, the number of arrests began to climb. In 1968, thirty-four people were charged in New Zealand courts. In 1970, the number had quadrupled.[13]

Though marijuana was primarily an urban phenomenon, it also fitted with a romantic pastoralism to which the counterculture was partial. Tolkien's hobbits had, after all, smoked something called pipe-weed. Local cultivation became increasingly common, and the soil and

A heavy night in Herne Bay, Auckland, circa 1971. Max Oettli photograph, Alexander Turnbull Library, PAColl-1386-1

climate usually proved favourable. 'Man Grew Cannabis at Porirua On Scale Never Before Seen', reported the *Evening Post* in November 1971, after a thirty-three-year-old man appeared in court charged with growing more than eighty plants in an area of wasteland behind the local marae. Though the size of this operation would soon be dwarfed by that of increasingly ambitious and professionalised growers, marijuana was mostly being distributed for modest profit by a small group of dealers, all smokers themselves, with a sense of camaraderie and a clientele comprised largely of friends and associates.

In 1971 David Riley, a postgraduate psychology student at Canterbury University, and Bob Gidlow, a psychology and sociology lecturer, conducted surveys of drug use among students. Discussing their research on National Radio's 'Aspect' programme, Riley said that marijuana was the most widely used drug on campus, and by equal numbers of males and females. Users were mainly atheists or agnostics, politically left of centre or apolitical. They tended to live in flats rather than hostels or family homes, and reported more sexual activity than non-users. They also tended to judge police 'much less favourably than did non-users'. Riley concluded: 'These things indicate that there is a particular lifestyle associated with marijuana use. Whether this is contingent upon marijuana use or whether this results in marijuana use is open to question.'[14]

For the new culture, marijuana use had become 'both a sacrament and a political act', as historian Redmer Yska put it, though as we shall see, it was not the only drug.[15]

SEIZING POWER IN THE UNIVERSE

A couple of years after he obtained the machine-gun that his friend John Gillies used in the Bassett Road killings, Bryce Peterson took LSD. For the first hour or so nothing seemed to be happening. Then he looked at his Dalmatian dog and noticed that its spots were moving down its body and congregating at the end of its tail. A spotted dog with a black patch over one eye was now a white dog with a black tail. That was odd. Nevertheless, Bryce and his wife, who had also taken a dose of the hallucinogen, decided to go for a drive. Somehow they made it across town to the Auckland Domain where they spent the rest of the day looking at trees and flowers, seeing them as they never had before, pulsing with colour and life. It was, Peterson said, 'the most beautiful day I've ever had in my life'.[16]

In its utopianism the counterculture would imagine many kinds of enlightenment: sexual, societal, spiritual and psychological. For some, the source of those imaginings, and the gateway to them, was drugs — in particular LSD.

> If we could sniff or swallow something that would, for five or six hours each day, abolish our solitude as individuals, attune us

with our fellows in a glowing exaltation of affection and make life in all its aspects seem not only worth living, but divinely beautiful and significant, and if this heavenly, world-transfiguring drug were of such a kind that we could wake up next morning with a clear head and an undamaged constitution—then, it seems to me, all our problems (and not merely the one small problem of discovering a novel pleasure) would be wholly solved and earth would become paradise.[17]

So wrote the English novelist and philosopher Aldous Huxley in 1931. He had got something like his wish in 1953 when a psychiatrist friend, Humphrey Osmond, gave him mescaline. Huxley recorded his experiences of the drug in *The Doors of Perception*, published the following year. Receiving a perplexed reception in reviews from the time, the book would become an essential text on the countercultural bookshelf. After further experimentation with a similar drug, lysergic acid diethylamide, or LSD, Huxley and Osmond, in a match of creative wordplay, invented the term 'psychedelic', while Huxley would go on to write the novel *Island*, a 'utopian blueprint for what a psychedelically enlightened society might be like'.[18]

Though LSD would come to be the most publicised hallucinogenic drug, and the one most associated with the counterculture, humans have been taking hallucinogens for thousands of years. In Mexico, pre-European religious ceremonies involved ingesting such substances as peyote, prepared from the San Pedro cactus, and psilocybin, found in so-called magic mushrooms, both of which can produce powerful hallucinations. German scientists in the late nineteenth century had already created mescaline, a synthetic version of the psychoactive alkaloid in peyote.[19] From the early twentieth century it was being used experimentally in the treatment of schizophrenia.

LSD was actually a mistake. In 1938, Albert Hofmann, a researcher at Sandoz Pharmaceuticals in Switzerland, had been trying to produce a remedy for asthma. He discovered the drug's psychoactive properties only when he accidentally absorbed some through his finger-tips. Riding home from work, he nearly fell off his bicycle. In a report subsequently filed with his Sandoz supervisor, Hofmann described 'an uninterrupted stream of fantastic images of extraordinary plasticity and vividness and accompanied by an intense kaleidoscopic play of colours'.[20]

By the late 1940s, Sandoz had begun to supply LSD to select researchers. One of these was Timothy Leary, a clinical psychologist based at Harvard. In 1960, during a visit to Mexico, Leary had taken psilocybin and called it 'the deepest religious experience in my life. I discovered that beauty, revelation, sensuality, the cellular history of the past, God, the Devil—all lie inside my body, outside my mind.'[21] On his return to Harvard, he started a project with colleague Richard Alpert to explore the use of psychedelics in treatment. Among his experiments was a programme with prisoners, combining psilocybin with psychotherapy as a form of rehabilitation, with apparently positive results.

Believing that psychedelics could be as revolutionary and world-transfiguring as Huxley had predicted, Leary looked to form alliances beyond the medical profession. He found one in the poet Allen Ginsberg, who declared that these new 'wisdom drugs' were at the centre of a major shift in human consciousness. 'It's time,' the poet said, 'to seize power in the universe.'[22] The university establishment started to see Leary's experiments as unprofessional and cultish, and he was eventually fired from Harvard, but by this time he had the fame and momentum to go it alone.

Another favourite book among the growing psychedelic cult was the *Tibetan Book of the Dead*. Alpert called it 'the most vivid description of what we were experiencing with psychedelics but hadn't been able to describe … and there it was, described in this book that was 2500 years old'.[23] The text would become the basis of Leary, Alpert and Richard Metzner's book *The Psychedelic Experience*, which in turn would inspire the Beatles' psychedelic opus 'Tomorrow Never Knows'.

PSYCHONAUTS AND TRIP ADVISERS

With proselytisers like Leary and Alpert, LSD became fashionable in the US in bohemian and intellectual circles. By the early sixties, as Jay Stevens noted, 'in a major city like Los Angeles it was as easy to go on an LSD trip as it was to visit Disneyland'.[24] Britain did not yet have an LSD subculture. A New Zealander would play a pivotal role in initiating one.

In early 1961, John Esam had left New Zealand for London, via New York: a 'would-be-Baudelaire' dressed in 'nuclear black', as he was described by the Australian novelist Patrick White, who had met him and favourably appraised his work.[25] Five days after his arrival in the English capital, Esam wrote: 'London is so full of awareness, like porcelain blood … The people here, each one is "getting on with himself", each living the real fate of his form in some way.'[26]

For the next couple of years he moved around Europe, a human connector in a circuit of poets, artists, seekers and dissenters that its members referred to as 'the Scene'. In Paris he stayed at a run-down guesthouse in the Latin Quarter that the American poet Gregory Corso had dubbed the Beat Hotel. 'You could go to London, Paris, Athens, and you would see the same people,' says Dan Richter, an American poet, mime artist and fellow member of the Scene, who became acquainted with Esam during this period. 'We all knew each other. It was very small.'[27]

Back in London, Esam and Richter organised what British histories of the counterculture have identified as its seminal moment: The International Poetry Incarnation at the Royal Albert Hall. Esam

London, June 1965: Allen Ginsberg (centre), with John Esam on his right, and Dan Richter beside Esam. John 'Hoppy' Hopkins photograph © 1965, Estate of J. V. L. Hopkins

had learnt that in June 1965 Allen Ginsberg, fellow poet Lawrence Ferlinghetti and Gregory Corso were all due to be in London. Also in town was Barbara Rubin, the New York experimental filmmaker whose photo had appeared on the back cover of Bob Dylan's electrified and electrifying *Bringing It All Back Home* album, released that March. Encouraging the team to think big, Rubin booked the Albert Hall. Richter's wife Jill paid the deposit with a loan from her mother.

A poetry reading in a seven-thousand-seat hall was unprecedented; most would have said wildly over-ambitious. But word rippled through the Scene and beyond, and on the night the venue was filled to capacity, with many turned away. In an early demonstration of flower power (the term was coined that year by Ginsberg), flowers discarded at day's end by the Covent Garden florists were handed out to the crowds. Marijuana smoke hung thick in the air. It was an ambience that by the end of the decade would come to typify rock concerts, but in London at this time there had not yet been a rock concert anything like this. The 'happening', as such events came to be known, was the preserve of poets. The four-hour programme paired the American Beat icons with notable contemporary poets on the British scene, including Adrian Mitchell, Alexander Trocchi, Tom McGrath and Esam.

Richter remembers standing with Esam in the wings as the night unfolded. 'We wanted it to be like a living room or pad or something so we had put couches and chairs and reading lamp in the middle of the ring and the poets would sit around and take turns to get up and read in the round. It was very dramatic. I remember saying to Johnny, "What happened? Where did all these people come from?" It was like it happened overnight.

'These people were listening to the new music that was out there, they were reading this stuff and they were starting to smoke dope and they were contemplating giving up their jobs. And suddenly everybody was there, and from that point it was out in the open. I really regard the Albert Hall as the turning point. From then on, suddenly there were be-ins and demonstrations. The whole thing just took off at that point. That's what John and I were realising that night. That this thing had happened.'[28]

Another friend of Esam's around this time was an Englishman, Michael Hollingshead.[29] Hollingshead had been a British cultural attaché in New York in 1961 when he first took LSD, legally obtained from Sandoz. Profoundly affected by the experience, Hollingshead contacted Leary, who invited him to join in his research programme. Eventually Hollingshead returned to Britain, arriving weeks after the Albert Hall happening, bringing with him several hundred copies of the *Tibetan Book of the Dead* and a quantity of LSD. Esam, who had already begun his own experiments with chemically altered states before he left New Zealand, soon became an advocate. Writer Barry Miles recalled Esam having 'a store of thousands of LSD trips ... and was evangelical about its beneficial qualities'. He noted that Esam's 'altered vision meant that his conversation often appeared to be elliptical, even far removed from everyday reality'.[30]

Dan Richter says Esam took his psychedelics seriously. 'If you're going to go on a spiritual quest you don't have to wear tie-dyed shirts, bellbottomed pants and a fright wig. He always wore normal dark clothes, was clean and had a haircut. I don't see him as a person who was out to party. He was on a serious quest.'[31]

By late 1965, Hollingshead and Esam were known in London as the two reliable sources of LSD. They would also prepare and accompany you on your trip: psychonauts and trip advisers. Hollingshead had set up a flat in Chelsea which he named the World Psychedelic Centre, and where he organised 'workshops for consciousness expansion', hosting such guests as Roman Polanski, William Burroughs, Donovan and the Beatles.[32] Esam's flat was just around the corner in Lennox Gardens. In nearby Kensington was the large Cromwell Road house where Esam's friend Nigel Lesmoir-Gordon lived with his wife Jenny and a revolving cast of creatives, the most famous of whom was Syd Barrett, founder of the band Pink Floyd. Barrett's experiments with LSD inspired some of his most adventurous music, though may also have been a catalyst for the mental illness that would ultimately curtail his career. Esam, a friend of Barrett's, was a frequent guest.

But the British state, already dealing with youth unrest in the anti-war movement, was about to intervene. In February 1966, Esam's flat was raided and he became the first person in Britain to be arrested on charges relating to possession of the drug. Though LSD was not yet illegal, he was charged with possessing ergot, from which LSD is derived and which was illegal under the Poisons Act.[33]

The prosecution seemed determined to make an example of the New Zealander, and mounted a long and costly case, which even included an appearance by Albert Hofmann, LSD's inventor, flown in especially from Switzerland. At the trial in April 1966, prosecutor George Schindler stated that LSD was a hallucinatory drug and it was an offence to sell it without a prescription, adding, as if to imply a conspiracy, that 'it is clear that Esam is in touch with people all over the world who are taking this drug'.[34] Esam, in his defence, called on the Nobel Prize-winning biochemist Professor Ernst Chain, who trumped Hofmann's evidence with the argument that LSD did not conform to the poison rules at the time of the raid and that therefore Esam could not be guilty. In January 1967, after a trial that had been drawn out over almost a year, he was finally acquitted.[35]

Esam swore off LSD after this, but he continued to write poetry and remained a significant figure in London countercultural circles. At the end of 1967 he co-organised the happening Christmas On Earth Continued, an 'all night Christmas dream party' at the Kensington Olympia featuring Pink Floyd, Jimi Hendrix, Soft Machine and the Who. He performed a dance scene in experimental filmmaker Conrad Rooks's cultish psychedelic drama *Chappaqua*, alongside appearances by Allen Ginsberg and Ravi Shankar. And a fortuitous meeting with Arthur C. Clarke resulted in him securing his friend Dan Richter an iconic — if unrecognisable — movie role as the ape in the opening scene of *2001: A Space Odyssey*.

UNSKILLED EXPERIMENTS

Although John Esam maintained a correspondence with family and a small number of close friends, few people back in New Zealand knew anything of his activities.

New Zealanders had been reading about LSD since 1954, when an article syndicated from the UK reported that 'scientists have invented a new drug which takes people back to their earliest childhood' and went on to describe hallucinations reminiscent of *Alice In Wonderland*. 'Under the drug a woman of 29 became a child of five or six years old. She felt her clothes were huge and hung loosely about her.'[36] Popular American magazines such as *Time* and *Life* had run features, noting the use of the drug by celebrities under the supervision of their doctors.

Local psychiatrists had begun to use the drug in treatment programmes. Over a two-year period from July 1964, Dr David Livingstone, working at Calvary Private Hospital in Christchurch, had administered LSD to fifty-five consenting patients in 131 sessions of up to eight hours each. In the October 1966 edition of the *New Zealand Medical Journal*, Livingstone wrote positively of the drug as a therapeutic tool, opining that it 'offers great promise of effectiveness in the correction of psychiatric illness ... In nearly all cases its proper use results in very significant acquisition of insight and self-understanding.'[37] But he cautioned about the dangers should the drug, with its 'life threatening personality disintegrating propensities', fall into 'the hands of unskilled experimenters'. This, he suggested, would 'seem to be akin to the release of atomic fission products in an agricultural irrigation scheme, or the handing over of a pressure-cooker to a nine-year-old child'.[38]

But by then New Zealanders were already conducting their own unskilled experiments. The anarchist Bill Dwyer had arrived in Auckland in 1963, leaving behind the various kinds of havoc he had created in Wellington and seeking a new audience. He found one in Myers Park, at that time the only area in central Auckland designated for public speaking. Every Sunday he would be there, loudly and colourfully haranguing the crowds.

'Bill had a rich Irish-accented baritone voice and was a fluent and entertaining speaker,' recalled Michael Morrissey, a regular attender. 'His targets were much the same every week: government, censorship, sexual liberation, freedom to take drugs. He got plenty of hecklers and seemed to enjoy the challenge of interruption. Soon he had a regular captive audience which included vocal members of left and right wing persuasion.'[39]

Dwyer's performances tested the limits of what was considered free speech in New Zealand, and in early 1966 he was charged with using offensive language after calling the Queen 'a bludger' and the YWCA 'a brothel'. He was fined £15. After that he returned to Wellington, intending to stop only briefly en route to Australia, but his departure was delayed by an accident. During a romantic tryst in the Town Belt, a fence had given way beneath him, sending the anarchist tumbling down a bank and breaking vertebrae in his neck. This forced him to remain in Wellington for longer than intended, sporting an elaborate neck brace. Rex Benson, a fellow anarchist whose girlfriend was rooming at Dwyer's, recalled waking one night to the 'fearsome sight' of Dwyer on the opposite side of the room, naked but for the plaster brace, attempting to accommodate himself, his girlfriend and the plaster protuberance in a single bed.[40]

Eventually Dwyer reached Australia where he resumed his public speaking role, this time in the Sydney Domain, where he would sometimes appear dressed as a clown or Santa Claus. 'Chaplinesque' is how he was described by Nicholas Pounder, who saw him in action there on several occasions.[41] By this time Dwyer had become an advocate of the transformative powers of LSD. He would dispatch Rex Benson, who had joined him in Sydney, to a post office in the outer suburbs to collect packages of blotting-paper sheets impregnated with the drug. Benson never knew where the substance was being produced, but understood it to be the work of 'a local scientist who knew what he was doing'.[42] Benson brought the sheets back to the flat he shared with Dwyer, and the pair would cut them into even squares, each containing approximately 2 micrograms of LSD, which Dwyer would then dispense from a central-city pad known by word of mouth as The Cellar.

To Dwyer, acid and anarchism went hand in hand. On one occasion he chartered two buses from the Sydney Transport Department for a party in the Wattamolla picnic area of Royal National Park. There would be live music, dancing and recreational drug use. Tipped off to the proposed picnic, the *Sunday Telegraph* became inadvertent promoters, reporting Dwyer's plans the weekend before. Its correspondent dutifully turned up on the day and his account appeared under the headline '80 Teenage Junkies Take LSD Trip':

> The LSD group arrived in the park shortly before lunch and unpacked Anarchist and 'Red' flags, a generator to power their electric guitars, and their drugs ... A long-haired youth had a 'hookah' or water-pipe which he used to smoke marijuhana ... A fourteen-year-old girl visited the lavatories three times in half an hour, always looking pale and drawn. Each time that she left the lavatories she staggered. She was laughing and giggling hysterically.[43]

The police had become interested in Dwyer's activities, and shortly after the picnic Dwyer was arrested, charged and convicted for selling LSD. In 1969, having served only part of an eighteen-month sentence, he was deported to Ireland.

Though New Zealand had often lagged behind the rest of the world, in 1967 it had its psychedelic summer right on cue. Some of Dwyer's LSD had found its way back across the Tasman, along with supplies from other offshore sources. At this stage, New Zealand Customs had no directive or protocols to search for the drug. Turned-on travellers returning from Sydney or San Francisco would carry sheets of LSD trips into the country barely hidden in their hand luggage.

With the recently released debut of the Doors (named after Huxley's *Doors of Perception*) and Jimi Hendrix's knowingly titled *Are You Experienced?* playing in the background, hundreds of New Zealanders experienced LSD for the first time. Deborah Yates, living in a community of Parnell flats, recalls friend and neighbour Murray Grimsdale returning from Australia 'raving about this stuff called

Civic Square, Wellington, 1972. Ans Westra photograph, Alexander Turnbull Library, PA-Group-00941

LSD. He had this friend who had been making it and he said he could get us some. It wasn't illegal yet. So he got this envelope of green blotting paper which we'd cut up and chew.' Yates added, 'We'd do it on a Saturday morning, we'd all dress up in our colours and feathers and blankets and things and just go across the road to the Domain and wander around. And it was amazing. It was very pure acid, nothing negative about it. I don't know how many times we did that but quite a few.'[44]

LSD users fell broadly into two camps: knowledge seekers and pleasure seekers. The former acknowledged the seriousness of the drug. 'It wasn't "come on Barbie, let's go party",' one sixties tripper told me.

'Acid was too scary to be just hedonistic. It was the bungy of the day. It was going into the mines of Moria, where the Balrog might get you.'

For the knowledge seeker, the payoff was in the glimpses of a greater truth, yet these could be experienced by the pleasure seekers too. Rachel Stace, who had followed her idols the Beatles down the psychedelic path, initially saw herself as one of the latter group. 'We put on our tripping clothes and went off to the park and we'd sit in the trees in our beautiful clothes. Goodness knows what people thought. But it was all very innocent, just sitting there giggling, looking at nature. In fact, it was the foundation of my spiritual beliefs now, because you just knew you were all interconnected and there was some sort of living force that you couldn't really see properly until you were on acid. And then it all became clear. Nature was beautiful, the world was beautiful, and it was all amazing.'[45]

Pat Hanly had returned to New Zealand with his family in 1962, and over the next few years became recognised as one of the country's foremost expressionist painters. Searching for ways to release himself and his work from what he called 'the control of habit reaction (physical and mental)', he became curious about LSD. In 1967 he took his first trip. 'Unbelievable tranquillity and awareness of all things,' he wrote in his journal the following day. 'Uncontrollable amusement at some things, very happy. Indescribable happenings all around, very calm today and finding awareness of trees and flowers etc still happening.' A further trip prompted him to note: 'The world glimpsed as it lives and dies in all things. Words for a description of this are not possible but the only thing that is constant is the … "IT IS" in everything, so clear. I saw a less afraid man watch me in the mirror. Gil, golden smooth and animal, eternal, indescribably beautiful and wonder full [sic].'[46]

The insights Hanly gained from the experience would inform his art. In a series of paintings, *'Inside' the Garden*, he attempted to convey what he had observed as 'the "molecular" difference of things, the chemical interaction'. The paintings showed people, plants, fruit and flowers with what Hanly's biographer Russell Haley described as 'the luminous interiority of their individual energies'.[47]

In Christchurch around the same time, a young art student, Philip Clairmont, was embarking on his own drug experiments. He was soon joined by fellow painter and psychic explorer Tony Fomison, recently returned from a spell in Britain. Clairmont's paintings, with their intensified colours and heightened details, are, as Martin Edmond notes, 'clearly psychedelic', while Fomison's darker canvases with their 'gallery of grotesques' are informed more by his use of opiates.[48]

A PSYCHEDELIC SOUNDTRACK

Drugs, especially LSD, were having a similarly unbinding effect on popular music, inspiring paisley sound palettes and ambitious long-form works that stretched way beyond the traditional three-minute pop song. With their ground-breaking *Sgt. Pepper's Lonely Hearts Club Band* the Beatles demonstrated that the long-playing album, once a collection of hits and fillers, could be treated as a complete work in the manner of a suite or symphony. The term 'pop' was beginning to be supplanted by the weightier 'rock'.

As authors of their own history, the boomers have tended to ascribe to rock—*their* music—a greater cultural importance than other types of popular music. In fact, music had long played a social role in New Zealand, from jazz-age dances in downtown ballrooms to the kind of rural knees-ups depicted so vividly in Peter Cape's song 'Down the Hall on Saturday Night'. Yet rock did provide more than just an accompaniment to dancing and courtship. Both sonically and lyrically it carried information about the changing world. On the sleeve of their first album, US psychedelic rock pioneers the Byrds had suggested that the volume and intensity of modern music was influenced by the arrival of the jet plane. Others heard a response to the existence of The Bomb. Where pop before the mid-sixties had concerned itself largely with idealised depictions of romantic love, rock gave voice to some of the generation's fears—of war, destruction and alienation—as well as its utopian longings. It dealt with sex in more explicit terms, explored Eastern philosophy and reflected on experiences with drugs. While some of it was undoubtedly pompous, there was also music of astonishing inventiveness and skill.

Little of this revolutionary music found its way onto New Zealand's publicly owned, conservatively managed airwaves. The commercial 'ZB' stations broadcast just one or two hours of contemporary music each day, usually in the early evening—'The Sunset Show' in Wellington, 'The Five to Seven Show' in Auckland, 'The Sound Show' in Christchurch. Playlists skewed to more conventional tastes—for every Byrds or Hendrix song approved by the programme directors, there seemed to be a dozen by Engelbert Humperdinck or Tom Jones—and singles were favoured over tracks from albums. The only local pop to reach the airwaves came from calculatedly mainstream acts groomed by the few local record labels. Nevertheless, the occasional piece of subversion would sneak through. With its insurgent chorus of 'Everybody must get stoned!', Bob Dylan's 'Rainy Day Women #7 & 35' had found its way onto the airwaves in 1966, the NZBC censors having perhaps been distracted from the lyric by the song's enigmatic title.

Personality disc jockeys such as Neville 'Cham The Man' Chamberlain and ('Hi there it's') Pete Sinclair interspersed their predominantly pop selections with a mock-hipster patter, diluted to match NZBC presentation standards. It was only the rare broadcaster such as Arthur Pearce who would air album tracks, often by artists who never had hit singles or exposure on New Zealand radio. Pearce had started out in the 1930s presenting a jazz programme. By the

1960s the Wellington-based broadcaster, now in his sixties and using the alias Cotton-Eyed Joe, was filling his weekly 'Big Beat Ball' with a connoisseur's selection of obscurities.

As the music of the era grew more eclectic, so did Pearce's programme, which spanned from American R&B to psychedelic rock. A typical half-hour might feature James Brown, Tarheel Slim, the Del Vikings and Moby Grape, the selections linked by a bewildering string of puns which Pearce delivered in his light, ageless voice. He would often speak to visiting international musicians, though never on air. These interviews, which he recorded in note form only, were simply to enhance his background knowledge or satisfy his curiosity on some obscure discographic detail. The visitors would be astounded by this conservatively dressed middle-aged man's knowledge of, and enthusiasm for, the most arcane pop. Visiting American pop star Gene Pitney called it 'the weirdest show I have ever heard in my life'.[49]

Pearce's broad yet impeccable taste would have an impact on local musicians whose horizons were immeasurably widened by his deeply knowledgeable presentations. For the teenage Rick Bryant, who would go on to sing with Mammal and BLERTA, 'Big Beat Ball' was appointment listening.

Radio Hauraki began in late 1966 in response to the pop music void left by the NZBC's monopoly and conservative programming. Inspired by the youth-focused stations he had heard in Sydney, and the much-publicised British pirate station Radio Caroline, former *Truth* journalist David Gapes had the notion to start a station of his own. To get around the rigid broadcasting regulations the private station would operate from a ship moored in international waters. On 1 December 1966, Radio Hauraki began broadcasting from the *Tiri*, moored in the Colville Channel to the west of Great Barrier Island, and could be picked up in Auckland and its environs.

While still focused primarily on pop singles, Radio Hauraki at least acknowledged the youth messaging of the new music. They would play the risqué pop records the state broadcaster deemed unsuitable. As music journalist Murray Cammick put it: 'Radio Hauraki did not need to worry about the meaning of "Lucy in the Sky With Diamonds" or what the Small Faces were doing in "Itchycoo Park".'[50] Their pirate status gave them a modicum of rebel cool. They branded themselves 'the Good Guys' (and they *were* all guys; no women DJs aboard the *Tiri*). Government regulators, state broadcasters and anyone else opposing them were, by implication, the Bad Guys.

Hauraki's countercultural moment was brief and more a matter of chance than stance. Gapes and his Good Guys were neither hippies nor revolutionaries. When they were granted a licence in mid-1970, they spearheaded what would ultimately become one of the most deregulated commercial radio markets in the world. But for a period in the late sixties they seemed to be on the same wavelength as those clamouring for freedom around the globe.[51]

Meanwhile in San Francisco, the crucible of the counterculture, the Summer of Love was unfolding to a soundtrack that would never be heard in New Zealand, on radio or anywhere else. Some have said it was a sound so mercurial it was never even captured on record.

San Francisco had spawned one of the original bohemian subcultures. In the 1950s this had been centred on North Beach, where cheap rents and a cosmopolitan community enabled a proliferation of art galleries, bookshops and bars. In the sixties an offshoot sprang up in the Haight-Ashbury district; by the middle of the decade this had become the world's most visible community of what were being called hippies.

Musicians formed a crucial part of this community. Bands such as Jefferson Airplane, the Grateful Dead and Big Brother and the Holding Company lived in the Haight-Ashbury, and embraced the same urban-communal lifestyles as their audiences. In Berkeley, on the east side of San Francisco Bay, Country Joe and the Fish reflected the more political mood of the university campus. Though these bands eventually made records, it was at live events that they came into their own. Their performances were collective happenings involving light shows, dancing and, inevitably, LSD. The template for these events had been the Acid Tests: drug-fuelled free-for-alls hosted by the writer Ken Kesey and his entourage known as the Merry Pranksters, at which LSD was handed out ritually.

Eventually New Zealand rock shows would come to emulate aspects of this scene, but in the sixties San Francisco's influence on local music was minimal. To New Zealand ears, San Francisco was represented by a couple of hit records by singers who were not from the city at all and whose music bore no relation to that of the Airplane or the Dead. Scott McKenzie, a soft-centred songster from Florida, scored a New Zealand number one with 'San Francisco (Wear Some Flowers In Your Hair)', a jingle for hippiedom penned by the Mamas and the Papas' John Phillips. Eric Burdon and the Animals got nearly as much attention with 'San Franciscan Nights', which sounded like a turned-on tourist commercial, its spoken voiceover urging listeners to 'fly Trans-Love Airways to San Francisco'.

The nearest New Zealand came to producing its own flower-power pop single came in 1968. Inspired by 'the most beautiful day' he had spent tripping with his wife in the Auckland Domain, Bryce Peterson went home and wrote 'Gracious Lady Alice Dee' (try saying the name aloud) and passed it on to peroxide pop star Lew Pryme. Opening with the lines 'We wandered through the multicoloured flowers, not knowing where the world might be', the song evoked the dazed and naive wonder of the newly turned on. It was not a hit, though it wasn't given much of a chance. In spite of Pryme abbreviating the title to 'Gracious Lady', the NZBC still refused to play it, and police reportedly removed copies from record stores. Peterson recorded another LSD-inspired song, the more overt and even more twee

'Slightly-Delic', with his own band the House of Nimrod, which fared no better.

But by this time the psychedelic summer had already been interrupted.

A CUP OF TEA FOR THE COPS

By 1967, New Zealand government authorities had begun a campaign against the drug, taking its cue from British and American responses, and bolstered by lurid newspaper stories from overseas. 'An LSD devotee might well jump from a window and kill himself on the "I can fly" assumption', reported the *Dominion*, quoting a consultant to the US Presidential Crime Commission under the headline 'Deranging Drug'.[52] 'New Mystery Drug Sending Hippies to Their Deaths' rang the headline in the *Evening Post*, which reported that in San Francisco LSD might soon be superseded by a 'new drug STP, which flies them farther out and keeps them higher longer than LSD'.[53]

Other reports suggested, misleadingly, that LSD was addictive. In mid-1967, Minister of Police Percy Allen had returned from a trip to the United States where he had met narcotics and law enforcement chiefs in California and Chicago convinced that the laws covering the use of LSD in New Zealand needed to be tightened. He had, he said, seen 'teenage LSD addicts' first hand in San Francisco, 'the real home of the hippies': 'I saw them by the hundreds in a park. Some wore shirts with the slogan: "Give LSD a try—it's the only way to fly." The addicts were dirty and unkempt. I was disgusted.'[54]

To Allen, as well as his US counterparts, controlling the use of LSD was evidently more than just a health issue or a question of public safety. The drug represented a way of life and a set of values that differed dramatically from his own and others of his generation. But though Allen blamed drugs for what he perceived to be moral and physical degeneracy, young New Zealanders had already begun to live their lives in ways that diverged radically from those of their parents before drugs came along. 'Until the early 1970s they were very hard to come by,' recalls Ken James. 'Most of us formed our views before their arrival. I believe that drugs had more influence on those who *didn't* take them, who realised that their thinking and way of life was under threat. Which it was.'[55]

On 7 July 1967, LSD was criminalised in New Zealand. In an antipodean echo of the Esam case, the first person in the country to be convicted of possessing LSD was a poet. Four days after the legislation was passed, Mark Young was arrested and charged with possessing the drug, along with a small amount of marijuana. In court, the magistrate, born in 1890, conceded that LSD had been developed for psychotherapeutic use but rejected the appeal of lawyer Frank Haigh that Young had found the drug helpful to his writing. 'Everyone who takes the narcotic merely for fun and games, or in the modern parlance for

Exploring consciousness in the Coromandel, circa 1973. Rachel Stace private collection

"kicks", is knowingly endangering himself physically and mentally and is helping to foster a nefarious public evil,' said the judge. He sentenced Young to six weeks in prison.[56]

It was the first of a series of rapid, well-publicised LSD busts. One day, Deborah Yates received an early-morning visit from Murray Grimsdale: 'Murray was living next door and came and knocked on the door, put his head in and said "Hi, have you got any milk? I'm being busted and I'm making a cup of tea for the cops", which was his way of letting us know.' If the bust was intended to scare straight the burgeoning hippie community to which Yates belonged, it didn't seem to have that effect. Yates's reaction to the raid was as insouciant as

Grimsdale's. 'We went across the road and rang Frank Haigh the lawyer, who went down to the police cells,' she remembers. 'And then we all dropped a trip and went off to the Domain—*schmerkling* we called it. *Schmerkle, schmerkle.* Colours everywhere. You could see the air and it was pink and blue, and once I saw Mickey Mouse and his children flying across the sky ... I was supposed to be at Teachers' College at the time.'[57]

In response to the law change and Young's sentencing, *Craccum* published a cover story on LSD by Michael Morrissey, which challenged the position adopted by state officials and the mainstream media. 'Where is the consistency in mores or morals in a society that permits the deaths from alcohol, tobacco and motor vehicles?' he asked. 'Has not the individual the right to try a new experience, even if it is merely for "kicks"?' he wrote, pointing out that climbing, skiing and motorcar racing 'all take their toll of life and ligament'.[58]

But the establishment was regrouping to drive home its own argument. Professionals such as Deputy Director of Health Dr William Murphy told the Wellington Lions Club in November 1967: 'Hippies, beatniks and other fringe groups are taking fantastic risks by using the drug with no medical supervision.' His speech was quoted in a *Dominion* report headlined 'LSD Drug Users "Play Russian Roulette"'.[59]

Whether the likes of Murphy and Allen believed that by simply removing drugs from the equation young people would go back to dressing conservatively, give up protesting and communal living, and return to their nuclear families is hard to say. But it is clear that to these officials, and to some of the civil servants charged with enforcing the laws, the strangeness of the countercultural lifestyle was taken as an affront, a challenge to their own way of life, and they would do all they could to shut it down.

Police were used to dealing with the criminal world; some maintained friendly relations with the old-school crims. They could talk to them about interests they had in common, like rugby, racing and beer. With this new generation of lawbreakers they wouldn't have known where to start. Yet psychedelic youth was not without its allies. In 1970, Tony Taylor, Professor of Clinical Psychology at Victoria University, whose research during the Beatles' 1964 tour had identified the special emotional needs of Beatles fans, addressed what he saw as society's hypocrisy when it came to the abuse of drugs. 'We live in a drug dependent community,' he told an inter-disciplinary seminar arranged by the Board of Health.

> The majority of our population seem to turn on at daybreak with amphetamines, to control diet with dexedrine, to moderate anxiety with tranquillisers, to lift depression with amitryptaline [sic], to socialise with alcohol, and finally turn off at night with barbiturates, all but one of which can be obtained under Social Security ...

However, this appellation 'drug abuser' is rarely given to the achievement oriented, anxiety ridden, depressed middle aged pillars of propriety, notwithstanding the severe social repercussions of their suicidal, alcoholic, aggressive and manipulative behaviour. Rather the scornful description is applied to the much smaller group of people who use narcotics, most of whom are from the younger generation, and as such form a relatively powerless minority group ...

The main difference between the groups would seem to be that those who use the narcotics, stimulants, hallucinogens and psychedelics try either to lift themselves or extend themselves, but the others use regular doses of their prescribed medication with which to tolerate, modify and support themselves.[60]

Taylor's sympathy for the young was echoed by DSIR toxicologist Ray Henwood when in 1968 he wrote that:

the goals and standards of our society which we claim are being rejected ... need some thinking about. I am convinced that the young in general are not particularly interested in wall-to-wall carpets and Siamese cats. Our present emphasis on our great technological advances seems to outweigh any thoughts on man's emotional technology ...

The worst thing we can do is send our law officers to America where the problem has reached such great proportions that the remedies used there could be quite harmful when applied to New Zealand ... It is of little use dismissing all drug offenders as a criminal anti-social element.

I am not here defending the unsupervised use of drugs but perhaps claiming that a 'Turned On' society has no chance— a 'Tuned In' one might have.[61]

But there was little hope that such guardians of the establishment as Allen and Walton would ever tune in to the new values of the counterculture. With the growing number of young people experimenting with LSD came an inevitable increase in the number, if not the proportion, of people experiencing bad trips. In 1971, Oakley psychiatric hospital medical superintendent P. P. E. Savage said he had seen 'perhaps about half a dozen ... during the last couple of years. The victims were in a state of utter confusion. One person said he saw running corpses, bloody and grotesque. He was being watched, he said, by "evil eyes".' Savage seemed to be in no doubt that in implementing strict prohibition, the police were doing the right thing. 'It must be stamped out at all costs,' he said.[62]

This view was backed up by a continuing stream of newspaper articles, cautionary tales from overseas now being replaced by lurid local headlines. 'A young man with a history of LSD-taking went berserk and tried to kill a male nurse in a hospital ward this week,' reported the *Sunday Times* in an article that would become the subject of a libel case [detailed in Chapter 5]. 'He had become hallucinated [sic] and deluded,' the paper claimed, 'believed the end of the world had come, that he was Jesus Christ, that the United States and Australia no longer existed and that Wellington Harbour had suddenly gone dry.'[63]

While such stories seemed to confirm the direst warnings of prohibitionists, these kinds of incidents were rare in proportion to the thousands of trips taken during this time. Though anyone in possession of LSD now risked steep penalties, use of the drug continued in a clandestine way, making ever wider the social gap between the turned on and the tuned out.

FREAK FLAGS, FREE LOVE

By the mid-sixties the Beatle moptop had been established as an essential accessory for any aspiring male pop musician. For most other young Kiwi men, the short-back-and-sides remained mandatory, alongside a bland and limited range of work and leisure clothing, while young women were expected to emulate the dress style of their mothers. Traditional notions of respectability combined with a broader authoritarianism to create a climate of conflict and uncertainty when some young adults began to break the mould.

Queen Street, Auckland, circa 1967.
Geoff Studd photograph, private collection

Alan Brunton recalled the first time he saw a male 'with hair down below his shoulders and a space around him as he walked down the street. "Who's that weirdo, what does this mean?"' But clothes played their part too. 'I remember, within my first six months at the university in Auckland, sitting in a history lecture, maybe there's six hundred, seven hundred students sitting there, and Julian Rosenberg walks in with his long, long hair and his silk and velvety totally mod look. And there was silence. It was a very intense experience and that was a moment when, in six hundred young minds, something changed.'[1]

For Tom White, a teenager attending high school in the Hutt Valley in the late sixties, long hair 'was a statement, absolutely. Letting my freak flag fly, like the Crosby, Stills, Nash and Young song, "Almost Cut My Hair". I'd walk past the hall and see the girls kneeling on the stage, and the deputy woman principal going around with a tape measure or a ruler, measuring between the floor and their hemline. That was what they had to deal with, and we had to deal with hair not being over the ears. I can really feel it to this day—it felt offensive and abusive, like my body is being managed without my say-so.'

Long hair, the school authorities said, was dirty, degenerate and made you look like a girl. After being issued a number of warnings, Tom, by now sixteen and legally old enough to leave school, was called into the office of the deputy principal. 'I remember him saying, "You either get your hair cut when I tell you to or you go. Come back and tell me what you decide." And I walked out of the room. I was barely a metre on the other side and I turned around and came back and said, "Right, I'm going. If that's what this is all about, if that's what school is about." I wasn't very articulate, but in other words, if this is what education is, then I'm out. I made that decision without talking to parents or friends or colleagues. I didn't leave myself a chance to cool down or reconsider. I was very clear he had crossed the line.'[2]

REBELLION STARTS ON THE CHIN

To grow your hair was to be aware of society's objections and do it anyway. It advertised your willingness to rebel, and acted as a signal to those who might be on your side. If you saw another person on the street with long hair you could assume they also opposed the Vietnam War, were in favour of smoking pot and had a liberal attitude to sex. And it was obvious that they had issues with authority.

'It was *épater la bourgeoisie*, shock the bourgeoisie!' says Roger Steele, quoting the rallying cry for the French Decadent poets of the late nineteenth century, among them Charles Baudelaire and Arthur Rimbaud. Steele had given up cutting his hair when he moved to Wellington for university in the late sixties. 'Why *not* grow your hair? Like why not be a pacifist? We've always had these norms. Actually long hair is beautiful. We've always thought it was beautiful on women, why can't it be beautiful on men? And it was beautiful on a heck of a lot of men. But yes, it upset our parents, and our parents stood for the establishment and repression and a lack of freedom.'[3]

By the same token, short hair could be seen to represent conservative values, confidence in authority and a vested interest in maintaining the established order. Institutions like the police force and the military, as well as schools, enforced strict hair regulations.

The rebellion had started on the chin. Until the middle of the decade, simply to wear a beard was enough to get you labelled a beatnik, a communist, a beardie-weirdie—and beaten up. Newspaper reports of local protest marches in the early sixties would note that some of the protesters wore facial hair, as though—along with corduroy trousers and duffel coats—this was confirmation of some dangerous otherness. Fidel Castro had a beard. The last New Zealand Prime Minister to wear one was Thomas McKenzie, briefly in office in 1912.

A few of the bearded also shunned the short-back-and-sides in favour of a slightly shaggier look, but in the mid-sixties even the matching fringes and collar-length straight cuts of the Beatles were considered unruly. As the decade went on, hair continued to grow. Hippies in San Francisco and other American cities simply stopped cutting it altogether. The men began to resemble Renaissance portraits of Jesus. Pop stars followed suit.

Hair became the subject of earnest newspaper enquiries. 'It is part of a protest by young people against the world they have inherited— a striving to assert individuality in a society which they see as having carefully-ordered surface values and hopelessly confused inner attitudes,' suggested the Christchurch *Press*'s David Brunton (no relation of Alan).[4] The *Auckland Star* seemed to heave a sigh of relief as it realised long hair was just another sign of conformity, before musing that perhaps a little non-conformity was not such a bad thing:

> What fearful threat to humanity is posed by the cultivation of long hair, that the defenders of the law and guardians of the establishment should raise their collective hackles in righteous horror? There is nothing intrinsically virtuous or evil about long hair—and questions of cleanliness and tidiness apply whatever the cut ... All the current fuss over long hair is simply one sign of the increasing intolerance being shown by modern society towards anyone or anything appearing to be different. There are many subtle pressures in today's world which seek to bend us all into a mindless conformity of views and behaviour.
>
> For all the sound and fury of its rebellion against its elders, the modern teenage generation tends to be as rigidly conformist as any other group ... One Auckland father recently confided: 'My teenage daughter has to know all the tunes in the top 10 or her classmates wouldn't speak to her.' And the hippies are another group which have merely traded one set of values for another which are just as inflexible ....

Papanui High School pupils protest a ban on long hair, February 1971. Christchurch City Libraries. CCL-StarP-00089A

But there is no need to be too pessimistic. There is a sufficient proportion of free-thinkers in every age-group in this country to make the vision of some future Orwellian brainwashed existence seem quite ridiculous … A civilisation exerts its pressures towards conformity only at the danger of extinguishing genius and breeding a uniform mediocrity.[5]

Some tried to rationalise their prejudices with safety arguments. An officer in the Lower Hutt Fire Brigade worried that long hair and beards could prove lethal for firemen, as 'toxic air can sneak in between the whiskers and the rubber of breathing apparatus'. A certain amount of regimentalism had to exist in the Fire Service, he added, so shorter hair should remain a requirement.[6]

In early 1972, as the school year was getting underway with headmasters ordering mass shearings, two Wellington secondary schools relented. Wellington High School principal Cyril Bradwell went on record as saying there were more important things in education than the length of someone's hair, while at Onslow College, where I was entering my Fourth Form year, a threatened strike by students (led by future historian James Belich who, at age fourteen, was coming to school sporting bushy mutton-chop sideburns) saw the board give way and abolish hair regulations. Around this time *Bullshit and Jellybeans*, the memoir-cum-manifesto of Tim Shadbolt (of whom more later), was published. The first page finds him arriving in prison:

> I thought about refusing a hair-cut but wanted to be with the boys and see prison life; for me to go into solitary would suit them just fine. So I submitted to the final act of mass conformity — dress / grey, head / bald, inspiration / nil, education / none. Discipline / uniforms / uniformity. An excellent preparation for New Zealand society, grey and dull. Off came fourteen inches of hair, my first haircut in six years.[7]

'FREEDOM. I'M DIFFERENT'

Women launched their own style of rebellion. Rosemary McLeod, at school in Wellington with Rachel Stace, explains that up until the time the Beatles came to New Zealand, 'young girls basically dressed like their mothers. They wore nylon stockings — flesh-coloured — and little high heels.'[8] But around the middle of the decade, taking their cue from fashion icons like Twiggy or the local pop star Dinah Lee, some began to cut their hair into a short bob — a sort of female version of the Beatle cut — or else grew it long and wore it straight like iconic English singer Marianne Faithfull, either way eschewing the layers and lacquers that had distinguished women's fashion in the fifties. By the end of the decade, long hair would, for both men and women, come to typify hippies and other countercultural types.

While hair got longer, skirts got shorter. Revealing more of the body than the previous generation would have dared, the sexual statement of the miniskirt was implicit: the wearer is comfortable in her body, ergo in her sexuality. To McLeod, the miniskirt said: 'Freedom. I'm different. I remember the feeling of walking out in a miniskirt for the first time. I was thirteen or fourteen and I thought, "This is the way to go!" We were made to be drab at school. Not only were you made to look like your mother, but you also had school uniforms that were universally designed to make you look hideous. You were controlled. Desexualised. Naughty girls pulled their tunics up a bit; bad girls like me and Rachel Stace, we'd put on makeup after school and go downtown to look at boys, and have it confiscated by bitch teachers.'[9] But when McLeod wore her miniskirt to an after-school job at a left-wing Wellington bookshop she quickly became aware of the lecherous motives of male customers who would ask her to climb the tall ladder 'to pass down the complete works of Chairman Mao'.[10]

Though such distinct items as long hair, miniskirts, tie-dye, denim and muslin are often lumped together in a general characterisation of sixties youth fashion, the shifts in style from the start to the end of the decade were dramatic and could be charted year by year.

One of them was 1968, evidently the year of the sandal. For a photo feature, New Zealand pop-culture monthly *Playdate* paid a visit to Rique, a Los Angeles-born sandal-maker who had taken up residence in Auckland. They find him, longhaired, bearded and wearing little John Lennon-style spectacles. Psychedelic posters adorn his walls, joss sticks burn, tea is served and Moby Grape spins on the stereo as he measures up the interviewer for a pair of sandals in a modified Greek style.[11]

In another issue of the same magazine, sandals stand for a whole series of social and sexual decisions. *Sandals of Indian Leather* is a short story narrated by a young woman who works in textiles and lives in a bedsit. At a party she meets a bearded Irishman who wears sandals 'made of carved leather the colour of coffee ... bulky and strong, yet refined'. He regales her with the adventures that have led him temporarily to New Zealand: hitchhiking across central Europe, partying in Paris with Bob Dylan, walking through Greece, motor-cycling through Africa, mining in northern Australia. They walk, and talk about freedom. He tells her: 'You have the city. The fabrics you design. Your home. All these things tie you down and stop your freedom. I have the whole world. I own nothing so I own everything. I'm king to myself. It's the only way to be, woman.'

A romance ensues, if entirely on his terms. 'Sometimes he would be home when I arrived (he insisted on climbing through the window).' One day he turns up on a motorbike: 'This baby and me are travelling the world.'

They ride to a beach. She looks in his face. Words swirl in her head, though it is not clear whether they ever leave her lips. 'I want to come Sean, I want to come,' she imagines herself saying. 'I want to ride on that black machine ... I want to sleep under the sky. I want to feel the dust around a pair of sandals of carved Indian leather.'[12]

In its rejection of a hierarchy in which power was symbolised in tailored clothing such as the suits worn by lawyers, accountants and other professionals, the counterculture opted for the utilitarian. There was a strong preference for denim, associated with labourers and prisoners. But it could also be fanciful. Where parents would put on their most formal clothes to go to church or to a wedding or funeral, their countercultural children might dress up especially to take an acid trip. Clothing reflected the counterculture's internationalism, its interest in, and appropriation of, other cultures. Headbands and animal skins referenced Native American culture; muslin, decorative cottons and jewellery invoked Asia.

By the early seventies unorthodox dress was becoming more common, though it still had the power to turn heads. 'Wild Gear? In Wellington? It can't happen here ... but it has' ran a 1971 headline in *Playdate*:

'We loved dressing up, we loved costumes...'. Rachel Stace private collection

[A]ny stranger, returning now to the staid capital after a few years absence, must be struck immediately by a new climate of hair and excess in gear. The rebels do not predominate, but, few though they are, in any lunchtime crowd they suddenly materialise in colours and combinations that have a stunning effect on the ogling citizens ... Amongst the wild ones are many who are attractively clad with cloaks, ponchos and tie-die [sic] gear ... embroidered coats and shawls.[13]

Rachel Stace, having left school and now living in a flat as a self-described hippie, remembers: 'We loved dressing up, we loved costumes—colour, texture, velvet, patterns, all that stuff. We'd go out of our way to look absolutely gorgeous. We didn't buy magazines. It was more from music. Jimi Hendrix, what is he wearing? The Rolling Stones, what are they wearing?'

Rachel and her friends would make their own clothes, taking inspiration from the photos on album covers.[14]

As the hippies moved out of the cities to communes and rural outreaches [discussed further in Chapter 8], their attire became even more wayward, and would remain so, long after hippie styles had been

FREAK FLAGS, FREE LOVE 103

Women in a mirror. Angela Middleton photograph, private collection

tamed and incorporated into urban fashion. A shortage of money, scant access to new clothing and primitive laundry facilities resulted in the modes of dress Miro Bilbrough describes in her memoir of communal life in the seventies, *In the Time of the Manaroans*:

> ... I acquire the habit of wearing second-hand forties crepe de chine and rayon dresses featuring tailored pleats, gores, cloth bows, buttons, belts, and soft collars that remind me of those droopy-faced flowers, violas ...
>
> I don't think twice about mucking out or composting the garden or fetching buckets of water in unravelling tea or cocktail dresses ... Under contour-skimming crepe you might layer an Indian wraparound skirt to dip in unconscious waves or a saggy, vintage viscose petticoat dyed leaf-green. It's cold in these climes. And yet no knickers. I never see a pair of knickers in all my years in the hippy world, unless they are a pair of post-war, peach cami-knickers hanging on a washing line ... Bras are not even in the lexicon.[15]

UNSPEAKABLE SEX

An absence of knickers and bras was symbolic of the way the counter-culture rejected the constraints of the past. In sex, as in other things, it aspired to the utopian. The hypocrisies of the previous generation—those clandestine affairs that took place within supposedly happy marriages, sexual identities hidden in closets, religious doctrines that declared sex outside of marriage a sin—would all be replaced by openness and honesty. Love would be liberated. Free love.

Like many ideas attributed to the counterculture, the idea of sexual revolution had existed long before the counterculture took it up. The first sexual revolution is sometimes said to have occurred in America in the 1920s, when Hollywood movies and a fad for Sigmund Freud seemed to indicate a pushback against morals inherited from the Victorians. Free love had been expounded even earlier in England by eighteenth-century feminists like Mary Wollstonecraft, who evinced the idea that sex is not just about reproduction, and that both men and women have a right to sexual pleasure without the interference of the church or state, and Romantics such as William Blake who compared the sexual oppression of marriage to slavery.

But whatever might have happened in historic Hollywood or ancient Albion, New Zealand at the start of the sixties was a long way from sexual revolution. 'Sex was absolutely, literally unspeakable,' says Hugh Young, who at the turn of the decade was entering his adolescence in a liberal, middle-class Christchurch family. 'You could not talk about sex in any detail. It was impossible to learn about sex. There was no sensible literature. None at all. You looked up masturbation in the dictionary and it said "self abuse". And unfortunately my parents, for all their liberality, thought I would learn by osmosis. I never had "the talk".'[16]

In Naenae, Terri Benning, too, was nearing adolescence. 'There was no sex education. We had biology at school but it was always very embarrassing when you got down to the reproductive bits. Mum never told us about what might happen to us when we got our periods or anything like that. I remember finding sanitary pads in my older sister's drawer and asking "What are these?" "Oh nothing, they're fine." I was probably eleven or twelve. At some point you put two and two together, but it just all happened without any explanation. When my period started I went, "I'm bleeding!" and Mum went, "Oh, you've got your period. Oh well, here's a belt and here's some pads and here's some safety pins." It was all pretty archaic. But there was no talk about how you could get pregnant or about sex or anything like that. It was just trial and error.'[17]

In their study of child-rearing patterns in New Zealand, based on interviews conducted with mothers of young children between 1963 and 1966, psychologists Jane and James Ritchie found 'an obliqueness and denial' that left them concerned 'for the development ahead of attitudes towards the child's own body and sexual pleasure in general. It seems very likely that most will only learn of such things from other sources than those which parents can regulate, control or even know about.'[18]

Wherever there had been hints of sexual rebellion, such as the incidences of teenage sex that gave rise to the Mazengarb Report, any attempts to understand the rebels, help them stay safe or provide them with useful information as they explored their sexual selves, were heavily outnumbered by efforts to suppress them.

Seemingly indifferent to unwanted pregnancy, the Mazengarb committee recommended that contraceptives be kept out of the hands of adolescents. Its report resulted in the Polices Offences Amendment Act 1954 which made it illegal for medical professionals to discuss contraception with persons under sixteen. The committee expressed alarm at 'the attitude of mind of some young people to sexual indulgence with one another, their planning and organisation of it, and *their assumption that when they consent together they are not doing anything wrong*' (my emphasis).[19] It would be far better, the report and its advocates appeared to be saying, if teenagers and other unmarried couples simply didn't have sex at all.

Merely to seek information about sex was problematic. The report referred to a set of questions submitted by a group of female students to a doctor who had been brought into a secondary school class to provide sex education. 'Having read the questions,' the report noted, 'the doctor commented that she must have prepared the wrong lecture—it should have been for an older group. A transcript of the questions was produced to the committee. There were inquiries which one would assume might be made by young women who had married or were about to marry.'[20]

Marriage, the report implied, was the only proper place in which sex should take place. The nuclear family was the ideal social unit, the key to identity, belonging and social stability, and this was reinforced in the literature produced by government. Soon after the Mazengarb Report, the Health Department was charged with producing a series of pamphlets available to adults on request to help them instruct their children in sex education, with titles such as *Sex and the Adolescent Boy*, *Sex and the Adolescent Girl*, and *Parents, the Adolescent and Sex: The Parents' Role*. Academic researcher Claire Gooder observed that these 'wholly associated sex with marriage, responsibility and love', without making it accessible to the unmarried or adolescent. There was no suggestion in this literature that anything other than heterosexual sex even existed. 'Sex can be a very beautiful thing,' *Sex and the Adolescent Boy* assured its readers, 'but it is very easily spoilt. It is only in the sanctity of marriage that it can be enjoyed freely, unashamedly and with the sanction of society.'[21]

Even sex *within* marriage was a subject rarely discussed, though this was beginning to change. The New Zealand Family Planning Association had been set up in 1936 by a small group of women including Elsie Freeman (later to become Elsie Locke) 'to educate and enlighten the people of New Zealand on the need for birth control and sex education'. Its original name was the Sex Hygiene and Birth Regulation Society. As Locke's fellow founder (and fellow communist) Mary Dobbie explained, '"hygiene" was not an emotive word and "regulation" seemed milder than "control"'.[22] Over the next few decades, Family Planning would perform a delicate balancing act as it tried to provide information, real choice, and support for women and their partners while placating dominant conservative forces within government, churches and the medical profession.

In 1953, the year pioneering American sexologist Alfred Kinsey brought discussion of sexuality and the art of sexual fulfilment closer to the mainstream with his report *Sexual Behaviour in the Human Female* (closely following his earlier *Sexual Behaviour in the Human Male*), Family Planning had placed its first advertisement in the *Woman's Weekly*, and received hundreds of letters in response.[23] Evidently sex was something New Zealanders *did* think about, even if they were too prudish, repressed, shy or inarticulate to discuss it in public.

But an innovation in contraception was about to create a new set of conditions that within a decade would transform sex and society.

A WORLD WHERE YOU COULD GET AWAY WITH IT

The counterculture did not invent free love or sexual revolution, and nor did it invent the Pill. Like LSD, the Pill came from the scientific/medical world, though it would become—along with drugs, miniskirts, Vietnam and the Beatles—part of a litany often recited as shorthand for the social upheavals of the era. Developed in the United States, it became available in New Zealand by prescription in 1961, marketed 'as a modern contraceptive for married couples, as a tool for marital harmony, equality and choice'.[24]

Its uptake was swift by world standards. For doctors, prescribing the Pill came as a relief from the complicated and awkward business of fitting diaphragms. By 1967, 20 percent of New Zealand women of reproductive age were using it, compared to 8 percent in the US and 3 percent in Britain, and user rates remained high.[25] Estimates suggest that by 1975 up to 35 percent of New Zealand women were using the Pill, compared to 19 percent of women in Britain.[26]

The Pill undoubtedly had some liberating effects for married New Zealand women. The number of women seeking part-time work once their children had started school began to rise. Though hard to assess without studies of intimate behaviour, anecdotes suggest that having been released from the anxieties of a possible unwanted pregnancy, some married couples began to enjoy more fulfilling sex lives. Then again, by relieving men of any responsibility for birth control, some began to expect that sex would now be available on demand.

But for unmarried, single or underage women, there was little chance of being prescribed the Pill and it remained difficult to obtain into the 1970s. The morality that had driven such propaganda as the Mazengarb Report continued to prevail. In 1967, Patricia Ann Rogers, aged twenty, was arrested in a vice squad raid on a Grey Lynn flat that a police prosecutor said 'could well be described as part of the hippie cult'. Three males were charged with narcotic possession. Rogers appeared in court for possessing fertility control tablets without a prescription, which she said she had obtained at a dance. Bail was set at $50 and she was ordered to report daily to the police.[27]

In the case of Carol, the subject of a 2017 RNZ 'Eyewitness' programme, becoming a solo parent in 1966 at age seventeen was still not deemed sufficient grounds to be prescribed birth control. When she made this request of her doctor, his only response was, 'Haven't you learnt your lesson?'[28]

A handful of doctors became known for prescribing the Pill to young and unmarried women, but it sometimes came at a price. One male GP in Wellington was well known for issuing prescriptions to teenage girls, but equally known for his inappropriate examinations and attempts to 'try it on' with his young patients. Even married women had to endure humiliations, abuses and moralistic diatribes to obtain the Pill. Doctors, given the power to choose who they would and wouldn't prescribe the drug to, implemented their own moral codes. In 1964, a Dr Dawson of Whangārei wrote to the Minister of Health requesting that his department issue a statement recommending the Pill 'for medical reasons only', fearing that 'hordes of importunate females are likely to descend on our surgeries demanding prescriptions … There are a large number of women who have no intention of accepting the responsibility of motherhood.'[29]

As a consequence of such attitudes, there were many unwanted pregnancies. Abortion was illegal and the range of circumstances under which they could be carried out in public hospitals was extremely narrow. Some women sought the services of clandestine 'backstreet' abortionists who carried out the procedures illegally from private premises throughout the country. These could be physically harmful and sometimes fatal. From the late sixties, women who could find the money flew to Australia where a legal ruling had set a precedent that abortion was lawful if necessary to preserve the physical or mental health of the woman concerned.

Thousands of young women each year would give birth to children in secrecy and have them immediately put up for adoption. When Terri Benning was twelve, her sixteen-year-old sister disappeared for several months. Terri was told she had 'gone to secretarial school'. In fact she had gone to Bethany, a maternity home in Napier run by the Salvation Army where pregnant unmarried girls and women went to give birth in secrecy. In almost all cases the babies were given up for adoption.

In the seventies, it became easier for young and unmarried women to get the Pill. When Dr Margaret Sparrow began working at the Victoria University Student Health clinic in 1970 she produced an elaborate contraception display, despite the protests of the clinic director and even some students. The following year the physician in charge of the student health services at Otago University announced that the Pill would be available to students, the first time a student health service had made an open statement on contraceptives.

Yet the mere fact of the Pill's existence may already have had a liberating effect on the emerging generation. In her study of sex in Britain, *The Long Sexual Revolution*, New Zealand historian Hera Cook notes that 'by 1965 there were debates on sexual mores occurring that, while theoretical, presented alternative ways of responding to actual choices and possibilities in the lives of young people. One major effect of these debates when combined with extensive media coverage of the Pill was that, for any girls during the 1960s, the idea of the Pill was as important as the reality.'[30] Cook cites a study in which an English woman who was a teenager in the first half of the 1960s reflected: 'Our generation was growing up with the knowledge that somewhere out there existed a contraceptive which promised you would be able to get away with it, in the way only men had before.'[31]

In New Zealand, where the Pill was taken up with more alacrity than in Britain, the promise of a world in which you would 'get away with it'—where sex without pregnancy was a possibility and perhaps even a right—was likely even more pervasive. Young New Zealanders had already begun to defy society's oppressive conventions on many fronts, and there was a willingness among young men and women to explore and enjoy sexual relationships in ways their parents had not. This generation might have had greater access to contraception than their parents had, but they were also more willing to take risks. Having

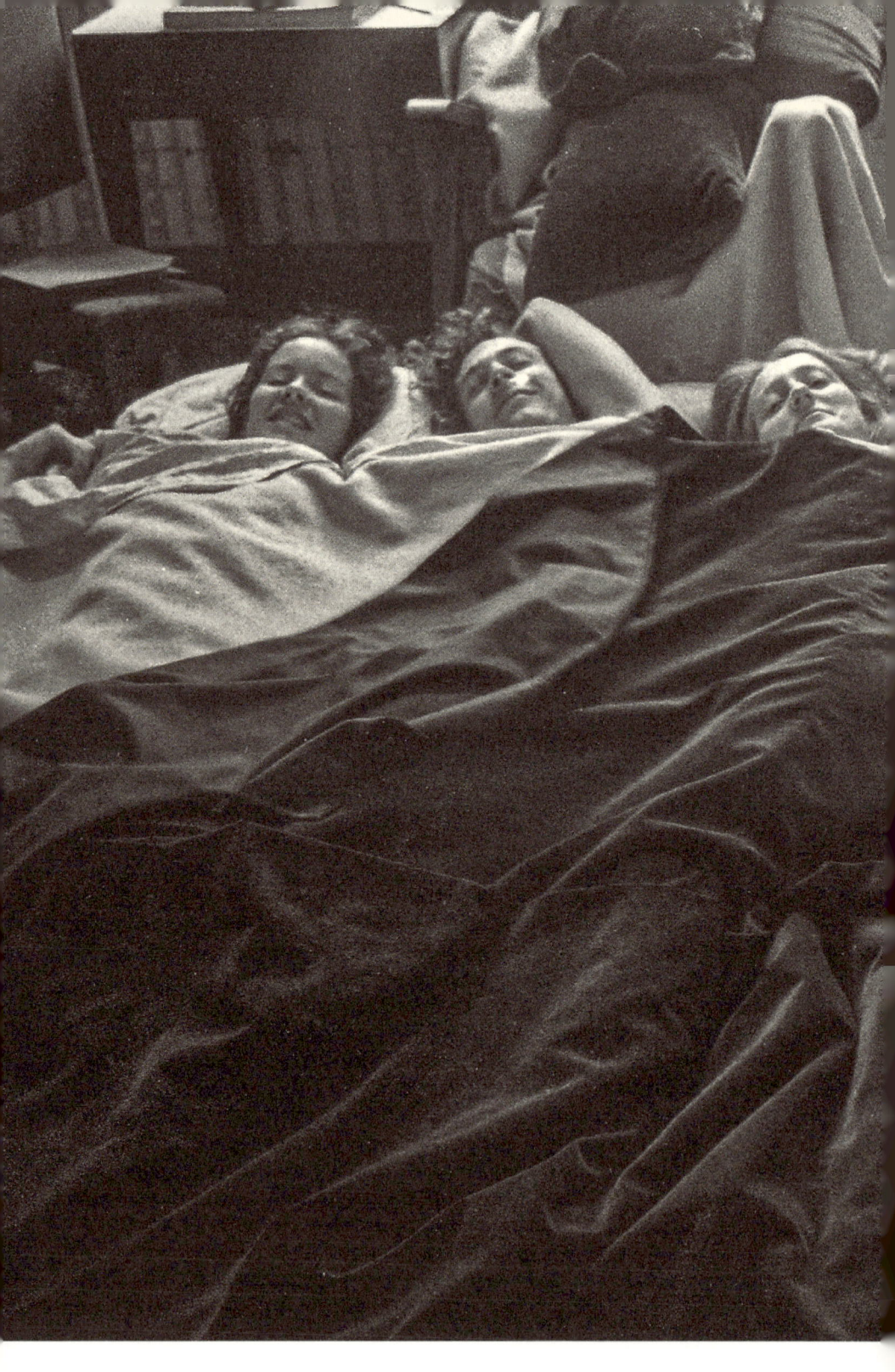

Herne Bay, Auckland, early 1970s.
Max Oettli photograph, Alexander Turnbull Library, PAColl-1386-1

sex was answering to a biological urge and could also be a philosophical act: an act of rebellion, like the rejection of religious conventions, marriage, or the use of illegal drugs.

Rachel Stace laughs as she reveals to me that her father had been a member of the Mazengarb committee. In retrospect, she says, her activities as a teenager were just the kind the report had been attempting to quell. 'The same year the Beatles came, this American guy came to Wellington College. We met at one of these ghastly dance classes after school and we fell madly in love at fifteen. We were sure this was it.' When the young American returned to his native Minnesota the following year, Rachel conspired to follow him there as an exchange student. Her parents agreed to let her go, on the condition that she passed School Certificate, which she did. Returning to New Zealand at the end of the American school year, she persuaded her parents to let her move from the single-sex Wellington Girls' to the co-educational Onslow College. Now armed with sexual experience, there were relationships with boyfriends at school. There was also a clandestine affair with a painter whose Saturday-morning art classes she had enrolled in. 'There was a mattress where the model had been lying and there was half an hour before Mum was due to pick me up.'[32]

Sometimes she would fake a dental appointment and visit the painter at his flat during the school day. Her attitude to sex—that it was a pleasure to be indulged in—was shared by many of the girls and boys in her social group. This point of view was reinforced in the literature popular among her peers. To the characters in On the Road, unrestricted sexuality was an expression of an inner holiness. It is one of the things that compels Kerouac's hero Dean Moriarty throughout the book, engaging in spontaneous encounters with a succession of mostly temporary partners as he rages down the road to enlightenment.

The growing availability of travel and interest in the beliefs of non-Western societies also saw the introduction of ideas about sex inspired by the ancient literature of Asia. The Kama Sutra is an Indian text on the philosophy of love, sexuality and fulfilment, written in the third century and translated into English in the late nineteenth. On its own, the section on courtship might not have caused too much anxiety for the typical New Zealand guidance counsellor in the 1960s. It suggests, for instance, that the young man seeking to attract a woman might 'hold a party and invite the guests to read poems and debate the arts'. But once it moves on to sections on kissing, biting, role-play and numerous variations on sexual congress, it goes well beyond the national Health Department manuals.

Although The Kama Sutra places value on the sexual pleasure of all parties, it does seem to favour the male experience over that of the female, if not as blatantly as Kerouac. It describes dozens of different sexual configurations, defined variously as high congress, low congress, supported congress, united congress and the congress of a herd of cows ('when a man enjoys many women altogether'). It is also steeped in the

Lovers from the Kama Sutra. Nepali art collection, Victoria and Albert Museum, London. Bridgeman Art Library, BAL4540

traditional class structure of Indian society. We are told, for instance, that 'the Auparishtaka [the book's term for oral sex] is practised only by unchaste and wanton women, female attendants and serving maids'.[33]

Still, it was all a long way from *Sex and the Adolescent Girl* and its influence spread osmotically. By the early 1970s, further imported literature had fed into the new sexual ideals, including *The Joy of Sex* by British physician and anti-militarist Alex Comfort, and *The Art of Sensual Massage*, with its moody images (nakedness and hairiness prerequisites for both the massager and the massaged), recommended accessories (oils, incense, candlelight), music tips (slow blues, rāga or chant) and warnings about waterbeds.

Perhaps the most insidious influence came from popular music. Through the sixties, song lyrics had moved from dewy-eyed depictions of romantic love to more explicit scenarios. Whether or not you believed the Beatles wanted only to hold your hand, or wondered how 'the things that you do' made them 'feel alright', the lyrics left enough room to hear the more chaste meanings. But in 1967 when the Rolling Stones sang 'Let's Spend the Night Together' there was little doubt as to what Mick Jagger had in mind. The NZBC promptly banned the record (or rather, euphemistically listed it in the corporation's ledger of censored material as 'not bought'), while the Troggs' 'I Can't Control Myself' was marked 'audition carefully'. Prohibition, as ever, only added to the allure.

There were other rock songs that presented the experience of sex from a female point of view, like Big Brother and the Holding Company's 'Turtle Blues' written by Janis Joplin.[34] Black American music extended the longstanding tradition in which male and female singers batted sexual demands back and forth in the form of witty 'answer songs', like the Otis Redding and Aretha Franklin versions of 'Respect'. Yet despite some notable exceptions, there was an overwhelming sense that men controlled the rock stage, even if the complex gendered identity of a rock star like Mick Jagger presented a very different image of masculinity from that of, say, All Black Colin Meads. The rise of the rock star was accompanied by the concept of the 'groupie', promoted in the underground press: a female music fan so much in the thrall of the music and its practitioners that she was willing to offer her sexual services for free.

Another idea enshrined at this time was that of the unholy trinity: sex, drugs and rock'n'roll. Among the prohibitionist warnings about marijuana was that it could be used as an aphrodisiac. For the counterculture, this sounded like a double win. But an even more popular drug for this purpose, though relatively short-lived, was Mandrax. Originally designed and prescribed as a sedative, and marketed in the US as Quaalude, Mandrax became popular as a recreational drug in the early to mid-1970s for its pleasantly relaxing effects on both the body and the inhibitions. Though supposedly available only on prescription, jarsful of the little pills found their way into the countercultural community. An infamous Herne Bay flat in Auckland, inhabited by musicians including members of Dragon and the future Hello Sailor, acquired the name Mandrax Mansion. At the time, Rachel Stace was living just up the road: 'You'd be swigging back Mandrax and next minute you'd be on a bed with six other people all writhing around, with or without clothes. Fabulous drug. Lots of orgies. It was great.'[35]

In an unpublished memoir, the musician Rick Bryant recalled, in a rhetorical style that reads part Hunter S. Thompson, part Victorian novel:

> There used to be a pharmaceutical recipe called Mandrax, that might just as easily and suitably have been called 'too much fun.' Gonzo it was. I AM NOT RECOMMENDING IT. But if you chucked a few dozen of them into an ordinary liquor fuelled party, you were likely to get an outpouring of generous spontaneity that very much approximated an orgy. Not a Roman orgy, just

Wellington, 1974. Keith Stewart
photograph, private collection

an ordinary one. Those among your number, who have parents about my age, who have not speculated much about what your parents got up to when they were forgetting all about the 60s — which stretched a long way onto the 70s, by the way — speculate away, you will not be guaranteed valid testimony. Some fairly matronly matrons may not rush to recall their nimble nymphery.[36]

As for the oral contraceptive, it arrived into a burgeoning counterculture in which songs, literature and a growing mythology already reinforced the idea of men as carefree rebels and easy riders. It was as though its mere existence now exempted boys from thinking about pregnancy. Where fear of being held accountable for a pregnancy had once acted as a handbrake, now some men started to behave as though women should be sexually available on demand. The new environment allowed attitudes that had existed latently to flourish unimpeded. Courtship was accelerated or done away with altogether.

Women, now given the possibility of control over their own fertility, were also able to initiate sex, and some did, though rarely in the way an aggressive male might. One well-known male musician would assail women at parties with the blunt inquiry, 'Wanna fuck?' They were free to say no, he reasoned, and sometimes they would say yes. Other men wouldn't take no for an answer. Sue Belt doesn't recall anyone using the word rape at the time, but says that what passed for consent would be viewed differently today. 'I was quite bolshy, but there would be more vulnerable women who someone would come on to and they'd think, "I don't really want to, but if I don't I'm unhip."'[37]

A new vocabulary, imported from psychotherapy, developed around sex and could be used for coercion. Not wanting to have sex, for whatever reason, indicated the woman was 'uptight' or had 'hang-ups'. Despite the counterculture's do-what-you-like ethos, social pressure could be powerful. 'It was almost as if this pseudo-liberation had deprived you of choice, rather than giving you choice,' said Rosemary McLeod. 'The only choice you had was that you weren't getting pregnant.'[38] The typical countercultural male, she remembers, 'liked his women horizontal. They were what we call cocksure, and you were bloody lucky to get the offer. "You should be bloody grateful." There was a lot of that.'[39]

In *The Making of a Counter Culture*, Theodore Roszak had idealised a new kind of man who displayed a 'feminist softness' in contrast to 'the *Playboy* version of total permissiveness' that he saw being promoted by the consumer society with its 'imbecile affluence and impersonal orgasms' and 'conception of femininity … indistinguishable from social idiocy'.[40] He would have been disappointed by the countercultural Kiwi. In re-imagining the world, the male of this species had not necessarily rejected the privileges society had bestowed upon him thanks simply to his gender. If he worked, he could still expect to earn more than a woman. If he spoke up, he was less likely to be shouted down. Few men questioned such privileges. And though there were undoubtedly exceptions, this imbalance of power often carried over unquestioned into the bedrooms.

Surveying the scene from the mid-1970s, New Zealand sociologist Debbie Jones saw the ideology of the sexual revolution had been essentially no different from that of the 'sexual establishment':

> [It] can be summed up as being what *men* want.
>
> A woman should be 'free' enough sexually to be an available and exciting sexual partner, without inconveniently asserting her needs. She should take responsibility for birth control and bring up any children the man may want. She should be sexually exclusive to 'her' man, but still accommodate his need for sexual variety.
>
> As long as men hold the real power, there can be no real sexual revolution. The whole counterculture movement is a good example of this. Despite the anti-owner, anti-work, pro-sex-and-love thing, the counterculture male was still firmly in control.[41]

In the spirit of anything goes, the counterculture gave non-heterosexual sex its tacit approval. Internationally known countercultural figures such as Allen Ginsberg and the San Francisco poster artist Steven Arnold were outspokenly queer. Gay and lesbian sex was, in some of the local underground literature, portrayed simply as part of the smorgasbord of sexual possibilities, in open resistance to the fact that in New Zealand homosexuality remained illegal for men, with a conviction potentially resulting in imprisonment or medical 'aversion therapy'.

In a 1973 issue of *Itch*, an underground magazine published in Wellington aimed at and largely written by secondary school students, an anonymous columnist wrote: 'It's important not to close your mind to things like fucking with people of the same sex … A difficulty of lesbianism and homosexuality is the very strong pressures from our society, but don't be afraid to explore the possibilities of all sorts of relationships whatever society says.'[42] Likewise *The Little Red Schoolbook*, published in 1972 as a kind of countercultural beginners' guide, embraced the principle of diversity. 'Everybody is different — in sexual matters too … In purely physical terms, homosexuals make love just like anyone else, although of course they can't have intercourse in quite the same way … Their love and their feelings are just as real and genuine and natural as anyone else's.'[43]

As historian Chris Brickell has observed: 'In some ways, same-sex relationships were defined as an integral part of the counterculture, even though in this particular book gay liberationist ideas about sexual

Graffiti, Victoria University of Wellington, 1973. Keith Stewart photograph, private collection

fluidity and universality were subsumed under an overarching symbolic opposition between sexual conventionality on the one hand, and an oppressed minority on the other.'[44]

To Alison Laurie, writing in 1973 in the short-lived New Zealand edition of *Rolling Stone*, homosexuality was an act of political defiance 'against this nuclear-marriage, consumer-unit, stereotyping role farm and its social structure … and is actually understood as such by the real controllers and manipulators who manage our society. Without the order and rigidity of sex roles, without the institution of the family, an economy based upon selling TV sets, washing machines, soap and cornflakes to each consumer-unit could not survive.'[45] Laurie had returned to New Zealand that year after almost a decade overseas, energised by the lesbian networks and wider counterculture she had encountered in London and New York.[46] As she would later write: 'I felt a strong urge to return to Aotearoa, New Zealand. Letters from friends implied that the revolution might actually reach there, too.'[47]

Gay issues began to be promoted and celebrated in the same spirit as other countercultural happenings. 'Come and freak out with good vibrations, free lollipops and music by Country Road', read the invitation to a 1973 Gay Liberation Fantasy Dance in the University of Auckland cafeteria. The Gay Liberation Front had been founded at the

University of Auckland the year before, after Ngahuia Te Awekotuku (then known as Ngahuia Volkerling) was denied a visa to the United States to study both the Gay Liberation and Native American 'Red Power' movements, having stated on her application form that she is 'a homosexual Māori woman'. She recalled: 'After a meeting at which I was told I was a known sexual deviant by the American consul I went up to the university forum, which happens at one o'clock every Thursday, and I picked up the mike and I said, "Who is crazy enough to come and do this with me?"'[48] The first activity of the newly formed group was a lively picket of the American Consulate, drawing a mixture of men and women, gay and straight.

Yet while gay and lesbian sex was embraced by the broader counterculture as another expression of freedom, real equality for homosexuals wouldn't be gained until the next century, with the fight for law reform left largely to those whose freedoms the laws most directly affected, along with a few individuals in public life—often members of institutions far removed from the counterculture—who were brave and principled enough to take a stand.

The counterculture's relationship with the transgender community was even more tenuous. This subculture had a presence in the urban zones of Auckland and Wellington, centred on particular nightclubs and coffee lounges, some of which were run by trans women, and identified by a few flamboyant figures like Wellington's well-known trans woman drag performer Carmen. Though being trans was not technically outlawed, employment discrimination saw many turn to sex work for survival, and the trans community was subjected to frequent harassment by both the police and the public. But the trans community would have little obvious overlap with the counterculture—other than perhaps sharing sources of certain drugs—until the late seventies when the Red Mole theatre troupe mounted a season at The Balcony, Carmen's Wellington nightclub, leading to some lasting friendships.

Thinking back to the Jumping Sundays in Albert Park, John Bower recalled the only negative thing that ever occurred there was an incident in which a trans woman or cross-dresser was chased away from the site by a group of revellers and pursued down Queen Street. 'I don't know why that happened but it was a mob mentality,' he remembered in 2019, still puzzling over the episode.[49] The aggressive mood of the pursuers had seemed out of place in the midst of the peace-oriented gathering. Though the counterculture challenged traditional attitudes to sex and gender, clothing, appearance and conformity in general, it was disconcerting how suddenly it could revert to a display of old-fashioned hostility towards a perceived outsider.

FREEING
THE WORD

Five

In the sixties, daily newspapers and weekly tabloids reinforced the image of New Zealand as a predominantly white, patriarchal place where crime was punished, sport revered, and anyone falling conspicuously outside the norm had some serious explaining to do. In its own way the press also propagated the idea of a counter-culture, sometimes through the inadvertent allure of negative publicity but also through the genuine curiosity of journalists. But the counterculture would cultivate communication channels of its own.

The Resistance Bookshop, Willis St, Wellington, 1972. **Keith Stewart photograph, private collection**

Even before *Time*'s influential July 1967 cover story, tantalising reports on the American hippies had begun cropping up in New Zealand's newspapers. On 1 April that year, the *Otago Daily Times* ran a syndicated piece by the Australian journalist Lillian Roxon, reporting from the United States. 'A new youth grouping, the Hippies, has sprung up in San Francisco and may spread over America and to Europe,' a subeditor wrote, telegraphing the essence of the article that followed. 'Hippies are still way out … but they have an essential gaiety and zest for life which the Beatniks, whom they replace, scorned in their Bomb-dominated philosophy.'

In case any readers thought the piece was an April Fool's Day prank, it was followed a few days later by an article, headlined '"Hippies" Seen In Sydney', reporting a clergyman's warnings that 'a strange "religious cult" whose members are known as "Hippies" is emerging among Sydney teenagers … It involves the use of the hallucinatory drug LSD … There are thought to be at least 50 "hippies" in one Sydney sect alone.'[1]

The revolution was getting nearer.

GOING UNDERGROUND

By this time there were young New Zealanders who had been to Sydney and even San Francisco and returned to tell of their experiences, whether or not they saw themselves as part of a 'strange religious cult'. Most people, though, got their first intimations of rebellion vicariously.

As the French writer and academic Robert Escarpit pointed out, the twentieth century saw new 'audio-visual mass-communication media' distribute 'ever-increasing quantities of information' to sectors of society which had previously been culturally ignored.[2] But while the impact of television was profound, in the dwellings of New Zealand's counterculture a shelf of paperbacks was more common than a TV set.

Penguin Books, the first major publisher of paperbacks, had been the brainchild of V. K. Krishna Menon, the Indian diplomat and scholar who would be a star guest at Alister Taylor's 1968 Peace, Power and Politics conference [of which more later in this chapter]. In the mid-1930s, as an editor for London publisher Bodley Head, Menon had realised his vision of democratising knowledge by flooding the market with affordable editions of quality titles from Homer to Hemingway. By 1960, the format had been adopted worldwide. In the United States paperbacks were outselling hardbacks. Penguin's notoriety exploded that year with the first unexpurgated edition of D. H. Lawrence's *Lady Chatterley's Lover* and the resulting obscenity trial in the UK. In New Zealand the cheap pocket-sized format saw beatnik bibles like *On the Road* and Hermann Hesse's *Siddhartha* changing hands, disseminating visions of freedom—sexual, spiritual and artistic.

Bookshops became hangouts. In Wellington there was Parsons with its coffee bar, and second-hand shops such as Smith's, where ebullient proprietor Dick Reynolds would press volumes of Rimbaud, Camus or Beckett upon budding existentialists like John Esam and David Mitchell. There was Modern Books, operated by a co-operative whose first elected committee had included the public intellectual Bill Sutch, historian John Beaglehole and long-time communist Elizabeth McGowan. Like Modern Books, Auckland's Progressive Books had begun in the thirties as a co-operative bookstore to sell literature with an internationalist socialist perspective, and was still going strong.[3]

It was not until the late sixties that the counterculture began to open its own stores. Sporting a name with revolutionary connotations, the first Resistance Bookshop was started in Auckland in September 1969 by a group of activists who had recently been involved in the liberation of Albert Park, including Sue Matthews (who would later become well known as Green MP Sue Bradford) and Roger Fowler. Alan Robson had obtained the lease on an empty, council-owned building near the top of Queen Street.[4]

Resistance was always about more than selling books. One of its first acts was to acquire its own printing press, enabling the shop to produce its own political leaflets. It was paid for in part with the proceeds of a student handbook produced for the Auckland Technical Institute.[5] The shop had a designated meeting room, which it made available to various political groups. It also had several bedrooms and became home to some members of the collective, as well as operating as a crash pad. In fact, it was not until early 1970 that it legally opened for retail. That year a Resistance Bookshop opened in Wellington, independent of Auckland, though run along similar lines. After its initial premises in Cuba Street burned down (some said as a result of arson, though it was never proven) it moved to the first of two Willis Street addresses.

A stocklist from the Willis Street shop circa 1972 finds titles arranged into categories: Drugs (Aleister Crowley's *Diary of a Drug Fiend*, Aldous Huxley's *The Doors of Perception*); Education (*Teaching as a Subversive Activity*, *Summerhill*); Black America (*Black Awakening in Capitalist America*, *Soledad Brother*); Religion (*An Introduction to Zen Buddhism*, *Tibetan Book of the Dead*); Anarchism (Kropotkin's *Memoirs of a Revolutionist*); Music (Lillian Roxon's *Rock Encyclopedia*, *Rolling Stone Interviews*); and Fiction (Anthony Burgess's *A Clockwork Orange*, Hermann Hesse's *Steppenwolf*). There are numerous titles relating to Marxism and Trotskyism, and to philosophers and political theorists like Jean-Paul Sartre and Herbert Marcuse. There are comics by Robert Crumb and books of poetry by James K. Baxter. Germaine Greer's *The Female Eunuch* and Patricia Grimshaw's *Women's Suffrage in New Zealand* are filed under Sex. Counterculture has its own section which includes Theodore Roszak's *Making of a Counter Culture*, Richard Neville's *Playpower* and Jeff Nuttall's *Bomb Culture*.

It was also a place where one could always find copies of *Cock*.

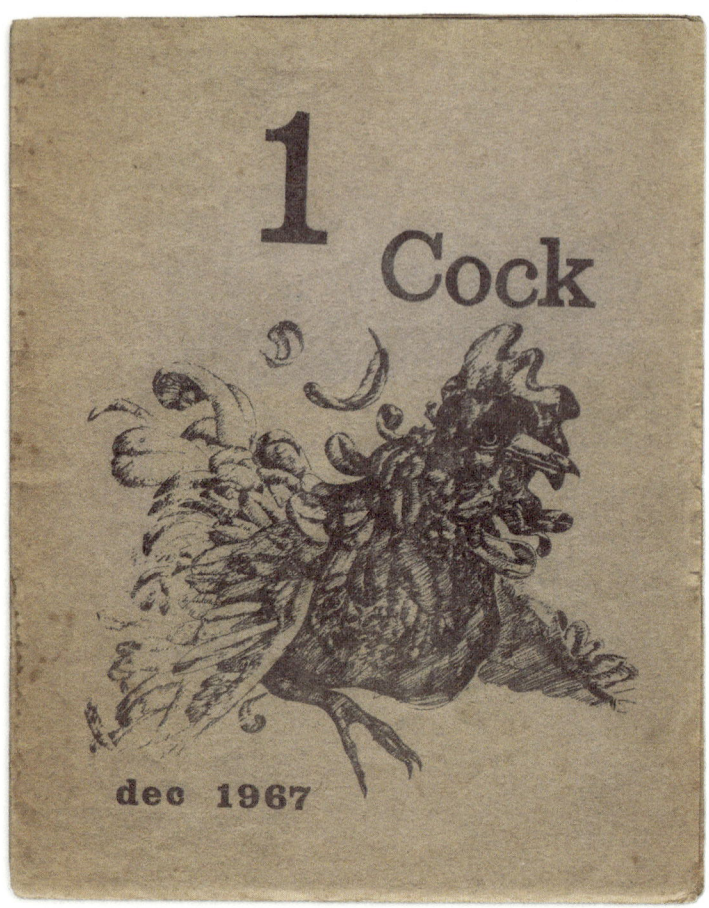

Cock 1, 1967. Private collection

*

In the early seventies, on my daily commute from the city to Onslow College in Johnsonville, I would sometimes encounter a cockseller at Wellington Railway Station. This was not, as it might sound, a male sex worker but rather a distributor of the magazine *Cock*. The seller, judging by their appearance, was a university student or recent dropout. One of our cohort would pay 20 cents for a copy, and the magazine would be eagerly passed around on the train and at the back of school assembly.

The first issue of *Cock* had appeared in December 1967: a sixteen-page compendium of fake news ('Mr K. J. Holyoake, second assistant lavatory attendant at Parliament Buildings, was this morning carried screaming from the front bench …'); jibes at the right-wing media ('In a close field *NZ Truth* looks like winning the Gisborne Sewage Farm Award for 1967'); a report on the latest decisions of the

Indecent Publications Tribunal, and a classified ad calling for persons 'interested in forming a Cannabis Sativa Growers Association'. The name and contact address given was that of Robin Thompson, head of the Wellington vice squad.

Most of the material was written by its editor, Christopher Robin Wheeler. There was also a bogus report on New Zealand Copulation Statistics, ostensibly issued by the Department of Health but in fact written by Wellington GP Dr Erich Geiringer; a ballad by James K. Baxter ('The Private Conference of Harry Fat'); cartoons by Bob Brockie and Brent Wong; and—the only deadly serious inclusion— an account of Greek government torture practices, smuggled out of an Athens prison and reprinted from *The Australian*. This mix of politics, satire, scandal, conspiracy theory and toilet humour was pretty much the template for future issues, which would appear initially every couple of months, then at wider intervals, over the next five years.

Wheeler was shaggy-haired and ginger-bearded, in constant conflict with various agents of authority either real or imagined: the

Chris Wheeler, standing, converses with a smoker in the *Cock* loft, early 1970s. Ans Westra photograph, Alexander Turnbull Library, PA-Group-00941

police, the security service, the mainstream media. To both straight society and the counterculture he was known as the man behind the country's most infamous underground publication.

He had not always been a non-conformist. Wheeler was a graduate of Christ's College, New Zealand's oldest, most traditional private boys' school, located in the centre of Christchurch. In 1957, fresh out of Christ's, where he had excelled at sea cadets, he received his notice for compulsory military training. With dreams of a naval career, he went willingly before the selection board, but was turned down on account of his poor eyesight. The rejection embittered him and a move to Wellington radicalised him. He found the city 'vibrant with intelligent and controversial activity of all varieties, and the type of eccentrics that were almost completely absent in Christchurch'.[6] Within months of his arrival he had read *On the Road*, bought a guitar, learnt a few folk songs and begun performing at the Monde Marie. He fell in with the left-wing political and bohemian crowd, among whom his ribald humour and energetic opposition to the status quo made him a popular figure. These became the chief characteristics of *Cock*, which he would produce from December 1967 to September 1973.

Commercial printers weren't just expensive; they could also be obstructive, as Wheeler had already discovered when dealing with Wellington printer Standard Press over a Committee on Vietnam publication he was helping with, *Vietnam Quote & Comment*. 'They were all old RSA-type geezers which was the standard problem of the era—"prove you're a real man and go to war" sort of thing, and "You should support the Americans in whatever they do because they saved New Zealand in World War II." I think we got one issue of the paper printed by them, then they obviously got pressure from on high—cops, SIS [Security Intelligence Service], ring from Parliament—and the price for printing and censorship started to rise.'[7]

What were the other options? The Xerox photocopier had gone on the market in 1960, but was expensive and remained relatively rare in New Zealand until late in the decade. The cheapest type of duplicator was the Gestetner, which involved typing text onto a wax stencil that would then be stretched over a rotating drum and fed between two ink-covered rollers. The process was manual, time-consuming, practical only for small runs, and produced a blotchy unprofessional-looking result. Political groups often printed circulars using this method, and their manifestos resembled school newsletters or classroom test sheets.

In the early sixties my father, an admirer of the British magazine *Private Eye*, had entertained thoughts of putting out his own magazine of political satire, but the demands of a young family had pushed the notion aside. So when Wheeler started talking up a similar idea, Con was happy to help. He told Wheeler about a Rotaprint press at the Public Service Association (PSA) offices on The Terrace where he worked. Someone had let the ink dry on the rollers, literally gluing them together, and the machine now sat abandoned. One weekend Wheeler, with the help of several recruits including his girlfriend Helen Whiteford and the actor Wi Kuki Kaa, loaded the press onto a trailer. They used creosote to unglue the ink, re-rubbered the rollers, and Cockerel Print was in business.

Andrew Delahunty, who in his early teens took guitar lessons from Wheeler and continued to visit him for coffee and conversation after Wheeler's folk singing had been replaced by radical publishing, remembers the imposing presence of the printing press. 'The weight of the thing and the space it took up—it wasn't a light undertaking to be an underground publisher.'[8]

After a couple of short-lived locations, Cockerel Print set up its ultimate premises in Aro Street, in the loft of a former bakery. Downstairs Andy Grant and Jim Marchbanks repaired vehicles under the name Mickey Mouse Motors. In the early 1980s the loft would be used as the location for a dope-smoking scene featuring Bruno Lawrence in *Goodbye Pork Pie*, Geoff Murphy's cinematic homage to the counterculture.

Though *Cock*'s logo was a rooster, Wheeler clearly intended the more profane meaning to offend in the right places. Deriving amusement from their own genitalia was an apparent feature of New Zealand's early underground publishers. Wheeler's *Cock* had been preceded by a primitive and short-lived Dunedin radical broadsheet, *Falus*—'The Official Organ of the Beards and Weirdies and the Industrial Union of Workers'.[9] It was followed by such vaguely suggestive titles as *Itch* and *Affairs*.

Wheeler maintained a verbal war against the established printing industry. 'The classic New Zealand printer is a sad little man,' he ranted in a typical broadside.

> Like Bob Dylan's Mr Jones, something's going on and he doesn't know what it is. Totally deprived of any critical faculty by years of exposure to the drivelling crap which chunders daily through his printing machines, he is totally in debt to all that is worst in the consumer society.
>
> This scabrous member of a slave class has for too long seen clear his duty to his Establishment owners. He has cut copy presented by New Zealand's few critical writers on grounds which vary from 'obscenity' to 'libel' and a thousand carping petty excuses in between.
>
> Now that this slave class is becoming increasingly monopolised by the shit-capitalist daily press barons it behoves every poison pen radical and anarchist muckraker to get into the Print Revolution. Free the Presses must become the new cry …[10]

Earwig had been launched in 1967, a few months before *Cock*, when Palmerston North Teachers' College student Jonathan Milne took over the college magazine. The first issue included an article of his own in which he took a formula to assess readability and applied it to the notes lecturers were giving to first-year students, finding that these were more difficult than Tolstoy, Shakespeare or Samuel Beckett. His conclusion, that the educators were rendering their ideas inaccessible through bad writing, did not endear him to the college's administration.

Milne's interest in graphics and photographic techniques, which he had begun to explore during an earlier spell at Ilam School of Fine Arts in Canterbury, saw the magazine pushing the primitive Gestetner printing process to its limits. He didn't stay long in the state education system, but his interest in printing and publishing continued. In 1969 he launched *Earwig* as a national magazine and shifted to Auckland.

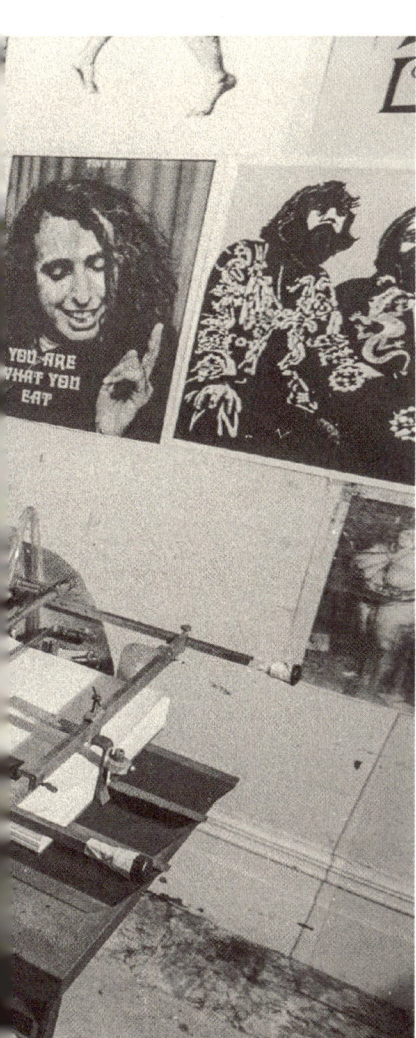

Heather McInnes with the *Earwig* printing press, circa 1972. John Miller photograph, private collection

A rented house in Norfolk Street, Ponsonby, became headquarters of the Earwig Collective, where Milne, Heather McInnes, Kubi Witten-Hannah and Hew Patterson collaborated on putting the magazine together. The cover of the first issue to come out of the new premises featured a striking two-tone portrait of Jimi Hendrix, black and white against a background of eyeball-frazzling orange. Milne hand-screened the covers, all five thousand of them. The issue also includes a photograph of Milne, naked except for a discreetly placed flower, overlaid with text.

Earwig featured a similar mix of radical politics and countercultural commentary to *Cock*, though without Wheeler's bawdy brand of satire and with a more refined graphic style and added emphasis on poetry. Notably, it also featured considerably more women contributors than *Cock*. Of the several dozen poets whose work appeared in *Earwig*, half were women.

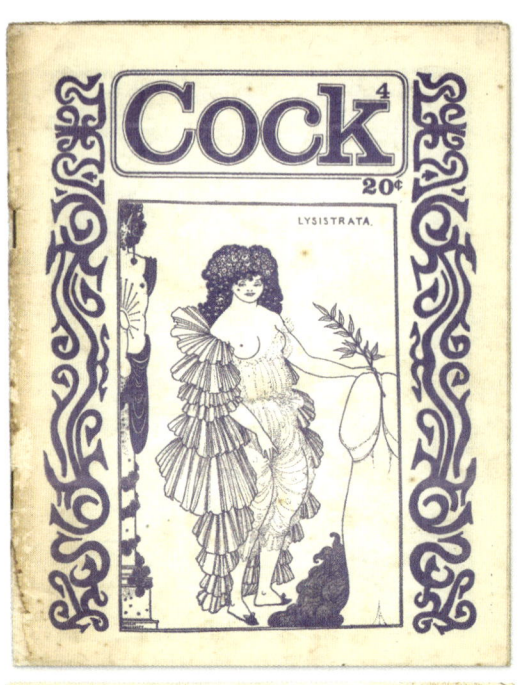
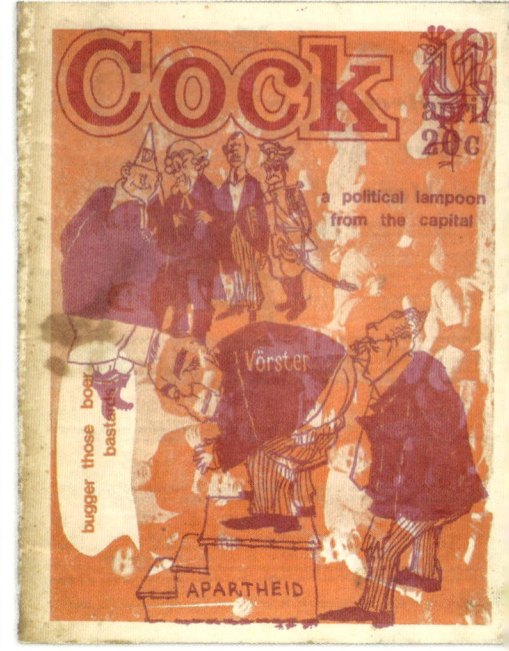

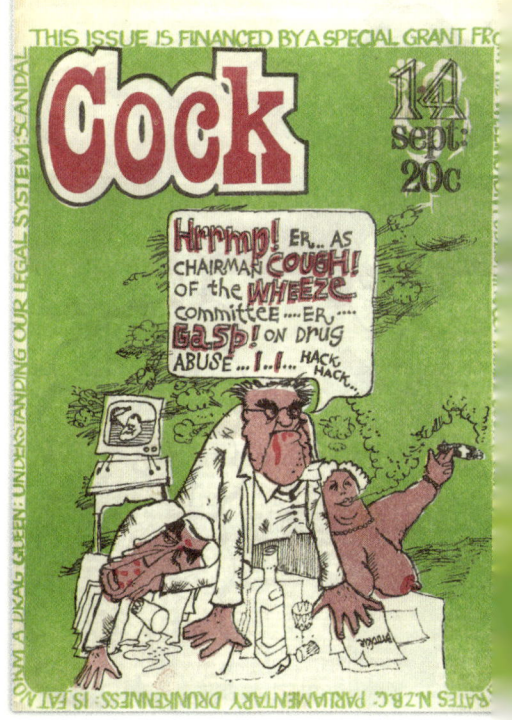

A selection of *Cock* covers, 1968–73.
Private collection

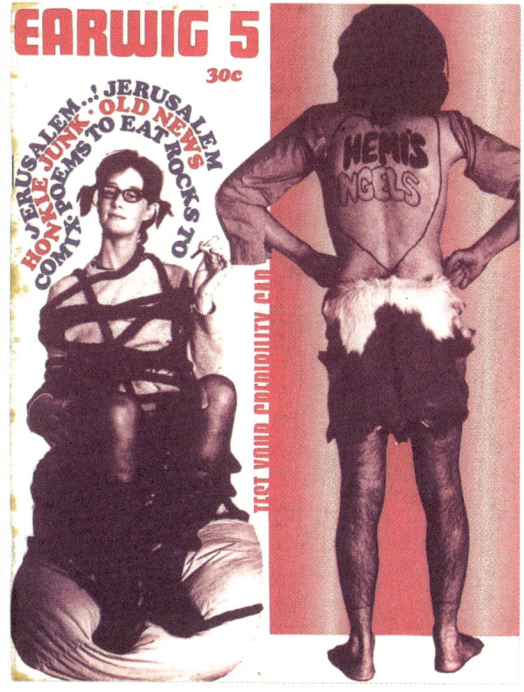

Earwig 2–5, circa 1970–72, covers by Jonathan Milne. Jonathan Milne collection

Just as Wheeler had discovered, the professional printers, fearful of breaching libel and obscenity laws, were reluctant to print the magazine, so *Earwig* purchased its own offset press. As a way of supporting the enterprise, Milne and McInnes began producing posters of countercultural icons such as Bob Dylan, Frank Zappa, Buddha and Tiny Tim that would soon adorn the walls of student flats around the country. At a weekend stall at the 1970 Easter Show they sold enough posters for the collective to be able to put the deposit on a $6500 house in Herne Bay. Catching wind of this, the Norfolk Street landlord, upset that he might be losing his enterprising if unorthodox tenants, made a surprising offer: would they like to buy his house as well? All they would need to do was keep paying the same instalments they had been paying in rent. *Earwig* soon owned two central Auckland properties.

Norfolk Street had become something of an activists drop-in centre. Tame Iti, an activist and artist who would help establish the Māori rights group Nga Tamatoa, moved in. Tim Shadbolt, an increasingly visible figure in the protest movement, was a regular visitor. The premises also received frequent visits from the police. One raid came after a homemade bomb had been used to set fire to a grandstand in protest against a rugby tour of South Africa. Milne remembers: 'This cop found a little plastic jar of carpet tacks, similar to the ones [used in the bomb]. Actually, I had an old barber's chair and had bought them to reupholster the chair. The police were obviously quite excited, but finding the tacks was still insufficient.'[11] On another occasion they came looking for drugs. An intensive search involving a dozen police turned up one Ritalin tablet and one Valium tablet but no prescription. Charges were laid against Witten-Hannah, but the case collapsed in court and damages were awarded against the police.

There were also telephone threats. 'Someone was going to bomb us, throw Molotov cocktails through the window. People answering the telephone described hearing noises in the background. One day I took a call that turned out to be from the police and I was quite startled to hear the same noises. We became fairly convinced that the police themselves were harassing us, trying to destabilise us.'[12]

Most often it was the content of the publications that prompted police visits to the underground publishers. *Ferret* magazine, run from a premises adjacent to the recently established Christchurch Resistance Bookshop by a collective calling itself Kosmic Krumbia and using the original Cockerel Print press acquired from Chris Wheeler, was launched to coincide with 1973 university orientation. Its first issue (titled *Ferret 2*, just to confuse) contained an article entitled 'The Mad Bomber's Handbook' which explained how to use gelignite and make a Molotov cocktail, resulting in charges against editor Martin Braithwaite for 'inciting violence'.

Cock's premises were raided numerous times for evidence of criminal libel. Wheeler's strategy for survival was to stay close to the poverty line. 'I could see that if I started accumulating assets then it would be worth suing me for libel—we were very libellous. [British journalist] Claud Cockburn's rule applies here. "Keep everything scummy and cheap looking but make sure your information is way ahead of everyone else's!" You need to survive, which I did on about five dollars per week which was my share to Andy and Jim for my loft, plus a few other dollars for food.'[13] Even so, this didn't deter two detectives, on different occasions, from suing Wheeler for damages over libellous material that appeared in his magazine. Wheeler was unrepentant. 'We're in the business of exposing this society as one which is basically corrupt and all the police raids and law suits do is help us underline our point that this "democracy" only gives you "freedom of speech" as long as you've got nothing to say,' he wrote in a *Cock* article entitled 'Of Libels and the Police Conspiracy Against the Free Press in NZ'. He admitted he made 'the odd mistake and when we do we try to take immediate steps to correct it ... We're not in the business of wanton dissemination of lies because the daily press does that job quite happily on its own ...'[14]

A number of booksellers, too, were served with writs for selling publications such as *Cock*. To Wheeler the whole thing had 'implications far beyond a simple attempt to stamp out *Cock* magazine'.[15] It was a battle between opposing forces: the counterculture and the status quo.

Christchurch's *Uncool* replicated the inky offset style of *Cock*. An illustrated front cover by Philip Clairmont showed an exploding head; the back (also by Clairmont) depicted a helmeted, truncheon-wielding member of the New Zealand police exclaiming 'Abortion Sex Death-War', and looked like it might have been printed in blood. Between the covers were articles on the anti-war movement, drugs and the Rolling Stones; a profile of Christchurch candy-floss seller and lifelong political activist Jim Andrews; and various comics and articles reprinted from the London and San Francisco underground. Though numerous contributors were thanked, including artist Tony Fomison whose short essay on 'head art' began 'Everyone can draw ... most heads know this', no editor was credited. 'We are who you are ... YOU ARE THE PEOPLE—YOU ARE THE POWER', explained the 'non-editorial'. 'The editors wish to remain anonymous and refuse to die.' In spite of such a defiant attitude, the magazine appears to have lasted only one issue.[16]

The southernmost periodical was *The Counter Culture Free Press*. Launched in Dunedin in 1972—though the date on the masthead was 3 A.W. (that is, three years After Woodstock)—it was an amplifier for the ideas of Malcolm Gramaphone, who had changed his name from Malcolm James to annoy his father. (He would name his own son Gabriel God Galaxy Gramaphone to annoy everybody.) He drove a yellow ambulance and was once fined for smoking cannabis during a visit to a friend in prison. His interests were chiefly political.

LEFT: *Counter Culture Free Press*, Krapotkin Press, circa 1972. Alexander Turnbull Library collection ALMA 993784363502836

BELOW: Deadline looms in the *Salient* office, Lenin looks on. Roger Steele is second from left. Keith Stewart photograph, private collection

He was a proponent of Republicanism and corresponded with the Ugandan dictator Idi Amin with whom he shared a hatred of the British monarchy.¹⁷ But his magazine covered a representative cross-section of countercultural issues.

A typical edition included a feature titled 'Drugs Used Positively: Seeking Transcendence', an exposé of rent racketeering in Dunedin, an article on organic gardening, and another that compared the covert planning behind the raising of Lake Manapōuri for a power station to the Watergate conspiracy. A section of shorter items headed 'News for People Who Don't Read the Pig Press' noted that marijuana was being used by a specialist in Florida for the treatment of glaucoma, NZ Breweries was profiting by keeping the deposit on beer bottles low, and a hat formerly belonging to Hitler had failed to reach its reserve at an auction in Munich. In contrast to the usual schoolboy humour and blatant sexism of *Cock* (which was echoed to varying degrees in the other underground papers), *Counter Culture Free Press* ran sophisticated pieces on gay and women's rights and sexuality. A feature by American feminist Leah Fritz entitled 'Liberated Orgasms', reprinted from the radical American newspaper *Berkeley Tribe*, heralded a 'clitoral counter-revolution'.¹⁸

All these publications had signed up to the Underground Press Syndicate (UPS), a network of countercultural publications formed in the United States in mid-1966. The agreement was that members were free to reprint each other's material in exchange for free subscriptions to each other's publications. For a long time it worked surprisingly well. Jonathan Milne remembers mailing off copies of *Earwig* to dozens of UPS members around the world and being inundated with exotic underground publications in return. San Francisco-based cartoonist Gilbert Shelton, creator of the Fabulous Furry Freak Brothers and Fat Freddy's Cat, belonged to UPS. His comics, which humorously celebrated the stoner lifestyle of three San Francisco hippies and their household pet, were reprinted everywhere, including in the student newspapers.

The major universities had student newspapers or magazines that were published weekly or fortnightly during term time by their respective students' associations. The earliest, *Critic*, was founded at the University of Otago in 1925; the most recent, *Salient*, at Victoria University in Wellington in 1938. They had, to varying degrees, traditionally been a magnet for left-wing and progressive thinkers. Through the 1960s they had all used their pages to raise awareness of nuclear disarmament and the Vietnam War, and to report on the growing protest movement. Ideas about drugs and sex, and the countercultural importance of film, literature and rock music, began to be reflected as well, along with the ubiquitous Shelton comics.

Bill Gruar had been marked as a troublemaker before he started Canterbury University in 1965 aged seventeen. During his final year at school he had been asked to give a talk on Vietnam. Knowing nothing about the subject, he chanced upon an article by Wolfgang Rosenberg in the *New Zealand Monthly Review* criticising American foreign policy in Southeast Asia, and used it as the basis of his report. 'The headmaster went ballistic at me,' he recalls. '"Where did you get this information? What are you talking about?" He was an old military guy from the Second World War. So I went to varsity armed with anti-Vietnam [War] stuff.'[19]

By the time he became editor of *Canta* in 1968 he had started smoking marijuana. Under his editorship the paper poked fun at Holyoake, promoted the protest movement, and ran backgrounders on drugs and their effects. In 1970 he moved to Wellington, encouraged by Geoff Murphy whom he had met through mutual friends, and took up a job as editor of *Focus*, the New Zealand University Students' Association's national publication. Continuing the campaign he had begun at *Canta* against what he saw as wilful scaremongering about drug use, he took issue with two articles written by journalist John Steed that appeared in the national newspaper the *Sunday Times*. Headlined 'I Am Scared of Drugs But I Must Have Them', the first article reported an interview with Lisa, a twenty-one-year-old receptionist who had begun smoking cannabis and claimed she was now unable to stop. The second, headed 'After LSD, Man Tries to Kill Nurse', reported on the exploits of a Canterbury University student who had recently been admitted to Wellington Hospital seeking treatment for drug dependency.

Gruar set out to debunk the articles, reporting that Lisa was sixteen years old, that she did not work as a receptionist but in the accounts department of a city firm, and that she had freely admitted lying to Steed. He added that Lisa was emphatic that she had never told Steed that she was in any way dependent on marijuana. He similarly disputed the second article, stating that 'No "tall, slim, 23-year-old Canterbury University student" or any other student for that matter, has been recently admitted to the Wellington Hospital "seeking treatment for drug dependency".'[20]

He had effectively accused the *Sunday Times* writer of lying. Steed responded aggressively, suing the New Zealand University Students' Association (NZUSA) for libel. Though Lisa had admitted lying to Steed, and the person who had been admitted to hospital was not a student, Gruar was unable to prove that Steed had known otherwise at the time of the articles. The case was costly for NZUSA and a blow for Gruar, who was forced to apologise and retract his statements. Now finding himself unemployable as a journalist, he threw his energies into moviemaking with Murphy.

More frivolously, the students' associations published annual capping magazines to coincide with graduation celebrations. These

Cartoon by Chris Grosz from *Superbag*, 1970. Private collection

traditionally mixed the programme of events with satire and sniggering boys' humour, but by the late sixties had taken on a decidedly counter-cultural hue. In 1970, under the editorial eye of Alan Brunton and Jim Stevenson, cartoonists and comic artists took over Auckland's annual capping book. It was renamed *Superbag* and presented as a plastic bag emblazoned with a bare-breasted female superhero (drawn by Dick Frizzell), and stuffed with assorted pieces of printed matter, including a booklet of cartoons by Chris Grosz and comics by Barry Linton.

Grosz was from Christchurch. His father, an Austrian Jew, had been part of The Group, an informal art association formed as an alternative to the conservative Canterbury Society of Artists. Over time The Group provided a platform for modernist painters such as Colin McCahon, Toss Woollaston and Rita Angus. Chris's inherited interest in visual arts was paralleled by his interest in music. He was a regular at the Stage Door, formed friendships with the members of Chants R&B, and played in the Band of Hope Jug Band with fellow artists Bill Hammond and Warwick Brock.

Barry Linton's strips, which would appear in various student publications over the next few years, 'read like abstract philosophical poems about love, life and nature'.[21] Though born in Auckland, Barry, like Chris Grosz, had spent much of his childhood in Christchurch. Early comic influences had been the American *MAD* magazine and the British *The Beano*. In the late sixties, after a spell at high school in Hamilton, he returned to Auckland, ostensibly to attend Elam School of Fine Arts, but soon threw in his studies to hobo about the country, where he lived in squats and 'hung out with druggies'.[22] During a spell in

Wellington he met and formed a lasting friendship with fellow cartoonist Gerald 'Joe' Wylie, who was on his way to art school in Christchurch.

The same year as *Superbag*, Canterbury University's capping mag was reborn as an underground comic in which some of Wylie's work appeared. In *Captain Kiwi Battles the Dope Fiends*, the stereotypical shorthaired, beer-drinking, rugby-playing New Zealand male—actually an undercover superhero working for the police—is defeated in a battle of wills, wits and pharmaceuticals by a bunch of countercultural anti-heroes including Pot Head, Hash Man and Acid Head (who appears astride a giant tin of LSD bearing the nationally iconic Edmond's Baking Powder emblem 'Sure To Rise').

But by 1971 Canterbury's capping mag, now renamed *Shard*, had slashed the comics. 'The past years ... the magazine was a paste up of other people's rather tedious sense of humour,' the new editors announced solemnly. 'We have attempted to emphasise two things—quality and creativity.' In fact, *Shard* had little humour at all, with several pages given over to a long story by Gary Langford about sex and desperation, and several more to profiles of Cabinet ministers.

THE WORD IS FREED

University of Auckland's *Craccum*, meanwhile, had taken on an arts editor who brought a countercultural sensibility directly to its pages.

'I was born in 1946. My dream was born in the Sixties,' Alan Brunton once wrote.[23] Originally from Christchurch, Brunton had been sent to Hamilton as a toddler by his unmarried parents to stay with his paternal grandmother and, having apparently made up his own mind not to return to his parents even once they had married, would remain there until 1965 when he left for university in Auckland. To an imaginative teenager already interested in Marxism and theatre, arriving in Auckland was 'like going to New York'. He joined CND and travelled to Wellington with other students for the Easter march. Halfway between the University of Auckland and the student hostel was the Kiwi Hotel, which he still recalled in awe when interviewed thirty-five years later by Chris Bourke: 'You'd open the door off the dusty street ... and the first thing would be the red carpet on the floor, the beer-stained red carpet. And there might be half a dozen people at eleven o'clock in the morning, and that might include Colin McCahon, Hamish Keith, Michael Neill, David Mitchell ... You would wonder who they were. I never thought of just bowling up and approaching these people. There was a magic and charisma about them, but just what they had done I wasn't too aware of.'[24]

He would soon find out who these and other members of the creative intelligentsia were and what they had done. One of the country's first contemporary art dealers, Barry Lett, a graduate of Wellington Teachers' College, had opened his own gallery in Auckland in 1965. There he developed a market for the works of McCahon, Pat Hanly,

'Captain Kiwi—Kiwi Battles the Dope Fiends' by Joe Wylie, from *Led Lettuce*, circa 1970. Adam Gifford private collection

'Captain Kiwi—Kiwi Battles the Dope Fiends' by Joe Wylie, from *Led Lettuce*, circa 1970. **Adam Gifford private collection**

Ralph Hotere, Toss Woollaston, Milan Mrkusich, Don Binney and Michael Illingworth: these days a roll-call of some of New Zealand's best-known modernist painters, then just a handful of fringe-dwellers trying to survive. Lett also hosted nights of poetry reading and live jazz. Some nights, after the Kiwi closed — in those days at 6 p.m. — Brunton would join the procession from pub to gallery, sometimes supporting a crate of beer on his shoulder. At the Barry Lett Galleries he would get to know Mitchell and fellow Wellington poet Mark Young, both nearly a decade his senior.

In 1968 Brunton went to Wellington to complete his Master's degree, which he did in between attending anti-war demos and sampling the new psychedelics. The next year he moved back to Auckland, and with his friend Jim Stevenson shifted into a flat at 5 Boyle Crescent, Parnell, recently vacated by junkies. It was unfurnished but for a couple of mattresses and a portable record player. 'We planned to set up the Cultural Liberation Front, for some ill-defined purpose like overthrowing society or changing consciousness or reinvigorating the imagination,' he would recall.[25] They called a meeting. The only people who turned up were the poet Russell Haley and a group of students led by Tim Shadbolt calling themselves AUSAPOCPAH — the Auckland University Society for the Active Prevention of Cruelty to Politically Apathetic Humans, who had formed as 'an insult to the quiet rational intellectual crap that's supposed to flow around the university precincts' and ran about the campus dressed in flowing red-and-black capes and bowler hats.[26]

Within an hour the groups understood that each had its own agenda with little to offer the other. While Shadbolt would go on to channel his sense of theatre into political statements such as the liberation of Albert Park and the handing out of jellybeans to a meeting of the Auckland City Council, Brunton took a purely artistic route. Under the auspices of the Student Literary Society, he and Stevenson mounted a series of multimedia happenings on campus, combining dance, theatre, films and music. Alistair Riddell's Original Sun Blues Band and Henry Jackson's Killing Floor played electrified blues while a light show devised by Philip Alpers involving projectors and coloured oil summoned the ambience of a San Francisco rock happening. Profits from the popular events were funnelled into a poetry magazine, *The Word Is Freed*. The first issue, edited by Brunton and Stevenson, appeared in July 1969. It contained writing by Brunton, Haley, Mitchell, Jan Kemp, Ian Wedde, Bill Manhire and Murray Edmond among others, along with the exquisite line drawings of Barry Linton. Surrealistic, oblique and as uncompromising as any of the underground mags, its stark black-and-white layout nevertheless displayed an aesthetic refinement that contrasted with that of its more haphazard counterparts.

While published under the sober moniker of the Auckland University Students' Association, *The Word Is Freed* was effectively the Cultural Liberation Front manifesto. Brunton had been electrified by the upheavals in Paris of May 1968 and the rock soundtrack of the

'My dream was born in the Sixties...'
Alan Brunton, 1970. Max Oettli photograph,
Alexander Turnbull Library, PAColl-1386-1

American counterculture; *Freed* was his response.²⁷ 'The idea of the Cultural Liberation Front,' Brunton said, 'was to free the imagination.' It was also a declaration of independence from the earlier generation whose work still dominated the country's small literary landscape. To Brunton, *Freed* 'demanded an abrupt end to the hegemony of the Elders and a new dispensation that was irregular, possessed, occult, disjunctive, slapstick and stuck together in a frenzy'.²⁸ Though it would continue for five issues (of which Brunton edited only the first two) its founders had always intended it to auto-destruct: another way in which it rejected established convention.

Brunton began 1970 as *Craccum*'s arts editor, peppering the magazine's main course of campus politics ('Fuzz Threaten Forum Free Speech' rang the front-page headline on the first issue that year) with poems, reviews which ranged across the spectrum of the arts but focused on the modern and the disruptive, and extended pieces of his own including a long interview with British author Anthony Burgess, whose novel of violent youth subculture *A Clockwork Orange* would soon be adapted as a controversial film. He also ran cartoon strips by Barry Linton. Though black and white, these were nearly always, as Linton put it, 'psychedelic in nature. Not in special effects, but in concepts.'²⁹

Comic by Barry Linton, from *Craccum*, 1971. Private collection

But by mid-year Brunton's name had disappeared from the *Craccum* masthead. By this time he was in Calcutta, headed for Kathmandu, where he would spend two months before continuing overland to Afghanistan and, eventually, London. It would be nearly four years before he saw New Zealand again, and the journeys, both physical and metaphysical, he undertook during this time would inform everything he did for the rest of his life. In Bali in September 1973 he met up with Sally Rodwell, with whom he had had a brief relationship in Auckland prior to his departure. 'Independent, silver-tongued and boundlessly energetic, she saw in Alan not only a soul mate but the chance to remain permanently on the road and beyond the reach of a dull suburban life,' Michele Leggott and Martin Edmond would later write.[30] Travelling together through Southeast Asia, Alan and Sally formed a romantic and artistic partnership that would sustain them for the next twenty-nine years.

The year 1971 began with Stephen Chan as *Craccum* editor, but he resigned after the student administration board refused to authorise sixteen-page issues. Chan had argued that this was essential for producing a paper of the standard that would 'offer news and commentary to counter the conservative sycophantic news media'. With him, in sympathy, went most of the paper's staff and contributors, including Sue Kedgley, Murray Edmond, John Miller and Kathryn (later Caterina) De Nave.[31] Cut loose from *Craccum*, he poured his energies into publishing the first collection of poetry by David Mitchell, *Pipe Dreams in Ponsonby*. He had first heard the poet reading at the Ponsonby Club Hotel—known as the Gluepot because, once ensconced there, drinkers tended to find themselves stuck. Chan used his student grant to pay the printing deposit and published the book under his own imprint, The Association of Orientally Flavoured Syndics. Chan saw himself making a stand on behalf of 'the lyrically experimental young', against a New Zealand publishing industry epitomised by the once-innovative Caxton Press, now 'dominated by old men with old ideas and old techniques'.[32]

The book, with illustrations by Pat Hanly, received plenty of attention, in spite of never having an official launch.

> I'd run out of money. In fact, although the book sold out very rapidly, my inexperience was such that I spent more money than I needed to in a whole raft of production and promotional activities. The hardback edition was bound by hand, for instance. I hawked it in person to hundreds of book shops throughout the country, hitch-hiking in order to do so. Back home I would wrap the orders by hand, scrawl out crude invoices, and then inveigle my alarmingly patient mother once a week to cart the lot down to the post office (and pay for the postage to the bookshops). It did mean that I had no money to be a student, so — in true late 1960s and early 1970s fashion — a number of elegant older women took me under their arms and paid off the printing and other costs. Because the third objective, apart from making a stand against literary conservatism and designing something beautiful, was to sell the book as cheaply as possible.[33]

A *Listener* review of *Pipe Dreams in Ponsonby* detected a variety of influences, including 'the Shakespearian plays (with their passionate ear for music) and the Beat poetry of Ferlinghetti and Corso' but ultimately declared Mitchell to be 'his own original'. Peter Crisp found in 'poem after poem ... brief glimmers of an ordered, mystical system of belief, full of light and intelligence' and 'frequent moments of clear-minded joy that make heart and head sing together in the new, bright air of Ponsonby'.[34]

BLOWING UP

Puritans like Oswald Mazengarb had believed that Hollywood images of American rebels corrupted the attitudes and behaviours of 1950s New Zealand youth. Now a new wave of popular cinema was exerting its influence on the young minds of the sixties.

In 1966, European auteur Michelangelo Antonioni's film *Blow-Up* splashed the style, sound and ambience of swinging London onto the big screen, complete with a pot party, an orgy, a troupe of street mimes and a guitar-splintering performance from Jeff Beck with the Yardbirds. For 1969's *Zabriskie Point*, Antonioni turned his lens to North America, where students rioted, hippies rolled naked in the dust, and symbols of bourgeois materialism were literally blown up. The battle lines between the counterculture and the straight world were clearly delineated that year in Dennis Hopper's *Easy Rider*, in which Hopper and Peter Fonda played a pair of drug-dealing, motorcycling, acid-dropping pilgrims on a journey that took them from Californian communes to the Mardi Gras in New Orleans, only to perish at the hands of murderous, hippie-hating rednecks. Stuart Hagmann's *The Strawberry Statement* shifted the conflict to a fictitious American campus, while Lindsay Anderson's *If . . . .* took place in an English public boys' school. Its publicity poster showed two students, one holding a pile of books, the other a machine-gun, above the logline: 'Which side will you be on?'

The films reinforced their rebellious messages with powerful rock soundtracks: the Yardbirds in *Blow-Up*, Pink Floyd and the Grateful Dead in *Zabriskie Point*, Hendrix, the Byrds and the Holy Modal Rounders in *Easy Rider*. And in October 1970 came *Woodstock*, the documentary of the previous year's festival. This more than any other movie codified the counterculture, presenting iconic musical performances—Jimi Hendrix deconstructing 'The Star Spangled Banner', the Who declaiming 'We're not gonna take it!'—alongside images and interviews about drug-taking, nudity, free love and long hair. You want a counterculture? This, it seemed to say, is how it's done.

All these films were shown in New Zealand cinemas, though cuts by a snip-happy censor left it for the Kiwi imagination to fill in the missing pieces of what were often already fragmented narratives. (Of the movies mentioned above, *Woodstock* suffered the most severely, with 418 metres—close to a quarter of an hour of screen time—cut for New Zealand screenings.[35]) Around the same time, popular mainstream films such as *Bonnie and Clyde* and *Butch Cassidy and the Sundance Kid* (also appearing after cuts) portrayed their titular anti-heroes more as countercultural rebels than ruthless outlaws.

New Zealand's own cinema would take a while to catch up. Local film-making had languished since the pioneering efforts of Rudall Hayward in the 1920s and '30s and consisted mostly of tourist documentaries and educational films produced by the state-owned National Film Unit.

There were a few exceptions. The far-sighted John O'Shea, of the small independent Pacific Films, had examined the underlying racial prejudice in New Zealand in his laudable if stilted 1952 feature *Broken Barrier*. It took him twelve more years to raise the finance for his second full-length film, *Runaway*, an on-the-road story starring Colin Broadley as a young accountant-turned-hedonist in search of the real New Zealand. He travels the length of the country and has relationships with several women along the way, including an innocent Māori maiden played by Kiri Te Kanawa. Barry Crump, whose hit novel *A Good Keen Man* had enshrined the boozy bushman as an archetype of Kiwi masculinity, played a convincing cameo as a lecherous pig hunter.

It had been shot by twenty-one-year-old novice Tony Williams, with an even younger Michael Seresin as his assistant.

Released in 1964, *Runaway* seemed dated on arrival, especially when held up against the Beatles' *A Hard Day's Night* which screened the same year. Retitled *Runaway Killer* for overseas release, reviewers tended to be more enthusiastic about the cinematography than the acting. Still, it both emerged from and reflected a different New Zealand from the one conventionally portrayed in popular culture. Michael Seresin recalled: 'I think John was trying to get a message across of this lost soul … in a nation of lost souls, rural people living relatively remote lives.'[36]

O'Shea was still running to catch up with *A Hard Day's Night* with his next feature, *Don't Let It Get You*, a musical starring Howard Morrison, Kiri Te Kanawa, Lew Pryme and Ray Columbus, released in 1966. Though the film hardly seems subversive, it portrayed a romantic, carefree side of New Zealand rarely seen at the time, as well as putting on screen such distinctly local traditions as Māori showbands.

Soon after its release, Seresin, who had again been camera assistant, left for London, where he almost immediately fell into a job with the Beatles, working on *Magical Mystery Tour*, their self-directed psychedelic television special. Seresin would go on to be director of photography on many notable films, from *Midnight Express* (1978) to *Harry Potter and the Prisoner of Azkaban* (2004). Looking back, he sees the Pacific Films that John O'Shea presided over as a cultural oasis in sixties New Zealand: 'They were cosmopolitan people who'd either been born abroad or travelled and were sympathetic to food, wine, ideas — discussing abstract things instead of the rugby score or the price of two-toothed sheep.'[37]

Back in Wellington, a bunch of musicians, storytellers and aspirant filmmakers who had spent a good part of the decade drinking, philosophising and fantasising in the Studio Jazz Club and the Duke of Edinburgh were getting closer to realising one of their fantasies: to make a movie. Geoff Murphy directed and came up with the plot of *Tank Busters* in which a bunch of dreamers, not unlike himself and his mates, conspire to rob a university safe.

Though aimed at television — the media heart of mainstream New Zealand — *Tank Busters* is both a product of the counterculture and a snapshot of it. Sets were constructed and painted in the rehearsal room of R&B band the Original Sin. The room doubled as a set for the pub scenes, where we meet the protagonists: half a dozen longhaired males, some sporting a moustache or paisley shirt, clustered around a couple of jugs of beer. Some of them are students, the others dropouts. Policemen ('Cops, you know, fuzz', as one of the hairy heroes is heard to mutter) are the enemy. The only woman in the story is a pay clerk, who doubles as the love interest.

The climax comes when the six guys, who have now divided into three duos and, unbeknownst to each other, hatched three separate

Geoff Murphy editing film in the basement of a condemned building, July 1972. *New Zealand Herald*

burglary plans, all try to rob the safe on the same night. The botched heist coincides with a rock concert in the adjacent Student Union Hall. Along with one of the first major screen-acting performances by Bruno Lawrence, the film features rare footage of homegrown guitar hero Harvey Mann fronting a late version of the Underdogs. It also features an early example of the special-effects explosion that would become a Murphy trademark. Blowing stuff up was one of the ways in which the counterculture communicated its contempt for the status quo, and there were more explosions to come.

Completion of *Tank Busters* was held up while Murphy, working on a shoestring budget, haggled, borrowed and even burgled to get the film finished. Knowing that NZBC employees often helped themselves to the unused ends of film rolls, Murphy had friends in the organisation divert thousands of feet of the already stolen stock to his project.

If middle New Zealand was to take any message from the movie when it was eventually screened nearly two years later, it might have been that these longhaired dreamers couldn't pull off a break-in at their own campus, so probably weren't too much of a threat.

A BIGGER STAGE

Alister Taylor believed that to really effect any change you needed to act on a bigger stage, as the establishment did. In 1966 he had left student politics for a job as a current affairs journalist with the NZBC, where he was instrumental in launching *Checkpoint* which, more than half a century later, remains a flagship programme of the state broadcaster. Perhaps he thought that by producing a national current affairs programme he could help sway the government policies of the day. Behind the scenes, he continued his involvement with the anti-war movement.

He was energetic, innovative and ungovernable. When his suggestion of recording telephone interviews for broadcast was rejected by management—they said the audio quality wouldn't meet broadcast standards—he went ahead and did it anyway. On this occasion he won. A journalist in Kuala Lumpur describing the riots in the Malaysian capital while machine-guns fired in the background brought a palpable immediacy to the events, and Taylor's initiative was commended.

But in early 1968 he was summoned into the office of the Director General of the NZBC Gilbert Stringer and given five minutes to clear his desk. His extra-curricular activities, he was told, compromised the impartiality of the programme. It transpired that Stringer had received a complaint from the American ambassador regarding *Checkpoint*'s coverage of Vietnam and American foreign policy. Taylor sought legal representation and support from the PSA, who succeeded in having him reinstated with full pay and legal costs. But on his return he found he had been taken off *Checkpoint* and assigned new duties supervising broadcasts to the Pacific, where he could have little influence on political reporting here.

Taylor resigned in disgust, but was already making other plans. In March he would launch the single most publicised event in the local anti-war movement's history so far. Timed to coincide with a meeting in Wellington of the South East Asia Treaty Organisation (SEATO) council, Peace, Power and Politics would be a three-day conference with a focus on Vietnam—and a roll-call of the international protest movement. An initial proposal to have Martin Luther King Jr speak never eventuated. Had he attended, he would likely not have been in Memphis, Tennessee, where he was assassinated three days after the conference ended. Those who did attend included Indian intellectual and Penguin Books founder Krishna Menon, *San Francisco Chronicle* journalist Felix Greene, Irish politician and historian Conor Cruise O'Brien, and a number of local anti-war intellectuals. These were not bomb-throwing radicals or hippie anarchists but mature heavy-weight figures.

Two weeks out, there was a sabotage attempt from a high level. The Reserve Bank, with the backing of Finance Minister Rob Muldoon, denied the organisers permission to pay the airfares of three overseas

Peace, Power and Politics poster,
1968, designed by Fred 'Cul' Cullen.
Ephemera Collection, Alexander Turnbull
Library, Eph-C-VIETNAM-1968-01

speakers. There was a public outcry. Unions, churches, the Labour Opposition and newspapers all expressed outrage. Even the normally anti-protester *Truth* declared: 'At one blow Mr Muldoon has … demonstrated that New Zealanders are ruled by a Government so intolerant of views opposing its own that it will interfere with the public's right to hear them.'[38]

It was great publicity, the event went ahead anyway, and the turnout exceeded Taylor's expectations, with two thousand people turning up for some of the talks. While the attendees represented the full range of anti-war supporters, the sense of an occasion rather than just another worthy meeting in a draughty hall accounted for the conspicuous number of youths and longhairs.

As for the airfares, Taylor was rescued by social activist Sonja Davies, who had a friend in the UK who was prepared to advance the money for the tickets. By the opening of the conference, however, it became clear that Taylor, whose lifelong habit of using one project to fund the next was already in evidence, had no intention of repaying the loan, so Davies took matters into her own hands. She positioned herself alongside Taylor at the front desk of the Wellington Opera House and personally collected the cash until she had been repaid in full.

Like radio, all the country's television was controlled by the NZBC and until 1975 each of the four centres had only one channel. Other than a brief regional news segment, the whole nation essentially saw the same thing. National news was covered nightly in a spoken bulletin, followed by an imported newsreel of overseas material. Tony Larsen, a schoolboy in Tawa, north of Wellington, remembers seeing footage in 1965 of the black civil rights marches from Selma, Alabama, to the state capital of Montgomery. 'All those cops with their billy clubs and helmets and snarling Alsatians and crowds of black people with the cops going up to them with the Alsatians straining at their leashes. Such a contrast to life in Tawa!'[39]

As the decade wore on, television's coverage of local affairs grew more sophisticated, with in-house productions such as *Gallery* and *Compass* presenting topical interviews and discussions, while local news crews were dispatched to capture on-the-spot footage of dramatic events like the 1966 visit of President Lyndon Johnson or the 1968 sinking of the *Wahine*.

News film continued to be received from overseas, to be recut by local editors. In this way images of the street riots around the 1968 Chicago Democratic Convention, the killing of students at Kent State University by the Ohio National Guard, and the My Lai massacre brought the Vietnam War into local living rooms in a way that war and its effects had never been before.[40]

'I can remember, as an editor, getting footage and looking through it and seeing dead bodies and thinking this was extraordinary,' recalled Sean Duffy, who worked in NZBC news at the time. 'We suddenly lost our innocence and our naivety about what was occurring in the world.' Though he added: 'There were strict rules about what we were allowed to put on television and the New Zealand audience wouldn't have got to see a lot of dead bodies, even though we were sent them.'[41]

Though Defence Minister David Thomson accused the NZBC of 'a lack of integrity', citing coverage of the My Lai massacre as a display of the broadcaster's anti-war bias, Major-General Walter McKinnon, chair of the NZBC, rejected the claims. In his previous role as New Zealand Army's Chief of General Staff, he had been an advocate of combat commitment.[42]

Protest groups had discovered the value of television as a means of promoting their cause, and began to tailor their protests with the camera in mind. Therese O'Connell, involved in a number of Wellington

protest groups, recalls: 'Our big discussion was often [around] what events would we create that television would want to pick up.' She remembers questions being asked in Parliament about how a television news crew knew to be outside the Prime Minister's residence in Pipitea Street late one night when an effigy was burned.[43]

No one had a better grasp of how to use the media to gain attention than Tim Shadbolt. Before long the entire country was familiar with his crinkly-eyed grin, unruly hair, flamboyant soapboxing and imaginative acts of political disruption. He was on television, in newspapers, parks, streets, schools and town halls, and both in and outside prisons. Wherever he went, he never shut up. It helped that he was extremely entertaining. His speeches, all recounted with humour, combined revolutionary rhetoric and ripping yarns of masculine derring-do.

It was during 1968 that he started to become a countercultural celebrity. Twenty years old and nominally studying history and political science at the University of Auckland, he had already ridden with bike gangs, worked as a miner on the Manapōuri dam and laboured on construction sites, and he tended to regard his lecturers and campus colleagues as ivory-tower elitists in contrast to the salt-of-the-earth blokes he had sweated alongside in the real world. But he was also passionately opposed to the Vietnam War and South African apartheid, smoked pot and lived in an urban commune.

Though his campus group AUSAPOCPAH numbered only eight, they published a weekly news sheet drawing attention to issues of war and injustice, picketed warships, held peace marches and urged students to get involved. In 1968 their high profile won them several places on the student executive. But Shadbolt's instinct for publicity proved stronger than his ability to organise. In his role as social controller he was put in charge of the university's end-of-term dance. He handed out flyers at local schools and drew a packed crowd to the Student Union Hall. Just one problem: he had forgotten to book the band. In a desperate ploy, a drummer was rustled up to play along to records while Shadbolt's brother Rod and a few of his mates clutched musical instruments and mimed, but before long the unsatisfied crowd was shouting, fighting and demanding its money back. Shadbolt was sacked from his executive office, after which he threw himself deeper into protest.

Over the next three years he would be arrested dozens of times, though what he was protesting was not always clear. Sue Bradford recalls: 'Tim would make these passionate speeches but you couldn't quite work out what the point was and where he was going.'[44]

'He was never really a political idealist,' says his friend and former AUSAPOCPAH member John Bower. 'He never had any real policies. He was always just ... "Get involved!" He could sway a crowd. And [he had] an ability to draw an analogy that just resonated with a great number of people, with the humour of it. Plus his smile.'[45] Jonathan Milne remembers an 'extraordinary instinct for showbiz. And on a good day he was hilariously funny and quick and quite endearing, and on a bad

Tim Shadbolt in Albert Park, with dog Brutus. Murray Cammick photograph, Simon Grigg private collection day he could be quick and stupid. He told the Resistance Bookshop they shouldn't be selling their books, they should be giving them away. They actually depended on selling a few for staying alive, but Tim doggedly failed to see that.'[46]

AUSAPOCPAH morphed into the Friends of Brutus, named for Shadbolt's Alsatian dog. There was talk of enrolling Brutus as an Independent candidate in the general election. When Bower was imprisoned (of which more later), Shadbolt led a hunger strike in Myers Park in protest. Every Sunday, between songs from the Frank E. Evans Lunchtime Band, he would address the crowds there. On the day the Myers Park contingent set off unannounced to liberate the forbidden Albert Park, Shadbolt was nearly left behind; he had gone to buy a milkshake, returning just in time see the crowd disappearing down Queen Street.

Attempts to have the new location legitimised gained Shadbolt further notoriety. When he led a group to a meeting of the Auckland City Council to plead their case, bringing streamers, flowers and cakes, and handing out jellybeans in the council chambers, he was arrested along with four others. Nevertheless, Mayor Robinson seemed to recognise the social value of the Albert Park events, perhaps seeing them as a safety valve at a time when more conventional protests were becoming increasingly heated, and admitting that they livened up a Sunday 'which is normally dull'.[47]

Though official restrictions would not be removed until the following year, for the remainder of 1969 the happenings continued under the banner Jumping Sundays, with Shadbolt one of the chief attractions. A *Waikato Times* reporter took in a typical Shadbolt sermon. The subject on this occasion was the New Zealand Army. Shadbolt advocated for a naked military—'I'll guarantee if they were all nude they wouldn't fight'—and mocked their recruitment drive: '"Join the army, be a man" they say. What they don't say is you might also be a corpse … The advertisements show Asian girls with slits up their dresses, and some of these young guys who've never had a girl think "that's the life for me". They plug duty free shopping in Singapore. What they should be telling you is that you'll more than likely be killed …'[48]

His audience was not restricted to the counterculture. He also ventured into union meetings and even Lions clubs. Addressing a luncheon club of the Clerical Workers Union, he praised Jesus Christ ('my favourite revolutionary'), Florence Nightingale ('another little beauty—she went off to care for the wounded soldiers who were mostly criminals') and the suffragettes ('they used to dash out in front of the King's horses and throw themselves under carriages. They really smashed into those cops'). In the lead-up to the 1969 general election, he was among the studio audience at a televised leaders' debate. He heckled when Prime Minister Keith Holyoake dithered over when troops would be withdrawn from Vietnam, and cheered Opposition leader Norman Kirk when he expressed the hope that they would be home by Christmas.

But what might have been the definitive televised showdown between the counterculture and the establishment never made it to air. Irish-born journalist Brian Edwards was a household name in the late sixties after fronting a series of television current affairs programmes. At the end of 1970, before a live audience in the Lower Hutt Little Theatre, he taped a pilot for what he hoped would become his own weekly programme, *The Brian Edwards Show*. Attempting to turn generational friction into a media coup, Edwards' featured guests were three of the country's most visible countercultural personalities: Shadbolt, Alister Taylor and Chris Wheeler. In the opposite corner: the country's most pugnacious politician, Robert Muldoon.

As soon as the debate started it became a battle of verbal barbs. Taylor called Muldoon 'a cost accountant who worries about dimes and cents while pensioners starve'. Wheeler called him 'pushy and arrogant ... everything New Zealanders want in a political leader', while Shadbolt's attack was strictly personal, focused on the distinguishing scar that affected the muscles of Muldoon's left cheek. 'It's the lump! I just can't stand the bloody lump on his face!'

'Two of you three young men are individualists,' Muldoon retorted. 'The other's an idiot. I'll let the audience decide.'[49]

To judge by his account, Edwards was delighted with the whole thing. Muldoon called it 'a most interesting piece of television'. But the NZBC rejected *The Brian Edwards Show*, claiming it did not meet the corporation's broadcast standards.

If Edwards was disappointed, Muldoon was indignant. 'I want the NZBC to show it,' he told a group of school duxes at a luncheon hosted by the Auckland City Council, 'because, while I took a hard knock the programme gives a clear insight into the real merit of these men's ideals. I am not going to be critical of these so-called leaders of the New Left, but I will say that they are false prophets as far as young people are concerned.'[50]

False prophets or not, Shadbolt, Taylor and Wheeler carried on communicating their ideas to the young, with and without the megaphone of the mainstream media. In 1971 Taylor launched his own publishing firm [detailed in Chapter 13] and was responsible for some of the most influential countercultural publications in the country, with Shadbolt one of his best-selling authors. 'Taylor's joined the establishment', hippies were heard to grumble. But, as he insisted to Marcia Russell of *Thursday* magazine in 1972, it wasn't a matter of joining the establishment. 'You let the Establishment teach you and then you move in and do it even better.'[51]

THE WAR AT HOME

Six

In October 1969, a month out from that year's election, Prime Minister Keith Holyoake sent a memo to Brigadier William Gilbert, Director of the Security Intelligence Service, asking for 'a report showing the origin, composition, motivating principles and activities of the Progressive Youth Movement'.[1]

Holyoake had been seeing and hearing a lot of the PYM recently, yet their membership, structure, agenda and affiliations still seemed unclear. He had found his business on the campaign trail increasingly disrupted by groups of young people identifying themselves as PYM who came to meetings to heckle and fight with police and National Party members. They had also made up the more militant element in recent protest marches, particularly those revolving around the August visit of American Secretary of State William P. Rogers.

Protesting the visit of Air Vice-Marshal Ky, January 1967. Dominion Post Collection, Alexander Turnbull Library, PAColl-7327-1-068

The month of Rogers' visit, an issue of the magazine *PYM Organiser* had carried instructions for making a Molotov cocktail and diagrams showing how to adapt this weapon to a rifle. As a result, Minister of Police Percy Allen ordered raids in Auckland that resulted in the confiscation of several rifles, including one belonging to Bill Lee, the Auckland PYM's nominal leader. Though it transpired that Lee had a licence for the gun, his possession of the weapon was raised by the prosecution when he was charged in the Auckland Magistrate's Court with intent to incite disorder, violence or lawlessness.

'A BUNCH OF ROUGH-LOOKING BUGGERS'

The Auckland PYM had begun in August 1965 at a meeting of two dozen or so people, all in their teens and early twenties. Roughly half were students, the remainder blue-collar workers and apprentices. That same month saw the New Zealand visit of controversial British band the Pretty Things, and their Auckland Town Hall concert was the focus of an enlistment drive by the newly formed organisation, who paraded outside with posters and successfully recruited some of the young R&B fans to their ranks. As the fledgling political group grew, tertiary students tended to drop out, and the proportion of young workers, apprentices and secondary school students increased. Initially they called themselves Youth Action Committee on Vietnam. As their interests widened over the next few months, the name became simply Youth Action Committee, then in April 1966 Auckland Progressive Youth, with Movement added some time later.[2]

'We changed the name to Progressive Youth Movement because it was clear that once you start questioning one issue, such as New Zealand being involved in the War, you start running into all kinds of interconnected things,' founding member Anna Lee told Paul Jackman, citing big business, American financial interests, and the relationship between the police and the status quo as other areas of concern.[3] As Jackman would observe, what the PYM emphasised was the radicalisation and mobilisation of young people as an end in itself.[4]

'Youth Power—France, Britain, Germany, USA, Peru—a new vital progressive force—A call to action' reads a handwritten plan for a PYM poster. Though the group's members were highly aware of overseas youth rebellion, particularly in America, their visions of a reformed society were founded not so much on hippie lines as a youth-led class uprising. According to Sue Bradford, who as a member observed them at close range, they were 'puritanically anti-drug, although they were quite happy with lots of alcohol at their parties'.[5]

To develop their movement, they planned a series of group activities at a farm near Auckland. An internal journal outlined the proposed activities and their ultimate purpose: 'confrontation between established society and mobilised youth'.[6]

PYM Organiser, 1969. Barry Lee Collection on the Progressive Youth Movement, Auckland Branch, Special Collections, University of Auckland, MSS-Archives-2011/03

P.Y.M. ORGANISER

Phone 869-097 or 609-697   P.O. Box 6736, Wellesley St. 5c
AUCKLAND

MOLLER'S FARM '69

Sunday, July 20, saw some of us on the 30-acre farm, together with the Hell's Angels, the V8 Boys, University Radicals, Samoans, and Maoris, Western Suburbs working youth, Hippies and other diverse elements —including some semi-admiring members of the Labour Party. Now what is the significance of this for PYM and the Left in general?

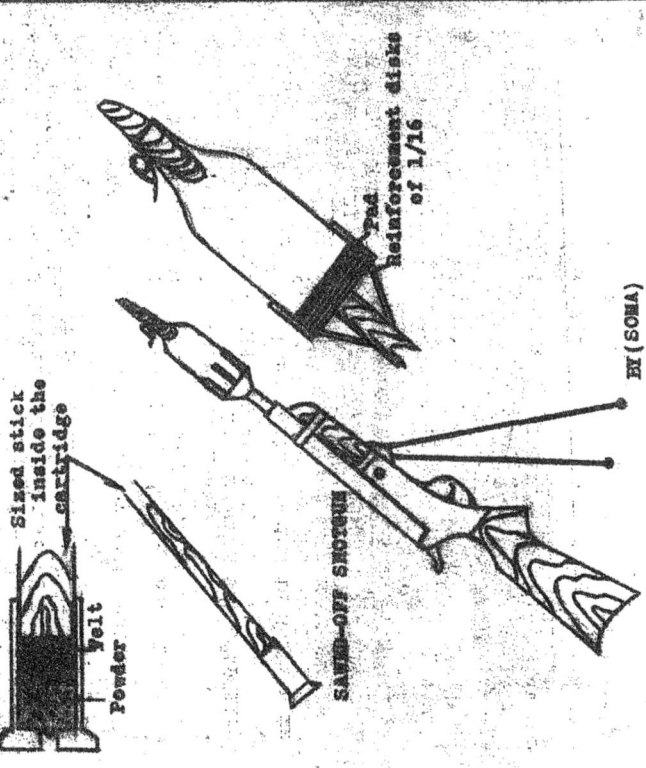

CONSTRUCTION of a MOLOTOV COCKTAIL

A Molotov cocktail is a bottle containing three parts kerosine and one part motor oil. The bottle is sealed and wrapped in waste cotton which is sprinkled with gasoline and ignited.

ADAPTION OF THE MOLOTOV COCKTAIL TO A RIFLE

This apparatus will fire the burning bottles a hundred metres or more, with a fairly high degree of accuracy. This is an ideal weapon for encirclements when the enemy have many wooden or inflammable material constructions, also for firing against tanks in hilly country.

BY (SOMA)

Starting from rifle shoots, motorbike scrambling, hunting, print making, hangis, films, music, dancing etc. we will move into the amazing, astounding, joyous phenomenon of street liberation. This involves presenting dance, drama and music happenings in Vulcan Lane on Saturday night … Fine—until the pubs, shops, dance halls and capitalists etc. start losing loot. They panic— how to break it up? Our friend in the street, the policeman, is their obvious answer. But the people are enjoying themselves. Result—confrontation. All the people are drawn in. If we have done our work well, it becomes completely political.[7]

They had also gleaned from worldwide media coverage of the black civil rights movement in America that protest acts generated the greatest publicity when they were met with violence. Always media savvy, the PYM understood the power of television. When Air Vice-Marshal Ky arrived at Māngere Airport in 1967, it was PYM member John Gabolinsky who committed the first major act of protest, throwing himself in front of Ky's car. He was quickly apprehended by police, but the event was captured by television news cameras. Talking to Jackman about the incident twelve years later, Gabolinsky recalled: 'When I arrived back at work the next day I was immediately surrounded by half the blokes and they agreed "You're right, all the stuff you told us was right" simply because they saw me on T.V. get planted.'[8] His interpretation of the value of such an act was a typical example of PYM thinking.

The next major confrontation between the PYM and the authorities came in October 1967 following an anti-Vietnam War march in Queen Street, organised by the Auckland Council on Vietnam. The march had attracted two thousand people and been an orderly affair, but after the formal demonstration had ended, the PYM issued a spontaneous invitation to marchers to carry on to Paratai Drive and the home of the US consul. Around one hundred took up the offer, giving the police an unwanted surprise. As the marchers neared the consul's mansion, scuffles broke out near a fence running along the edge of a steep cliff.

At some point Bill Lee found himself backed up against the fence by one of the policemen. Other PYM members came to his rescue, and in the ensuing melee Police Inspector Grynwyd Rees either fell or was pushed over the fence, catching himself just short of the sheer 100-metre drop. 'Pitched Battle with Vietnam Demonstrators: Police Inspector Is Pushed Over Cliff', read the *Herald* headline the next day. For the PYM it was another publicity coup. 'It frightened a lot of people off but also a lot of people were brought in,' remarked Gabolinsky. 'We did have a sudden burst of growth after that.'[9] It was clear the PYM was cut from a different cloth from the middle-class, student-led Youth CND. They weren't the kind you could imagine putting on puppet shows for children.

Bill Lee had grown up in Panmure. His father was a carpenter in the railway workshops, and had a strong trade union ethos.[10] His younger brother Barry had always wanted to be a policeman and in 1966, fresh out of school, was taken on as a police cadet. Influenced by his father's left-wing views, Barry spent his spare time at training camp reading up on Vietnam and other political issues. In August 1967, his training complete, he was posted to the Auckland Central Police Station. He didn't last long. A week before the Paratai Drive incident, he was taken aside by Inspector Rees and quizzed about his political views. A few days later he was summoned by the Chief Superintendent of the Auckland Police and informed of his dismissal. Though the action was later deemed unlawful and Lee was paid compensation, his brief policing career was over. 'I was escorted to empty my locker and to my room in the barracks to collect my belongings. From there I went from being in the police to being active in PYM.'[11]

Deborah Yates, a founder member of Youth CND, remembers encountering the PYM that year at a bacchanalian gathering at the Bethells Beach home of Andy Wilcox: 'It was a hāngī that didn't work, so they got the lambs out on sticks and cooked it on the bonfire, and the PYM were there, a bunch of rough-looking buggers. I didn't take to them at all.'[12]

Wilcox, a charming, barefooted beach boy and mechanic who would die young in a boating accident, was the son of Vic Wilcox, long-serving secretary of the New Zealand Communist Party. Since the Soviet invasion of Hungary in 1956, the party had been undergoing a series of splits in which large numbers would either jump or be pushed, with the different factions accusing each other of 'revisionism', 'propagating the bourgeois line' and other ideological transgressions. By the late 1960s the senior Wilcox, an adherent of Mao Zedong, was seeking to boost the party's declining numbers by strengthening alliances with youth movements such as the PYM. In his 1994 memoir Ron Smith, a member of the party's Wellington District Committee since 1941, noted that 'Wilcox and the Party National Centre backed this whole youth revolt with unstinted praise. Youth Branches of the Party were formed in Auckland and Wellington. *The People's Voice* hailed youth in general, and the PYM in particular, as harbingers of the revolution.'[13]

Wilcox encouraged his members to unite with the young revolutionaries. 'By joining in their fight against restrictions on peaceful protest and demonstration, we show that we are "with it" in their eyes,' he told the National Committee in March 1970. 'It is not a matter of concern if they wear long hair or miniskirts. We could never previously attract young people to Marxist study classes but now they are coming in numbers from three to fifty ... Of course there have been mistakes made by the youth and we cannot treat them lightly. But we must not adopt a grandfatherly approach or show complacency, passivity or communist conceit and arrogance. We must be in there with them.'[14]

Auckland Town Hall, circa 1971.
Max Oettli photograph, Alexander Turnbull Library, PAColl-1386-1

But while Wilcox continued to argue with other Old Left factions over who espoused the purer form of communism, some of the PYM had another agenda altogether. A student who had recently begun to hang out with the Wellington PYM at the time of the second Radical Activist Congress, held at Victoria University in 1970, recalled:

> There was a debate between the two chief currents of the day: the Maoists and the Trotskyists. I stood with the PYMers at the back of the raked auditorium and watched as things got more and more heated. Before long someone produced a record-shop bag and slid out an LP. 'Have you heard this? It's really good.' I looked and saw that it was MC5, *Kick Out The Jams*. I'd seen mention of it in books but, being at that point a junior folkie, had never heard it, let alone seen a copy. One of his friends began opening a zip-up bag and asking 'Can you see a wall socket?' Then he produced a little Dansette-style portable record player, balanced it on the balustrade running behind the topmost row of seats, plugged it in and held out his hand for the album. Of course the effect even at full volume was hardly electrifying, but the intent was obvious and provoked an instant response. A guy from one of the factions, I couldn't tell which, bounded furiously up the aisle, shouldered his way past the knot of us clustered around the machine, whipped the disc off the turntable while it was still turning and flung it towards the front of the room. It sailed over the heads of the audience and disappeared from sight in front of the stage while they all seemed to stare in our direction. Seemed like a good time to go.[15]

Though PYMs also sprang up in Whangārei, Hamilton, Rotorua, Kawerau, Hawke's Bay, Palmerston North and Christchurch, there was little co-ordination or even common strategy among them.[16] 'Membership of the PYM is often a state of mind,' a Wellington member told a *Dominion* reporter.[17]

Like the Auckland branch, the Wellington PYM had close ties to the local Resistance Bookshop, but it was largely comprised of students, and combined politics with pranksterism and pot. A 1971 pamphlet published by the Wellington branch declared that 'the oldies are fucked in the head ... we're freaking them out in the streets ... PYM wants headmasters kicked out, apprenticeships ended. free grog, grass and contraceptives. cheap rents and records. prices frozen. factories controlled by the workers. american bases kicked out of New Zealand. the land belonging to all New Zealanders, not just a few ...'[18] In naming their magazine *PYM Rabble* the Wellington group appeared to be parodying their Auckland counterparts, whose publication had recently changed its brand to the more earnest *PYM Rebel*.

The Christchurch PYM had working-class roots, and an ethos of forging alliances between students and workers like that which almost brought about revolution in France in 1968. For a while they had the strong support of the Lyttelton branch of the Seamen's Union, who came to their aid when bike gang the Outcasts tried to disrupt an anti-Vietnam War rally on the banks of the Avon. The first speaker had just begun to address the three hundred demonstrators when twenty motorcyclists began chanting 'Sieg Heil'. Seconds later, the bikies were charged by a roughly equal number of demonstrators, most of whom had been parading under the Seamen's Union banner, driving them out on to the road. Bikies were beaten with banners. When banners broke, the seamen laid into them with poles. The bikies retreated.[19]

But the Christchurch PYM, like their Wellington counterparts, also showed a hippie influence, with theatrical, media-attracting gestures, including the provision of free public bicycles (an idea initiated in Amsterdam by the radical Dutch Provos), the laying of wreaths to Vietnamese victims of American atrocities at Anzac Day ceremonies, and the distribution at school gates of *The PYM Colouring Book*. ('Here is a policeman pulling a demonstrator's hair. Policemen do nasty things when they are told to. The army men are worse. They will even kill people if the government tells them to ...'[20])

After a raid on the offices of the Christchurch PYM in which printing equipment was confiscated, a hundred or so youths took to the streets with banners, chanting 'Overthrow the fascist state' and 'Take a trip, walk around, see the pigs that run our town'. The PYM came to be identified with a new confrontational and inflammatory language, adopted from the American protest movement, in which police were 'pigs', 'fascist pigs' or 'the fuzz'. In fact it was the mainstream media that amplified the new language in sensationalist headlines. The PYM's own literature seldom used such terms, preferring the commonplace 'police' or, occasionally, 'copper' or 'cops'.

Nevertheless the PYM changed the face of protest in New Zealand. Where others hoped to bring about change with banners, vigils, chants and marches, they were ready to put their bodies on the line. As Jackman puts it: 'The PYM saw conflict between the state and members of society as having innate value. Thus, without in any way casting doubt on the sincerity of the people involved regarding the various causes championed, it may be said that the PYM sought conflict and controversy as an end in itself.'[21] And yet they never organised themselves in any formal way for violence or initiated any violence against the police. As Jackman concluded, '[T]he PYM's contribution to opposition to the Vietnam War was essentially one of style.'[22]

In his briefing to Holyoake, Brigadier Gilbert noted that the Communist Party 'makes little secret of its belief that the destruction of the general machinery of state would suit its revolutionary purpose in New Zealand' and its encouragement of 'any form of youthful rebellion'.[23] This youthful rebellion, according to the briefing, included not only the PYM, but also various university socialist groups and the recently formed 'Secondary School Pupils Association' (actually the Secondary School Students' Association or SSSA). The briefing also noted such publications as Chris Wheeler's *Cock* and the *Socialist Forum* newsletter as reflecting the influence of the New Left.

But there were other sources of rebellion that the Brigadier did not yet seem to know about, possibly because these were operating without the public face of an organisation, and so far beneath the radar that he and his agents had not yet heard about them.

BOMBER BOWER

'Bomber Bower, we call him,' Gerry tells me as he gives me his friend John Bower's number. Though Bower's bombing days are nearly fifty years behind him, the legend has stuck. For the past few decades he has run a trucking firm in Auckland. When I meet him at his house in 2019 he is dressed in black shorts and a black T-shirt over a beer belly, and is sweating as though he has been unloading a shipment of something heavy. 'Just in from work?' I ask. Bower, now in his late sixties, chuckles. 'Well, no. Actually, I've been dancing *Swan Lake*.' I have a moment of cognitive dissonance before he explains that there's a former ballet dancer at his gym who has offered to teach a few of the old boys some steps and, well, why not?

John Bower grew up in Whangārei with a shellshocked, alcoholic father and a schoolteacher mother whose fragile mental health meant frequent spells in hospital. While his parents struggled, John did his best to look after his three younger brothers, and occasionally got them into trouble. Once he stole some gelignite from the local quarry, and he and his siblings let it off in the creek. By his early teens he had been made a state ward and put into foster care. He spent his final school year at Westlake Boys' High where he proved to be a good student, excelling in physics and maths. In 1968 he went to Auckland University and fell in with a political protest crowd centred on the charismatic Tim Shadbolt. He moved into a flat next door to Shadbolt's in Gibraltar Crescent. Bower hadn't known much before about the Treaty of Waitangi or the Vietnam War, but life had already given him a strong sense of what was and was not fair.

One of his earliest acts of protest involved a sit-in at the US Consulate, involving a couple of dozen students and a lecturer in French, Walter Pollard. This anti-war protest had been conceived by Alan Robson, and inspired by some of the more theatrical headline-grabbing demonstrations taking place in America and Europe which had been largely absent from the New Zealand protest scene. The invasion was unexpected and met little resistance. Bower remembers making himself at home in the consul's office as Pollard read aloud from Bertrand Russell, while the flustered consul remained seated at his desk pretending to read a newspaper. The paper, Bower noticed, was upside down. Eventually police arrived and the protesters were arrested, removed and charged with trespass.

Smoke bomb at a National Party meeting, Wellington Town Hall, November 1972. Dominion Post Collection, Alexander Turnbull Library, PAColl-7327-1-044

A socially sanctioned occasion for misbehaviour came each May when graduation ceremonies took place on the major university campuses. During what was known as Capping Week, various drunken student pranks, including a costumed procession through the city, were shown more tolerance by the police than usual. By 1969, radical activism and carnival anarchy had merged in the guise of capping stunts. That year a few pranksters, including Bower's younger brother Colin, had the idea to open up the network of tunnels under Albert Park, originally built as an air-raid shelter but sealed off since the end of the war. Bower offered to help. First they would need to get the plans from the Auckland City Council. Bower remembers: 'I went up and said I was going to do an engineering project on the feasibility of turning it into a carpark and the guy there said, "Oh no, it can't be done", and I said, "Well, if it can't be done I've got to say why it can't be done", and so he took me down to the plan room and showed me the plans. Next day I went back, went down there, took them out, photographed them all and put them back again.'[24]

That night Bower and half a dozen others started digging at the foot of Constitution Hill, 500 metres or so from the park. After a couple of hours they got tired, so hid their shovels and, covered in mud, adjourned to the Kiwi Tavern. This set the pattern for the next few evenings. Eventually they broke through to the tunnel, but found it extended only 60 metres or so into the hillside before stopping abruptly. The only way to get any further, Bower reckoned, was with explosives. He knew where those could be found: a quick trip to Whangārei and he was back with two cases of gelly. But before they had time to prepare the blast, the police stumbled on the digging operation. They didn't find the gelignite and dismissed the whole thing as a harmless lark, but the project now had to be abandoned.

But other stunts, more clear in their political symbolism, would go ahead. One group drove 380 kilometres to the Waiouru Military Camp, where they successfully stole two army jeeps, drove them back to Auckland and abandoned them on campus. Another group had the notion to pay homage to Hone Heke, who chopped down the flagpole at Kororāreka/Russell in 1844 in protest against British authority over Māori affairs. With the recent passage of the Maori Affairs Amendment Act, seen by radical Māori as another land-grab, it felt like the right time for a reprise of Heke's act. The axemen shifted their sights to Waitangi, where another famous flagpole stood, but on their arrival at the meeting house where the historic treaty had been signed they found the current pole encased in stainless steel. Their blade made little impression.

John Bower had a way to deal with that, and a few nights later the group — Don Cooke, Bill Bone and Bob van Ruyssevelt, plus Bower — once more made the 200-kilometre drive, leaving Auckland sometime after midnight in Bob's green-and-white 1959 Ford Customline which could comfortably do the ton. A crate of beer bounced in the back alongside the box of explosives. At Waitangi, they placed four sticks of gelignite around the base of the flagpole, someone ignited the detonator and they all piled back into the Ford. By the time the fuse had burned down, the bombers were already on the road, laughing, drinking and singing their way back to Auckland.

Around 4.30 a.m. a telephone exchange clerk, on night duty at the Kawakawa Post Office, received a message that there had been an explosion in the Paihia district. Not long after, he heard the sound of a motor vehicle travelling at high speed. The clerk stepped outside in time to see a green-and-white Customline speeding south down the state highway. It didn't take too long for the cops to find it. A vehicle matching the clerk's description had stopped for gas in Whangārei a few hours earlier, and the garage attendant, noting the 'scruffy appearance' of the car's occupants, had taken down the licence-plate number. The suspects were questioned and searched, but before any charges could be laid they had taken off for Australia, their fares paid by a sympathetic 'businessman protester'.[25] 'As you can see, the foxes are on the run,' Bower wrote from Bundaberg to a friend back in Auckland. 'I cannot underline the necessity for keeping our whereabouts in Australia and our address secret. Because believe me [name redacted] if they get us back in New Zealand we face a rap of up to 7 years' jail.'[26]

But life in Queensland turned out to be its own kind of punishment, sleeping rough, with little money, no work and scant sympathy from the local students who seemed to favour theory over action. The whereabouts of the bombers was soon known to the New Zealand police, who intuited that extradition would be unnecessary. Within a few weeks, homesickness and destitution had brought them back and they handed themselves in on arrival. Cooke was sentenced to four months' periodic detention, van Ruyssevelt to three, and Bone and Bower received nine-month prison sentences, eventually commuted to fines.

'A REVOLUTION-INSPIRED DYNAMO'

Historians have memorialised 1968 as the year of political upheaval in the Western world. There were riots at the Democratic Convention in Chicago, student–worker uprisings in Paris. New Zealand, lagging slightly behind, had its 1968 in 1970 when confrontation reached new, more violent levels.

In November 1969, Keith Holyoake had been re-elected, beating Labour's Norman Kirk and leading National into office for a fourth consecutive term. The announcement that US Vice-President Spiro Agnew was to visit New Zealand in early January 1970 was the next focus of a protest movement that was becoming increasingly restive. Accompanying Agnew on the three-day visit would be the astronaut Eugene Cernan (who, a few years later, would become the last man to walk on the moon). As a gift to the nation, Agnew would proffer four pieces of moon rock, brought back to Earth the previous year by the crew of Apollo 11. But the climax of the Vice-President's stay would be a state banquet hosted by Holyoake.

Official demonstrations against the visit were planned and arranged in the authorised manner, with the usual notifications being given to police. But there were also those planning their own activities, separate from the main demonstrations. These included someone whose name I recall from my childhood only because, as a six-year-old, I found it amusing that he sounded like he had been given the same name twice: Lyle Carlisle.

When I was growing up, my dad was sometimes visited by bearded men. They were usually younger than Con, and I guess they regarded him, with his history of activism, as a kind of mentor.

They would turn up on the doorstep around dusk, and he would welcome them into his study where they would sit for hours, locked in earnest conversation. I was too young to follow what was being discussed and I never knew who most of them were. I had never seen Lyle Carlisle's name written down and had not heard it spoken aloud in more than fifty years, but, as I flicked through a 1970 issue of *Cock* magazine, it leaped from the headline of a double-page spread: 'Lyle Eric (Lemming) Carlisle 1953–1970.'[27]

As was the fashion in underground design, the text was overprinted on a monochrome illustration, rendering parts of it almost illegible. The picture was a bust drawing of a bearded, bespectacled, bright-looking man of indeterminate age. The tribute was written by Carlisle's friend John Parkyn. Yet it read not just as a eulogy for Lyle Carlisle, who had been 'quiet, gentle, intelligent and really loveable', but for a particular innocence: one that would soon be lost, though perhaps few at the time saw this as keenly and presciently as Parkyn.

I learned that at twenty years of age Carlisle, known to his friends as Lemming, had been a proofreader for veteran publishers A. H. & A. W. Reed. Six years later he would be 'earning his colours of courage in the forefront of a political riot'. Somewhere in the course of that transformation must have been the occasions he visited my dad.

Parkyn had first met Carlisle in the early sixties, just as the first wave of the counterculture—'the beats and their impossible dreams of smiling nations, squatting side by side, laying down their nuclear arms while Joan Baez bleated in Esperanto'—was mutating into the second. As the early passion of the CND marches faded, Parkyn saw his contemporaries retreating from hopeful protest into art, alcohol, marriage, in some cases jail or insanity. Yet as politics fell out of fashion among his peers, Lemming went against the grain, becoming increasingly politicised. Parkyn told how, from being an essentially apolitical observer, Lemming became an active presence 'found at events and happenings from Auckland to Christchurch to Wellington and back again, arguing, soaking up new ideas, gaining in self-confidence all the time, evolving his own credo, which he was to stick to with tenacity, sense of justice, lack of cant, loyalty to friends, tolerance and generosity'. While others were distracted, Lemming could 'see through the US State Department bullshit and predict what was to happen to the world pretty soon'.

While Parkyn was overseas in 1968, the quiet Lemming turned revolutionary. At Vietnam demonstrations he tussled with police. In Albert Park he preached direct action. In a letter to Parkyn written during this period, he told of taking 'inspiration and indignation from Cleaver, Malcolm X, Guevara, Fanon, Mailer. I read about Bobby Seale. I read about the Panthers, I read about the massacres and I burn … this is something I can't ignore. I've tried it.'

Around this time Lemming was ominously heard to mutter about 'hoisting the Jolly Roger on the parapet in Molesworth Street' (the location of Parliament Buildings). This growing toughness 'became transmogrified into political aggression'. At a public meeting featuring Holyoake at the Auckland Town Hall, he came into direct physical conflict with the police. As Parkyn put it: '[H]is character was being honed down into a revolution-inspired dynamo.'

Knowing the police would be preoccupied with the main group of protesters on the night of the Agnew rally outside the state banquet, Lemming began secretly planning his own protest. Some say he and a small group had acquired weapons and explosives and were ready to use them. While the police were occupied at the Hotel Intercontinental, where Agnew would be staying, they planned to hit Queen Street where the head offices of the banks were. They would smash the windows, create mayhem and launch the revolution.

But on the eve of Agnew's arrival, the normally clear-headed Lemming, perhaps in an effort to calm his nerves, took something, either heroin or a combination of alcohol and barbiturates, went to bed and never woke up.

It was a particularly hot and sticky Auckland summer. The official demonstrations went ahead as planned, and were the most violent New Zealand had seen since the country's involvement in Vietnam began. They commenced as soon as the Vice-President arrived for his three-day visit on Thursday 15 January. Things came to a head late on the second night as demonstrators maintained their noisy vigil outside the Hotel Intercontinental. By breaking their slogan of 'One, two, three, four, we don't want your bloody war!' into a stereo call-and-response chant, they were able to sustain a continuous racket. But while the five hundred or so protesters showed little sign of flagging, the hundred or more cops were getting tired and testy.

At around 11.45 p.m. an observer saw police approach a few people in the front of the crowd, as they had been doing from time to time throughout the evening. Only a handful of the demonstrators would have been able to see the interaction or hear what was said.[28] 'Almost immediately afterwards a wall of police charged into the crowd, the majority of whom were still seated on the footpath in a tightly packed mass.'[29] John Bower was among that crowd. As he remembers it, 'The cops got upset and just waded in. Basically the cops beat us up … just went mad. I don't know who was in command. Obviously they were getting it in the neck because the noise was just carrying on.'[30]

Demonstrators were forced into nearby Albert Park, yet even after they had been dispersed 'a small number of constables', according to a journalist, 'perhaps six or seven, pursued them into the trees, still assaulting them'.[31] Bower was among them. He was helping another protester, Janet Neville, to escape over a fence when he was set upon, knocked to the ground and beaten.

Waterloo Quadrant during Spiro Agnew's visit,
17 January 1970. John Fields photograph, Museum
of New Zealand Te Papa Tongarewa, O.040775

In the days that followed, a committee of concerned citizens was formed to lobby for a public inquiry to establish whether or not the common expectation of freedom from undue or arbitrary violence by the police had been eroded.

John Bower would respond in his own way.

In the small hours of the first Sunday in March, Alan Brunton — poet, performer, existentialist — was walking home through Parnell. He had just come from a party in Remuera Road for his future partner Sally Rodwell, and had given her *Let It Bleed*, the latest Rolling Stones album. 'A totally radical record for the time,' as he would say. 'It was physical, it was sexual, it was biological …' It had been a great party, and he was feeling high in every sense. 'I was a totally happy person that night. I felt some sort of achievement about my life.'[32]

He had walked through Newmarket and down Parnell Road, had just passed the Hearst chocolate factory and was approaching his flat when suddenly up the rise came several speeding police vehicles, lights flashing. They screeched to a halt beside Brunton. He was immediately jumpy, hoping there was nothing in his pockets. A primal fear: a few grams of marijuana could mean six months in prison.

Out of dark vans came police with torches and dogs. 'The dogs are crawling all over me,' he recalled. 'I'm thrashed around to the wall, hands up against the wall, top to bottom search. They're yelling and screaming something at me I don't recognise. I had no idea where they came from, what they wanted, what on earth was going on.' Then, as suddenly as they arrived, they were gone. Arriving home, Brunton's flatmates told him there had been an explosion that evening at the RNZAF base in Fox Street, just a few blocks away.

At the scene of the explosion, police had found a note which read:

> This bombing is one of the initial steps in a plan to render the military establishment incapable of continuing its immoral war in Vietnam. We intend to increase our action against more military bases until the Govt. withdraws its troops from Vietnam. (signed) Revolutionary Activists.

The police contacted the SIS with a view to establishing the identity of the 'Revolutionary Activists' but the service was unable to assist. It was five months before John Bower appeared in court, charged with damaging the Fox Street Air Force Number 1 Port Depot by means of an explosive. He was also charged with a failed attempt to blow up the Army's Number 6 magazine at Ardmore, just south-east of the city. In evidence, a detective read the note found under the door of the depot, purportedly bearing Bower's fingerprints.

There had been no one there at the time of the explosion. The only equipment damaged was a pair of old Singer sewing machines, valued at $10 and $14, held in storage pending transit to Fiji.

In sentencing, Justice Beattie told Bower: 'It is one thing to express dissent by words or proper demonstrations, but we will not tolerate violence. You take no warning ... you show resentment towards authority.' He sentenced Bower to four years' imprisonment.[33] He would serve much of it in the maximum security block at Paremoremo.

'REBELLIOUS, INTERNATIONALIST, CONFIDENT'

No sooner had Vice-President Agnew and his astronaut departed, than demonstrations began mounting against a tour of the All Blacks to South Africa due to start mid-year. The movement against apartheid had begun in New Zealand before CND or the Vietnam War and, though it developed more slowly, it would ultimately have an even more dramatic impact, forcing New Zealanders to consider the structure, values and injustices of their own society.

South Africa had been stratified along racial lines ever since the Dutch colonised it in the eighteenth century. Since 1948 it had

Damaged articles—No.1 Port Depot Incident, 3 March 1970. Archives New Zealand, R23566404

been governed under a white supremacist system known as apartheid, under which the white minority forced millions of black South Africans into segregated neighbourhoods and severely restricted their political, civil and economic freedoms. Abhorrent as this practice was, it would never have received as much attention in New Zealand had South Africa not shared the Kiwi fanaticism for rugby. Showdowns between New Zealand's All Blacks and South Africa's Springboks were seen as a clash of the Titans, and tours by both teams were eagerly anticipated. Those in New Zealand opposed to the apartheid regime, however, advocated boycotting matches to ensure the South African government would feel the nation's—and the world's—opprobrium and be forced to change its racist system. This belief would ultimately lead, in 1981, to the biggest and most divisive protests ever seen in New Zealand, and contribute to the eventual fall of apartheid.

Initially, though, protests focused only on the fact that, under its racist laws, South Africa would not allow the visiting All Blacks to include Māori in the team. In '81, Prime Minister Robert Muldoon would brand anti-tour leaders as traitors and communists, but the first high-profile advocate of a sporting boycott was in fact a highly decorated war hero. In 1948, the year he was elected president of the Returned Services Association, Major-General Sir Howard Kippenberger declared at an RSA function in his honour: 'I had the Maoris under my command for two years, and in that time they had 1500 casualties, and I am not going to acquiesce in any damned Afrikanders saying they cannot go.'[34]

Despite Kippenberger's stand, an All Blacks tour went ahead that year without Māori players. The 'No Māoris, No Tour' platform received some support, particularly from Māori, but there was still little focus on South Africa's treatment of its black population, nor had the notion yet developed that the Springboks should not be welcome visitors to New Zealand. Only the Māori Women's Welfare League voiced opposition to a 1956 Springbok tour that otherwise seemed to unite the country in a rugby-induced fever. Even the Communist Party approved.

In 1960 the Springboks again invited the All Blacks to visit South Africa. When it was stipulated once more that no Māori be included, former National Minister of Maori Affairs E. B. Corbett elegantly stated that 'sport without morality no longer deserves the name'.[35] Students took to the streets, with more than five hundred marching on Parliament. Then, two months before the tour was scheduled to begin, sixty-nine black South Africans demonstrating against pass laws were shot dead outside a police station in the black township of Sharpeville. In the face of this shocking illustration of apartheid's brutality, the New Zealand Rugby Football Union continued with its tour plans. When the government made no attempt to intervene, protests grew massively. At a state farewell to the All Blacks a thousand people rallied outside Parliament, with more than twice that number protesting in Auckland. When the team departed from Whenuapai Airport 'about 20 demonstrators mostly students, suddenly rushed across the tarmac, shouting and waving their fists. The Electra roared past only about a plane's width from the nearest demonstrator.'[36]

A 1964 tour by a South African cricket team met an unambiguously anti-apartheid protest with pickets in Wellington, Christchurch and Auckland. Wellington newspapers called the demonstrators 'unwanted and unmannerly limelight seekers determined to spoil other people's pleasures'.[37] In 1965 another visit from the Springboks went ahead despite Matiu Rata, MP for Northern Maori, speaking out against the New Zealand Māori Council's decision to welcome the team, while Sir Eruera Tirikatene pointed out that 'the very composition of their [all-white] team is a visible manifestation of apartheid'.[38]

By this time, apartheid had become part of the package of global injustices mobilising the new, younger generation of protesters. An assortment of anti-apartheid organisations sprang up, the most visible of which was HART, formed in 1969 just ahead of the 1970 All Blacks tour of South Africa. The name, an acronym of Halt All Racist Tours, was the invention of Māori activist and PYM member Tama Poata. Acting chairman was Trevor Richards, a young student politician who

Trevor Richards leads the march, 1973. John Miller photograph had started at Auckland University in the mid-1960s and in 1968 become chair of the Students' Association International Affairs Committee. Looking back, Richards would call HART 'a typical child of its time—rebellious, internationalist, confident, optimistic ... Its rebellion was against a specific scheduled event ... [b]ut like much of the social and political activity of the sixties, it also went further, calling into question fundamental values in New Zealand society.'[39]

Richards looked like a cross between Trotsky and one of the Furry Freak Brothers. With his bushy black hair and walrus whiskers, he became the very recognisable face of New Zealand's anti-apartheid movement. To the establishment, he had all the distinguishing features of an enemy. The distaste was mutual. 'In 1970 we perceived the political establishment and those in it to be the antithesis of all that we stood for,' Richards wrote in *Dancing on Our Bones*, his history of the anti-apartheid movement. 'We thought they were narrow, insular, petty, small-minded, smug, screwed up, conservative, joyless, repressed, authoritarian, dull, short-haired, hypocritical and racist.'[40]

In contrast to his rhetoric, Richards in person was mild and congenial. Though protest was his profession, persuasion was his preference. He would talk anywhere that would have him—schools, workplaces, even rugby clubs—about the evils of apartheid and what New Zealand could do to help end it. He was aware that to change New Zealand's thinking, HART had to be in the mainstream media, but the conservative newspapers, with their scare-mongering headlines ('Protesters Arrested As Anti Tour Marchers Roam Town') and loaded language (protesters were repeatedly referred to as 'a mob'), reinforced the rugby world's view of the anti-apartheid movement as made up of communists and free-love-practising hippies. That some were envious of the protesters' supposed lifestyle was evident in a question put to Richards by a rugby club member from the Waikato after one of his talks: 'When I come down to Wellington to farewell the team ... can I stay the night with one of your protest birds?'[41] More menacing and even more stupid was one of what Richards called his 'fan letters' that threatened to 'string him up' and warned that 'the Third World War will wipe all hippies off the face of the earth as the Second World War did to Jews. You are all dirty hippies. Get out of New Zealand.'[42]

While HART pursued its protests largely through traditional and legitimate channels, there were some who applied more radical strategies. With the violence of January's Agnew visit still fresh in the minds of both protesters and police, there was a charged atmosphere to the 1970 tour protests. At the All Blacks trials in Wellington, roads to Athletic Park were blocked by hundreds of protesters, while the goalposts at Christchurch's Lancaster Park were sawed down in the night. In Auckland the offices of the Rugby Football Union were set on fire with a Molotov cocktail. On the last day of the trials a man doused himself with petrol but was arrested before he was able to light a match.[43]

Things boiled over in the final seventy-two hours before the All Blacks' departure for South Africa from Wellington Airport. A vivid if overheated account can be found in *The Whole World Watches*, a 'Cock special' written by Alister Taylor, published by Chris Wheeler, and rushed to print as the tour and protester trials went ahead. With recent showdowns between protesters and police still fresh in his mind, Taylor appeared to be in no doubt that the time to do battle with the state had arrived. Little mention is made in the bulletin of apartheid or the plight of black South Africans. Instead he chronicled in detail the injustices suffered by New Zealand's student-dominated protest body at the hands of the police, and quoted the protesters' cries of 'Cops are pigs!' and 'Pigs of the State!' The greatest violence was recorded during the Friday-night march Taylor dubbed 'the battle of Willis Street', during which he himself was arrested.

> I was dragged, upright, to the front of the Kiwi Cafe, about fourteen or so feet in front of the demonstration, and held there by two constables. I was still in agony, trying to adjust my arms up my back so they didn't hurt so much. Two more constables ran up from Manners Street and grabbed me. The four then pounced on me, as witnesses will tell in court, and I was beaten to the ground. I can't remember much at all, except for the pain, and the fact that my bladder proved too much.[44]

'Mailer like,' he added, comparing himself to the macho American writer Norman Mailer whose celebrated account of the Chicago demonstrations, *The Armies of the Night*, had recently been published and was a bestseller.

But the way Taylor reported an incident at the airport on the morning of departure undermines some of his moral authority. Taylor (who by this time was in a police holding cell) cited the testimony of protester James L. Graham who said: 'I was one of many surrounding a Maori policeman who didn't have his number showing ... Everyone was chanting "Where's your number you bastard?" He appeared to break down and lashed at some male demonstrators.'[45] Photos show the group taunting the policeman before he 'went berserk' were predominantly, if not entirely, Pākehā. That the policeman's outburst might have been a reaction to what he construed as racial abuse was not apparently considered by Taylor.

Looking back, Trevor Richards wrote:

> *The Whole World Watches* painted a picture of people who were angry and confident, who were not intimidated, and who knew they were right. It was a knowledge born of quintessential sixties values, inspired by a desire to make a difference, and in tune with changing international realities. It is easy now to describe it as naive, self-righteous, overblown. That is to miss entirely its significance. It was, and remains, an important statement of

where a number of the post-Second World War generation were in June 1970.⁴⁶

As the All Blacks' Electra readied for takeoff, two protesters, Tim Shadbolt and Peter Verschaffelt, leaped over a high fence and ran towards the aeroplane. Hundreds of others, who had spent the night at Victoria University's Union Hall then marched at dawn to the airport, cheered them on. (Months later, a local newspaper pictured a healthy marijuana plant discovered in a garden by the airport. The homeowner speculated it grew from a seed flicked by a passing protester.) Verschaffelt, a student politician who would go on to become a television journalist and evangelist for the neoliberal reforms of the 1980s, was wrestled to the tarmac as the plane began taxiing. Shadbolt didn't even get that far, felled by a fullback-type tackle from a plainclothes detective just a few metres past the fence. Blurry images of his attempt put him on the front page of that night's *Evening Post*, giving another boost to his rising public profile.

Such guerrilla acts would be taken to greater and more creative extremes in 1981, by which time opposition to apartheid had merged with a wider social unrest, resulting in some of the biggest and most sustained displays of civil disobedience the country had seen. But at the start of the seventies they represented the political face of a youth rebellion that was asserting itself on several fronts at once.

AQUARIAN EXPOSITIONS

Seven

Music provided a rallying point for the counterculture, and helped project its ideals into the mainstream. The musical *Hair* opened on Broadway in early 1968. Written by a pair of American librettists, Gerome Ragni and James Rado, and Canadian composer Galt MacDermot, it wove topical themes of sexual revolution, communal living, drug use, anti-war protest and mysticism into a memorable set of songs in a wide sweep of pop styles.[1] For the next four years, while productions of *Hair* ran everywhere from Tokyo to Yugoslavia, New Zealand would experience it only through an original-cast LP, salacious newspaper reports and a string of pop hits by artists covering some of its better tunes. 'This is the dawning of the age of Aquarius,' chimed Los Angeles showband the Fifth Dimension in their 1969 hit, heralding the coming astrological age which astromancers predicted would bring 'mystic crystal revelation and the mind's true liberation'.[2] Local easy-listening acts John Rowles and Garth Young jumped in with their own cover versions.

Scratch Orchestra (NZ) in the crater of Maungawhau/Mount Eden, 1971.
Max Oettli photograph, Alexander Turnbull Library, PAColl-1386-1

That year singer Jenny Parkinson was one of several New Zealanders to successfully audition for a role in the Australian production. Returning to Auckland after a twenty-three-month run in Sydney as a member of the chorus, she said she thought the show was now quite dated, though the production had offset this with a few changes of emphasis, such as making the African-American characters more militant.[3]

AQUARIUS ON TRIAL

Hair finally reached New Zealand stages in early 1972. Almost immediately upon opening in Auckland, the producers were charged with indecency under Section 24 of the Crimes Act. It was the first time a stage show had been prosecuted in New Zealand. In fact, it was the only time a prosecution against the show had been taken anywhere, though attempts to ban it in Boston had wound up in a Supreme Court hearing that eventually found in favour of the production.

In Auckland, prosecution witnesses included Detective Chief Inspector E. G. Perry, who had seen it five consecutive times; deputy editor of the *Auckland Star* Pat Booth; and Mrs Margot Jacqueline Hudson, a Whakatāne secretary with a background in amateur dramatics. All of them said they had been upset by the show's four-letter words and simulated sex acts. Along with depictions of drug-taking and *Hair*'s anti-war message, it was as though all the values of the counterculture had been conveniently wrapped up in a single package and put on trial.

Defence witnesses included Presbyterian minister Rev. Francis Rex Hamlin; playwright and critic Bruce Mason; and journalists Iain Macdonald and Marcia Russell. They would not only argue against the obscenity charge but also maintain that the show was highly relevant in its anti-war and anti-hypocrisy themes. The Rev. Hamlin found the nude scene in particular to be of 'profound religious significance ... the hope of mankind in all its troubles is to drop all barriers. The symbolism of nudism was this; all barriers had to be down, we had to completely expose ourselves to others.'[4] He went on to compare the character of Claude, drafted into the Vietnam War, to Christ in his vulnerability.

After listening to evidence from both sides, Justice McMullin suggested that the jury might consider 'why, in 1972, matters of obscenity were dealt with by a law made in 1908' and that 'if the overriding effect of the show is to call the attention of society to matters in which society's attention should rightly be awakened then the public good may be served'. The jury returned a not guilty verdict and the show went on.[5]

HOMEGROWN HAPPENINGS

As a witness for the defence in the *Hair* trial, Jenny McLeod, Professor of Music at Victoria University, had spoken of being especially moved by the moments that allowed the audience to 'transcend themselves, able to get beyond their petty concerns and join in the brotherhood of man', comparing the effect to that of the Bach Passions. 'In terms of what I would call emotional highpoints or climaxes in *Hair*, I found more than I have found in any other live experience I have seen. I would be proud if I could do the same thing myself on such a scale.'[6]

In fact McLeod had already produced work on such a scale. In 1968, the year *Hair* hit Broadway, New Zealand had seen the debut of McLeod's *Earth and Sky*, a three-act musical theatre work based on the Māori creation narrative, featuring costumed dancers, several choirs, woodwind, brass and percussion orchestras, two pianos, electronic organ, pre-recorded voices and three hundred primary school children on stage. Composed before she was twenty-seven, it would establish McLeod as a public figure, one who would cheerfully and uniquely traverse the worlds of both the mainstream and the counterculture until she ultimately threw in her lot with the latter.

There had always been something countercultural about Jenny McLeod. When she arrived at Victoria University in 1961 wearing a leather jacket, clutching a motorcycle helmet and dragging on a cigarette, Frederick Page, professor and founder of the university's Music Department, had wondered what this bikie was doing in his palace of learning. She didn't look like a student, let alone one enrolled to study classical music. But she would turn out to be the most brilliant protégé Page ever had. Within the decade, she had succeeded him as head of the department, becoming at twenty-eight the youngest professor of music in the Commonwealth.

Fred Page, in his faded, chalk-streaked academic gown, was unlike anyone McLeod had met either. She had grown up in Levin, with two younger brothers, a bookseller father who took his buying tips from the sales reps and rarely read anything himself, and a Methodist mother who channelled her creative urges into needlepoint and prop-making for the local Little Theatre. Once, as a pre-schooler, Jenny had overheard her parents arguing about money. Aghast that anyone could be squabbling over something so ephemeral, she decided then and there that they had no idea what life was about, and resolved never to take any notice of anything else they said. At five she recognised that the lines and shapes on a classroom mural were the same as those in the book her schoolteacher used when playing the piano, and persuaded the teacher to show her how to read music. She practised obsessively and was soon a competent sight-reader. Though classical music was not part of her parents' world, they eventually bought her a piano. By her mid-teens she had won an American Field Scholarship which took her to study in Decatur, Illinois, where she startled the school's graduation ceremony by playing Chopin's challenging 'Revolutionary Etude' entirely from memory.

Fred Page was in his late fifties when McLeod became his student. He introduced her to modern composers like Webern and

Jenny McLeod conducts a rehearsal of *Earth and Sky*, Masterton, August 1968. **Wairarapa Times-Age Collection, Wairarapa Archive**

Schoenberg, and lent her books of poetry. She became a regular guest at the Thorndon home of Fred and his wife, the painter Evelyn Page. Jenny had never met people whose lives revolved so passionately around music, literature, painting, food, wine and conversation. 'The Pages became like my substitute parents,' she says. 'I told my parents, "You can't really give me what I need" and they thoroughly agreed!' The Pages, she adds, 'loved my family too. They had never known any other family quite like it.'[7]

Her next awakening came at a Cambridge Summer Music School, where she first heard the music of Olivier Messiaen, the mystical French composer. In 1964, having graduated from Victoria and determined to study with Messiaen, she set off for Paris. Messiaen's process for selecting the elite group of students for his Paris Conservatoire class involved a rigorous month of ear tests, to be undertaken as a group. McLeod confesses her strategy for passing these tests was not entirely ethical. 'Messiaen would ask people questions. I would pretend I hadn't noticed that he had directed it at someone else, not me, and if I knew the answer I would say the answer, no matter who he asked. The others must have hated me.'

Ethical or not, she impressed the maestro with her knowledge and got into his class. A season with Messiaen was followed by spells in Darmstadt and Cologne studying with Pierre Boulez and Karlheinz Stockhausen respectively, both former students of Messiaen's. Of the controversial Stockhausen, she says, 'He had fantastic ideas about music, about the structure and how to do things, but you could have put any kind of notes into them half the time.'

By 1966 homesickness had brought her back to Wellington and a lecturing position at Victoria, where Fred Page's Music Department already included established composers David Farquhar and Douglas Lilburn. That year she began writing *Earth and Sky*. The first production was mounted in Masterton to ecstatic reviews. This was a homegrown happening, legitimised in the eyes of critics by McLeod's background in classical music, and gained her national media attention of a kind never before lavished on a local composer. Over the next couple of years *Earth and Sky* was staged again in Christchurch, Tauranga, and finally in Auckland where a gala performance at the newly established Mercury Theatre was attended by the Queen.

THE MĀORI HENDRIX AND OTHER HEROES

Rock music continued to be a crucial meeting point for the turned on. There was nothing in New Zealand as organised as Ken Kesey's Acid Tests in San Francisco or Timothy Leary's workshops, but rock concerts could be informal psychedelic communions, and none more so than those of the group Space Farm, whose fluorescent posters, designed by Archie Bowie and inspired by the visions he had had on LSD, hinted at the experiences the events would offer.

Space Farm. Design for album cover and poster by Archie Bowie, 1972. Archie Bowie private collection

When Space Farm took the stage at the Wellington Town Hall one night in 1971, the second act in a double-bill with Ticket, all four members of the group were tripping. Bass player Billy Williams recalls: 'We had been fasting and abstaining from drugs for a month before that gig, so when we took a cap of mescaline each while Ticket were playing, it took effect very quickly. The walls in the band room were colourfully swirling when someone knocked at the door and said it was time to play. Walking out on stage was surreal.'[8] Many in the audience that night were tripping too: 'When Space Farm played, people knew we would be tripping on acid so they would do likewise and take the magic carpet ride with us.'[9]

Whatever the altered states of the musicians, the instrumental work showed a high level of discipline, as a recording of the concert made by audience member John Pilcher attests. Other than the singing of guitarist Harvey Mann (never a strong vocalist, but on this occasion he seems particularly untethered to pitch), the music has an intense cohesion. Mann's guitar and the drumming of Glen Absolum sync up to sound at times like a single instrument. Mann intends no irony when he attributes it to 'chemistry': 'It was a total interplay that almost operated like one mind. The unity was that strong.'[10] Williams agrees.

'There were moments of otherworldly magic when we played. We were aware of some other force driving the musical chariot.'[11]

Mann had first gained attention a few years earlier as guitarist with the Underdogs, a blues band taking its cue from the recent British revival of this quintessentially American form. With the groups John Mayall's Bluesbreakers and Cream, the British blues exponent Eric Clapton had repurposed the music as a loud, flashy guitar-based brand of rock. Mann was cast as the Kiwi Clapton, and walls around Auckland began to be daubed with the graffito 'Mann Is God', a theologically challenging parody of the slogan 'Clapton Is God' which had famously appeared in the London Underground a year or two before.[12]

But the most influential of all of Britain's blues-rock exports was in fact an American import. Jimi Hendrix, a guitarist of African-American and Cherokee ancestry, had been based in Britain since 1966. There his inventive fusion of blues, rock and psychedelia earned him the star status that had eluded him in the US, where the music industry had black musicians locked into a narrow commercial stereotype. Hendrix's Kiwi acolytes included Mann, Doug Jerebine and Eddie Hansen, but his most profound and lasting influence was among Māori musicians, many of whom adopted his afro hairstyle and flamboyant dress sense, along with his guitar pyrotechnics.

In Wellington, guitarist Reno Tehei formed the Joyful Crye, a trio that was essentially a Hendrix tribute act. In 1967, a dapper, sportscoat-wearing Tehei had gone to Britain with the slick soul-pop showband Sounds Unlimited. 'When he came back he was Hendrix,' remembers Sam Gossen, who had been a roadie for Sounds Unlimited. 'Dressed like him, played like him, the whole bit.'[13] Along with a newly coiffed afro and velvet flares, Tehei had mastered Hendrix's full box of tricks: playing the guitar with his teeth, behind his back and through a new device called a wah-wah pedal. It was rumoured that Tehei had swiped the pedal from a London stage when the resident musicians weren't looking.

In the last months of 1967, the Joyful Crye played regularly at the Psychedelic Id, a short-lived club in Marjoribanks Street, Wellington, set up by canny promoter Wally Martin in an attempt to cash in on the hippie craze. 'Psychedelic and Pop Music! Colour! And Hippy Surprises!' promised the *Evening Post* ad. 'KING OF THE HIPPIES. Is It You?' another of his promotions demanded to know. 'King of the Hippies will be Crowned at Wellington's FIRST "LOVE IN" Next Month'. No record can be found of anyone claiming the title.

Billy Te Kahika, otherwise known as Billy TK, came from Bunnythorpe and spent the early sixties playing Shadows and Everly Brothers covers around Manawatū. Everything changed when he heard the distorted and sustained guitar on 'Stone Free', the B-side of Hendrix's first local release. He mastered the essence of Hendrix's style in time to join long-running club band the Human Instinct (formerly the Four Fours) in 1968, just as the group was transitioning to a heavier, blues-rock sound. In Auckland they held a late-night residency at the

Bo Peep. Other musicians, after their own gigs had ended for the night, would come to listen to the Instinct jam into the early hours.

Bruce Cavell, writing in *Craccum*, tried to capture the experience of seeing Te Kahika:

> He plays this Gibson—it's claret coloured—very tasteful, nothing flashy—and he just kind of stares out into the middle distance—from 20 feet away he looks bored—but, well, he couldn't play what he does if he was bored and if you go up and have a closer look you'll see he's not there, in the room … he's up up and away on a volume high, his eyes glazed, blank as behind him and beside him these incredible sounds—well, actually, they don't appear to come from anywhere—they cram into the whole room, they feel as though they've been there forever, waiting for someone to release them—and his fingers, these really nimble fingers flitting up and down, pausing as he eases a long, long feedback note out, but then they group intro chords, big powerful rich chords, hard chords, and then he textures them with the fuzzbox … and all the time the drums are going and the cymbals are crashing into your heart and further back still is the bass … they're not just making music, they're building an environment. It's *the* total experience …[14]

Unlike the Joyful Crye, the Human Instinct was well represented on record, thanks to the entrepreneurship of drummer and lead singer Maurice Greer. They made three albums with Te Kahika, of which *Stoned Guitar* is definitive, capturing the skill and energy of the band in gritty, bluesy rock like 'Black Sally', and the long improvisational title track in which Te Kahika employs feedback and an echo unit to create otherworldly textures, evocative yet not wholly derivative of Hendrix.

Other prominent Māori Hendrixes included Kemp Tuirirangi of Sons and Lovers and BLERTA, Steve Apirana of Butler, Tama Renata of Bulldog, and Horace Mahauriki of Storm, but there were many less familiar ones as well. In Christchurch, dance-band musician Peter Carter began to call himself Jimmi in homage to his hero. Though Jimmi Carter was never well known, in the eighties his son Shayne Carter would become one of the county's most recognised guitarists, fronting the bands Straitjacket Fits and Dimmer, and displaying a marked Hendrix influence.

While Pacific Island musicians, too, fell under Hendrix's spell, they were almost all young. In his fictionalised memoir *A Boy Called Broke*, Fa'amoana John Luafutu (whose son Malo would find fame in the early 2000s as the rapper Scribe) illustrates the generational divide. It is the early 1970s and a party is raging at the Ponsonby flat of a member of the newly formed civil rights organisation Polynesian Panthers. One of the Panthers, Foof, is playing a guitar. A senior Panther, Sefo, is singing. But there's a clash over repertoire. Sefo wants to sing older, sentimental songs like 'She Wears My Ring'. Others are calling for

Evan MacGregor of Heathen Grace, 1972.
One of countless musicians who emulated
both Hendrix's playing and his pyrotechnics.
Dominion Post Collection, Alexander Turnbull
Library, PAColl-7327-1-025

Hendrix: '"Come on, Bouss, play 'Stone Free'." Foof plays the request but Sefo is not happy with the new music that his younger bros are into … All this new music he terms "hippy music", belonging, he thinks, to those drug-taking, flea-ridden hippies, who appeared outta nowhere it seems …'[15]

Why did young Māori and Pacific Island musicians identify so strongly with Hendrix? For a start, he was clearly a master musician. Music plays a significant role in both the social and formal cultural life of Māori and Pacific Island communities, and a good musician is valued, more so than in Pākehā society. But perhaps there was also something they recognised in Hendrix's displacement—the fact that he had had to move to England to make it, a black man fronting an otherwise white band in a musical world that had been appropriated and overrun by white men. There was even an urban legend circulating in the early seventies that Hendrix was part-Māori, though the slightest bit of research would have disproved it.

Still, the Māori Hendrix was a phenomenon that outlived Hendrix himself. Hendrix died in September 1970, and for the rest of the decade Māori and Pasifika Hendrixes could be heard up and down the country. A few still exist today. It was only in the early eighties that Bob Marley supplanted Hendrix as the pre-eminent role model for Polynesian musicians, and once again he represented something more than just a great musician.

'A BIT OF A REVOLUTION'

In August 1969, around half a million people spent a muddy weekend on a 600-acre dairy farm in upstate New York. 'An Aquarian Exposition', or Woodstock as it came to be known, entered popular mythology. Despite bearing all the characteristics of a disaster—overcrowding, bad weather, poor sanitation, food shortages, dangerous drugs, financial loss, death—the event declared itself a triumph; proof that the counter-culture's ideals of peace, love and freedom under the banner of rock music were enough to sustain an entire city, at least for a weekend. It signalled that the counterculture had reached critical mass. *Rolling Stone* reported: 'Out of the mud and hunger and thirst, despite the rain and the end-of-the-world traffic jams, beyond the bad dope trips and the garish confusion, a new nation had emerged into the glare provided by the open-mouthed media.'[16]

But rather than acknowledging the festival's social significance, the mainstream press focused on issues of public safety and the problematic consequences of the crowd size. New Zealand newspapers picked up these threads and wove them into a cautionary tale. 'Giant Hippie-Style Festival Turns Sour', ran the headline in the *Otago Daily Times*. 'Huge Folk Scene Leaves Chaos and Casualties', reported the *New Zealand Herald*, buttressing the implication that this whole scene was dangerous with an adjacent headline that read 'Hippies Sought for Murders'. On closer inspection, the latter item was revealed to have nothing to do with Woodstock but concerned the hunt for the killers of actress Sharon Tate and several others found dead in Los Angeles six days before the festival. There was no mention yet of anyone named Manson.

Before the year's end, Abbie Hoffman, self-styled spokesman for the New York-based Yippies and author (under the pseudonym Free) of anti-establishment manifesto *Revolution for the Hell of It*, had rushed out a new book ('a talk-rock album'), *Woodstock Nation*. Crystallised in its title was the idea that Woodstock had represented more than just a gathering of individuals with a shared taste in music and recreation; more, even, than a temporary city run on utopian ideals. Woodstock was a nation, one that would match historian Benedict Anderson's 1983 definition as 'an imagined community ... imagined because the members of even the smallest nation will never know most of their fellow members, meet them or even hear of them, yet in the minds of each lives the image of their communion'.[17]

Pickers in a paddock, Hamilton, circa 1970. Ian Baker photograph, private collection

That image travelled far beyond the physical borders of the Woodstock festival site, and moved quickly. Even before the *Woodstock* movie hit New Zealand cinemas in late 1970, enshrining Hendrix's deconstruction of the American national anthem and MC Chip Monk's warnings to stay away from the brown acid, there was a feeling that New Zealand wanted its own event.

Within weeks of the Woodstock festival came Jumping Sundays. Though more like low-key versions of the San Francisco Human Be-Ins of a couple of years earlier, they were nevertheless a first response to a post-Woodstock world. And Woodstock also had an immediate impact on the already established gatherings. The folk boom of the early sixties had spawned a number of annual festivals, the largest of which was the National Banjo Pickers' Convention: an Easter weekend rally that, between 1967 and 1970, would draw fields full of bluegrass enthusiasts to the outskirts of Hamilton, where they sat around their tents trading Earl Scruggs licks and refining their clawhammer technique.[18] But, as organiser Michael Grace noted, by the time of the final Banjo Pickers' Convention 'the whole sort of Woodstock thing was starting to creep in and we were finding that it had become, as indeed festivals have been ever since, a place where there's quite a lot of drug use. But it was all pretty new and experimental in those days. I just didn't want it to go that way at all.'[19]

The spirit of Woodstock was more welcome at the National Blues Conventions at Moller's Farm in Oratia, where the music was louder, unruly and experimental, and the longhaired organisers, teenage guitarist Alistair Riddell and his friend Selwyn Jones, embraced the countercultural milieu. The first Blues Convention pre-dated Woodstock by eight months. The second, held in December 1969, featured performances by Riddell's Original Sun Blues Band, jug band the Greasy Handful (featuring a young Graham Brazier) and Rick Bryant (with Gutbucket), as well as poetry readings organised by Alan Brunton. Its alternative title, the Electric Picnic, implied turning on. Rick Bryant recalled: 'A lot of people were having their first LSD trips. A lot. Hundreds and hundreds. There were these specs going round where the lenses were pyramids and colours. It was like wearing an acid trip: "Here, have a trip with your trip." It was a very pleasant occasion. A micro-Woodstock. Entirely pacific.'[20]

After all the publicity about Woodstock, veteran Auckland entrepreneur Phil Warren set out to capitalise on the festival fad. Redwood 70: The First National Music Convention would be an all-weekend event at Redwood Park in West Auckland. Applying the commercial instincts that had seen him successfully managing clubs, labels and recording artists since the mid-1950s, Warren stacked the bill with names familiar to the general public from television and radio — Ray Columbus, Shane, the Rumour, the Chicks. Among these mainstream pop acts he scattered a handful of bands with credibility in the Auckland underground scene, including Fresh Air, Killing Floor and the Arch. The headliner and sole international act was the thoroughly middle-of-the-road Robin Gibb of the Bee Gees, just setting out on what proved to be a short-lived solo career.

Such grinding incongruities turned out to be typical of the event, as revealed by an NZBC documentary shown on television not long after the festival. We see punters arriving, a mix of long and short hair, Māori and Pākehā, ponchos and walk shorts. There is a visible police presence. There are no painted buses or house trucks, just an ominous black van bearing the insignia of a security firm. MC Pete Sinclair, with the same manufactured exuberance he brought to his role as frontman of television pop show *C'mon*, introduces 'the first happening in the happening decade!' as the Arch launches into a blues-rock riff with frontman Rangi Williams singing, with more significance than anyone seems ready to acknowledge, 'Please, please, listen to the children!' Out front, half a dozen young Māori men are grouped on a patch of grass enjoying the music in the afternoon sun. One wears a combat helmet with a handpainted swastika. Another has a cap bearing an SS symbol.[21] The one in the cap is speaking to an off-screen interviewer. We never hear the question, but can assume it concerns his reasons for coming to

Redwood 70. 'You get to know more people and you get to know more songs and you get to party up large,' he explains good-naturedly. 'You know what I mean? No you don't.' He flashes a gap-toothed smile.

'I came to see a bit of a revolution,' asserts a young Pākehā. He fiddles with his mid-length hair. His mate, whose hair is almost identical, gleefully picks up the thought. 'If any old ladies look out their window they're going to get a bottle through it tonight. It's going to be a sea of glass! It's going to be a revolution!'

Now it's Saturday night and Robin Gibb is about to come on. 'But first,' warns Sinclair, a schoolmasterly tone sneaking into his deejay schtick, 'I've got to remind you, the police and the security service have promised to remove anyone from the grounds who creates any sort of disturbance at all. So let's cool it and have a groovy scene!'

Gibb appears, 'a slight figure in a brown suit and white turtleneck sweater', as the *Auckland Star*'s Tony Potter will describe him, with 'no stage act to speak of'.[22] While the band, augmented by local orchestral players, launches into a syrupy Bee Gees ballad, a piece of fruit whizzes past the singer's ear. He pauses, momentarily nonplussed, then carries on with the song. In the final bars of the song a girl leaps onto the stage and throws herself at him. It might be a moment out of the Beatles' 1964 tour. Losing his balance, Gibb staggers backwards into the band. The girl is wrestled off by several policemen and the singing resumes. But no sooner has the fan made her exit than the stage is rushed by a succession of young males, one of whom knocks over both the cameraman's tripod and the singer's microphone stand. It's hard to determine what the boys want, but it doesn't seem to be a hug from Robin. Missiles begin to fly from the crowd as policemen hurl the intruders off the stage and back onto the lawn. Gibb retreats into the wings while the stage swarms with police and security guards.

One of the police has requisitioned the microphone and is commanding the audience to 'get back behind the wire. We want you behind the wire!' His stance and language are a flashback to the Agnew demonstrations in Auckland only days before. Gibb does not return to the stage, and the night ends with the musicians packing up while a section of the crowd chants 'We want Robin! We want Robin!' Whether they want to love or lynch him is unclear.

Scenes filmed the following day seem a little more relaxed, as though some pressure valve has been released in the violent night. The sun is out. A priest conducts the Eucharist in the open air. Possibly the least funky gospel choir ever sings 'Angels Watching Over Me' in stiff 4/4 time. The invisible interviewer interrogates a few more punters on their way out the gate. 'There were fights all over the place but if you kept out of it, it was okay,' says a young Māori woman, with a smile. 'There might have been a bit too many jungle bunnies and that, but on the whole it was alright,' says a longhaired Pākehā male as he leans out the window of a departing car. The casual racism was just one expression of the divisions Redwood exposed. There were the gang members' swastikas, symbolically defying social norms. There were the boys who had come 'to see a bit of a revolution', which sounds more like a euphemism for a beery Saturday-night brawl. At Woodstock, the music had brought people together, but these disparate groups were evidently not yet ready to come together as members of some globally imagined nation. And while others may have come hoping for a vicarious glimpse of the infamous counterculture, the real counterculture seems to have kept a wary distance, understanding perhaps that this uneasy mix of television entertainers, middle-of-the-road pop stars and the occasional underground rocker would be a long way from an Aquarian exposition.[23]

SANTA'S LIQUID DREAM AND OTHER HAPPENINGS

Phil Warren failed to make back his investment on ticket sales at Redwood 70, and it would be another couple of years before anyone tried such a large-scale festival again, but the interim saw numerous smaller, truly countercultural events.

Scratch Orchestra (NZ) in the crater of Maungawhau/Mount Eden, 1971. Max Oettli photograph, Alexander Turnbull Library, PAColl-1386-1

Phil Dadson's idea of a musical happening was probably about as far from Phil Warren's as you could get. Having witnessed Thelonious Monk criss-crossing jazz and kinetic art in Auckland in 1965, Dadson had spent a year in London, where he studied with Cornelius Cardew, Britain's leading experimental composer. Cardew, a former assistant to Karlheinz Stockhausen, introduced Dadson to his concept of the Scratch Orchestra: an orchestra composed of beginners — 'scratch players' — rather than trained initiates, using a combination of traditional and homemade instruments and devising their own notation, thereby liberating music from the institutions.

After returning to New Zealand in 1969, Dadson set about forming an 'antipodean twig' of the orchestra. By 1971 Scratch Orchestra (NZ) had performed a number of times, including *Solar Plexus*, a large-scale, dawn-to-dusk drumming event held in the crater of one of Auckland's dormant volcanoes, Maungawhau/Mount Eden.

Though it may have achieved Cardew's egalitarian ideals, Dadson soon became frustrated with the orchestra, feeling that their performances were more like 'therapeutic free-for-alls'.[24] In 1974 he launched an offshoot, From Scratch, a smaller, more disciplined ensemble with Bruce Barber, Geoff Chappell and Gray Nicol. From Scratch made their debut in Wellington as part of Sonic Circus, a six-hour experimental music event at Victoria University run by composer and teacher Jack Body, with continuous music played in eight locations. Among these were the Dream Room ('a music-sculpture environment') and the Resonance Room (a room of bells), while the law library was taken over by electronic music.

Wellington had already witnessed other musical happenings centred on the university music scene, including *Embryo* and *Santa's Liquid Dream*, both of which involved composers Tony Backhouse and Ian McDonald. 'We'd have rehearsals where we'd toss the I Ching to see what we'd do next,' Tony remembers. 'At one point we even swapped the beginning and the middle around and it seemed to make just as much sense.'[25] Though hardly an unqualified success, *Santa's Liquid Dream*, which had involved a good chunk of Wellington's musical underground, inspired musician-filmmakers Geoff Murphy and Bruno Lawrence to form their multimedia band BLERTA, who would go on to be a regular feature at happenings and festivals throughout the early seventies.

This milieu also produced a new generation of theatre practitioners who rebelled against the orthodoxy of imported plays and sedate venues. Ken Rae formed the Living Theatre Troupe in Auckland in 1970 with a group of fellow students who at various times included Sally Rodwell, Paul Carew, Frances Edmond and Murray Edmond, and like many rock bands of the era toured the country in a brightly painted bus. They devised original and experimental work that would be variously performed in streets, parks, beaches and warehouses and on marae. In Wellington, Paul Maunder founded

Australasian Architecture Student Association Congress, Warkworth, 1971. David Mitchell photograph, private collection

Highway at the Jam Factory, 1971.
Max Oettli photograph, Alexander
Turnbull Library, PAColl-1386-1

the Amamus Theatre Group, which included future international film star Sam Neill, drawing on songs, speeches, improvisation and the actors' own experiences to create works that aimed to 'interpret and mirror New Zealand society, where it exists'.[26] To Maunder, school halls and factories were preferable to 'the artificiality of cozy little theatres' inhabited by 'the new fur coat brigade'.[27]

Other events imagined a new society altogether, and abandoned or derelict industrial sites provided symbolic settings. In summer 1971, a disused lime factory in Warkworth was the site of a week-long experiment in alternative dwellings and communal living under the deceptively formal banner of the Australasian Architecture Student Association Congress. In fact it was a happening by any other name. Students and their entourages lived for the duration in temporary, self-designed dwellings made variously of tubular scaffolding, cardboard, canvas, paper and wire. Suspended from one tree was a carousel-like series of platforms, each bearing a single-person tent. There was a gigantic dome. Hilltops and riverbanks hosted lectures from international guests such as pioneering eco architects Sim Van der Ryn and Serge Chermayeff. In the evenings there were rock bands, light shows, mime acts and movies.[28]

Later that year the University Arts Festival drew a thousand people to a former Auckland fruit-bottling plant for Jam Factory. Effectively a festival within a festival, the idea, according to organiser Paul Carew, arose 'from dissatisfaction with the type of music being provided by professional promoters, who seem to stick to safe middle-of-the-road groups'.[29] Interspersing live music with films, the event ran continuously from Saturday morning to Sunday night ('bring a blanket' advised the ads), and was headlined by Wellington bands Highway and Farmyard. It combined the light shows of Peter Frater, that were already a psychedelic institution in Wellington, and Keir Volkerling who had lit the Warkworth congress. Pot was plentiful.

Though some established music venues tried to capitalise on the new culture, the proprietors tended to be old-school entrepreneurs whose priority was to make a buck. This meant reining in the bands' more experimental impulses in favour of material that the casual club-goer would recognise. These bands were often more comfortable and better appreciated in less traditional venues. The Barry Lett Galleries hosted the Australasian Rock Squad (featuring Harvey Mann), playing what was billed as 'cosmic rock and spontaneous music'.[30] Fresh Air was an Auckland-based line-up of mostly transplanted Wellingtonians, including Chris Seresin, George Barris and Chaz Burke-Kennedy, who were in their element jamming in the fresh air of Albert Park on Jumping Sundays.

In Wellington the Original Sin could be found at the Mystic, a venue that struggled to live up to its name. 'It was primitive. I don't recall any special lighting,' recalls occasional Mystic visitor Andrew Delahunty. 'It was just the upstairs of an empty house with the Original Sin playing in one corner.'[31] In Dunedin, the courtyards and back yards of central-city flats provided temporary and spontaneous venues for bands such as Pussyfoot, Noah and Stash, whose covers of Hendrix, Traffic and Led Zeppelin reflected the underground tastes of the countercultural cognoscenti.

Rock came to the campuses relatively late. Though there had been small jazz enclaves and odd chamber music groups, for most of the sixties the highest-profile music on campus was folk. Untainted by commerce, associated with left-wing politics and carrying a touch of hipness thanks to Bob Dylan, folk appealed to the idealistic and high-minded.

It was through the Victoria University Folk Club in 1968 that Graeme Nesbitt made his first forays into music promotion. With his long hair, beret and Afghan coat he looked like Che Guevara might have after a month in Haight-Ashbury. While he sometimes performed as a member of the folk and blues group Country Deal, his real gift was as an organiser. In 1970 he was elected Victoria University's cultural affairs officer, and thus put in charge of that year's National Student

Arts Festival, which it was Victoria's turn to host. The week-long festival usually presented a predictable programme of drama, poetry, chess tournaments and law moots. In Nesbitt's hands it became a countercultural happening.

To launch the festival and greet out-of-towners arriving by the all-night railcar, he had the band Mammal (a recent outgrowth of the Original Sin) playing a dawn chorus of psychedelic rock just inside the colonnaded entrance of Wellington Railway Station. To close, he held a concert at the Paramount Theatre headlined by Highway, a new amalgam of Wellington musicians including guitarist Phil Prichard, bassist George Limbidis and drummer Jim Lawrie, whose all-original

Mammal, illuminated by Peter Frater, Victoria University Student Union Hall, 1973. **Keith Stewart photograph, private collection**

repertoire, guitar escapades and spring-tight rhythms were enhanced by the pot that Nesbitt had been disseminating throughout the week to those in the know. Bruce Cavell enthused in *Craccum*, calling it 'the best local thing I've ever been to' and 'rock'n'roll played the way you wish it would always be played'.[32]

The Highway concert drew such a turnout that Nesbitt hastily arranged a second show later that same night. The festival's good vibes were disrupted only when Tim Shadbolt, down from Auckland for the week with a guerrilla theatre group, tried to stage a spontaneous sleepover in the Student Union building. When the campers refused to leave, Nesbitt called the police, and Shadbolt and several others were charged with trespass. A few hours after his release, Shadbolt was picked up at the Duke of Edinburgh and arrested again, this time for non-payment of fines, and spent the remainder of the festival in prison. There were mutterings about Nesbitt's ego and the dominance of rock music over other activities. Yet the festival was widely judged a success; it even turned a profit, and became the template for student arts events for the next few years.

After the festival, Highway hit the road on a tour of university campuses. Accompanying them was Peter Frater, who brought along his do-it-yourself approximation of a San Francisco light show, with a Heath Robinson-like arrangement of projectors, food dyes and molten oils. Chris Knox, who in a few years would emerge as a pivotal figure in the punk scene, saw Highway's first show in Dunedin and was so impressed he went back to hear them again the following night. Not only was he seeing 'for just about the first time in my life, that there were New Zealand musicians doing original stuff' but 'both nights they did a long free-form thing, which went for about 40 minutes each night and was totally different each night, and I was highly impressed by that'.[33]

Highway were a festival favourite that year and also headlined at Pekapeka on the Kāpiti coast. Though Pekapaka, like Redwood, drew a range of punters, the afternoon event was notable mainly for a series of fights between members of two gangs, the Mongrel Mob and the recently formed Satan's Slaves. A reporter from Wellington student newspaper *Salient* remarked with affected jadedness: 'The bulk of the "audience" were there to drink in the sun and watch the crowd, and listen to the music when it was good. They probably soon got bored. At least as the afternoon wore on many were waiting for the fighting they knew would break out. Looks like they weren't disappointed.'[34]

Graeme Nesbitt and his Students' Arts Council successor Bruce Kirkland continued to supervise concerts and campus tours by bands that fell outside the commercial mainstream, played original music and in many ways gave the counterculture its musical voice. The most ambitious bands to tread the campus circuit in this period were Dragon and Split Ends (soon to adopt the sensational spelling *Enz*), both of whose stories have been well documented and who would both, by the end of the seventies, find substantial success overseas.

Other frequent flyers on the circuit included Tamburlaine, who played an intricate, psychedelically tinged folk-rock, and Ticket, a power-trio-plus-singer from Auckland. They had finessed their tight sound during 1970 with a residency at a Christchurch club Aubrey's, where their audiences included US servicemen stationed in the city as part of the Antarctic research programme or on rest and recreation leave from Vietnam. The soldiers would sometimes provide gifts of marijuana and LSD, which they were able to bring into the country unchallenged because the air base was exempt from Customs checks.

Particularly dear to Nesbitt was Mammal. Formed at Victoria University, where several of the group either studied or taught, Mammal were as eclectic as a Cotton-Eyed Joe radio show, incorporating obscure R&B, psychedelic jams, and long, intricate original songs, though the finer details were sometimes lost in the faltering frequencies of a substandard sound system. Barefooted guitarist Robert Taylor would play himself into a dervish trance. Vocalist and junior English lecturer Rick Bryant looked gruff and sang with a wounded soulfulness, while Tony Backhouse, responsible for much of the songwriting, complemented Bryant's coarser tones with his pure soaring tenor. In combination with a Peter Frater light show, a Mammal gig was always a happening. On one occasion they primed a group of students assembled in the Victoria University quadrangle in preparation for a Vietnam War march with an incendiary version of the Stones' 'Street Fighting Man'. They travelled the country in a painted bus, dropped acid, smoked pot, and subsidised their ventures with Nesbitt's and Bryant's cannabis dealing. In 1972 they recorded their only album, in collaboration with the poet Sam Hunt, with whom they sometimes toured. The title song was their setting of Hunt's poem 'Beware the Man', and in Mammal's live shows it rang out like an anti-establishment anthem. It begins with the lines:

> Beware the man who tries to fit you out
> In his idea of a hat
> Dictating the colour and the shape of it

and concludes with the caution:

> Beware! He's fitting you for more than that.

BLERTA carved a circuit of their own. This sometimes included universities, but more often took them to halls and theatres in the provincial backblocks where a band of any kind was seldom seen, let alone an anarchic multimedia collective of men, women and children travelling in a psychedelic house bus.

BLERTA—Bruno Lawrence's Electric Revelation and Travelling Apparition—was started in 1971 by Lawrence. After a decade as a professional drummer, he was looking for an alternative to the pub circuit and collar-and-tie cabaret gigs: something more compatible with his lifestyle, which now included a wife, four children and a lot of hippie hangers-on. In each new town, BLERTA would drive around the streets announcing their arrival, publicising the night's performance and sometimes scaring the citizens. In Christchurch, Veronica Lawrence parked one of the entourage's cars in a suburban street and returned to find it surrounded by police. They had been summoned by a citizen who had 'felt threatened' by the vehicle.[35]

A BLERTA rāga, Serenity 1972. From left:
Greg Taylor, Chris Seresin and Fane Flaws.
Hamish Horsley Collection, Sarjeant Gallery

LEFT TO RIGHT: Donald McLeod (left) and Hamish Horsley assembling Serenity, December 1972. Hamish Horsley Collection, Sarjeant Gallery

Serenity dancers, 1972. Hamish Horsley Collection, Sarjeant Gallery

South African drummer Bauxhau jams at Serenity. Hamish Horsley Collection, Sarjeant Gallery

BLERTA children's show at Serenity. Hamish Horsley Collection, Sarjeant Gallery

AQUARIAN EXPOSITIONS

Bruno Lawrence with BLERTA,
Ngaruawahia Festival, January 1973.
John Miller photograph, private collection

The original core of BLERTA were the members of Littlejohn, a Wellington-based nightclub group that included singer Corben Simpson and guitarist Kemp Tuirirangi, which Bruno augmented with various other musicians, moviemakers, actors and hippies-without-portfolio. Chris Seresin of Fresh Air brought his piano and sitar. And there was Bruno's old friend and brother-in-law Geoff Murphy. 'Bruno is King Arthur and I'm Merlin,' said Murphy to Sue McCauley, who wrote about her travels with the band in early 1972.[36] The music, directed by Bruno, combined elements of jazz, pop and psychedelic rock, but a BLERTA show also included film, skits, and explosions engineered by Murphy.

BLERTA's painted bus, all-ages repertoire and communal ethos were a natural fit with the kids and kaftans at Serenity, a festival held in December 1972 at Pūtiki, just across the river from the township of Whanganui. Consistent with its name, Serenity was an entirely peaceful affair.

It began as the brainchild of Donald McLeod and Hamish Horsley, two hippies in their early twenties, energetically committed to exploring art, drugs and Eastern religion. Horsley, known as Kapok on account of his mop of fluffy blond hair, had grown up at Pūtiki and had friends at the local marae who agreed to make their paddock available for the festival site. The nearby Four Seasons Theatre also loaned its premises. Along with BLERTA, those who responded to invitations included South African drummer Bauxhau; Aboriginal didgeridoo player Peter Wilson; poets Hone Tuwhare and Sam Hunt; drama groups Amamus and Theatre Action, and another led by George Webby of Wellington Teachers' College. Yoga instructors and the Society for Krishna Consciousness offered workshops. Composer Jack Body requested helium canisters and bird whistles for a purpose-written environmental piece which he would perform in the hills above the site.

A week before the event, a representative of the Satan's Slaves gang stopped by the festival headquarters, a house belonging to the iwi. He left his card ('You have just met a member of Satan's Slaves — 1 per cent') but never returned. By this time, volunteers were already at work on the site. BLERTA arrived early and helped build the stage. Though disaster threatened in the form of an opening-night storm, there was a Woodstock-style triumph when the clouds parted the following morning. In all, between fifteen hundred and two thousand attended, around half of them camping out for the full four days. Adults and children from the marae mingled with the longhairs. On the final afternoon, everyone still at the festival was invited to a hāngī at the marae; there was even a vegetarian option.

Serenity's success stemmed from its being the co-operative effort of young hippies and local iwi who showed a genuinely reciprocal interest in each other's cultures, and found a common value in communing around art and music. Yet Serenity failed to break even, and McLeod and Horsley would spend much of the following year working odd jobs to pay off the debt, after which Horsley headed for Kathmandu where he would spend the next few years as a monk.[37]

Serenity was never repeated, though early in 1973 the organisation put out the *Serenity Letter*, a handbill advising of an Aquarius Festival to take place that May in Nimbin, New South Wales ('crops are already growing there ready for distribution at the festival'). BLERTA would be crossing the Tasman to perform there, and anyone wishing to join a party of New Zealanders to accompany them was invited to sign up immediately.

Though New Zealand's only real connection was BLERTA, the festival altered the course of history for Nimbin 'from a declining banana and dairy economy, to countercultural capital of Australia'.[38] Four decades later, a travel story in the *New Zealand Herald* headlined 'Nimbin: The Weed Capital of Australia' would describe the tie-dye and hemp store-bestrewn town as 'a throwback to the seventies'.[39]

WOODSTOCK WAIKATO

New Zealand was still waiting for its Woodstock when, on the first Friday of 1973, young people began to arrive at the 250-acre dairy farm on the edge of the Waikato River that would be the site of the Great Ngaruawahia Music Festival. 'Woodstock Planned in Waikato' ran the *Herald* headline.

Ngaruawahia was the brainchild of two bright young entrepreneurs with close enough connections to the counterculture to know they would need a more credible headliner than Robin Gibb. By the time he was twenty-one, New Zealander Barry Coburn and his Australian associate Robert Raymond had already successfully mounted Elton John and Led Zeppelin concerts at Western Springs stadium, the biggest rock shows the country had seen.

Raymond drove a Mercedes and had a posh Remuera home where he had entertained Led Zeppelin. Coburn, by contrast, was unassuming and, according to Dick Nicholls' profile in New Zealand's *Rolling Stone*, 'a health food faddist passionately concerned about pollution and the French bomb tests ... incredibly sincere and could almost pass for a Bible-Class leader'.[40]

To headline their festival, Coburn and Raymond signed two international bands, Fairport Convention and Black Sabbath, a pairing that represented the extreme poles of British rock at the time: folk-rock and heavy metal. The wide middle ground was left to be filled by local acts. There would be forty food stalls, fifty showers, a hundred toilets and a crèche, along with a forty-strong medical team with hundreds of metres of Band-Aid, gallons of sunburn cream and five hundred tetanus shots. In anticipation, the two nearest hotels stocked up with almost a quarter of a million beer cans.[41] The Earwig Collective was commissioned to produce *The Ngaruawahia Chronicle*, a four-page broadsheet containing the festival programme, profiles of a few of the acts, and features on health food and ecology.

People began to arrive several days early. 'A myriad of tents and coloured domes housing people, children, food, drink, medical supplies and musical equipment have transformed dairy-cow paddocks into a multi-coloured tent town,' the *Dominion* reported before the first notes had sounded.[42] The Merchant Adventurers of Narnia, Wellington-based importers and retailers of hippie accoutrements [of which more in Chapter 13], filled a bus with friends and merchandise—Indian clothes and fabrics, incense and essential oils, rolling papers and roach clips— and set up their on-site shop in a tent.

Unlike the uneasy mix of mainstream and underground performers at Redwood 70, the Great Ngaruawahia Festival bill favoured local acts with some countercultural cachet. Though padded with a few pop-chart voices (Shane, Shade Smith), most bands played original material of a kind seldom heard on New Zealand radio. The La De Da's, based in Australia since the late sixties, returned as

TOP: Ngaruawahia Festival, 1973.

BOTTOM: Treefoot, centre, with headband. David Stone photographs, private collection

a stripped-down power trio. Another expat, Reggie Ruka, fronted Aussie band Itambu, and made an impression with his cartwheels and 'erotic spider walk'.[43] Tamburlaine and Tolepuddle provided folksier flavours.

To add drama to their entrance, Black Sabbath had ordered the construction of a giant wooden cross, to be set alight at midnight on the hill overlooking the amphitheatre. Though ostensibly evoking some ancient pagan ritual, no one seemed to consider the more recent association of this symbol with the racist and murderous Ku Klux Klan. To oblige the band's request, Coburn, in time-honoured Kiwi DIY fashion, instructed members of the local stage crew to knock together a cross out of a few pieces of four-by-two. Come showtime, however, they had difficulty getting the wood to ignite. Eventually this was achieved with the help of various flammable liquids that disgorged a plume of toxins into the evening air.

Sabbath's set, too, was more smoke than fire.[44] Among the underwhelmed was Billy Williams, formerly of Space Farm, playing

that weekend with Ticket, who had been booked to tour Australia with Black Sabbath following the festival. 'It was rough and the music wasn't tight. When they had finished, we went back to Robert Raymond's caravan and were sitting inside when Robert came to the door. He asked what we thought of Black Sabbath's set. Someone said "It sounded terrible!" and we saw Robert's face contort awkwardly and with raised eyebrows, gave a strained laugh, closed the door and left. Robert came back sometime later and told us Black Sabbath's manager was standing right behind him at the caravan, had heard our response, and didn't want us to tour Australia with them anymore.'[45]

Black Sabbath's Sunday-night squib had been preceded by smouldering sets from campus-circuit perennials Billy TK and the Powerhouse and Mammal. The weekend also heard the homegrown hard rock of Arkastra, Butler and Mandrake. Split Ends gave their first performance outside Auckland, though the mixed response to their semi-acoustic art-songs suggested crowds weren't quite ready for them. Nor were the Ends quite ready for the crowds, despite the confidence

Corben Simpson cools off at Ngaruawahia, 1973. David Stone photographs, private collection

shown in them by festival organiser Coburn, who was also their manager. The newly formed Dragon, still several years away from Australasian stardom, also gave their first major performance that weekend, to a less than rapturous reception.

BLERTA performed both a children's show and a typically anarchic jazz-rock set. It was their singer Corben Simpson who provided the festival's determining moment during a solo performance on the first day. After a few songs he declared he was hot, stripped off his clothes and played the rest of his set in the nude. Simpson's gesture drew a line in the sand: society's conventions did not apply here. Nudity, onstage and off, provided salacious fodder for the mainstream media. It was the primary focus of a feature in the *Sunday Times*. 'Oh! Oh! Naked Ngaruawahia!' gasped the headline as photos depicted unclothed women unselfconsciously drinking beer, flashing peace signs and enjoying the festival.[46]

Despite some early alarm about the possibility of widespread use of LSD and marijuana ('The farmland site of the Ngaruawahia Music Festival could grow an unwanted crop of cannabis sativa—marijuana or "pot" to the uninitiated', warned the *Sunday Times*[47]), drugs featured little in the subsequent reporting, though there was no doubt plenty available. Only two arrests for drug offences were reported. Nor was alcohol reported as a particular problem, in spite of the quarter of a million cans in circulation.

Other papers purported to examine such expressions of 'the new morality' more seriously. A *Dominion* editorial the Wednesday after the festival suggested that: 'if one is offended one need not have been there'. It noted that while

> the philosophy of those who converge in gregarious droves to perform their own thing in an elemental earth setting is as hard for uninitiated to understand as the primitive appeal of their music beat ... on reflection ... the festival went rather well. There was no crippling larrikinism. The entertainment was not corrupted to serve malicious ends.
>
> Society must continue to guard against public obscenity and corrupting influences, though definitions necessarily adjust to changing standards. Like other youth-inspired and no-doubt short-lived manifestations, the well-run pop festival may serve as a useful brief release from any tensions and hang-ups of a conformist technological age.[48]

The overall tranquillity of the festival may have had something to do with the light-handed approach to security. Much of this task fell to Eden Security, a predominantly Māori firm run by Hugh Lynn, a former child tap-dancing champion and go-go dance instructor, whose first venture into security provision had been during the Pretty Things' visit in 1965. As he told Cushla Donaldson in her impressionistic documentary, *The Great Ngaruawahia Music Festival*, 'Māori were very comfortable with large numbers of people — tangi, marae, that sort of thing — and there was an ease in communicating with people. We're not going to arrest you for smoking dope or having sex. Taking your clothes off isn't hurting anybody and we didn't worry.'[49]

Though attendance figures never reached the twenty-five thousand Raymond and Coburn had hoped for, the eighteen thousand who came represented the greatest concentration of countercultural youth the country had seen. But while even the conservative press generally conceded that the long weekend had been something close to Arcadian, its aftermath played out in the courts. In June, Corben Simpson was convicted and fined for 'wilfully and obscenely exposing his person' during his performance. By 1974 Raymond, who had bought out Barry Coburn's shares in the production company, was in court, answering claims of more than $16,500 owed to six creditors as a result of the festival. The Earwig Collective, who had published the festival's programme, got in early. Jonathan Milne remembers: 'I had to throw — it wasn't exactly a tantrum, it was anguish, because they weren't going to pay. We'd been commissioned to do this thing … and I begged and pleaded because we were on the bones. And they actually did finally pay. There were other creditors who were in line, but I think we got cash.'[50]

In 1975 a court hearing was told that the organisers of the festival had incurred a $50,000 loss. Robert Raymond recalled in 2020 that it took two years to pay the creditors, but he looks back on the event with fond memories. 'We still celebrate occasionally, along with many folks who devotedly were an enormous part of the successful organisation. We were all pioneers really.'[51]

It would not be until the late seventies that anyone would attempt another festival on such a scale. It seemed that if Coburn and Raymond couldn't make it pay, no one else was willing to risk it. Yet despite its messy aftermath, Ngaruawahia was generally agreed to have been the real thing. If Woodstock represented the apogee of the rock festival as countercultural event — a microcosm of a world living on peace, love and music — then New Zealand had had its Woodstock in the Waikato.

SCENES FROM THE REVOLUTION

While live music was an important part of the emerging culture, records remained the primary carriers of musical information, as crucial in their own way as films or literature. To the English writer David Hepworth, the long-playing album was 'a semi-precious object, a mark of sophistication, a measure of wealth, an instrument of education, a unit of currency, a banner to be carried before one through the streets, a poster saying things one dare not say oneself, a means of attracting the opposite sex, and, for hundreds of thousands of young people, the single most cherished inanimate object in their lives'.[52]

If the LP held such significance to Hepworth growing up in West Yorkshire, to a young inhabitant of a colonial island nation in the South

Pacific it meant all that and more. LPs brought messages from the other side of the world. They were a precious connection to a global movement of ideas, sounds and meanings. Many of the tantalising titles one read about in the sea-freighted music magazines were not available locally and so became the stuff of myth. To have actually heard *Trout Mask Replica*, *The Gilded Palace of Sin* or the self-titled third album of the Velvet Underground was to have gained admittance to an exclusive sect.

Of the albums that saw local releases, a few acquired a totemic importance, and none more so than the Rolling Stones' *Let It Bleed*. Released at the tail end of 1969, it would be the counterculture's ubiquitous soundtrack until the Stones superseded themselves with *Sticky Fingers* eighteen months later. It was the perennial party record, an accompaniment to endless varieties of free-expressive dance, yet it doubled as a dispatch from the frontlines. Bookended with scenes from the revolution — 'Gimme Shelter' ('war, children, it's just a shot away') and 'You Can't Always Get What You Want' ('I went down to the demonstration, to get my fair share of abuse') — the album burst like a volley of Molotov cocktails aimed at bourgeois morality. Its title song makes fun of the Beatles' pious 'Let It Be' with allusions to menstruation and oral sex.[53] In 'Monkey Man' it's all junkies, satanic messiahs and 'lemon-squeezers' (a sexual euphemism borrowed from the bluesman Robert Johnson), while 'Live With Me' lampoons the peccadilloes of the English upper class. But there is also the sexual violence of 'Midnight Rambler', a blues boogie with gothic overtones, in which Jagger plays the role of a psychopathic rapist. If the effect could be called psychodrama, it also amplifies the casual misogyny of many a countercultural male.

As the sixties rolled towards the seventies, *Let It Bleed* seemed a long way from the songs of idealised, innocent love that had filled the air less than a decade earlier — a measure of how much the world had changed. The week of its release, California had hosted an event that history would record as the anti-Woodstock: a hastily arranged one-day festival at the Altamont Speedway that had disintegrated into an orgy of violence and bad vibes. The Stones were the headliners.

A few weeks after the Great Ngaruawahia Music Festival, the Stones returned to New Zealand for the first time since the mid-sixties. By this time the countercultural landscape of the northern hemisphere they had observed so acutely in *Let It Bleed* had, in many ways, been replicated down under. There had been violent demonstrations and a fair share of abuse; lots of sex, some of it falling conspicuously outside the societal conventions of marriage, monogamy, heterosexuality and the missionary position. And there were drugs — marijuana, psychedelics and now, increasingly, heroin.

Rachel Stace was at Western Springs to see them, nearly nine years after she had screamed for the Beatles as a schoolgirl in Wellington. Those days seemed so innocent now. Her life since had become more dangerous, thanks to a recreational diet of marijuana and acid supplemented with Mandrax and opiates. A photograph taken

Listening to *Let It Bleed*. Max Oettli photograph, Alexander Turnbull Library, PAColl-1386-1

at the concert shows her and a group of her closest friends standing among the mostly seated, summer-afternoon crowd. Rachel, in round wire-rimmed glasses, stands near the centre of the group, holding a cigarette and sporting a peacock feather. To her left is Grant: tall, longhaired, in mirror shades, beads and pink crushed-velvet jacket slashed to reveal a bare chest—a rock star in search of a band. To her right is Jane in flowing headscarf, bracelets and rings. Beside Jane is Sally. 'He was a real queen,' Rachel remembers. 'Apparently he was called Sally because he was brought up by the Salvation Army, but his real name was David.'[54] The group looks glamorous and decadent, as though they really belong on the stage. The photo appeared in *Craccum* alongside a review of the concert, and has since been reproduced in newspapers to illustrate nostalgia stories about the hippie era. But to Rachel the image is bittersweet. Both Jane and Grant would die prematurely after struggles with addiction. Sally, to Rachel's surprise, is still alive.

In his short story *Best Intentions*, Bill Payne recounts the adventures of three druggy Stones fans—Flynn, McCain and Sid, the story's narrator—who, along with their beer-drinking buddy Beck, drive up from Wellington to Auckland in early 1973 to see that same summer show. He writes: 'Once we heard the news we forgot our best

intentions. We forgot about family and girlfriends, about back rent and bad debt and utility bills. We forgot about anniversaries and appointments, about previous engagements and long-standing obligations. Good morals, personal responsibility and owning up for our sins no longer seemed important ...' He adds: 'All we talked and cared about, all we could remember was this: the Rolling Stones were coming, and there were things we had to do.'[55] Their first task was to burgle a chemist's store. Then, stocked up with 'pills and potions, oils and capsules, bottles and packets and sundry other illegal-without-a-

prescription sledgehammer miracle cures', they hit State Highway One in Flynn's old heap, shouting along to Stones songs and intermittently shooting up drugs as they go.

In the story's black-comic conclusion, it is the beer drinker who ends up in hospital and misses the event. The others make it to Western Springs and enjoy a stoned afternoon in the sun, though, as Sid later reflects, it was not as good as in Wellington in 1965 when Brian Jones was alive and teenagers were mobbing the stage.

Rachel Stace, with cigarette and peacock feather, standing with friends. Western Springs Stadium, 1973. Rachel Stace private collection

GIMME SHELTER

Eight

New ideas about sex, marriage, work and domestic life brought young people into increasing conflict with the established institutions. In 1967, acting under the discipline regulations of the University of Otago Council, Vice-Chancellor Robin Williams enforced a ban on mixed flatting, making an example of a nineteen-year-old final-year psychology student by ordering him to move out of a flat he was sharing with three women. The students' parents and landlord had sanctioned the arrangement, but the idea of young unmarried people of mixed gender cohabiting was still a bridge too far for many.

Child in Colville, Coromandel Peninsula, 1974. Ian Baker photograph, private collection

Outrage at the Chancellor's action was enough to draw a thousand students to an illegal overnight 'live-in' in the Student Union, 180 of whom slept over. It also prompted a response from the poet James K. Baxter, resident in Dunedin that year as recipient of the Burns Fellowship, who took up the cause of flatters and fornicators in a poem that first appeared in *Falus*:

> A thousand founding fathers lie
> Well roofed against the howling sky
> In mixed accommodation—Hush!
> It is the living make us blush
> Because the young have wicked hearts
> And blood to swell their private parts.
> To think of corpses pleases me
> They keep such perfect chastity.
> O Dr Williams, you were right
> To shove the lovers out of sight;
> Now they can wander half the night
> Through coffee house and street and park
> And fidget in the dripping dark,
> While we play Mozart and applaud
> The angel with the flaming sword![1]

Baxter's defence of young lust went a step further than the situation demanded: the male student in question had not been sleeping with any of his female flatmates, merely sharing the same roof. But to Dr Williams' supporters, the issue was about more than cohabitation anyway. Writing under the pseudonym 'Teach Them', a correspondent to the *Otago Daily Times* declared:

> This controversy started over mixed flatting only, but is now extended to a general moral freedom ... We of the older generation left school at an early age, and worked to help support ourselves, our sick and our elderly during the depression. What freedom did we have? We are the ones who suffered six years of war to keep our country free for our children. We gave up many freedoms during the war, and since, to establish a better way of life ... We have given our children a chance to develop their talents, only to find that we have also given them too much freedom. It has become the only word in their vocabulary. They know nothing of gratitude, appreciation, pride of nation, race, country or even pride of family. Modesty, self-respect, courtesy have all fallen to the axe of this horrible word 'freedom,' which is not freedom at all but abuse.
>
> Put a stop to this. Close the universities to all but a few well-chosen young people who can prove they are worth spending our money on. Send the others out to the 'freedom' of finding work for themselves and a chance to do something better than waste

their time and ours with childish demonstrations.

>   Let the students realise that their job is not to fight for more freedom, but to preserve and maintain the freedom which can only be enjoyed by law-abiding citizens.[2]

To which one student, writing as 'An Ever Trying Failure', responded:

> It is now twenty-two years since World War II, since I was born, and many more years since the depression ... Must we have the hard-time stories stuffed down our throats year after year? What do you expect us to do? Crawl to you every five minutes and thank you for the wonderful world you have made for us? This world is not such a mightily fantastic place to live in anyway ...[3]

URBAN NETWORKS

Mixed flatting became increasingly common, particularly in the university towns. Sue Belt was eighteen when she moved into a flat in Thorndon with her musician boyfriend Peter Kennedy, his bandmates Rick Bryant and Julie Needham, and student politician-turned-music promoter Graeme Nesbitt. But, like many, she kept her living arrangements under wraps. 'Mum and Dad would come round and I never really told them I was living with boys. I remember they came upstairs to Peter's and my room and I had to kick all his shoes under the bed, because even though I'd said I believed in free love I'd never quite admitted to them that we were living together.'[4]

Flatting didn't just make it feasible to sleep with your partner. Flats could be conscious experiments in communal living, making it possible for all the accepted conditions for the survival of the species — food, shelter, clothing, sex — to be reconsidered in ways that diverged from societal norms. It was possible for flatters to work in paid employment only for as much or as long as was necessary for survival, enabling the maximum amount of time to be reserved for the things that mattered most, whether creative, spiritual, political or recreational.

By the early seventies, Rachel Stace was living with thirteen others, whose shared interests included drugs, sex and music, in a rambling two-storey villa in Herne Bay, paisley scarves tied around hanging lamps, the back garden overgrown. An outhouse and adjoining cottage were included in a total rental of $36 per week. 'We could afford to spend $40 on acid at the weekend and still have enough left over for food.'[5] Rachel worked as a postie, then as a clerk in the Department of Social Welfare, leaving each job once she had amassed enough money to pay her way for the next few months. Other members of the household took a similarly pragmatic, career-averse approach to employment. One or two were students living on bursaries.

Some flats were furnished by landlords, others by their tenants. Used chairs, couches, tables and other suburban cast-offs could be bought cheaply from second-hand shops, or were contributed by parents. Bed bases and bookcases were constructed from found materials such as pallets and bricks. Flats seldom had televisions. A single stereo would be set up in the main living area and used by all residents; collections of records and books were frequently pooled. The ethos was non-acquisitive and non-materialistic. As household members came and went, they would often leave items behind for the continued use of the household. 'You didn't accumulate things then,' recalled Nicholas Pounder. 'You left them on the floor or on the wall.'[6]

Brent Morrissey had grown up in Christchurch but gone to Australia as a teenager in search of adventure. In Sydney he took a job as a mail sorter, only to discover that young New Zealanders working for the Australian government could be conscripted and sent to Vietnam. When officials turned up at his flat one morning, he hid under the bed while his Australian girlfriend told them he had returned to New Zealand, which he did at the first opportunity. In Auckland, he headed for a St Marys Bay address he had been given by a friend. It was a huge Victorian villa with a large second-storey veranda and a collection of larger and smaller flats. He was welcomed in, and within a short time was part of an enclave of young activists, artists, academics and drifters—the Auckland Push, as they were sometimes called—for whom 10 London Street was its citadel. Lyle Carlisle, 'Lemming', the thoughtful revolutionary who would die on the eve of the violent Agnew demos, occupied an upstairs flat where he would hold court, talking about jazz and revolution. For the next few years London Street would be a site of vigorous discussions about politics and art, experiments with sex and drugs, and constant parties.

On the other side of town in the suburb of Grafton, adjacent to the Domain and close to the university, a network of rented villas housed a floating population of students, artists and dropouts. Deborah Yates had 'run away from home' and moved into a villa in Park Road in 1967. She remembers first hearing *Sgt. Pepper* there the week of its release. Marijuana and the soon-to-be-made-illegal LSD were in common use among her neighbours and flatmates, and while this may have exacerbated their alienation from the wider society it helped bond the community. 'It was a very small scene and it was in a very straight world, so [you] had to hang on to each other and support each other from afar. You couldn't really survive being a serious painter or writer without having these connections.'[7]

Alison McClean, also in her teens, moved into a house in nearby Grafton Road. Flatmates built a mezzanine floor out of materials lifted under the cover of night from a construction site across the road. In the back garden they erected a stage where friends, including future Hello Sailor frontman Graham Brazier, would give impromptu concerts. The landlord turned a blind eye to the various renovations and modifications, possibly because the house was one of many in Grafton due to be demolished for a motorway cutting. 'People became physically close,' Alison remembers. 'A house full of people were quite bonded. I remember one boy said, "We should knock all the walls out and all sleep in the same room" and I thought that was quite a lovely idea. We didn't do it, but we loved each other, listened to each other. There was a lot of talking, a lot of reading. You felt loyalties.'[8]

Social networks were fluid, with both visitors and residents moving freely between neighbouring households, but the sense of community extended nationally as well. During a 1974 hitch-hiking trip to visit alternative communities around New Zealand, Tim Jones met Alan Admore, who was just about to launch *Mushroom*, 'a magazine for alternative life styles'. 'When he heard that I was heading for Christchurch, he said, "Go straight to 9 Berwick Street and make yourself at home."' Jones found it empty 'except for three large dogs, any one of which looked capable of eating me for breakfast. However, the dogs proved amazingly friendly … So I went inside and had a bath, during which time someone came home. When I emerged from the bathroom, that someone said "Hello," and went about her business without the slightest concern or curiosity as to who I was!' The house, as it turned out, had six full-time inhabitants who shared the rent and power bill; each contributed $4 a week towards food, which was often bought from a food co-op. Five were students, while Alan worked full time on the magazine.

Jones noted that 'outwardly the flat was organised like thousands of others, but the spirit was different … All housework and cooking was done without any roster, prior arrangement or talk. There was a flow, a harmony, happiness, which pervaded everything right down to the smallest act or word.'[9]

Closely related to the communal flat, but with some distinct characteristics of its own, was the crash pad: a property, rented or perhaps squatted, with an unfixed roster of residents. Some occupants would be semi-permanent; others might stay a night, a week or a month. Crashers had usually learned about the place by word of mouth. They would turn up unannounced, perhaps offering the name of some shared acquaintance by way of reference, and stay wherever they could find available space.

Some crash pads were simply flats turned feral; others were crash pads by conviction. When Nicholas Pounder arrived in Auckland from Sydney in 1971, he found the crash-pad concept far more established than in Australia. 'I'd read about crash pads but only in the context of Haight-Ashbury. In New Zealand there was a network. Crash pads were a social gesture.'[10]

In 1969 Alan Brunton and Jim Stevenson had moved into a crash pad at 5 Boyle Crescent in Grafton, from where they would launch the Cultural Liberation Front. They had been alerted to its existence by the musician Trix Willoughby, who lived in a crash pad next door

Young man with puppy, Auckland, circa 1970. Max Oettli photograph, Alexander Turnbull Library, PAColl-1386-1

at number 7. By this time, James K. Baxter had completed his Burns Fellowship, experienced a life-changing vision and was ready to move. Writing to fellow poet Louis Johnson, he mused: 'If I went entirely by my own will I'd probably shift up to Auckland and work on and off and do some shagging and found a local chapter of the Hippies.'[11] Which is more or less what he did. Brunton recalled 'a disturbing man with a beard' turning up one day at 5 Boyle Crescent. 'He said Trix had left next door and he was the boss and therefore our rent-collector and he wanted five dollars.'[12]

Baxter's conviction that the soul-sapping loneliness of suburban life was the seedbed of the country's social ills had begun long before he wrote his 'Small Ode to Mixed Flatting'. For many years he had expressed such beliefs in poetry and polemics, which he would air in journals, letters pages, and interviews on radio and television. In a 1967 television documentary, a still-beardless Baxter reported in dour tones an observation he had made a few years earlier as a Wellington postman: 'You'd go around, take the letters round, and people would come out and it seemed as if their only contact with the outside world was through the mail that you brought. And this wasn't only old people. It was housewives with families and so on, as if they were living in a very deep solitude which they hadn't chosen, but which had been rather forced on them.'[13] Eventually he decided it was his task to provide not just words but a practical gesture: to create a place of refuge for some of society's casualties, particularly the young whom he saw falling victim to mental illness and drug addiction.

However much Baxter's actions were driven by altruism—and there are plenty of accounts to show they were—it is evident that he was as ill-suited to suburban family life as any of the lonely housewives he spoke of, and that in pursuing his communal ideal he was not simply creating a refuge for others but also seeking an escape for himself. His relationship with his wife Jacqui Sturm, to whom he had been married since 1948, had been damaged by his own abuses and infidelities.

In early 1969, Baxter left his family and headed north. His physical appearance changed. His hair and beard grew long, unkempt and apparently lice-infested. He dressed in shabby second-hand clothes, usually without shoes. As he had prophesied in his letter to Johnson, in Auckland he worked on and off, including a spell at the Chelsea Sugar Works, and evidently did some shagging. Over the next couple of years several women would become pregnant to him.

The Boyle Crescent crash pads were already familiar to Auckland's young junkies prior to Baxter's arrival. Shortly before Brunton and Stevenson acquired the keys to number 5, seventeen-year-old Philip Sharples had died in the washhouse of a heroin overdose. By inserting himself into an existing drug scene, Baxter, a recovering alcoholic and practising member of Alcoholics Anonymous, acquired an instant community of outlaws and outcasts. Though he was joined by the occasional contemporary such as Gill Shadbolt, most of the people coming and going from Boyle Crescent were half his age or younger. Baxter's seniority and charisma made him the inevitable leader.

Brunton retained a degree of scepticism towards his new neighbour. 'Over the next few weeks he opened number 7 to any freak who could stand the anomie. One of them sold my record player ... When Baxter got tired of casualties screaming out their demons, he would come over to us to get some rest.'[14]

GETTING IT TOGETHER IN THE COUNTRY

Around New Zealand other kinds of communities, more expansive than flats and more organised than crash pads, were beginning to form. In December 1971 a journalist for the *Evening Post* visited a country house in Tai Tapu, 20 kilometres out of Christchurch, where a group of '17 to 20 year olds ... have formed a commune'. The group were remnants of the Winchester commune, an urban community founded on anarchist principles, who had gone rural after being evicted from their central Christchurch premises. The commune was based on sharing, explained seventeen-year-old Anna Bonnevie. 'We do casual work and the money we get goes into a tin. We all live out of the tin. Sometimes we do go short, but when that happens we all budget and we all help one another.' Addressing the public's prurient preoccupation with what was going on in the bedrooms of the communards, Bonnevie said: 'Sex in the commune? Do we believe in free love? A lot of people can't understand it, I know, but I would say there would be a lot less sex in our commune than in a single girl's flat in the city.'[15]

Closer to Christchurch's city centre, twenty or so young Cantabrians, including schoolteacher and future MP Marian Hobbs (then Marian Logeman), set up a community in a pair of Victorian mansions on back-to-back sections that became collectively referred to as Chippenham. A third site of the community was a 40-acre farm, Gricklegrass, near Oxford, 50 kilometres out of town. The farm provided a livelihood for some of the community, while several others ran a bakery. And just outside Dunedin, in the seaside town of Waitati, an assortment of former holiday baches were taken over by a loose collective of alternative lifestylers including *Counter Culture Free Press* editor Malcolm Gramaphone and *Mushroom* founder Alan Admore. Members of the community became involved in the production of the magazines, and the little township became a testing ground for many of the experiments proposed in the presses. In the absence of a sewerage system, Waitati saw the development of composting toilets. It also hosted the birth of the Waitati Militia, a group initially formed to protest the Vietnam War that grew to perform such gonzo stunts

Lynda and Leo Thompson leaving Freemans Bay for Huia, West Coast. Auckland, 1976.
Sally Griffin photograph, private collection

as the naked hijacking of a train, taking hostages and demanding beer and money from the passengers.[16]

Then there were those who felt the need to go even farther afield. The city, they believed, was spiritually and socially poisonous, representing everything the counterculture rejected. For these utopians the answer was to start again from scratch. This was not a new idea, though it was one to which New Zealand, with its unpopulated rural expanses, was well suited. *Time*'s influential 1967 cover story on the hippies had drawn attention to the burgeoning commune movement in the United States, making specific mention of the Drop City commune in Colorado and Morning Star commune north of San Francisco, adding that there were now some thirty such entities spread across North America.

New Zealand had a tradition of intentional communities, going back at least to the 1930s. There was Ray Hansen's Beeville community in the Waikato, and Riverside, at Lower Moutere west of Nelson, founded in 1941 by Christian pacifist Archibald Barrington. But it was not until the start of the seventies that the counterculture began packing up and moving to the country. The move was driven in part by Americans and Europeans who had come looking for an alternative way of life. Some had already been involved with communes overseas. With plenty of open space and available land, New Zealand seemed ideal.

Long Louis, one of the first rural New Zealand communes of the counterculture era, was established in Hokianga by a woodcarver called Pipi, whose real name was Philip Rutherford and who claimed to be a descendant of Nelson-born physicist Ernest Rutherford, and a recent arrival from San Francisco known as Treefoot.

Treefoot had once been Larry Pischoff, but had been through a number of names since his San Francisco schooldays. Sick of jokes about his surname, he changed it to Bischoff, then his Christian name to Max. By the end of the sixties, Max Bischoff had graduated from Stanford University and was living in Haight-Ashbury, attending Grateful Dead and Jefferson Airplane concerts, smoking dope as often as he could, and working as a hospital orderly. Though he had been given a low draft status and was not likely to be sent to Vietnam, the ongoing war offended his pacifist beliefs. When four students were shot dead by members of the National Guard during an anti-war demonstration at Kent State University in May 1970, he knew it was time to leave. He considered Canada, Sweden and Australia, but in the end he opted for New Zealand, the country he knew least about, working his passage south on a Norwegian freighter. On Jervois Road in Auckland, a few hours after docking, he crossed paths with a long-haired stranger who gave him the address of a crash pad and said he would be welcome there.

Some months later, stoned at a party in a Ponsonby flat, he was told that one of the women living there had just had a baby. What was the child's name? he asked. Treefoot Sam, came the reply, or so he imagined. In fact, the baby was just plain Sam, but the name Treefoot

Geodesic dome in Grafton, Auckland, early 1970s. Max Oettli photograph, Alexander Turnbull Library, PAColl-1386-1

had inexplicably entered his head and kept knocking around in there. It sounded to him like a Native American Indian name, or something out of *The Lord of the Rings*. At some point in the evening he went to change the record—it was the Rolling Stones, as usual—and the sudden silence seemed to turn everyone's attention towards him. Sensing the moment was his and that it was his duty to make something of it, he spluttered out a spontaneous announcement: 'I have just changed my name. To Treefoot.' He heard applause.

Treefoot fell in with a group who were raising money to buy land for a commune. Neil Young's new song 'Are You Ready for the Country?' rang in his ears like a summons. In November 1971, the group moved into a rented farmhouse in Waiotemarama, Hokianga. This disparate bunch—which included a Krishnamurti follower and an American exile from the aerospace industry—didn't hold together, but in Hokianga Treefoot met Pipi Rutherford, who was living in a bus with his wife Mani Barr and at least one child. Rutherford had heard about a piece of land in a damp valley that had belonged to a bushman, hermit and former gumdigger known as Long Louis. Treefoot gave Pipi the $500 he had saved, and the land was purchased from Long Louis's nephew.[17]

Alison McClean, living in urban Grafton, was an occasional visitor to Long Louis. 'You got off the bus on the way to … somewhere. You had to first traverse farms and then go up and down bushy valleys to find the commune. You had to camp out overnight, or I did because I got off the bus late, and I had a little baby. She was good at wiggling under electric fences. It was land that was too steep to mill the kauri out of so [the kauri] were there in all their pristine glory, way deep in hill country. It was really rough country.

'They lived in houses they built themselves. There was a guy called Snail who did superb woodcarving. He made a magnificent rocking horse on ropes. You could put a toddler on this rocking horse and sail across the bush.

'The only place you could grow any vegetables was where there was bracken. Bracken would grow where there was a little bit of mud, so they would take out the bracken and grow vegetables there. They were all vegetarian. But it didn't take long before they gave up on vegetarianism and the boys got guns and they became goat eaters.'[18]

It was around this time on a Hokianga back road that an encounter took place between a member of the counterculture and a Member of Parliament.

In early summer 1972, the general election campaign was underway and Matiu Rata, MP for Northern Maori, was on the campaign trail. With him in the Chevrolet Impala were two helpers, both Māori like himself, all three wearing suits. They were hot, uncomfortable and in a hurry. Moving slowly towards them came a horse and its rider, a hippie dressed only in what looked like a kind of loincloth. He was an American and had spent the past couple of years subsisting on a remote piece of land. For Rata it was both a paradox and an epiphany. Here they were, three Māori, 'sweltering in suits in this ostentatious American car' while the barely clad Pākehā seemed 'comfortable, indifferent, with all the time in the world', apparently living a life more akin to that of pre-colonial Māori.[19]

Over the next year Rata would devise a scheme for making tracts of Crown land available for a peppercorn fee to any young people wanting to start their own communities. It was one taken up with alacrity by the newly elected Labour Prime Minister Norman Kirk. Though Kirk could hardly have been mistaken for a hippie, he was a thoughtful, solitary man who shared some of the counterculture's distaste for materialism and wish for more communal values. As his private secretary Margaret Hayward noted, the Ohu Scheme, as it became known—'ohu' meaning communal working group—appealed to Kirk 'as an antidote to the ills of modern society, as well as a means of showing people the virtues of a simpler life'.[20]

Matiu Rata, addressing the Ohu working party in August 1974, enlarged on this point of view. 'The over-emphasis on the gross national product, perpetual greed, speculation, profiteering, unethical practices and the cult of individualism can only result in the further alienation of those who seek a return to community and group feelings. I share with other Government members the hope that the Ohu will, in some way, lead the way to a more concerned society and recapture anew the deep links of people and land.'[21]

Pete Pharazyn went to an early meeting of groups interested in the scheme. For two or three years he had been living in Wellington in semi-communal flats going-on crash pads. There had been a lot of LSD around, and the young musician and photolithographer was feeling 'the need to ground'. The pastoral folk songs of Cat Stevens were starting to appeal to him more than the psychedelic rock of Quicksilver Messenger Service. As a kid growing up in Hawke's Bay he had spent a lot of time outdoors, hunting and trapping possums; now he had a hankering to get back to the land.[22]

By this time, twenty-five groups wanting to start communities had been approved; one, a Coromandel-based community calling itself Sunburst, had already begun. Yet despite the enthusiasm of Kirk, Rata and some other government members, opposition at lower levels of bureaucracy would ultimately undermine them. Federated Farmers, which had a representative on the Ohu Advisory Committee, vocally criticised the scheme. Margaret Hayward had already noted in March that 'press officer Peter Kelsey, who has transferred from our office to work on the scheme, of which he is an enthusiastic advocate, tells me the Lands and Survey Department has decided that applicants should have only land designated as suitable for nothing else "and that's pretty bad land to go onto"'.[23]

Ohu bath. Angela Middleton
photograph, private collection

Where suitable land was found, other problems arose. The idea of small communities of artisans springing up in the wilderness might have appealed to Kirk, but it horrified some of the county councils responsible for issuing building consents. Croixilles Ohu in Marlborough was denied its application to build extra dwellings on the grounds that it would 'promote sporadic residential development in a rural zone'.[24] When another group chose an area surrounded by private property, the property owners denied its request to build an access road.[25]

And there was the ill-preparedness of the founders themselves. Pete Pharazyn's group was offered a site on the Ahu Ahu Stream, a remote tributary of the Whanganui River where First World War veterans had once tried to farm. They set off up the River Road in two cars, one with a canoe strapped to the roof, bringing with them a few tools, a little food, two dozen marijuana plants and a lot of wire netting. After leaving their vehicles at the landing, they ferried themselves and supplies to the opposite bank of the Ahu Ahu, then made the one-hour trek up the steep, narrow track to the communal site. They found the original farmhouse, now roofless, and set up camp in its derelict remains. Over the next few days, attempts were made to turn over the soil. Vegetable seedlings were planted; wire mesh arranged to protect the marijuana. If it was already dawning on these urban refugees that the project might be more challenging than they had imagined, it was confirmed when they made their second trip a month or so later. Rabbits and possums had decimated the garden; they had even got through the wire mesh and eaten the marijuana. Pete recalls: 'It was at that point that I realised that the compadres that I'd chosen to go onto the new frontier with had absolutely no rural skills at all. I became fairly disillusioned.'[26]

Another group, further up the valley, were better prepared; their commune, the Ahu Ahu Ohu, survived until about 2010. Pete's group never returned. Others, seeing the barricades of red tape that had to be broken through before they could set foot on a piece of land, opted for private purchases instead.

If the fate of the Ohu Scheme was just about sealed, Norman Kirk's unexpected death in August 1974, followed closely by the election of a National government, finished it off. Venn Young, Minister of Lands for the incoming government, said: 'If Ohu is to continue and if the Government is going to be involved, I must be sure these people are making a contribution to the wider society.'[27] Tauranga MP Keith Allen expressed National Party sentiments less discreetly when he referred to Ohu residents as 'a pack of bludgers'.[28]

Nevertheless, ohu or no ohu, more than forty intentional communities were established between 1970 and 1975, and dozens more would spring up over the remainder of the decade, with several lasting into the current century. Their names have touches of Tolkien, William Blake and hippie folksinger Donovan, and reflect the utopian romanticism of their founders: Clearwater, Earth Extract, Goodwill,

Gricklegrass, Moonsilver Forest, Renaissance, Sunburst, Rainbow Valley, Happisam.

The founders and inhabitants of the assorted communes represented a range of intentions. There were those who were attracted by ideals of self-sufficiency. They farmed, grew things and built elaborate shelters. Some developed crafts such as pottery, weaving, silversmithing. Some were motivated by ideals of living sustainably in harmony with the environment. Some sought an alternative way to raise their children than in a suburban nuclear family. Some went to have sex with a lot of different people. Some wanted to be left alone to take drugs; native bush, rugged clifftops and rambling riverbeds offering idyllic settings for acid trips. Remote rural locations provided opportunities for the clandestine cultivation of cannabis. The police, it was hoped, would be many valleys away. Some went to be closer to God. At Sunburst, one of the ohu that came to fruition, some members followed Guru Mahara Ji. For a while the Sunday Creek commune was almost entirely made up of orange-clad followers of Bhagwan Shree Rajneesh. A few were organised around particular charismatic individuals, sometimes with disastrous results, as in the case of Centrepoint [see Chapter 14].

Systems of organisation were as varied as the inhabitants. Some were highly structured, with committees, regular meetings and rules. Others were essentially anarchist. Some pooled resources and shared possessions. At others, individuals or families retained a degree of autonomy. They might have their own dwelling, while cooking and eating took place communally.

Julian Rosenberg was part of an urban collective from Auckland who were drawn to a piece of land at the northern tip of the Coromandel Peninsula. 'We were talking about, wouldn't it be good to have a place to just go and be ourselves, basically? To have a place that was completely safe and undisturbed, to experience the joys of exploring our relationship with the landscape and wild New Zealand? We were also interested in psychedelics.' They realised that 'if we grouped our money we could buy a farm on a postman's wage. I was a postman, my girlfriend was a postman, we worked six months and contributed 50 percent of a share each, and we were one of sixteen, and it went ahead. We could even employ a lawyer!'[29]

The communes engaged with the outside world to varying degrees. Some essentially operated as small businesses, selling produce or crafts. Sometimes communards would forge relationships with 'straight' farming neighbours, and work for them as labourers.

Artists and musicians were drawn to the rural communal lifestyle as a source of both inspiration and cheap living. For rock bands, 'getting it together in the country' became a credo, having originated with the British band Traffic, who had famously left the bustle of Birmingham in the summer of 1967 for a communal cottage in rural Berkshire, and Bob Dylan and his sometime backing group the Band, who had based themselves in the Catskill Mountains of upstate New York.

TOP: Jeff Scholes' pottery, Waitākere, 1974. Ian Baker photograph, private collection

BOTTOM: A house at Mahana, Coromandel, early 1980s. Peter Aagaard photograph

It was in this spirit that the Wellington band Highway headed over the hills to the Wairarapa where they rehearsed in a barn. Miles from any neighbours, they could play as long and loud as they liked. But though the pastoral setting inspired an entire album's worth of new material, no one thought to record or notate any of it, and it became lost in the fog of time.

Billy Te Kahika quit the Human Instinct in 1971 and formed Billy TK and the Powerhouse, an ensemble of up to fifteen players who took up residence in a rural mansion in Cheltenham in the Manawatū. Each member had his or her own room. There was space to rehearse and tennis courts to relax. 'We weren't worried about money,' Te Kahika remembers. 'Money wasn't the issue. It was for the art. We just used to all try to help each other, like one big family. That held us together.'[30]

Bruno Lawrence had left for Australia in 1973, taking the BLERTA bus and a version of the group that included founding members Kemp Tuirirangi, Chris Seresin and Ian Watkin, plus new recruits Fane Flaws, Patrick Bleakley and Greg Taylor, leaving co-founder Geoff Murphy behind to concentrate on his filmmaking. In BLERTA's absence, Murphy, cameraman Alun Bollinger, and actor and writer Martyn Sanderson and their young families co-operatively bought a piece of land at Waimarama Beach in Hawke's Bay. There they set up what would come to be known as Snoring Waters but is often referred to as the BLERTA commune, though initially its creative focus was more on movies than music. Alun Bollinger says: 'It was purely pragmatic because it was too expensive to live in the city. The Murphys had five kids, the Sandersons were on the bones of their arses, having been repatriated from India where they had been living with their five kids. [My wife] Helen and I had been looking around north of Auckland but never liked that idea because then you would be stuck with Auckland between you and the rest of the country.'[31]

Painters, too, headed to the hills. Michael Illingworth, whose visions of a return to nature had caused trouble in 1965 when his painting *Adam and Eve* was the subject of an obscenity complaint, went to Coroglen on the Coromandel. For years he had railed against mainstream society and parodied it in his paintings. Now he would turn his back on the mainstream altogether. Initially the Illingworths lived with others, but in the end it was just Michael, his wife Dene and their children. Money was scarce, and though the Illingworths remained in Coroglen from 1973 until Michael's death in 1988, the demands of living off the land impinged on his artistic output.[32]

There were those who believed that dropping out was copping out; that to change the system or bring about the revolution you had to be in the thick of it, not on a remote hilltop smoking grass, nursing a child or talking to God. An educated elite seeking self-sufficiency in a commune or other closed, minority community was betraying its social role, Russian-British architect Serge Chermayeff told students at the Warkworth congress in early 1971.[33] Others insisted that dropping out was itself a political act. 'Dropping out of the system ... is the most effective way to influence and ultimately destroy the Establishment', Malcolm Gramaphone had opined in the first issue of his *Counter Culture Free Press*.[34]

Tahuna Farm was set up in 1974 by a group sharing an idea that Olive Jones summarised as: '"the Establishment" was corrupt ... society was over-regulated and ... capitalism was responsible for an unequal and money-obsessed world'.[35] It was situated on four acres outside Nelson and leased from Dominion Breweries. Its founders chose to remain independent of city utilities such as electricity or sewerage, reinforcing, as Jones notes, 'the fiercely independent and cynical attitude of the founding group towards "the Establishment"'.[36] It was an almost nineteenth-century existence. Horse and cart were used, and the land was farmed organically, in contrast to the chemical-reliant approach of most New Zealand farmers at the time.

And there were those who were aware of the debate, had not decided but were exploring the possibilities. By the age of twenty, Catherine Delahunty was already a veteran of CND, SSSA, Vietnam War and apartheid protests. Now she had gone to live on the same communally owned land as Julian Rosenberg at Colville Bay Point. 'Sometimes it feels like preparation for a new order after the collapse of urban consumer capitalism,' she wrote in 1975. 'Sometimes it's a much blinder struggle of each person to live and feel productive. I cannot be more specific about what we are doing or describe inventions or successes (technical or social) as these are yet to come, only that there is a good spirit in it and a willingness to change.'[37]

UP THE RIVER

As for Matiu Rata's ohu vision, what survived? His initial passion for the scheme had derived, in part, from what he saw as values shared by the new communards and Māori. Though the vast majority of these communards were Pākehā, it must have been heartening to Rata to see Pākehā taking a step towards Māori values, rather than trampling over tikanga in their customary rush to embrace a Eurocentric concept of progress. Many of the communes established in this period were known by Māori names: Marahau, Moehau, Parapara, Tahuna, Tauiwi Takakau, Opuhi, Rangiputa, Timatanga, Whenua Pa, Tauhai, Puketa, Mahoe Farm, Ahu Ahu Ohu, Wharekahika, Whareroa. In reality, few of the communards seemed to give much consideration to Māori ways of doing things, in practice or principle. Some espoused a collectivism that might have been closer to that of tikanga Māori than other more individualistic structures, but the similarities were largely coincidental.

An exception was James K. Baxter's commune which he founded at Jerusalem, on the upper reaches of the Whanganui River, specifically for its proximity to a Māori community, from which he believed he, his fellow communards and perhaps the rest of New Zealand had much to learn.

In 1968, after two years as an honorary academic in Dunedin, the forty-one-year-old poet was in 'a state very close to despair'.[38] He found himself 'violently crucified by sex, anger, self-pity, hatred of self and life'.[39] Forever fretting about society's ills, his relationship with God and his own bothersome libido, he reached a personal crisis when his wife Jacqui, 'finding the strain of life too heavy—went away for a few days without saying where she was going or for how long … In the darkness of my wife's absence … I abandoned myself to God's guidance and mercy … And when I woke in the morning, the first thought in my mind—an entirely new and unprecedented, and as it were radioactive thought—was "Jerusalem."'[40] He didn't mean the city in Palestine, but the small remote mission station on the Whanganui.

While the thought may have been unprecedented, it spoke to all the elements that swirled constantly, if not always harmoniously, within his being: those of the poet, the moralist, the social worker, the Catholic, the student of taha Māori.

To the poet and the Catholic, the symbolism of a place called Jerusalem must have been irresistible. How much he already knew about the mission station is uncertain. In the late nineteenth century it had been run as a home for the children of unmarried mothers by the dynamic and socially committed missioner Suzanne Aubert. Baxter was aware that the local community was mostly Māori and, as he outlined in a series of intense letters, he would go there to 'learn the spoken Māori from a man whom God would provide for me'.[41]

By the time he headed from Auckland to Jerusalem some eighteen months later, he had consolidated the idea that his new home would also provide a type of refuge for 'young people with drug problems'.[42] This is what he told the Superior-General of the Home of Compassion in Wellington, who gave him permission to stay in a cottage near the Jerusalem convent.

John Newton, whose book *The Double Rainbow* details the story of the Jerusalem commune, notes that the poet founded 'the country's first and most influential experiment in hippie communalism' almost in spite of himself.[43] As he points out, Baxter's vision 'of a community where the people, both Māori and Pākehā, would try to live without money or books, worship God and work on the land' is not entirely typical of the sixties-style countercultural commune, and Baxter was in many ways an anomalous figure.[44] He was of the wrong age and wrong religion, and had the wrong temperament. And yet Baxter was attracted to the hippies, and by the time he got to Boyle Crescent in Auckland he had grown to look like one—or rather a cross between a hippie, a homeless person and an Old Testament prophet. Though he had long given up alcohol, he was partial to hashish. And while his sexual appetites seemed to cause him more anxiety, guilt and convoluted self-justification than free love was supposed to, he undoubtedly slept around.

There is no obviously comparable character in Britain or the United States. Though almost exactly the same age as American Beat poet and countercultural icon Allen Ginsberg (Baxter was six days younger), the two had little in common. One was a gay, ebullient Buddhist Jew; the other a dour, heterosexual Catholic convert. Baxter's poetry owed far more to classical sources than the Beats' did, and despite relating strongly to Kerouac's *On the Road*, which he called 'that masterpiece of the psychology of flight — flight from marriage, from settled occupation, and from what other people think of us', the writing of Kerouac, Ginsberg and their peers had no apparent influence on his work.[45]

For the first few months at Jerusalem, Baxter lived mostly by himself in what became known as the Nuns' Cottage. His relationship with the sisters in the convent was uneasy, but in Wiremu Hakopa Toa Te Awhitu he felt he might find both a mediator and the teacher of te reo Māori he had been counting on. Originally from Okahukura on the upper river, Father Te Awhitu had experienced a traditional Māori upbringing but had gone to Catholic boarding schools and, in 1944, become the first Māori to be ordained as a Catholic priest. He had returned to the river as the resident priest the year before Baxter's arrival. Baxter attended the Catholic services and gradually gained the trust of the pā.

The summer of 1969–70 saw a small but steady influx of young people Baxter had befriended during his time in Auckland, but from Labour Weekend, October 1970 the numbers swelled. By this time Ngāti Hau had given Baxter the use of a second dwelling which became known as the Top House. It had no windows or doors, blackberries grew through the floorboards and there was a hole in the roof, but it was made habitable with help from Father Te Awhitu (a skilled carpenter) and other local Māori. Eventually a third dwelling, also derelict, was cleaned up, occupied and christened Bag End, after Tolkien. An illustrated cover story in the January 1971 issue of the *New Zealand Weekly News* attracted further communards as well as curious on-lookers. Over the course of the year Jerusalem would receive much more publicity, a lot of it courted by Baxter himself.

In Suzanne Aubert's day, Jerusalem had been a refuge for orphans; now Baxter drew orphans of a different kind. He called his largely Pākehā tribe Ngā Mōkai — for which he offered the translation 'the fatherless'. Some were struggling with addictions and psychiatric problems, others were just disillusioned with mainstream society. In trying to mirror the Māori example, Baxter would offer them unconditional aroha. How did it work out? By Baxter's reckoning, pretty well. In 1971, in his *Jerusalem Daybook*, he wrote: 'In the course of the community's existence three persons have had to go from here to the mental hospital. It's not a bad record, considering the fact that at least fifteen hundred people have passed through the community, and some who were well out of their skulls when they arrived were able to recover.'[46]

TOP: James K. Baxter, Curious Cove, 1970. Nick Bollinger photograph, private collection

BOTTOM: Bag End, Jerusalem, 1971. *Wanganui Chronicle / New Zealand Herald*, Alexander Turnbull Library, PAColl-7327-1

In his tramp-like appearance, his living without income and trusting to the kindness of strangers, Baxter actively embraced the idea of poverty. Yet he was also a showman and loved an audience. Though he talked of working the land, and soon after his arrival had planted crops of kūmara and potatoes, Jerusalem was never the kind of experiment in self-sufficiency that most of the other communes aspired to. Don Franks—known around Wellington as Guitar Don, because he was rarely seen without an instrument in hand—dropped into Jerusalem after dropping out of university. 'There was always a packet of cheap tea, a packet of flour and a packet of porridge and some milk powder, but there was never anything much more than that,' he recalls. 'Sometimes we'd shoot goats and stuff. There was a pathetic attempt at a garden. But it wasn't an alternative way of living at all. It was a crash pad. There was a bit of dope, there wasn't much. People would sit around talking or playing guitars. Most of us were smoking cigarettes then, and you'd smoke a cigarette like a joint because people didn't have much. It was wasting it to let it burn in your fingers, so you would pass it round.'

People would generally stay a week or two, but Guitar Don stayed for several months. 'You'd hitch-hike up to Auckland or back to Wellington and you'd work for a week, like you could in those days, and come back with a whole lot of groceries and cigarettes and stay for a couple of days and when everything was eaten someone else would go off.'[47]

But a reciprocal relationship also developed between Ngā Mōkai and the pā. As Newton says, Baxter 'inscribed Māori values at the heart of his own communal household' but also stressed, to both Ngā Mōkai and the media, the household's collective dependence on the pā. And the arrival of Ngā Mōkai filled a demographic void left when urban drift had depleted local Ngāti Hau of their youth.

The hippies helped out, painting and labouring around the pā. Don Franks remembers: 'I did a bit of work for Toro Poutini. He was the farmer, like the squire. Him and his wife Alice talked Māori most of the time. He thought Baxter's religious stuff was silly. He said "He likes the fella upstairs! I don't think there's a fella upstairs ... "'[48] Eventually, Franks returned to Wellington and became a factory worker and trade unionist, having decided that organised labour was a more effective path to achieving social justice than sitting on a country porch playing guitar.

The commune attracted the salacious interest of the media, which had already shown a tendency to equate a lot of young people living together with an orgy of sex and drugs. Baxter's admirers shrugged it off, yet when a man in his mid-forties cultivates a group of acolytes mostly less than half his age there is a question of safety. Biographies by Baxter's contemporaries W. H. Oliver and Frank McKay, published in 1983 and 1990 respectively, refer to the poet in this period as 'still ostentatiously pious and irrepressibly randy', and note that the police 'disliked seeing him walking down Queen Street holding the hands of young girls', yet neither writer interrogates such behaviour.[49] There was an inevitable power imbalance in Baxter's relationships with the young women, some of which involved consensual sexual relations, others in which he appears to have been coercive. The publication of Baxter's letters in 2019 revealed an admission that he had raped his wife. In the wake of this, Ros Lewis would write that while she was living at Jerusalem when she was eighteen, Baxter had tried to rape her.[50]

In September 1971 it was reported that owing to the complaints of Pākehā farmers about trespassing hippies, and of some Ngāti Hau who believed the publicity was hurting the community, the commune began to disband. In fact, Baxter's relationship with Ngāti Hau was much more complex and enduring, and by summer he was back with a smaller group. He would continue to come and go from Jerusalem until his death from a heart attack, aged forty-six, in Auckland in October 1972.

Baxter was buried at Jerusalem. His tangi drew hundreds up the river road and received widespread publicity, after which the media turned its gaze away. Without its charismatic and conflicted figurehead, the Jerusalem commune, as far as mainstream New Zealand was concerned, was over. And yet the next few years saw it not only continue but flourish as it never had in Baxter's time, with Ngā Mōkai becoming increasingly involved in the life of the pā and hippies scattered through the wider community. The real end didn't come until 1975 with the death of Toro Poutini, who had been one of the strongest links between Ngāti Hau and Ngā Mōkai, and the departure of Greg Chalmers, who at just twenty-two had largely assumed the role of commune leader following Baxter's death. Even then, many of Ngā Mōkai went on to other communal situations around the country.

Baxter excepted, the counterculture, while producing a variety of templates for alternative living, seemed for the most part to give little consideration to biculturalism and what it might learn from tangata whenua, or notice that a communal culture already existed in New Zealand and had done so for roughly a thousand years. In a 1992 essay, Māori filmmaker Merata Mita reflected on the commune movement with a mixture of bemusement and irritation. 'The Sixties was a decade of reaction to an authoritarian system and the fact that life since World War II had not been much fun. A concerted effort was made by my generation to improve the quality of life by looking for humanistic alternatives ... Like many other Māori, I found myself part of the puzzled audience being expounded to on the virtues of communal life, by white urbanites who had gone back to *our* land.'[51]

THE NEW SEEKERS

nine

In the sixties the motorcycle was a symbol of rebel freedom. The Hells Angels Motorcycle Club (which had a New Zealand chapter from 1961) and other two-wheeled troupes had enshrined the vehicle as an image of danger and defiance. Bob Dylan wore a Triumph logo on the cover of his epochal *Highway 61 Revisited* album, and almost brought his career to an early close when he crashed his motorcycle on a Woodstock back road. The film *Easy Rider* set its rebel heroes on a road through the deadly heart of a conformist society, while Robert Pirsig's novel *Zen and the Art of Motorcycle Maintenance* used the road trip as a philosophical journey in search of harmony between the rational and the romantic. Jack Kerouac's road trips had usually involved cars rather than bikes. A murderous quantity of greenhouse gases will have been released in pursuit of his visions, though no one was thinking about such things back then. What mattered was being on the road.

Hitch-hiker and dog, Wellesley Street, Auckland, 1972. Ans Westra photograph, Alexander Turnbull Library, PA-Group-00941

ON THE ROAD

> To the casual observer, his life must have seemed an endless series of repetitive grubby excursions, campings, borrowings, ripoffs, bad deals, specious survival techniques. To those who subscribed to the cult of Chink, he was 'on the road': free and spaced, a gypsy freak. But those closest to him could see that Ngaruawahia was Marrakesh. Xanadhu ...[1]

The protagonist of *Dick Seddon's Great Dive*, a novella by New Zealand writer Ian Wedde, is a free-loving, motorcycle-riding, pot-smoking, blues-singing and ultimately doomed youth called Chink. The closer you zoom in on this freewheeling individual, the more his journey seems to spin outward, to places mystical and mythical.

The novella was first published as an edition of the literary magazine *Islands* in 1976, but seems to have been set a few years earlier, when those roads, either real or imagined, were still wide open. As the decade went on, house trucks—an even more visible statement of the freewheeling philosophy—began to make an appearance: mobile homes handbuilt out of packing cases, corrugated iron and other recycled materials, often to elaborate and eccentric designs.

But going on the road didn't actually require your own truck, motorcycle, car—or any wheels at all. At a time when there were fewer than a million vehicles on New Zealand roads (there are more than four times that number today), it was common to hitch-hike. The year Wedde's novella came out, I was seventeen. One morning I took the train from Wellington to Paraparaumu, strolled over to Highway 1 and stuck out my thumb. Thirteen hours and half a dozen rides later, I was in Auckland. The last 200-odd kilometres was as the passenger of an off-duty policeman who insisted on walking me to the open door of the Grafton flat where I would be staying, and who stood on the doorstep for an uncomfortably long time, peering suspiciously inside while my pot-smoking art student friend Simon greeted me.

At that time hitch-hiking was my primary mode of transport to any destination further than walking distance away. Longhaired, with neither a vehicle nor a driver's licence, I never had to foot it far before I got a lift, though it sometimes transpired that the driver had mistaken me for a girl. Occasionally my host would ask where I was from, what I did for a job, but more often they just wanted someone on whom to offload their own thoughts. I heard opinions about rugby, race relations, students, drugs and whatever had been on television the night before. Because I was availing myself of their goodwill, I tended to remain tactfully silent, even if I disagreed with them.

While I usually knew where I was headed, more intrepid hitch-hikers would trust rumour and chance to be their guides. Alison McClean would hear about a new commune somewhere in Coromandel or Hokianga, and on a whim hit the road to check it out, sometimes hitching with a male friend, sometimes alone. 'Truck drivers were allowed to pick you up in those days and they did because they were lonely. And Māori always stopped. They'd pull up, squash in, sit on knees, even if the car was crammed to bursting they'd fit you in somehow.'[2]

But the exploratory spirit carried some travellers much further afield. In 1973, Zeke and Judy Alley, in their early twenties and recently married, were living in a large Wellington flat on the side of a hill overlooking the harbour. That year a particularly strong variety of marijuana called Buddha had arrived in Wellington. There was a lot of LSD around as well. Zeke remembers one visitor running down the hall towards the balcony thinking she was an aeroplane. He was relieved when she stopped before the end of the runway. One day an old flatmate turned up, just back from Afghanistan. Zeke remembers: 'Listening to his stories of wild and exotic places I thought, That's what I want to do.' He and Judy went to Sydney, saved some money and hit the road.[3]

HIPPIE TRAILS

The hippie trail, as it became known, had been carved by intrepid North Americans and Europeans travelling overland from Europe to India and Nepal. Using local transport, eating whatever the locals ate and staying in the cheapest accommodation, they could make their money last far longer than it would in any Western city. Along the way they would pass

On the road. Angela Middleton photograph, private collection

through countries where drugs were readily available, clothes were colourful and the way of life was eye-opening.

New Zealanders began returning from European trips via this route around the mid-sixties, bringing home hashish and hepatitis. Before long, some were making the journey in the opposite direction, starting from New Zealand or Australia, travelling via Southeast Asia to India, the Middle East and Europe.

Zeke dug out an old diary for me and retraced the trip that he and Judy made.[4] In early September 1973, they flew from Darwin to Baucau in what was then Portuguese Timor. They hired a jeep and driver to take them to the border of Indonesian Timor and flew on to Bali. Then it was a bus to Surabaya in East Java, and a train to Jakarta. By mid-October they were in Singapore. From there it was another bus to Malacca in Malaysia, and a taxi—ridiculous but cheap—to the Malaysian capital, Kuala Lumpur. They hitch-hiked to the east coast beach town of Kota Bahru where they met a Malaysian liquor salesman who offered them a lift back to KL. On the way he stopped to look up an old friend who turned out to be the Sultan of Terengganu. At the Sultan's palace, Zeke and Judy were left alone while their friend the liquor salesman conducted business with the Sultan. It was Ramadan, so this demanded even more discretion than usual.

In late October they took the ferry to the island of Penang. Hearing about a coastal village where the locals rented out rooms to hippies, they headed to Batu Ferringhi which was full of young travellers like themselves. 'Every so often you'd come upon a nexus where west-bound travellers like us would meet people coming the other way. We'd all share advice on where to stay, where to eat, how much to score, things to avoid,' Zeke recalls. On several occasions they crossed paths with a couple of junkies they recognised from Wellington who were travelling with a young child.[5]

After a side trip across the Straits of Malacca to Belawan in Sumatra, it was a ferry from Penang back to the Malaysian mainland, then a train to Thailand, heading for Bangkok. It wasn't possible to cross the land borders into Burma, and Bangladesh was generally avoided owing to war and cyclones, so from Bangkok it was a bus to Chiang Mai in the north, a jumping-off point to the hill-tribe villages nearby which they accessed by minibus, river boat and foot.

In mid-December they took another river boat to Ban Huai Sai on the Mekong where they bought Air Lao tickets to Luang Prabang. They arrived in the Laotian capital Vientiane on the back of a truck just before Christmas, and checked into a hotel where a three-room suite, with plumbing, cost NZ$3.50 per night. They splashed out on Christmas dinner in a French restaurant. It cost them NZ$5 each.

On Boxing Day they returned to Thailand, taking a rickshaw to the bus station, then a bus to Udon Thani (Asian headquarters for American bombing missions in Laos and Vietnam), and on to Bangkok.

In early January they flew from Bangkok to Burma. In Pagan they watched the sun set over the Irrawaddy from high in the grand pagodas. The dust in the air turned the sun red and the river appeared to be made of gold. They left Pagan in a horse and cart, but returned to Rangoon by overnight train before flying to Calcutta.

By now they were well acclimatised to Asia. An English brother and sister they had met in Bangkok invited them to stay in Sri Lanka with their aunt and uncle, former tea planters whose estate had been nationalised. They travelled there via the east coast of India, reconnecting on the way with several friends they had made further back down the trail. They moved around Burma by bus and train, visited temples and coral beaches, and eventually returned to India by ferry. They spent the hot days of early March in the cool hill station of Ootacamund, or Ooty as the colonials called it, the original home of the East India Company, with its rose gardens, Anglican churches, hunting hounds and billiard parlours (snooker was invented there) giving it a surreal Englishness.

Mysore, Bangalore, and on to Goa, a heroin haven where used syringes glinted in the sand. From Bombay it was four consecutive train rides to the Nepalese border; then a bus to Kathmandu over dangerous roads on which you had to trust the drivers whose own faith rested with the deities depicted on the fronts of the vehicles.

Varanasi, New Delhi, Agra, back to New Delhi, and into Pakistan at the Wagah border. A bus from Lahore to Rawalpindi, and up into the cool Kaghan Valley. Eventually they returned to the sweltering plains and took a bus to Peshawar, the gateway to the Khyber Pass, and into Afghanistan. In Bamiyan, they saw the giant Buddhas carved into cliffs that would be destroyed by the Taliban in 2001. In early August they crossed into Iran, then under the Shah's rule. Tehran was strikingly modern by comparison with any city they had seen in months. Men and women wore Western clothes.

From there it was an eighty-hour bus trip to Istanbul. Greece and Turkey were fighting over Cyprus, but Zeke and Judy were still able to cross into Greece. After a few days in Athens they took a ferry to the island of Ios, where the hillsides were covered in temporary shelters, recently abandoned by European travellers. Lying in one of the shacks, a full moon shining in their faces, they knew they were getting ill. They moved to a furnished room in the village, but by then it was clear they had both contracted hepatitis. They made their nauseous way back to Piraeus, the port of Athens, where Judy collapsed in the street. A crowd gathered and helped her to a seat, then hailed them a cab back to the city. A few days later they flew to London, where their gaunt appearance shocked their friends. It was almost exactly a year since they left New Zealand.

Along the hippie trail, 1973. Zeke Alley in Pakistan (top) and a picnic in Nepal (bottom). **Zeke Alley private collection**

Travel helped create the counterculture. Before the sixties, leaving New Zealand meant a long and costly journey, usually by ship. It took six weeks to sail to Britain, the most common destination, where many Pākehā had relatives. Over the decade airfares came down, wages went up and an increasing number of New Zealanders began moving about the globe. In her history of the Kiwi tradition known as OE (overseas experience), Jude Wilson estimates that between 1960 and 1970 the average weeks' earnings required to fly from Sydney to London dropped by more than half.[6] Through its colonial relationship with Britain, many young New Zealanders were able to stay and work there as long as they liked. There would be work for them on arrival, and plenty of jobs back in New Zealand whenever they decided to return home.

Others took roads less travelled. In contrast to their risk-averse parents, who had lived through a world war, experienced austerity and loss, and tended to value comfort and security over adventure, boomers saw a world of ideas and possibilities, and they were eager to get out and explore it. Previous generations had been to places like Malaysia or Turkey as part of New Zealand's war effort. Now hippie trailblazers were travelling there to live among the locals, and gain insights into their lives and customs. They grew to appreciate different kinds of food, music, clothing and belief systems. The travels, the tales and the movement of ideas all contributed to a new and less insular way of seeing the world and New Zealand's place in it. Injustices in countries as remote as South Africa or Czechoslovakia came to be viewed as a global concern, and had young New Zealanders taking to the streets in protest.

For Zeke Alley, a year on the hippie trail had changed his goals and expectations. In London, his degree got him a job as a biochemist, but he hated it. 'My head was still back in India where we had seen a lot of other possibilities of life and how people live, a diverse range of people, both travellers and people who lived there.'[7]

In Nepal he had got talking to a fellow traveller and, as was the custom, offered to share his chillum. To Zeke's surprise, the pipe was politely refused. His new friend explained that he had just completed a course in meditation at a monastery just out of Kathmandu and it had given him plenty to think about without the help of hashish. Curious to know more, Zeke visited the monastery himself and resolved to return there one day. In the meantime, he began to read all he could about Buddhism. Though brought up a Methodist — his father taught Bible class and Sunday school, his mother played the organ, and the family went to church every Sunday — he had decided, before he left home, that he was an atheist. He says, 'The thing I liked most about Buddhism — in the Western tradition there's always people telling you what's right and what's wrong. In Buddhism they educate you to make your own decisions about what's right and wrong. They assume a bit more intelligence on the part of the user.'[8]

Not long after his return to Wellington he saw a sign in a window advertising a meditation course. It was being run by one of the devotees from the temple in Kathmandu who had heard there was a demand for meditation teachers in New Zealand.

COSMIC VOICES

In 1960, 90 percent of New Zealanders identified as Christian—mostly Anglican, Presbyterian, Catholic or Methodist—though few went to church very often. The first sign that the decade might see meat-and-potatoes Christianity replaced by an exotic spiritual smorgasbord was a visit in 1960 from George King.

Born in Shropshire in 1919, King had for many years been a practitioner of yoga—unusual for a white Englishman at that time. He was fanatical about it, and practised up to ten hours a day. One day in 1954 while taking a break from his asanas to wash the dishes in his Maida Vale flat, he was startled to hear a voice, though there was no one else in the room. 'Prepare yourself!' it commanded him. 'You are to become the voice of Interplanetary Parliament.'

The meaning of this perplexing, unexpected instruction was revealed a few days later when he received another surprise: a visit from an Indian yogi who, according to King, arrived and departed without ever opening the apartment's locked door. The mysterious voice, the yogi explained to him, had belonged to a being from Venus known as the Master Aetherius. Thus satisfied, King founded the Aetherius Society, and devoted himself to spreading the teachings of this cosmic intelligence, whose instructions he found he could receive by placing himself in a meditative trance.[9]

In preparation for the arrival of Aetherius, whom he believed would descend to Earth in a flying saucer, King identified nineteen sites around the world charged with cosmic energy. One was Mount Wakefield, near Aoraki/Mount Cook, which he and an assistant visited on Christmas Eve 1960. It nearly killed them. On their descent they ran out of daylight and wound up spending a freezing night on the mountain, rubbing each other's backs for warmth. But the trip was not in vain. According to King, during the climb he was contacted by Jesus who charged the mountain with spiritual powers. The pair graffitied 'Holy Rock' on a slab of greywacke at the spot where the rendezvous occurred, so that future pilgrims would know where to go.[10] A branch of the Aetherius Society was established in Auckland and continues to this day, while Mount Wakefield still waits for the cosmic master.

Though King's belief system was of his own invention, and his Venusian voices seem like something out of *The Twilight Zone*, his study of yoga, with its origins in Northern India dating back thousands of years, pre-empted a Western interest in non-Western spiritual practices that would grow massively through the 1960s and '70s.

George King (right) and fellow Aetherians practise yogic breathing while keeping an ear out for the cosmic voice. www.aetherius.org.nz

Maharishi Mahesh Yogi became an international celebrity in 1967 when his spiritual services were sought by the counterculture's most famous figureheads, the Beatles. But the Beatles were still barely known outside their native Liverpool when Maharishi paid a visit to New Zealand in 1962.

He had been born in central India as Mahesh Prasad Varma, the son of a mid-level tax official. Sometime in the 1950s, after a decade spent as assistant to the spiritual teacher Swami Brahmananda Saraswati, Mahesh came up with his own method of spiritual teaching which he branded Transcendental Meditation (TM). He became known as Maharishi Mahesh Yogi: 'Maharishi' denoting a teacher, 'Yogi' meaning one who has achieved a high level of spiritual insight. After introducing TM to India, he began touring the world.

A reporter for *Salient* paid six flowers, three pieces of fruit and a week's wages — the going rate — for an audience with the yogi. The recently established Wellington-based Spiritual Regeneration Movement, which hosted the Maharishi's visit, consisted of 'a number of youngish people', several of whom were familiar figures on campus. Others attending ranged from 'sceptics to deeply-convinced advocates' of the Maharishi's philosophy: 'One woman tucked fourteen pounds into her white envelope and carried six expensive blooms; there were also two men who sacrificed a pound each and confided that they had found their sacrificial flowers on a vacant lot on The Terrace.'

After a long wait in a dark corridor, the reporter, now 'bored, irritated and sceptical', was ushered into the Maharishi's presence. The teacher, barefoot, longhaired and white-robed, gave him a mantra — it sounded like *hanginmah* — and instructed him to return to an outer room and wait with the other initiates while repeating the mantra in his head.

'I deliberately sat in front of an open window,' he recalled. 'The cold fresh air was slightly tinged with the smell of fish and chips floating up from a nearby restaurant, and this combination effectively blotted out the gusts of thick, incense-laden air which escaped from the Maharishi's office each time the door was opened.

'I closed my eyes and thought of *hanginmah*.'

Eventually the Maharishi reappeared, but only to bid farewell; he was off to give the evening's lecture. 'I heard him say to one of the girls at the desk "They will meditate for ten minutes in that room, then go home," rather as a soup manufacturer might say "Bring to the boil and simmer."'

Returning to the streets, *Salient*'s reporter thought about the fruit and flowers he had bought as part payment for the session, and wondered what would become of them. He was extremely happy that, as a student, his weekly wages had been non-existent. Still, in spite of his reflexive cynicism, he found himself feeling 'peaceful yet alert' and 'tremendously, unusually energetic'.[11]

TM was just one of many Eastern spiritual movements that would develop followings in New Zealand over the next few years. A growing interest in Zen Buddhism was generated in part by the American author Alan Watts, who had introduced this Indian faith to a Western audience in bestsellers like *The Way of Zen* (1957). Others included Subud, founded in Indonesia in the 1920s by a Javanese mystic called Muhammad Subuh Sumohadiwidjojo; and Bahá'í, which originated in nineteenth-century Persia and, like Subud, did not specify a religious deity for worship, regarding all faiths to be more or less unified in purpose. Subud and Bahá'í established branches in various parts of the country and went about their business in relative privacy.

A group that attracted more attention, because its activities often took place in public, was the Hare Krishna movement. You heard them before you saw them: a tinkling of bells like the approaching of Santa's reindeer, a rhythmic drumming and a chant, 'Hare Krishna, Hare Krishna, Krishna Krishna, Hare Hare, Hare Rama, Hare Rama, Rama Rama, Hare Hare ...', over and over, set to any one of a number of simple interchangeable melodies. Actually, you could *smell* them before you heard them, as they often carried burning sticks of incense. As they rounded the corner, sway-dancing down the footpaths, pedestrians would step aside and stare. The male and female devotees, mostly Pākehā in their late teens to mid-twenties, wore loose white cotton robes and shaved heads, sometimes leaving an uncut tuft at the back. It was like some exotic festival had come to town.

The movement was born in Bengal in the sixteenth century out of the belief that chanting the names of God is good for all, and had been branded the International Society of Krishna Consciousness. Brought to America in 1966, Krishna followers can be seen cavorting in film footage of the 1967 Be-In in Golden Gate Park. From there the movement fanned out across the Western world. By the early seventies, the first local Krishna temple had been established in Landscape Road, Mount Eden, where fifteen or so devotees lived together. One of them, a nineteen-year-old former law student called Kevin Humphrey, told the *Listener* in 1972: 'Most people have become so materialistic, so impersonal, that they regard the universe as a machine with no intelligence behind it.'[12]

Though he lived at the Auckland temple, he had not yet been fully initiated. When the time came, the group's spiritual master would give him a new name and the assurance of release from the painful cycle of birth and death. For now, though, he remained Kevin. His mother had cried when he first joined the movement, but now she visited the temple each week to deliver fresh fruit and vegetables. On a trip to Fiji she had brought back a harmonium, and the devotees gratefully used it to accompany their chanted mantras. Though she was disappointed that Kevin had dropped out of university, she could appreciate other aspects of his lifestyle. As Kevin said, 'We don't get drunk, gamble or engage in illicit sex. In that way it's what every mother wants.'[13]

The Krishna movement drew a number of people who until then might have identified as hippies. They rejected the materialism of the mainstream, and their beliefs included vegetarianism and the existence

Harvey Mann (centre) after moving into the Hare Krishna temple with other members of Space Farm. Ans Westra photograph, Alexander Turnbull Library, PA-Group-00941

and pursuit of higher consciousness. On the other hand, their disciplined regime excluded sex outside marriage and drugs of all varieties.

It was a jolt to the hedonistic hippie crowd when the three members of the band Space Farm, who had been leading high-decibel psychedelic communions in rock venues around the country, appeared in Queen Street in early 1972 with shaven heads and white robes, chanting and handing out fruit and flowers. The entire band had become Krishna devotees. Harvey Mann and Glen Absolum moved into the temple. Along with making other lifestyle changes, they would give up hallucinogenic drugs. 'It wasn't that difficult to move on really,' Harvey Mann told me in 2018, 'because these types of drugs were not really social drugs. Basically you took some, then spent a few days bouncing back and then maybe taking again several days later. At a certain point, I decided I could no longer be bothered doing that.'[14] They recorded one further album as Space Farm, with song titles like 'Message to the World' and 'Krishna' addressing their new-found spiritual beliefs, though it would remain unreleased. Eventually Mann and Absolum re-emerged, pious and drug-free, in the thoroughly Krishna-centric Living Force.

✱

Abstemiousness was also required of members of the Divine Light Mission, an international organisation introduced to New Zealand in 1973. Its leader was a fifteen-year-old guru, Mahara Ji, who had taken over from his father, Divine Light's founder Hans Ji Maharaj, when he was eight. The local spokesman for Divine Light was Dennis Cooney, a prominent protester and Resistance Bookshop radical who had smoke-bombed the US Consulate during a Vietnam demo and attempted to stop a train taking compulsory military trainees to the Waiouru army camp.[15] He had also been arrested for chanting obscenities during the trial of Germaine Greer [of which more in Chapter 12]. Cooney had become a convert of Mahara Ji while attending a festival in Australia, where the Divine Light Mission had recently been established.

Cooney's conversion exposed the rift between the spiritual and political wings of the counterculture when the Auckland Resistance Bookshop prohibited him from using its duplicating machine — which he had helped them buy — to produce Divine Light literature. 'We're competing with you to win the minds of youth,' he was told by an unnamed guardian of the Gestetner.[16]

In late 1973, New Zealand Divine Light followers numbered around thirty. Within six months there were reported to be at least four hundred.[17] Divine Light was often in the headlines. Local newspapers focused on the tender age of its leader, who by sixteen had married a twenty-five-year-old American flight attendant, and had a palatial home in Malibu, several expensive cars and two small aeroplanes. Though it might have been hard for the common onlooker to square Mahara Ji's conspicuous wealth with pronouncements like 'You, in the western world, are crippled with materialism. Come to me, for I shall heal you from your disease', any irony was apparently lost on his devotees whose donations funded his lifestyle.[18]

In the first half of 1974, several emissaries of the guru visited New Zealand to 'reveal the knowledge' to local followers. Then in October the perfect master himself flew into Auckland, to be met by four hundred followers at the South Pacific Hotel. Among his more prominent converts were guitarist Billy TK ('playing better than ever since receiving Knowledge', reported *Centrepeace*, Divine Light's local newsletter) and the composer Jenny McLeod.

When her mentor Fred Page retired in 1970, McLeod, age twenty-nine, had taken over as head of Victoria University's Music Department. Now on a professor's salary, she could afford to buy a large old wooden villa on the side of Brooklyn Hill. She followed her musical theatre epic *Earth and Sky* with *Under the Sun*, an even bigger-scale extravaganza, produced in Palmerston North in 1971 and featuring — in addition to the choirs, orchestras and hundreds of children — a rock band. This time the critical reception was not quite as ecstatic and McLeod ultimately expressed her own dissatisfactions with the piece. One aspect she enjoyed, though, was playing with the rock band comprised of Palmerston North-based brothers Gary and Paul Hunt, who would later record their own quirky psych-folk album as the Forgiving. After spending her days and evenings in exhausting rehearsals with the cast and orchestra, she would jam with the Hunt brothers into the small hours and find herself rejuvenated, before making the two-hour drive back to Wellington. She recalled: 'I found there was a whole natural and spontaneous side of myself that had got lost, or had never been there, because I had never improvised. I'd spent so many years concentrating on the written note. And I found that the aural capacity of a lot of pop musicians was one hell of a lot better than mine.'[19]

And she was learning from her students as well as teaching them. They played her rock music, and introduced her to marijuana and LSD. She began to have doubts about the social value of being a classical composer when her contemporaries were all listening to rock. Meanwhile, the Brooklyn villa was becoming infamous for its parties and community of transients. One temporary occupant, a friend of McLeod's brother Craig, had returned from Thailand with a large quantity of cannabis. Acting on a tip-off, the drug squad arrived one night in the middle of a party at which the usual cross-section of academics, artists and hangers-on were present. Joints were hastily extinguished and stuffed down the backs of couches; a bag of grass was stashed in a bookcase. A guest, the author James McNeish, whispered to McLeod, 'Is there anything you want to hide?', and sequestered away some LSD. A cop found the marijuana in the bookcase, sniffed it and put it back. In the end, only the smuggler was apprehended. 'One law for the rich ...' the sergeant in charge was heard to mutter.

But for McLeod, drugs were just a step on a journey. 'I'd never thought about philosophy or religion but sometimes one would have those experiences with dope that made you think there was something inside of you, that you hadn't suspected.'[20] She began exploring Hindu and Buddhist beliefs. In 1974 she attended a meeting of the Divine Light Mission and, before long, the Brooklyn house had filled with an ashram's worth of Mahara Ji's followers. McLeod never knew who half of them were. In *Soul Talk*, the Divine Light newsletter, the Brooklyn address was given as the organisation's office. 'Professor Joins Mystic Cult' read the headline in the Christchurch *Press*.

Returning to the university after a sabbatical in 1975, she found herself increasingly estranged from the institution that had once embraced her eccentricities. 'My intellectual life was becoming fairly remote from what was happening in the classroom,' she would later reflect, 'and I began to introduce things that I'm sure just left everybody miles behind. I was losing touch with my teaching and things developed spiritually to a point where I realised that I needed something else.'[21]

She formed a rock band comprised largely of Divine Light missionaries, and began writing a rock opera about a time machine and a search for truth.[22] Eventually she resigned from the university and, for a long time, gave up music altogether to become a full-time organiser for Divine Light. She had found a terrific inner joy, she told the *New Zealand Woman's Weekly* in 1978. She and Dennis Cooney were interviewed together, and the pair laughed gleefully when the matter of Mahara Ji's material wealth came up. 'Of course he has a fleet of Cadillacs,' said Cooney. 'And an Aston Martin. You know how he gets them? We give them to him. You know why we give them to him? Because we love him.'[23]

Another who signed up to Mahjara Ji's mission around this time was Treefoot. After spending time at several different communes in the Hokianga, he had left Northland to attend and perform at the Great Ngaruawahia Music Festival. Still restless, he returned to Auckland, worked in orchards and began sampling different spiritual systems. He had been raised a Catholic, had even attended seminary for one semester in San Francisco, finding the 'attitude of service and kindness that comes with Christ's message' compatible with that of the hippies, though he ceased to call himself a Christian.

'I had taken LSD maybe twenty times and they were generally very positive experiences. I felt more alive, my consciousness felt wider, my senses sharper. I wanted to experience that, but didn't want to depend on a drug to get there. I thought I could get there through meditation.'

Billy Te Kahika, after receiving knowledge. Keith Stewart photograph, private collection

He dallied with Ananda Marga, a missionary organisation founded in India in 1955 to spread the teachings of Prabhat Ranjan Sarkar, who believed the task was to save the planet from destruction and help humanity to advance spiritually. Then he was introduced to Divine Light. 'I was going to say "suckered into",' he tells me. 'I went to one group meeting where someone said, If you go to this big gathering in Houston, Texas — Millennium 73 it was called — just by being there you will achieve enlightenment. And I thought, Wow, even if that's an exaggeration it's got to be something special.'

Hooked by the sales pitch, Treefoot scraped together the airfare and flew to Texas. But outside the Houston Astrodome, spirituality seemed in short supply. Merchants were selling overpriced posters, tapes, T-shirts and other souvenirs of the occasion, like at a stadium rock show. Inside the cavernous venue, among a crowd of tens of thousands, he heard dull speeches and amateur-sounding bands on a distant stage. Even the radiance of Guru Mahara Ji himself did not seem to project to Treefoot's corner of the auditorium.

Returning to New Zealand, still a few steps short of satori, he found carpentry work and took up Vipassana, a Buddhist meditation practice that had been preserved in parts of Southeast Asia since the fourth century, finding it had 'more integrity and less of the hyped-up, high pressure sales approach'.[24]

THE MONK DUDE

Mulling over these stories of spiritual searching, I remembered Danny, a friend from childhood. Born in 1955, he had grown up in Wellington in a liberal, left-wing family. His mother was a Quaker, his father an atheist. Our parents had been involved in CND and the Committee on Vietnam, and as kids Danny and I had walked together on some of the same marches.

When Danny was ten he wanted to be a wizard, 'wise and kind and strong like Gandalf'. *The Lord of the Rings* was his Bible. At secondary school he got heavily into music. He saw Led Zeppelin's 1972 concert at Western Springs. When he told his mother, with whom he sometimes attended Quaker meetings, that he no longer believed in God, that was fine with her. He left school, moved with friends into a flat they called Hatfield and the North after an obscure British band, studied Renaissance literature, smoked marijuana and listened to a lot of Yes. He read *The Lord of the Rings* again. And again.

In March 1975 he took his first LSD trip. It was a variety known as Clear Light, a thin square of gelatine or cellophane, which he divided four ways with three friends. They spent most of the day walking in the Botanic Garden, then went back to their flat and listened to music. It was a fantastic experience, but not one that he wanted to repeat again immediately. That single day had 'felt like the length of the previous nineteen years of my life', he tells me, and he needed time to reflect.[25]

A month later he took a second trip, California Sunshine this time. He and two friends tripped all day and the effect was similarly euphoric, though perhaps not quite as intense. By the evening it had worn off. Some marijuana was passed around. Suddenly Danny began to feel as though he had gone back into the LSD trip, but with more intensity than before.

'I had this feeling of incredible joy and it got stronger and stronger and I didn't know what was happening ... the feeling was going on inside me and it got so intense I felt like I was going to explode with ecstasy. And then I felt a force take control of me and I said these words in a language I didn't understand and I felt this energy rush up my spine like a bolt of lightning and I had this vision of infinite bliss. Like John Lennon's song "Across the Universe"—"limitless undying love which shines around me like a million suns"—it was that.'

There is a gap in his memory before his next recollection. 'I was in the next room lying down, and I had all these realisations, just things that I knew now that I didn't know before. You could call them intuitions that came as a result of this experience or whatever, but I actually had this idea, and in a weird way I think it's somehow true, that this experience had actually been induced by a yogi in India from the other side of the world and I basically had a set of instructions about what I was to do with my life.

'Number one was I was never to take drugs again. I had to learn meditation. The purpose of all human life is to pursue enlightenment. And that our role in the world is to save the world from human beings destroying themselves and lay the foundations for a spiritual civilisation.' For someone from Danny's background this was a tall order. He had little interest in spirituality or even philosophy. 'I hadn't read a single spiritual book in my entire life. All I knew about yoga was that some people do some kind of postures.'

He combed the shelves of the university library, where he chanced upon *The Varieties of Religious Experience: A Study in Human Nature*, written in 1901 by American philosopher and psychologist William James. 'It was enormously reassuring because it was about the experiences of hundreds of people from all different cultures, religious and non-religious backgrounds, and many of them had had experiences comparable to my own. So I thought great, but where do I go next?'

He tried teaching himself to meditate, read books on Buddhism and Taoism, and ordered *The Autobiography of a Yogi*. Meantime, the Renaissance poets he was learning about at university began to seem more and more like spiritual visionaries. By chance, next door to his girlfriend's family home in Wadestown was the Wellington headquarters of Ananda Marga. The Wellington centre had been set up in 1973. By the end of '75, Danny had signed up for an Ananda Marga training programme in Sydney, then carried on to Kathmandu where he trained as a monk.

These days he lives in California and is known as Dada Nabhaniilananda, or The Monk Dude. Though we hadn't spoken in forty-five years, he wasn't hard to find; he's on Facebook, has a website and gives TEDx talks on YouTube. Now profusely bearded, dressed in orange robes and white turban, his bright eyes and wide smile haven't changed since childhood. The details of Danny's epiphany didn't sound all that different from the Englishman George King's, yet coming from my old friend they seemed less like science fiction and more like, as he puts it, 'something to do with being human'.

Not long after Danny left town, another colourful brand of devotee began to be seen around parts of New Zealand. These ones dressed only in maroon or dark orange. They called themselves sanyasi; others called them the Orange People: followers of Bhagwan Shree Rajneesh, a philosophy graduate from central India who around 1970 had begun to teach a practice he called Dynamic Meditation, 'a whirling active form of dance followed by silence'.[26] He established a residential therapy centre in Poona, India, which quickly drew members and patrons from all over the world. Unlike the teachings of the Hare Krishna and Ananda Marga movements, The Bhagwan, as he was known, believed religion should help people get enjoyment out of life, and told his followers not to repress their sexuality. His discourses seemed to draw on Zen, Sufi, Tao and Buddhist traditions, but would also refer to Christianity as well as Freudian, Jungian and other psychologies. Some suspected he was making it up as he went along. His move to the United States and the establishment in the early eighties of Rajneeshpuram, a community in Wasco county, Oregon, is covered in detail in the Netflix series *Wild Wild Country*.

In New Zealand, sanyasi gravitated to the Sunday Creek commune in Tasman Bay. At first the mood there was harmonious, but eventually the non-sanyasi, who at one point made up just three of the total group, began to be irked by what they saw as blind obedience to an outside leader.[27] Eventually an instruction from the Bhagwan to urbanise saw many of his New Zealand followers move to cities.

Elsewhere an ever-widening array of mystical systems seemed to be on offer, some requiring no more than a temporary suspension of disbelief. At markets and festivals you would find fabric-draped tables at which fiery-eyed men or women, dressed in raiments from the East, would, for a fee, tell your fortune with the use of Tarot cards, I Ching coins, palm reading or astrological symbols.

If you happened to be wandering around the bottom of Auckland's Queen Street any time in the mid-seventies, you might be approached by a smiling man with a clipboard who would invite you to take a 'personality test'. If you agreed, he would lead you to a room on the second floor of the Imperial Buildings where you would be asked to complete a 200-question sheet, the results of which would be recorded on a 'personality graph'. Inevitably, you would rate distressingly poorly, but a solution to your personal deficiencies would be immediately offered in the form of a course in Scientology.

Invented in the fifties by American science fiction writer L. Ron Hubbard, the Church of Scientology — which would apply for religious status wherever it set up shop in order to avoid taxation — wasn't much like a religion but caught the wave of interest in psychoanalysis. New Zealand was in fact the first country outside America to establish a Church of Scientology.[28] A local branch was founded in 1955 by Frank Turnbull of Christchurch who had taken a Scientology Doctorate course in Philadelphia and been awarded by L. Ron Hubbard the title Scientology Bishop of Oceania. Over the years Scientology snared enough followers to eventually be able to buy the grand Methodist Theological College building in Auckland's Grafton Road.

Then there were the Moonies, the name popularly given to followers of Sun Myung Moon, leader of the Unification Church. Moon was born in North Korea and raised in a Pentecostal brand of Presbyterianism. When he was sixteen he had a vision of Jesus, who handpicked him to complete his messianic mission. Initially based in South Korea, by the early sixties the Unification Church had missionaries in Japan, North America and Europe. The first Moonie to land in New Zealand was Siegrun Kuhaupt, a German woman sent from Berlin to Wellington in 1973 to make converts and raise funds. At first her small local contingent sold peanuts and ginseng tea door to door. Before long, many were travelling around the globe as Moon missionaries, engaged in further recruitment.

Part of Moon's theology was specifically anti-communist. Marriage and the family was the vehicle to experience God's love. Your marriage partner was chosen for you by Moon, who conducted mass wedding ceremonies of thousands of people at a time. Drugs were out, as was pre-marital sex. Even after marriage, couples were expected to abstain from sex until Moon gave the word, which could sometimes take years.[29] Such tenets were the diametric opposite of the libertine and broadly left-wing values of the counterculture, yet hippie types turned out to be prime recruitment material for the Moonies. In an unpublished account based on his ten-year experience as a Moonie, Michael Butler drew a picture of a typical Unification convert: a dope-smoking, acid-dropping rock musician, living with his girlfriend, and with a vague interest in philosophy and spirituality.[30]

Both the Scientologists and the Moonies would be the subject of allegations by New Zealand families that their children had been manipulated, coerced, abducted and brainwashed. There would be a number of protracted battles in which professionals were hired to retrieve and de-program young converts, often without success. Many families were ultimately forced to accept their children's choices.

What drew people from the counterculture to religion? For some, like Danny, it was a way to explain and explore the insights he had apparently gained from his experiences with drugs. For others it was a continued search for a set of values to replace the ones they had abandoned. For yet others who had rejected the rules imposed on them by society but now found themselves psychically and spiritually unmoored, it offered an alternative structure, albeit one sometimes more rigid than the one they had been brought up with.

But at a time when Christianity was in decline, perhaps the most rebellious act of all was to turn to Jesus. And indeed, a new breed of Christian hippie, known as the Jesus Freak, began to appear. A *Time* magazine cover story in June 1971 had proclaimed 'The Jesus Revolution' with an image of Jesus looking like he had stepped out of *The Art of Sensual Massage* and illuminated in the dayglo colours of an Acid Test poster. New Zealand, too, had its adherents.

Marcus Ardern, a young, pot-smoking, anti-war activist with an interest in Eastern religion, had come to Auckland from Tauranga, and quickly became involved with the PYM. He was a visible presence at the Jumping Sundays: longhaired, bearded, be-robed, frequently holding court on a variety of subjects but often focusing on the contradictions in the Bible and the hypocrisies of its followers. In Albert Park he established his first Love Shop, a place where people could obtain without charge things they needed and give away things they didn't. He spent time at James K. Baxter's Boyle Crescent crash pad and later followed the poet to Jerusalem. 'I went there a hard-headed atheist,' he told the *Listener* in 1972. 'I thought the idea of a God absurd. But I began to have all sorts of religious ideas I found I could indulge to the full, because Jerusalem was so far out in the sticks you didn't have to be very rational anyway.'

Peace Rally, Auckland Domain, 1973. John Daley photographs, Museum of New Zealand Te Papa Tongarewa, 1286522

For a while he moved to Wellington where he started another Love Shop, shifting the focus of his social services to the pensioners he saw living in substandard accommodation and sometimes without enough money to eat properly. One day he was visited by an old friend, a former heavy drug user, who was now peddling 'ambiguous phrases like "I've been washed in the blood" and "I've been born again"—mystical things that didn't mean anything'. One day, figuring he had nothing to lose, Marcus locked his door and asked God to change his life. He wasn't sure anything happened, though halfway through the next day he realised he was no longer craving cigarettes, which he had been having trouble giving up. A few days later, still sceptical, he asked for a stronger sign and was plunged into what he initially thought was an LSD flashback, something he had experienced once before. He began speaking in a language he didn't know.

Not long after this he went to speak to a meeting of the Rotary Club, an international non-denominational association of service organisations founded on Christian principles and run by suit-wearing professional and business people. As a novelty, the club had booked the outspoken hippie to teach them about Love Shops, Jumping Sundays and life in the counterculture. Instead he told them about Jesus.[31]

HOMEGROWN GURUS AND PSYCHEDELIC SALESMEN

The notion of the spiritual teacher that had originated with the Hindus before the time of Christ was now being enthusiastically embraced by young Westerners worldwide, their minds newly opened by drugs, travel, literature and songs. 'Don't follow leaders, watch your parking meters', Bob Dylan had warned, and yet the counterculture seemed to

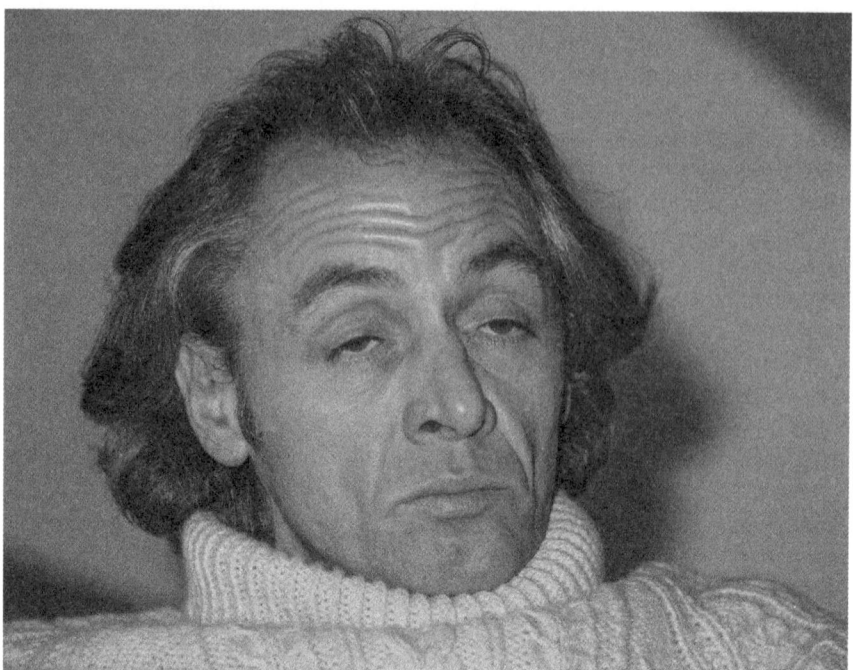

R. D. Laing in Wellington, 1973. Keith Stewart photograph, private collection

want leaders anyway. Some, like Dylan, would have guru-dom thrust upon them. Others seized it themselves.

In 1960, Gridley Lorimer Wright was a Wall Street stock trader and far-right Republican. During his trading days he had begun experimenting with marijuana and LSD, and before long had swapped high finance for high times. In 1967 he founded a short-lived Californian commune named Strawberry Fields, envisioned as 'a place of accelerated evolutionary change' where people could trip on acid and expand their consciousness without society's interference. But society interfered anyway, and after serving eighteen months in prison for drug possession, Gridley (as he was simply known) headed East to continue his pursuit of enlightenment through a combination of Asian spirituality and psychotropic drugs.

He arrived in New Zealand some time in 1970, having been deported from Bali where he had attempted to establish another community. In early 1971, he ventured to Jerusalem with an entourage that included several 'wives' and an apparently boundless supply of LSD.[32] Baxter, who had established the commune partly as a refuge for casualties of the urban drug scene, was away at the time. Over a period of days, Gridley handed out trips to all comers, including to some who had never taken the drug before. A resident described the scene to historian John Newton, who depicts a battlefield with 'comatose bodies strewn across the hillside while the abstainers and the more capable …

tended to the fallen'.[33] Baxter returned and, in a rare display of authoritarianism, gave Gridley his marching orders.

Gridley's trip to New Zealand went below the radar of the media. More widely noted was the visit of R. D. Laing, the Scottish psychiatrist and author who wrote that 'in the context of our present pervasive madness that we call normality, sanity, freedom, all our frames of references are ambiguous and equivocal ... The statesmen of the world who boast and threaten that they have Doomsday weapons are far more dangerous, and far more estranged from "reality" than many of the people on whom the label "psychotic" is affixed.'[34] As the author of several other challenging and influential books on psychotherapy, including the 1967 *The Politics of Experience and The Bird of Paradise*, inspired in part by his personal experiments with LSD, he had become a celebrated figure in the counterculture.

The word guru was frequently used for his radical experiments in treating the mentally ill. Most notable of these was Kingsley Hall, a residential treatment centre in the East End of London where from 1965 to 1970 a group of psychiatrists lived together with their patients, many of whom had been diagnosed schizophrenic, in a radical upending of traditional medical practice. To a generation who had come to question the social and political roles that their parents took for granted, Laing's work was a vindication. He questioned the use of antipsychotic drugs in treatment, though he took LSD himself and sometimes shared it with the other Kingsley Hall residents. He also had a taste for marijuana, and during his 1973 New Zealand visit some of his admirers helped him source it. However, it appears Laing was not prepared for the strength of the local variant and, to the horror of his hosts at a Wellington party, he took ill and collapsed. The doctor apparently recovered in time to deliver his lectures, but whether it was an effect of the marijuana or the free-associative method of meditation, aimed at breaking down cognitive filters, he was practising during this period, the talks were an ordeal for anyone in attendance, thanks to Laing's incessant blinking, twitching, paper-shuffling and interminable pauses.

Often found next to books by Laing were those of Carl Jung, the Swiss psychiatrist and colleague of Sigmund Freud. Jung saw the human psyche as fragmented and divided, and believed that all people, knowingly or not, are searching for their souls. As a process for differentiating the self from the individual's conscious and unconscious elements, he came up with a concept called individuation.

Jung, who died in 1961, had many followers around the world, some of whom set themselves up as gurus in their own right. One was Aysha Dayshur. She had been born Wendy Wootton and grown up in Hollywood where her parents worked in the film industry, but came to be known by a number of names including Wendi Love, Shamar, Shemura and Aysha Love. In the 1970s she married a New Zealander, Richard Dayshur, moved to New Zealand and began offering workshops in individuation. Jung had seen individuation as a lifelong process; for

Aysha it provided a group of long-term dependants. She set up a government-funded programme in Auckland aimed at assisting at-risk youth, giving employment to a number of her followers whom she described as her 'family'.

Eventually Television New Zealand's *Eyewitness News* investigated complaints about drug use, mistreatment of children, coercion of staff and clients into sexual relationships, and the use of government money to fund her own overseas trips. After the programme's screening and subsequent questions in Parliament, Aysha moved back to the States, taking the core of her New Zealand family with her. Her legacy continued to be debated after her death in 2004. In 2007, writing on a forum on the website culteducation.com, *recovering addict* recalled:

> Aysha would befriend young people, usually with very troubled family lives, and offer them what they were looking for: a mother figure who cared about them and loved them as they were and took an interest in them. She thought you were smart and special and told you so all the time. She treated you almost like you were her own child, except that she spoke to you as an equal. Her home and family seemed like everything you'd ever wanted and had been missing all your life. She was this unending fountain of love and caring ... But she also had no concept of right and wrong. She didn't hold you accountable for what you did to yourself. She never tried to get you to see your part in creating your family's troubles and reconcile with your parents, she never said you needed to quit using drugs because you were killing yourself and your future ... She never made you take responsibility for improving your own life, because she wanted you dependent on her forever ... She was also very beautiful and sexy and knew how to use that. Every young male has a fantasy about a beautiful older woman teaching him how to make love and not laughing at him like the girls his age sometimes do. She not only took advantage of this, she made it seem mystical and holy and like you were someone really special for being chosen by her.[35]

To which *infoneeded2* responded:

> There is nothing more to do, she is after all dead. The world is moving into greater love and truth and consciousness despite what they always do to the pioneers that bring in new paradigms after so much darkness. They killed Christ they always do but what he did lives within our cellular memory and goes on lifting us up. Aysha was one of those great lights who the dark side pursued but they did not stop her they cannot stop her ...[36]

In the mid-2010s, the US television series *Mad Men* looked back on the way the counterculture had been ripe for co-option and exploitation by manipulators and con artists of various stripes. Beginning in the early sixties, the programme follows the adventures of successful Madison Avenue ad-man Don Draper, who for most of the series seems cynical and estranged from the cultural revolution that is going on around him. But the final episode takes us to a community on a Californian clifftop overlooking the Pacific Ocean. Uncharacteristically, Don has gone there to check out a spiritual retreat. He participates in a group therapy session and cries. The last scene finds him in a meditation workshop, seated in the lotus position, eyes closed. A beatific smile crosses his face. Has he finally attained satori? No, he's just thought of what will become one of the most successful advertising campaigns in the history of Coca-Cola. As the jingle 'I'd like to buy the world a Coke ...' plays over the closing credits, Draper has figured out how he will prosper in the seventies.

Draper's fictitious Coke epiphany takes place in a community clearly modelled on the Esalen Institute of Big Sur, established in 1962 as a live-in community by psychologist and meditation scholar Michael Murphy, and Richard Price, a beatnik associate of Ginsberg and Kerouac. It offered workshops on everything from yoga to Gestalt psychology, and it was here in the mid-sixties that the future Aysha Dayshur embarked on the study of Jungian analysis which she would use as the basis for her cult.

By the end of the decade, Esalen was hosting thousands of visitors a year from as far away as New Zealand. Among them was Herbert Potter, a former Electrolux vacuum-cleaner salesman and now founder of his own successful pest-control business. A course run by Dale Carnegie—famous for self-help books like *How to Win Friends and Influence People* and *How to Stop Worrying and Start Living*—had inspired him to run self-help courses of his own. The visit to Esalen provided him with further material, which he poured into what he called encounter groups, borrowing the name used at Esalen: live-in workshops combining elements of psychotherapy, meditation and massage. These would take place at his home in Auckland and last eleven hours a day, for a week or more, costing the participant $75 (roughly $1200 today). Encounter groups grew in popularity, especially among the urban middle class who had first learned about them in imported magazines and were now seeing reports in the local press.

The idea had originated with a group of psychologists in the United States who, after the Second World War, developed the idea that training in human relations skills was an important but overlooked skill in modern society. Encounter groups spawned numerous variations under a variety of names—T-groups, Gestalt therapy, Sensory Awareness—all centred on an intensive group experience facilitated by a leader. By 1971, Bert Potter was hosting encounter groups in different parts of New Zealand.

Joanna was eleven when her mother returned to her family's Christchurch home after a week at one of Potter's encounter groups.[37] Her father, a clinical psychologist, was away in America, attending, as it happens, a workshop at the Esalen Institute. Her mother, after five children and fourteen years in a marriage that had begun to feel constraining, had for once done something for herself. She appeared to be transformed. 'She was radiant with happiness,' Joanna remembers, 'and told us she had met a really interesting man and she would like us to meet him too.

'She had never told us anything like this before. She had never *done* anything like this before. And she told us, among other things, that he had long hair. My little sister who was six at the time got really excited because she thought, He'll be like David Cassidy from the Partridge Family. But he wasn't.

'I remember opening the door and there he was wearing a poncho, a leather Stetson, bare feet, corduroy jeans, this ashy blond hair down to his shoulders and electric blue eyes — pale blue eyes, like the cricketer Shane Warne. A switched-on look like there was a current running through him.'

Over the next few months Bert would visit a number of times, always staying for several days. The change in Joanna's mother was palpable. Until then she had dressed like a typical suburban housewife of the 1960s; shift dresses, cardigans. Suddenly she was wearing V-knee jeans and was often barefoot. Even the kind of underwear she wore was different. It had been 'hold-you-in knickers with suspender thingies hanging off'; now it was 'little elasticated bras and briefs like girls would wear. Her hair grew longer. She seemed younger, she seemed lighter, she seemed enormously happier.'

As for Joanna, she could tell from the effect Potter had on her mother that he had magician-like qualities, yet she and her siblings were wary of him. 'He was very free to give his opinions on anything and everything. I remember him saying to my older sister who was fourteen, "Virgins are the scourge of the earth."' And his self-confidence appeared to be boundless. He would say things like, 'I'm in a state now where it's beneficial for people just to be in a room with me. Everybody has a lot to learn from me. The people who think they don't have anything to learn from me are the people who need me the most.'

That summer Potter took Joanna, her siblings and her mother for a holiday in a remote part of the Marlborough Sounds. 'Anything you want we can get the launch to bring it,' he promised the children, who requested the most luxurious and unattainable items they could think of. 'We said, "We want Coca-Cola" and "We want roast chicken!" And big trays of Coca-Cola cans were brought on the supply launch and we felt super-rich.'

During one of Potter's Christchurch stays, he offered the children massages, also foreign experiences in the family. 'Would you like it to be knickers on or knickers off?' he asked the young girls. 'Knickers on,' they answered unequivocally.

'All of this family has missed out on touching but you have missed out the most,' Joanna remembers him telling her.

Though the massage offer was not repeated, it coincided with the arrival of a new lexicon in the household. 'There was the word "uptight". Being "uptight"—that was not a cool thing to be. You've got "hang-ups", that was another thing. You've got to be happy with total sharing, you've got to be happy with total openness, things like doors on bedrooms or whether or not you even own the clothes you're wearing. He [Potter] put that message out there to anyone that he came across who put up any resistance to him. If you're uptight and shut-down you're not going to get the full benefit of the magic that is me.'

Joanna's father returned from America and her parents separated soon after. By now Bert Potter was living in a semi-communal situation in Auckland. He invited Joanna's mother to move there and bring the children, but she demurred, valuing her independence. One day Bert turned up at the Christchurch home with another woman in tow. His visits stopped after that.

In November 1973, Sandra Coney interviewed Potter for a piece in the feminist magazine *Broadsheet* titled 'Everything You Ever Wanted to Know About Housewives ... but never bothered to ask'. He gave the opinion that housewives led a life that was 'too easy. They create work for themselves to fill in empty time.' Instead of creating work he suggested they should engage in such activities as 'looking at a cloud or making love'. He also explained his focus on middle-class women. 'The working-class housewife is so rigid—so stuck in a rut—she can't see any other possibilities in life.'[38]

What Sandra Coney didn't mention in the article was that Potter, whom she interviewed in his Campbells Bay home 'on the edge of a bed in a room filled with dirty-looking mattresses', suggested that Coney should participate in his groups or perhaps join his community. 'You are completely free here to try anything you like with whoever you like,' he offered.[39] She declined, though others took up the invitation [as will be seen in Chapter 14].

ROOTS AND BRANCHES

Ten

The history of this country reveals profoundly contrasting ideas about the land. Before the arrival of Pākehā, Māori practised a sustainable model of gardening and gathering, based on a view in which the land is a visible sign of something spiritual. As the WAI 262 Waitangi Tribunal Report noted in 2011: 'They enabled human exploitation of the environment, but through the kinship value (known in te ao Māori as whanaungatanga) they also emphasised human responsibility to nurture and care for it (known in te ao Māori as kaitiakitanga).'[1]

Mahana commune, Coromandel, early 1980s. Peter Aagaard photograph

To the colonists, the land was 'ripe for the picking and full of prospect'.[2] Exploitation began with seals and whales, moved on to kauri and the other forests, and continued with kauri gum, coal and gold. As those resources became depleted, attention turned to farming cattle and sheep.

Though the counterculture was dominated by Pākehā and centred largely on imported ideas, it moved away from the colonial view of the land as a source of resources to exploit, and reconsidered the relationship between the land and the people—dependently, spiritually and artistically.

BACK TO THE GARDEN

The staple diet of the colonial Pākehā was meat-and-three-veg. It represented the good life. In pre-industrial Britain, large meat-based meals had been a luxury and the privilege of the rich, but in New Zealand, with its abundant farms and illusion of equality, everyone could eat like lords. As Dave Veart says, it was part of the colonial pitch. 'Emigrate to New Zealand and you'll have a full stomach.'[3] Meat, James Belich writes, 'symbolised human domination of nature, and was a marker of prosperity and status'.[4]

The colonists brought Shorthorns, Anguses and Herefords for beef, bred Perendales and Coopworths for lamb. They grew traditional British vegetables: potatoes, carrots, cabbages, peas. The Kiwi dinner was the British supper, super-sized. New Zealanders often ate meat three times a day, and the diet made the colonials grow taller and larger than their European counterparts. Surveys show a steady increase in the height and weight of children over the course of the twentieth century, especially between the 1930s and mid-1950s. The few who deviated from this regimen were seen as eccentric and possibly subversive.

Vegetarianism was rare, but often existed in enclaves connected to a wider belief system. The Humanitarian and Anti-Vivisection Society had been set up by First World War conscientious objector Norman Bell; the Food Reform and Humanitarian Society was established around the same time by Dunedin pacifists; and the New Zealand Vegetarian Society was formed by Theosophists in the forties. Occasionally one of these culinary non-conformists would sneak their ideas into the pantries of middle New Zealand. The Sanitarium company, founded by vegetarian Seventh-day Adventists, was the maker of the Kiwi breakfast staples Marmite and Weet-Bix, and from 1907 operator of a chain of healthfood stores.[5]

Like their maverick forebears, the counterculture challenged traditional attitudes to food in a variety of ways and for a variety of reasons: moral and ethical, biological, environmental and economical. For some it was bound up with pacifist and anti-war sentiments. There were those for whom it was a logical step to extend the humanitarianism of the anti-war movement to other living creatures. There was also the

TOP: Organic apples at Beeville commune, Morrinsville, 1971. Ans Westra photograph, Alexander Turnbull Library, PA-Group-00941

BOTTOM: Gardening at Mahana, Coromandel, early 1980s. Peter Aagaard photograph

influence of Eastern religions, many of which included vegetarianism in their practices.

In some cases, food was the meeting point between a religious group and the wider community. From the time the Hare Krishna opened their first New Zealand temple in 1972, they shared their cuisine with anyone adventurous enough to try dahls, chapatis and whatever they called that bright pink stuff. They held Sunday feasts at their temple where they would give the food away for free, and did the same at rock festivals. Before long they opened their own restaurants, selling food at prices affordable to hungry hippies.

Some were extending the traditions established by pre-countercultural pioneers, like the practice of organic gardening. When the Hansen family established Beeville near Morrinsville in the 1930s, one of the community's founding principles was the cultivation and consumption of natural, organically grown foods. Tim Jones went to live there in the early sixties and found that 'crops of corn, potatoes, watermelon, pumpkins thrived along with the vegetable gardens and fruit trees'.[6] This focus on growing organic produce for the community was transferred to Wilderland, the new community Dan and Edith Hansen started in Coromandel in 1965.

Visiting Wilderland in the seventies, Jones noted that 'the soil is basically poor, but in the garden and orchard areas it has been enriched by compost, hen manure, fish waste, blood and bone', and he rhapsodised about the quality of the food it yielded. 'I find that the salads have a distinct effect on me. My body quickly feels light and a sense of wellbeing pervades it, making me feel quite high. I'm not sure whether it is the number of ingredients, the richness of the soil or the loving care with which the gardening is done. Perhaps it is all of these things.'[7]

The other major pre-counterculture community at this time was Riverside, near Nelson. Until the 1970s, the Riverside orchards were run along much the same lines as other orchards in the district, using sprays and artificial fertilisers.[8] In the early sixties, a group within Riverside began to protest against meat-eating and promote organic husbandry in the community, but they were considered fanatical by some of the other members and did not stay for long. Rex Cooper, a new arrival in the late sixties, put forward a proposal for 'a small research unit' to look into 'improved methods of irrigation and water conservation, weed and insect-pest control (by non-toxic means where possible)'. His proposal appears to have won tacit approval, but community support was insufficient for him to feel he could proceed, and by 1971 he too had moved on. It was only as the seventies got underway that a groundswell for organic growing began at Riverside, with an influx of baby boomers bringing ideas about organics and vegetarianism.[9]

As for Jerusalem, James K. Baxter may have cast himself as a shepherd, but from all accounts he was not much of a gardener. So even he might have been surprised to learn that he had played a part in the birth of the country's organic gardening movement.

Jim Kebbell was a priest when he first encountered the poet. Driving home one wet Wellington winter's evening, he spied a homeless man stumbling towards an uncertain night's rest. Out of nowhere, Baxter, at that time employed by day as a postman, appeared on a bicycle, dismounted, placed his coat around the vagrant's shoulders and rode off into the night. Though the incident would appear to have all the elements of a classic piece of Baxter stagecraft, it made an impression on Kebbell and provided him with material for his sermon the following Sunday.

Over the next few years the priest would make the acquaintance of Baxter, who was in constant argument with members of the Church about what its role in society ought to be. Agreeing with Baxter that war was theologically unsound, Kebbell became involved in the Vietnam protests. One day on the golf course the Dean of the diocese informed him that he had been seen on the streets with the demonstrators and that the hierarchy did not approve.

Kebbell discussed the matter with Baxter during a 1970 crossing of Cook Strait. Baxter, by this time living in Jerusalem and looking much like a homeless person himself, had been invited to speak at Student Congress in Curious Cove. Kebbell, who was attending as a chaplain, offered him a ride there on his yacht. He recalls: 'It was pretty rough in Wellington Harbour and Jim got out and rebuked the sea and the waves on the deck, did a solemn proclamation. Then, as there was nobody there to watch, he went down below and went to sleep. He woke up just when we got through Tory Channel.'[10]

At Congress that year Kebbell met Marion Wood, and the couple embarked on a relationship. Kebbell sought dispensation from the Church to marry. Baxter wrote a letter to the Pope on the couple's behalf. 'It said, this man is a very good priest and he's doing God's work so God has seen fit to put upon him the burden of a wife,' Marion recalls. 'Very Baxter. Dreadful misogynist.'

His Holiness remained unpersuaded and Baxter advised the couple to 'do something the Church can find no fault with'. So Kebbell left the priesthood and, with fellow Catholic activist Tim Dyce, he and Marion established an urban outpost of Jerusalem. Like Baxter's commune, the McFarlane Street house was essentially a crash pad. Marion: 'The idea was that there was not a "them" and "us". Our concept was one of community, that everybody was equal, that everybody shared in the chores, everybody basically did what they wanted, but it was very non-hierarchical.'

There were a few rules, Jim remembers. 'No illegal activities on the premises. You couldn't operate drugs. And if you were a thief you couldn't bring your stolen goods home.' Though, Marion adds, 'When the chicken turned up for lunch with the price tag still sticking out of it, you thought, Oh well, it's fresh ...'

The household usually numbered around twenty. Baxter would stay when he was in Wellington; others came and went. Marion: 'We'd go away for a week, come back to McFarlane Street, walk in, and people would say, "Who are you?"'

Jim: 'But we hardly ever went away, in fact. We moved out of McFarlane Street [in 1973] to Allenby Terrace, which was slightly less crowded but [with] more difficult people.'

At Allenby Terrace, housemates often included recently released offenders, including New Zealand's longest-serving prisoner, the murderer Dean Wickliffe, and a former residential patient of Cherry Farm psychiatric hospital known as Mac, who suffered from claustrophobia, drank water compulsively and frequently wet his bed.

Jim: 'What [the residents] had in common was they came from dysfunctional families, for the most part. People who came to live with us could live there for life, that was the deal, and that gave them the sort of stability they had never had much before.'

Marion: 'We didn't see it as a task. We saw it as life. This was the way life was going to develop. There would be much more equality. Flower power. And everybody's going to love everybody. Hugs were huge. What we provided was some kind of a structure, and by and large people looked after each other.'

Jim and Marion would try to impart to the residents a few life skills such as cooking, and this led to the thought, 'Why don't we get a bit of land and try to start growing things?' So in 1975, while Marion was pregnant with their daughter Lucy, they purchased land at Te Horo, in rural Horowhenua, with four other families. It was Marion's mother Frances, who had recently moved out from Britain, who insisted that the land, which they named Common Property, should be farmed organically. Jim, coming from five generations of farmers, was initially sceptical, but was persuaded after reading about the effects of industrialised chemicals on the food chain.

For the most part, the urban flotsam showed little interest in the project. 'They were city folk,' says Marion. 'I remember one guy up there saying, "This is what we did inside [prison] ..."'

Nevertheless, they persisted with the farm to supply the vegetable needs of the collective families. Before long they were producing far more than the collective could consume, and began to sell their produce. Having created one of the country's first organic farms, the couple went on to establish Commonsense Organics stores, still operating nationwide today.

Jim and Marion are notable for their success and longevity in the organics business, but throughout the counterculture there were people similarly rethinking their relationship to the land, on both smaller and larger scales.

DAMNING THE DAM

When the Save Manapouri Campaign was launched in 1969, it was the first time an environmental issue became the focus of public protest and national debate. But it wasn't started by members of the counterculture. It was founded by Ron McLean, a Southland sheep farmer and former president of the Southland division of Federated Farmers, a bastion of the rural establishment. It was a rare issue on which the counterculture found common ground with conservative rural New Zealand.

The idea of harnessing the waters of the beautiful southern Lake Manapōuri to produce hydro electricity had been kicking around since the early twentieth century, but it wasn't until the 1950s that a proposal to build an aluminium smelter at Bluff gave rise to a plan to dam and raise the level of the lake in order to generate the required power. It took another decade before a formal agreement was signed between the various interested parties, by which time a few citizens had begun to question the despoiling of one of the country's natural beauties, especially because raising the lake level by the proposed 8.4 metres would yield only 4.5 percent more power. The early sixties had seen petitions and pamphlets opposing the scheme from long-established conservation groups the Scenery Preservation Society (established 1891) and Royal Forest and Bird Protection Society (1921), but the campaign shifted gear in 1969 once the power station had been completed but the lake level was still to be raised.

Following a crowded public meeting in Invercargill on 30 October 1969, the Save Manapouri committee was established, with related groups springing up around the country. There were marches in the capital and a new petition which drew more than a quarter of a million signatures—at that time the largest ever presented to Parliament. The government responded by setting up a commission of inquiry, which confirmed that raising the lake would cause serious and permanent environmental damage but concluded that the government's contract with the aluminium company Comalco meant it might be unavoidable. It also revealed that politicians, journalists and senior civil servants had been offered shares in Comalco.[11]

By early 1972 there had been threats of 'radical action' against the dam. But November's election brought victory to Labour, whose leader Norman Kirk had campaigned against raising the lake. Labour made good on Kirk's promise, and to remind him how strongly people felt about the issue there was the inescapable 'Damn the Dam', a top five soft-rock hit in 1973 for local singer-songwriter John Hanlon. He had originally written the song, with its deathless refrain, 'Damn the dam cried the fantail as he flew into the sky, to give power to the people, all this beauty has to die', as a commercial for fibreglass. Hanlon's fantail was finally put out of its misery when National announced its policy on the lake for the 1975 election. It was identical to Labour's.

The Manapōuri issue had resonated with a counterculture that by the late sixties was well attuned to injustice of various kinds. Ecological awareness was a recurring theme of Roszak's *The Making of a Counter Culture*, in which he lamented that 'the flora, fauna, landscape and increasingly the climate of the earth lie practically helpless at the feet of technological man'.[12] Charles A. Reich, in his countercultural treatise *The Greening of America*, asked: 'What have we all lost?' before going on to annotate a checklist that included 'the experience of living in harmony with nature'.[13] The idea of sacrificing nature to progress was another tenet of the establishment that was ripe for rejection.

The fact that, in the case of Manapōuri, the sacrifice would be for the benefit of major corporations pitted the counterculture against a familiar enemy. But for the greater populace, Manapōuri represented a significant shift in perspective. Ever since the colonial invasion, the dominant Pākehā view of the land had been that it was something to be tamed and exploited. Words like resource, ecosystem and sustainability weren't in the vocabulary. Native forests had been razed for timber, then replaced with exotic trees or, more often, grass to farm sheep and cows. The farms were regularly and heavily fertilised, mostly with phosphate stripped from vulnerable Pacific islands. And yet erosion was making it increasingly clear that this approach was pushing the land beyond its ecological limits.

At the same time, New Zealand's parent–child relationship with Mother England was coming to an end. For more than a century, New Zealand had been Britain's Farm, enjoying the security of a guaranteed market for meat and agricultural exports. But Britain's decision to join the European Economic Community (later renamed the European Union), set to take effect in 1973, meant such favours were about to end, and with it came a reconsideration of the country's national identity. At the start of the sixties, 'God Save The Queen' had played in every picture theatre before each screening, and everyone other than the occasional republican, anarchist or bohemian automatically stood in Her Majesty's honour. By the time of Manapōuri, the Amalgamated cinema chain had given up the practice as no longer appropriate, and its rival Kerridge Odeon soon followed suit. You might say the whole nation was feeling the stirrings of a change of consciousness.

BEECH BRAWL

No sooner had the threat to Manapōuri receded, than another major environmental campaign was underway, this one with its origins in the counterculture.

To anyone casually scanning media statements put out by the Forest Service in the early seventies, it might have appeared that the proposed conversion of South Island native forests to exotics would threaten hardly a single native tree. But reading past the spin, it had become apparent to a group of bright twenty-somethings, most of them students at the University of Auckland, that roughly one-tenth of remaining South Island natives were in fact destined for logging, including virtually all of the remaining lowland beeches.

The Beech Forest Action Committee (BFAC) was founded in Auckland in 1973 by a group that included young poet and photographer Denys Trussell, and future writer and critic Diana Wichtel. Sharing artistic backgrounds and a previous involvement in political demonstrations and happenings such as Jumping Sundays, the group had creative ideas about how to get attention. Wichtel came up with the slogan: WE WILL FIGHT THEM ON THE BEECHES. It was screenprinted on posters and plastered onto walls all over Auckland and beyond. Their first demonstration was outside the Central Post Office in Lower Queen Street at morning rush hour, and featured reliable crowd magnet Tim Shadbolt (who, incidentally, had been a labourer on the construction of the Manapōuri dam) addressing the passers-by. David Gapes, station manager of Radio Hauraki, was enlisted as a member and used his influence to circulate a fast-growing petition.[14]

Recognising that they were too far from both the South Island and Parliament to run a national campaign, BFAC quickly sought to establish regional branches. In Wellington they teamed up with Guy Salmon, son of scientist and conservationist John Salmon. Guy was in his early twenties and already making his name as a passionate and charismatic champion of conservation. Cautioning that he didn't purport to be 'Mr Young Person', he nevertheless described in the 1971 publication *Focus On Youth* the young (male) New Zealander with whom he shared a feeling of solidarity:

> [He] somewhere along the line ... has been infected with a little idealism and it has saved him. The idea that his society, and indeed his own life, could be better, has enabled him to put the world into perspective. He has risen above it, seen beyond it. He has perceived hypocrisy perhaps, exploitation or deprivation, injustice, false values ... More young people than ever before are unsatisfied with the path laid out for them and their country. They are critically aware, motivated by a moral concern, a sense of justice, and wanting to do something.[15]

Salmon's flat in North Terrace, Kelburn, previously occupied by activist and publisher Alister Taylor, became the nerve centre of BFAC. Some of the members had other enterprises that helped fund the campaign. Philip Alpers printed psychedelic posters under the trade name Cerebral Vortex, and operated a light show for rock bands. Salmon and Gwenny Davis ran a small factory making scented multi-coloured candles.

The committee set up working groups with different areas of responsibility around the country. Alpers and Salmon ran activist training sessions on campuses. They forged alliances with other conservation groups such as CoEnCo (New Zealand Conference on Environment and Conservation), set up by Salmon's father. But they increasingly found themselves at odds with the staid Forest and Bird, which paid lip service to the beech campaign while making apparently contradictory statements that showed support for the commercial arguments of the Forest Service.[16] Before long BFAC adopted establishment figures such as Auckland Mayor Sir Dove-Myer Robinson and Save Manapouri's Ron McLean as members of an 'honorary board of advisors', deliberately steering the group's image away from that of a bunch of countercultural radicals. Nevertheless, they continued to be portrayed in radical terms by the likes of Institute of Foresters president Jim Spiers who referred to people on BFAC's board as 'gurus of the new environmental cult'.[17] And the core of the group still looked to an international radical movement for inspiration. Needing a Manapōuri-scale focus for their campaign, they took a leaf from the Arusha Declaration, Tanzanian anti-colonialist leader Julius Nyerere's 1967 manifesto for African socialism and self-reliance, and came up with the Maruia Declaration: a petition based on six principles for the protection of virgin forests. The campaign would be a long one, marked by small victories, compromises and eventually, in 1986, an accord signed by government, industry and environmental groups. By then BFAC had morphed into the Native Forest Action Council, which in turn became the Maruia Society and later the Ecologic Foundation, which would continue to promote environmental issues and sustainable development into the twenty-first century.

Meanwhile the idea that environmentally destructive schemes driven by overseas companies demanded organised opposition was taken up by others such as the Campaign Against Foreign Control of Aotearoa, formed in 1974 by Murray Horton of the Christchurch PYM. The acronym CAFCA echoes the surname of the Prague-born novelist Franz Kafka, whose nightmare tales of the shadowy machinations of power it aptly brought to mind.

IDIOSYNCRATIC INNOVATIONS

Other characters from the counterculture made their own positive if sometimes idiosyncratic contributions to the environment, and helped change New Zealanders' attitudes. Dick Nicholls was originally from Taranaki where his interest in plants had begun in childhood. Living in Christchurch in the late sixties he met *Canta* editor Bill Gruar, and they bonded over a shared love of jazz and interest in drugs. Gruar introduced him to his Wellington musician friends Geoff Murphy and Bruno Lawrence. 'Not only was he highly intelligent,' Murphy recalled, 'but he was seriously eccentric.'[18] Murphy and Lawrence decided he must be a great philosopher. He played a bit part in *Tank Busters*, and almost caused the film to be banned when the broadcaster discovered that, as per Nicholls' request, Murphy had identified him in the credits as Rigid Nipples. After some negotiation, the scandalised broadcaster had the credits re-shot in time for screening.

The year 1973 saw Nicholls writing for Alister Taylor's short-lived local version of *Rolling Stone*. He followed the American blues star Muddy Waters on a New Zealand tour, filing an 8000-word report that offered both an intimate observation of the musician's routines, on stage and off, and a sprinkling of Nicholls' philosophising:

> It's no coincidence that blues and blues-based negro music are enjoying something of a revival at the same time as there is a thriving Jesus freak movement and a growing number of dropouts. With politicians commanding less respect and more contempt, and intellectuals writing books on 'the meaning of meaning', meaning seems to have lost all its meaning, and we have to rely on feelings, to live by intuition ... On and off stage Muddy Waters is a man of feeling. So long as he has got that empathetic blues feeling the world doesn't have to have meaning. We are all strangers in this strange world and we can learn from Muddy Waters that the blues make a joyful noise out of an absurd world.[19]

Living by intuition, a stranger in a strange world, Nicholls would find his way to the Parapara Inlet at Golden Bay. He was squatting in a car case there, entertaining vague thoughts of organic gardening, when someone suggested he try to do something with an adjacent 400-acre coastal area that seemed to have been written off as wasteland. Already softened up to unorthodox ideas by the Ohu Scheme, Lands and Survey approved Nicholls' proposal to establish native plants on the wasteland. Though the natives failed to take root in the boggy soil, his experiments with Australian eucalypts took off and eventually he planted more than eighty different varieties there. Despite mutterings of 'fire hazard' from some of the entrenched locals who had already been unnerved by an influx of dome-dwelling hippies, Nicholls would develop the area into the Milnthorpe Park Scenic Reserve, today a popular haven for walkers, sculptors and native birds. Eventually native ferns would appear.[20]

While Nicholls' ferns were budding in Milnthorpe, a vacant lot by a busy intersection in the centre of Wellington had produced a crop of cabbages. The former site of the Duke of Edinburgh hotel on the corner of Willis and Manners streets, the local counterculture's favourite watering hole, had lain dormant and dusty since the pub's demolition in the early seventies. The idea of planting it with cabbages occurred to Barry Thomas while he was lying in bed recovering from an illness as 'just the right kind of art challenge. My motivation was to bring something into the heart of the metropolis that shook its grey concrete edifices into a new reckoning with nature. For too long the city had driven humankind into a usury relationship with the natural world and for me that had to stop. So by bringing it about alone, albeit with some help on the day, I had to feel confident that such an act of art trespass was really going to work. There was no permission.'[21]

Thomas bought a truckload of topsoil for $34 and, by cutting through a wire fence, illegally entered the site, raked the soil and arranged 180 seedlings to spell CABBAGE. Not only did the cabbages grow, but in the weeks that followed passers-by would also take it on themselves to weed and water them. Others brought their own additions to the site: a bed, a bath, living-room furniture and a television set all appeared. Poets, musicians and political activists adopted it as a venue. Though developers would eventually build there, until late 1978 it functioned as both an art installation and improvised happening, challenging conventions of ownership and relationship to the land. Like Jumping Sundays, it would help inspire a more formalised programme of free public events and festivals in the years that followed.

The idea that the land is fundamental to who we are, and that it should be respected as such, was not new; it had existed as long as Māori had been here, though Māori concepts of land use had been treated mostly with contempt by Pākehā. But the rise of the environmental movement, along with such idiosyncratic innovations as Dick Nicholls' eucalypts and Barry Thomas's 'vacant lot of cabbages', was part of a maturing relationship with the land and developing sense of nationhood, to which the counterculture made a creative contribution.

Barry Thomas plants his 'vacant lot of cabbages', Wellington, 1978. Justin Keen photograph, Museum of New Zealand Te Papa Tongarewa, CA001114/001/001

ROUZE UP!

Eleven

On the opening page of Roszak's *The Making of a Counter Culture* is an epigram by the prophetic poet William Blake:

> Rouze up, O Young Men of the New Age!
> set your foreheads against the ignorant Hirelings!
> For we have Hirelings in the Camp, the Court, and
> the University, who would, if they could, for ever
> depress Mental, and prolong Corporeal war.

The Māori Land March on State Highway 1 outside Wellington, 1975.
Christian Heinegg photograph, Alexander Turnbull Library, 87561-4-F

Though Blake's exhortation was written in the early nineteenth century, part of the preface to *Milton*, his illuminated epic with its famous lines 'I will not cease from Mental Fight, Nor Shall my Sword sleep in my hand Til we have built Jerusalem ...', he might have been addressing the young rebels of the early 1970s with their own mental fights and dreams of Jerusalem.

YOUNG WARRIORS

Blake's poetry spoke to Rawiri Paratene, a teenager in South Auckland whose broad love of literature inspired him to apply to the QEII Arts Council Drama School in Wellington, which he would attend in 1971 and 1972, and from which he would be the first Māori to graduate. He arrived in Wellington with Blake's visions in his head, but also a strong sense that life in colonial New Zealand was unfair.[1]

'Growing up in Ōtara helped politicise me,' he would recall forty years later. 'I was a prefect and top student but looking around I could see that my people were struggling. There was no library, no gymnasium. There was a feeling that we'd been dumped there. And that made me angry.'[2]

In Wellington he moved into a flat with several other young Māori. Just down the road was a communal house occupied by members of the band BLERTA, whose painted bus sat on the street outside. Among Rawiri's flatmates was the young activist Tame Iti. Tame had grown up in Rūātoki in the eastern Bay of Plenty, speaking Māori as his first language. His activism had begun at the age of eight when his headmaster told the school assembly that the students were forbidden to speak te reo on the school grounds. The punishment was a choice of picking up horse manure or writing 'I must not speak Maori' a hundred times on the blackboard. 'I must have written it a thousand times, and I started to smell like a horse', he recalled in a TEDx talk in 2015. Yet at eight he had realised that the headmaster, in asserting his authority, had lost the respect of the students, lost his mana. Resistance worked.

At sixteen Tame left Rūātoki and spent time in Christchurch and Auckland where he 'started to meet new people—Māori, Pasifika, Pākehā ... questioning authority about all kinds of things: Women's Liberation, anti-apartheid, the Vietnam War, socialism and the rights of the working class. I started to hear the story from other cultures that sounded like old Tūhoe stories: stories about stolen land, communities displaced, stories about police brutality, stories about military rule. I learned the art of protest and political activism: occupy their space so they can't avoid you, draw attention to the issue and make them uncomfortable, make them face you and make your voice heard.'[3]

Rawiri Paratene (still known at the time as David Broughton) formed strong bonds with his teachers and fellow students at Drama School, though he sometimes got into trouble for missing classes. His absences were invariably due to political activities. He and Tame took part in an encampment on the steps of Parliament to draw attention to the erosion of Māori rights and language, and went to Waitangi to protest the annual Treaty commemorations.

They helped found the Wellington branch of Nga Tamatoa—the Young Warriors. Inspired in part by the American civil rights movement and the revolutionary Black Panther Party, Nga Tamatoa had been started in Auckland in 1970 by a group of Māori, mostly in their early twenties, among them Syd and Hana Jackson, Donna Awatere and Taura Eruera, who could see and powerfully articulate the injustices and social damage resulting from colonisation. Though issues such as protection of te reo Māori and honouring Te Tiriti o Waitangi were not new, Nga Tamatoa viewed these through a modern lens.

At the start of the 1960s, most Māori still lived in rural areas, and Pākehā, who lived mainly in the cities, could hum the mantra that New Zealand had 'the best race relations in the world'. Their state of bliss—'where ignorance is valued as innocence', as Donna Awatere put it—was interrupted only by the occasional reported incident such as the refusal of service to Dr Henry Bennett at the lounge bar of the Papakura Hotel on account of a 'colour bar' imposed by the publican, apparently at the request of his Pākehā patrons.[4] But the urbanisation that had begun after the war was rapidly accelerating, and the social cost of such sudden major social upheaval was evident in statistics relating to Māori health, education, employment, housing and crime.

Members of Nga Tamatoa on the steps of Parliament, 1971. Rawiri Paratene is front centre; Tame Iti is back right. **Dominion Post Collection, Alexander Turnbull Library, PAColl-7327**

Commissioned to find a solution, J. K. Hunn, in his 1961 Report on the Department of Maori Affairs, essentially proposed that integration should be acknowledged and promoted wherever possible as official policy. The report was a product of what historian Richard Hill calls 'Crown assumptions and priorities', and did not reflect the aspirations of Māori for Crown recognition of rangatiratanga (self-determination or chiefly authority). Recognising that the fundamental tenets of communal Māori culture and of 'individualistic and self-centred' European culture were 'incompatible', Hunn concluded that it was for Māori to adapt to the European world.[5]

Ironically, rather than resulting in integration, urban life fuelled the political consciousness of a new generation of Māori. In a similar way to the PYM, Tamatoa groups quickly sprang up in different centres, employing a range of strategies but all broadly sharing the same goals: opposing racism, spreading the Māori language and seeking redress for loss of land. With such scene-stealing stunts as the Parliament encampment, they got flak both from Pākehā who portrayed them as threatening militants and from Māori who saw their protest methods as undignified and an emulation of the kind used by Pākehā. As Aroha Harris points out, Nga Tamatoa challenged not only the Pākehā institutions but also the relatively conservative leadership of state-sponsored organisations like the Māori Women's Welfare League, established in 1951, and the New Zealand Māori Council, set up by the Crown in the wake of the Hunn Report.[6] 'We've achieved more in one year than the Maori Council in the ten years it has been going,' Syd Jackson told the *Listener*.[7]

✶

Almost concurrent with the rise of Nga Tamatoa was the formation of the Polynesian Panthers. The period that had seen the greatest urban migration of Māori had also seen an unprecedented influx of Pacific migrants lured by promises of work and education. Cook Islanders, Niueans and Tokelauans were New Zealand citizens, while New Zealand also had an agreement to accept migrants from its former trust-territory of Western Samoa.[8] Living mostly in the yet-to-be-gentrified inner city of Auckland, they were subjected to stereotyping and scapegoating, blamed for crime, rising unemployment and housing problems, while their cultural traditions were seen as strange and anti-social. Cooking in an umu or outdoor oven, for instance, drew complaints about the smoke.

Some young Islanders, seeking solidarity and a vent for their frustrations, formed gangs and got into trouble. The Polynesian Panthers were acting on their frustrations too, but the outlets they sought were practical and political. Like Nga Tamatoa, many of the founders were students. They took their name from the Black Panther Party, and inspiration from the writings of its leaders: Huey Newton, Bobby Seale, Eldridge Cleaver.

Nga Tamatoa and Polynesian Panthers at an anti-Vietnam War demonstration, circa 1971. Tame Iti is with megaphone. John Miller photograph, private collection

In his novelised memoir *A Boy Called Broke*, Fa'amoana John Luafutu recounts the genesis of the Polynesian Panthers. A Tongan student Willo (recognisable as Panther founder Will 'Ilolahia) hectors his friends, a lively assortment of gang members, musicians and drinking mates, into organising themselves as a political movement. He ponders the name Polynesian Panthers — 'Hmmm ... It's gotta nice ring to it. The time is right' — while one of his cohorts strums a guitar and starts to sing the revolutionary pop hit 'Something in the Air': *Lock up the streets and houses, because there's something in the air* ... 'In no time, an office is established above some shops at the end of Ponsonby Road in Three Lamps. Also joining are three dynamic Polynesian sisters who passionately believe in the kaupapa. They have roles in public speaking and running a youth recruitment drive.'

At one such venture to the Mount Albert shopping centre, Panther member 'Sister Ma'a' 'brings out anger and resistance from shop owners' but draws an attentive crowd of mostly brown faces, as well as the occasional Palagi 'of the hippy/student variety, holding sticks of incense'.[9]

Tigilau Ness, who would marry Māori Panther member Miriama Rauhihi, was seventeen when he joined the Panthers. As a student at Mount Albert Grammar, he was an avid reader and excelled in English but had been ordered out of school for refusing to cut his hair, which he had styled into an afro in homage to his hero Jimi Hendrix. Despite explaining to his headmaster that it was the Niuean custom for the eldest boy to wear his hair long until his coming-of-age ceremony, the expulsion stuck. He recalled: 'As I was walking out the front gate of Mount Albert Grammar, there was a whole lot of Auckland University students protesting. "Racist school! Racist school!" People like Tim Shadbolt and Will 'Ilolahia were there, all because I wouldn't cut my hair.'

Projected into political activism by a combination of cultural pride and a love of Hendrix, he began swotting up on the black American experience. 'Up till then I had read *Lord of the Rings* — the whole trilogy — and Shakespeare. As I started getting into the Polynesian Panthers I read a lot more political books — Malcolm X, Angela Davis. I suddenly realised that this thing wasn't only happening here. I could relate to what was going on over there, the stark racism. I felt the same thing here.'[10]

The Black Panthers had been founded in Oakland, California, initially with the aim of patrolling black communities and keeping them safe from police brutality. But with their quasi-military apparel and conspicuous wielding of weapons, they were seen by politicians and media as a violent threat to American society. It was a characterisation that was transposed to New Zealand media's coverage of the Polynesian Panthers.

Though the Polynesian Panthers consciously adopted the facade of their American counterparts — the black leather jackets, berets, afros, Panther insignia and generally staunch demeanour — it would be hard to find a more locally engaged group of citizens. They ran community dances and social events and after-school homework centres for students, assisted the elderly with their shopping, and provided places for prisoners on release from jail. After two children were killed on a dangerous road in Ponsonby, they ran a campaign to have a pedestrian crossing installed. They also provided legal aid to the Pasifika community, in consultation with a South Auckland lawyer, David Lange, yet to make his entry into national politics.

'REVOLUTIONARY INTER-COMMUNALISM'

While Pākehā protesters could be vehement about racial injustice in South Africa or Vietnam, recognition of racism in their own country was sporadic. HART paid lip service to domestic issues, but as an adjunct to their main cause. CARE — Citizens Association for Racial Equality — had formed in 1964 with a mixture of Pākehā and Polynesian members to draw attention to discrimination in the community, as well as throwing its weight behind the South African protests.

Then there was the People's Union. At Jumping Sundays there had been one voice that could be heard as loudly, and almost as often, as Tim Shadbolt's. That was the voice of Roger Fowler. But unlike Shadbolt, Fowler could sing, and tended to express his politics through songs rather than soapboxing. That year, with pianist Dave Neumegen (later to become Arif Usmani), he had formed the Frank E. Evans Lunchtime Entertainment Band, belting out popular songs of the twenties and thirties in an acoustic jug-band style. Often he would rewrite the lyrics. 'When the red red robin comes bob-bob-bobbin' along' became 'When the red revolution comes ...' Humorously named after the USS *Frank E. Evans* which had recently been ignominiously cut in half in a collision during training with the Royal New Zealand Navy, they were the embodiment of the slogan borrowed from the Furry Freak Brothers and graffitied on walls around the world: 'While you're out there smashing the state, don't forget to keep a smile on your lips and a song in your heart'.

Fowler had an engaging smile and a heart full of song, but he was also a natural organiser and a driving force in The People's Union for Survival and Freedom. Formed in 1971 and operating out of premises at 15 Ponsonby Road, the People's Union was a collective, committed to helping people in inner-city Auckland who might be struggling to make ends meet. Practising what Fowler called 'revolutionary inter-communalism', it was a broad church that encompassed students, hippies and dropouts, Māori and Pasifika radicals, immigrant families and others.[11]

They ran a community food programme, buying bulk fruit and vegetables from the city markets and reselling them at cost, saving members between a third and half the amount they were charged by retailers. They gave assistance to tenants by organising rent strikes, pressuring landlords into repairing their run-down properties, and

Wayne Toliafua of the Polynesian Panthers (left) and Roger Fowler (with banner), circa 1973. **John Miller photograph**

barricading themselves into buildings where renters were facing eviction. They organised the charter of a bus which would make a trip every Sunday from the central downtown bus station to Paremoremo maximum-security prison on the North Shore so that friends, families and supporters could visit inmates.

Fowler was familiar with the inside of a prison. In 1968 he had been a student teacher, nineteen years old and fired up about the iniquities of the Vietnam War, when his number was called for compulsory military service. He went to the medical test, passed with flying colours and was summoned to training camp. But instead of boarding the train to Waiouru with the other conscripts, he leafleted the station with anti-war material and went home. When he was found to be absent at the start of training, he was issued a fine. He refused to pay and was sentenced to a fortnight in Mount Eden. Since then, he had been arrested twenty-odd times in relation to various protest activities.[12]

The People's Union published its own newspaper, which included a '10 Point Statement of Direction' demanding 'an end to all oppression, be it class, racial, sexual, cultural or any other ... an education system which teaches us the skills we need in order to survive and build a society where all people's needs are met and all talents can flourish ... [that] our community select and control its own police force ... create our own courts ... [and] full and meaningful employment, controlled by the community and workers involved'.[13] Elsewhere, the paper stated:

> This society must be changed ... from one where the community is employed to enrich a few who own the businesses, dwellings etc., to one in which the community runs the businesses and dwellings for the benefit of all the members of the community ... In the short run we join together and force concessions from those few individuals who control our community's resources without concern for the people. In the long run the people will become strong enough to take over completely and run things according to human needs.[14]

The People's Union forged strong bonds with the Māori and Pasifika communities, who were especially vulnerable to exploitation by unscrupulous landlords and abuse by the police. It became what Fowler calls 'a sister organisation' to the Polynesian Panthers, sharing resources such as transport, printing and design equipment, and combining forces in the food co-op.

It was also involved with the Panthers in the PIG (Police Investigation Group) patrols that were set up in response to the Auckland Police Task Force, which the government had commissioned in 1973 to target Pacific Islanders suspected of overstaying their working visas. As the cops made their evening rounds of bars frequented by Māori and Pasifika, PIG patrols would trail them in their own vehicles, handing out leaflets, informing people of their rights, and occasionally intervening between them and the police.

✱

While some young Māori and Pasifika came into contact with the counterculture through shared activism, some crossed paths in other ways. Pākehā-dominated biker gangs such as Hells Angels had been around for a good decade; in the early seventies Māori and Pasifika gangs were starting to become a visible presence, and a loose interaction between gang members and the countercultural community was not unheard of, though neither was it entirely comfortable. Gangs were frequent attenders at rock festivals, where they would sometimes be involved in fights, more often with other gang members than with regular punters. There was a glaring contrast between the gangs with their appropriation of fascist iconography and apparent readiness for violence, and the hippies with their rainbow-coloured clothes and espousals of peace and love, but some counterculturists saw the gangs as fellow dissidents and dropouts from straight society. And evidently they liked a lot of the same music.

Some developed a liking for the same recreational substances too—though not everyone. One Pākehā pot-smoker became acquainted with some foundation members of predominantly Māori gang the Mongrel Mob, who had moved from Hastings to Wellington in the late sixties and were now living in the flat next door to his. There was some socialising between the households: if not quite revolutionary inter-communalism, it was convivial enough. Although the Mongrel Mob would later become associated with drug dealing of various kinds, he recalls that when he first met his neighbours 'they wouldn't have anything to do with drugs; some because they thought they would make you go mad or they didn't want to get hooked, some simply for the entirely practical reason that it was an easy lever for the cops, who were already on their backs'.[15]

Someone who understood the worlds of both the counterculture and the gangs was Denis O'Reilly. A Pākehā from Timaru, O'Reilly had not long abandoned a training in the seminary when he became a patched member of the Black Power gang: an unusual transition for a Pākehā and even more unusual for a student priest. Inspired by the poetry and polemics of Baxter, he had briefly run an open house for mostly Māori youth in Temuka, before being waylaid by BLERTA who in late 1971 were passing through the South Island town on their first tour in their brightly painted bus. Working part time in his father's garage, he had been called on to make some repairs to the band's vehicle, and wound up joining them for the remainder of their tour, and was introduced to hashish and the hippie lifestyle along the way.

Moving north to Wellington, he became involved with the McFarlane Street crash pad that had been established on Baxter's advice by Jim Kebbell and Marion Wood. Before long he had set up his own gang-oriented crash pad, as well as a workers' co-operative made

Storm, 1974. Gang associations saw this band barred from the pub circuit.
Ross France private collection

up of Black Power members which successfully tendered for labouring contracts around Wellington, establishing a long-term relationship with the City Council.

In conjunction with a group of activists involved with *Salient* who, according to editor Roger Steele 'believed there was a revolution happening and that the *Salient* office was pretty much the centre of it', O'Reilly brought gang members and students together in a number of radical acts, including an occupation of the Ministry of Maori and Island Affairs, picketing the premises of unethical landlords, and the establishment of a pop-up crèche in the Student Union building.[16]

He also kept a foot in the music scene, taking on the management of Storm, a gale-force rock band fronted by two brothers, guitarists Horace and Phil Mahauriki, and bass player Danny Makamaka, all friends of the Wellington Black Power, plus a couple of Pākehā: drummer Dave Alexander, and singer and recent law graduate Ross France. (Having seen them on several occasions, I can testify that Storm were terrific; their version of 'All Along the Watchtower' is unsurpassed, while the rest of their set was similarly majestic, with powerful vocal harmonies stacked on furious guitars.) With a grant from the Arts

Council, O'Reilly bought Storm a bus and, following in BLERTA's diesel fumes, they set off in the summer of 1974 on a tour of the North Island: Hawke's Bay, Gisborne, Coromandel, Auckland and beyond. O'Reilly booked the venues, depending mainly on word of mouth for publicity and local marae for accommodation. Remarkably, given the underground nature of the venture, they drew good crowds, especially in the Far North where they packed out the Whangārei Town Hall two nights in a row. The tour culminated in a free concert in Albert Park.

Storm had the ambition and the musical goods to become a successful, full-time touring band. But their association with Black Power was enough to have them barred from the crucial Lion Breweries circuit, which was run along tsarist lines by entertainment manager Richard Holden.[17] When the band split up in 1975, singer Ross France moved to Auckland where he became involved in both the People's Union and the fledgling Pacific reggae band Herbs. The others remained musically active in New Zealand and Australia. Though barely noted in local music histories, which skew towards bands with a legacy of recordings, Storm were nevertheless important: an expression of commonalities between Māori and the counterculture at a time when each was engaged in its own struggle against society's institutions. As a life member of Black Power, Denis O'Reilly has continued to be a prominent voice in the public conversation about gangs and society.

✷

As in music, there were overlaps in politics between the counterculture and Māori and Pasifika organisations. Māori had been active in anti-apartheid protests since long before the inception of the counterculture, and would continue to be active right up to the nation-splitting Springbok tour of 1981. The Vietnam War had also drawn Māori and Pasifika groups to mobilisations. But the reasons for protesting could be subtly yet significantly different. Māori and Pasifika solidarity with the North Vietnamese reflected an empathy particular to colonised peoples. 'Our enemy is the white man, not the Viet Cong', declared a Polynesian Panthers placard that no one could imagine Pākehā carrying. Rawiri Paratene remembers one of the first Vietnam mobilisations he attended as an opportunity to wave the Nga Tamatoa banner and attract new recruits as much as to protest the war. And where HART, the most prominent group opposing the rugby tours, were focused almost exclusively on the evils of South African apartheid, it was left to Māori to point out the related issue of racism in New Zealand.

The counterculture, in large part, consisted of Pākehā who had grown up with all the privileges Pākehā institutions offered and were now consciously rejecting them. Māori and Pasifika, on the other hand, had never been welcomed to those institutions in the first place. What organisations like Nga Tamatoa and the Polynesian Panthers wanted was for the Crown and government to admit that the system was racist, to overhaul the institutions and honour Te Tiriti o Waitangi and tino rangatiratanga or Māori sovereignty.

Eventually this would spur new movements such as the 1975 hīkoi that came to be known as the Māori Land March, which called for an end to land laws that excluded Māori cultural values and asked for the ability to establish legitimate communal ownership of land within iwi. Led by eighty-year-old Whina Cooper, who in 1951 had been the first national president of the Māori Women's Welfare League, it grew out of a hui Cooper had chaired at Te Puea marae in Māngere, that had brought together representatives of a range of iwi and other Māori groups, both radical and conservative, to agree on the need for more direct action on land loss. The hīkoi left Te Hāpua in the Far North in mid-September and reached Parliament in Wellington forty-three days later. The marchers had made their way down the centre of the North Island, with a core of fifty people marching the entire way, a retinue of support vehicles, and an estimated thirty thousand to forty thousand other people joining for different parts of the journey.[18]

While a number of Pākehā joined the march, and the issues at stake were close to home and arguably of more relevance, the hīkoi never became a rallying point for the counterculture in the way Vietnam, and the anti-apartheid and anti-nuclear movements, had. Behind the Land March was the question of rangatiratanga. For the counterculture to embrace rangatiratanga, it would need to change its orientation. Drug legalisation, sexual freedom, nuclear disarmament —under rangatiratanga, such issues would be addressed in terms of tikanga Māori. As Donna Awatere summed it up in one of the *Broadsheet* articles that became her 1985 manifesto *Maori Sovereignty*: 'It is not up to "the (white) people" to allow Maori the right to redesign this country "after the revolution". It is up to the Maori to allow white "people" this privilege.'[19] For all their perceived struggles, she observed, 'whites share a common culture in which the differences are *part* of that culture ... white people's protest is done within the boundary of the western capitalist culture which is their heritage'.[20]

If Māori and Pasifika alliances with the counterculture were not stronger, it may be because Māori and Pasifika societies are essentially collectivist, while Pākehā society is, as Hunn observed, individualist. The counterculture sought in many ways to reject the tenets of mainstream society, but old habits die hard. Despite the aspirations espoused by certain communards, rabble rousers, hippie idealists and fallen priests, the counterculture, with its overriding notions of freedom, would increasingly show itself to be a group of loosely affiliated individuals doing their own thing.

BULLSHIT AND GELIGNITE

Twelve

New Zealanders can be awfully sensitive about how the rest of the world perceives them. 'So what do you think of New Zealand?' visitors are routinely asked, often moments after they have arrived, while we pass judgements on the way our own representatives conduct themselves on the world stage. Sue Kedgley was interviewed in 1973 by Alan Whicker, the tweedy English television presenter, visiting as part of his long-running *Whicker's World* series. Kedgley, he explained in his British army officer tones, 'leads the "Women's Lib" movement in New Zealand'. Dispensing with foreplay, Kedgley got straight to her subject: the number of New Zealand women who have never achieved sexual satisfaction. She attributed this to the lack of sensitivity of the New Zealand male whom she described as being typically 'hefty, aggressive, and who probably would never have heard of a clitoris'.

A woman walks into a bar, 1970.
Dominion Post Collection, Alexander
Turnbull Library, EP1970/3763/8-F

Even if he *had* heard of a clitoris, this might have been the first time the hefty New Zealand male had heard the word spoken aloud, let alone on television. While Whicker blinked behind his glasses, Kedgley went on to describe the frustration of New Zealand women, 'particularly New Zealand women who have been overseas, been on the Continent. One of the most frightening things coming back to New Zealand is the sexual dissatisfaction ...'[1]

Some viewers sniggered, others entertained violent fantasies. In the *Auckland Star,* television reviewer Robert Gilmore worried about what 'our kinsmen 12,000 miles away' in the land of *Coronation Street* would think: 'Len Fairclough might have asked why some New Zealand male hadn't thumped some sense into beautiful, intelligent Sue Kedgley. Is Kedgley serious in this daft women's lib thing ...?'[2]

FREE WOMEN, FREE SOCIETY

Sue Kedgley was already one of the most familiar faces in the local Women's Liberation movement. She had grown up in Wellington in middle-class Roseneath. At fourteen, the Beatles' visit had been the most exciting thing in her life. It had also marked the start of a rebelliousness that saw her threatened with expulsion from Wellington Girls' College. Her parents moved her to the private Marsden School to complete her secondary schooling. In 1966 she arrived at Victoria University, where issues from student bursaries to the Vietnam War were being loudly debated. Defying the male dominance of student politics, the natural public speaker with the Marsden accent stood for the student executive and was duly elected.

In 1970, on her way back from a visit to her parents in Papua New Guinea where her father was helping establish a university, she picked up a copy of the just-published *Sisterhood Is Powerful*, American Robin Morgan's anthology of feminist writings, and a switch was flipped: 'the feminist click', as converts would refer to it. That year she arrived in Auckland to study for her Master's degree. In the offices of *Craccum* she asked where she might find the campus branch of Women's Liberation. 'There isn't one,' editor Stephen Chan told her. But he thought there ought to be.

'Stephen Chan was hugely influential with me,' Kedgley says. 'Here's this guy who never wore a shirt, just these jeans and hair down to here, very cool, and he said, "Well, start one yourself."' Kedgley and her friend Sharyn Cederman called a meeting, and Auckland Women's Liberation was formed.[3]

That year, eighteen-year-old Therese O'Connell arrived in Wellington from New Plymouth, her sense of social justice already kindled by television coverage of the civil rights movement in the US and by conversation in her Catholic household about the British occupation of Northern Ireland. In the capital, the young psychology student encountered demonstrations about one cause or other almost every Friday night. The sight of veteran communist and political agitator Rona Bailey pulling up in her sports car to an all-night vigil and lavishing the protesters with fish and chips impressed on her that activism could be both glamorous and altruistic. She joined the PYM and got involved in street theatre. When word arrived on the eve of the university capping procession that four protesters at Kent State University had been killed by national guardsmen in the US, she stayed up all night with a group making cardboard coffins with the names of the dead to carry behind the parade.

But it was a part-time job at the Students' Association cafeteria that moved her to launch the first branch of Women's Liberation. 'I found that guys doing the same work as me were getting paid more than me. I'll never forget the outrage of that.' By the time the *Dominion*'s 'World of Women' section profiled the new organisation in July 1970, the Wellington group was thirty-strong and growing.[4] As distinct from later groups, they would name themselves the Women's Liberation Front, in solidarity with other organisations fighting for what they saw as issues of human rights, such as the National Liberation Front in Vietnam.[5]

In early 1971, a mixed-gender group calling themselves Women for Equality organised leafleting and guerrilla theatre outside the Miss New Zealand Contest at Auckland Town Hall and, in combination with Kedgley and Cederman's Auckland University Women's Liberation group, conspired to take over a bar of the Great Northern Hotel, where women had been refused entry.[6] The latter episode had elements of farce. The Sports Bar of the Great Northern was, in fact, a popular gathering place for gay men: something Ngahuia Te Awekotuku, the only 'Māori lesbian' involved in the action, tried to point out to the group. At first the women were turned away by security guards, but police eventually granted the women permission to enter, provided they could show ID. Drinking continued there for several weeks before the publican opened another bar for males only — as he was entitled to do under the law. The protests fizzled soon after, though Te Awekotuku and her girlfriend continued to receive 'harsh words' from their 'gay brothers' who had not welcomed the fracas. But such stunts attracted publicity as intended, and turned both Kedgley and Te Awekotuku into nationally known figures.[7]

Adopting the brand of an existing international movement, Women's Liberation quickly became the most prominent of the various radical women's organisations. Within a few months, there were at least twenty groups meeting around the country.[8] In its early stages, Women's Liberation was closely connected to the broader counter-culture. Its demands echoed those being heard everywhere, from anti-war marches to Acid Tests: liberation for the Vietnamese people, liberation of the mind. Women's Liberation meetings were held in urban communes and their flyers were printed at Resistance Bookshops. Taking their cue from their American counterparts, they used

Group hug. Angela Middleton photograph, private collection

the term 'consciousness raising' to promote their workshops, sharing a vocabulary with such explorers of human consciousness as Timothy Leary and Richard Alpert. The consciousness-raising groups usually consisted of ten women or fewer who would discuss, in confidence, aspects of female experience, drawing on personal knowledge as well as the work of outside writers and researchers. An awareness of widespread illegal abortion was just one of many issues acknowledged within these groups. The trust built through sharing of experience and knowledge was valuable in developing a base for political action.

Yet sexism continued to thrive, even in the world of progressive politics. Sue Bradford, a teenage member of the PYM and one of the founders of the Auckland Resistance Bookshop, recalls getting up to speak about Vietnam at one of the political forums regularly held in the Auckland quad—the same forum that received Tim Shadbolt like a rock star—only to be shouted down, assailed with missiles and sexual invective.[9]

'Someone like Stephen Chan was thoughtful, philosophical, and very much supported Women's Liberation, and was encouraging to me and others, so there were a few exceptions,' says Sue Kedgley. But to many men of the counterculture, it seemed Women's Liberation just 'meant that now women were liberated we could all have sex with them'.[10]

When Rose Beauchamp married Ian Wedde in Auckland in 1967, they were both just twenty years old. Rose remembers it as 'a questioning kind of marriage. Getting married was the only way I perceived that I could actually get away from my parents' house and move into a freer world. You made alliances and I could see how Ian and I could support one another.' They were part of an affiliation of young writers, performers and painters that included Alan Brunton, David Mitchell and Russell Haley. But already it was clear where the power lay. 'At that time the men were the stars and the women just watched everything. I was a pianist but I was just watching and listening. I think I watched and listened for about ten years.'

The division between the sexes seemed to further widen once Rose and Ian had children. 'I personally was just trying to create some domestic stability at a time when there was so much alcohol,' she recalls. 'So many drugs and such a destructive level of behaviour going on in the marginal community — people wiping themselves out, killing themselves. And my main objective, seeing as I had a child, was just to try and maintain some stability.

'I was talking to a friend the other day and he said, "LSD changed everything" and I said, "Well, it didn't change everything for me." I had one trip and thought, Ooh, this is ghastly, I hate this feeling. I didn't want to be out of control like that, see the world in brighter colours. I didn't want to live in a dis-reality. I also realised that you were going to confuse your children terribly if you were in that world and they were trying to interact with you. I didn't see how that would work.'[11]

For a mother in the counterculture, turning on, tuning in and dropping out were not necessarily priorities. More worldly goals like equal pay, day care for their children and the right to control their own bodies were enough to be going on with.

Sandra Coney was at the first meeting of Auckland Women's Liberation. At the time she was living in Papakura, a housewife with two young children. She had married at seventeen, having already completed one year of tertiary study. In 1966, worrying about how she might provide for herself and her young family should anything happen to her husband, she went back to university. Her husband supported her decision, which was more than could be said for most of the university administration. 'There was a huge opposition to mothers with children being at university, which was a complete eye-opener to me. Everybody was fairly anti, even the Students' Association.'[12]

Finding allies among a small group of students and staff members, she helped found the Student and Staff Nursery Society, and opened a campus crèche. The experience helped focus her thinking on society's systematic oppression of women, and at Auckland Women's Liberation she found her soulmates. At first they came mostly from the urban middle class. A few were living in experimental arrangements such as urban communes. Others, like her, were in traditional nuclear-family situations and looking for a better way.

When Coney, writing in the 1980s, characterised the 'real business of being a New Zealand man' as being a matter of physical ability as opposed to effete pursuits like art or music, she was speaking from experience.[13] It was her father, Tom Pearce, who had taken an all-white All Blacks to South Africa in 1960; who had vehemently opposed Mayor Robinson's Auckland welcome for the Beatles in 1964, and had similarly decried the council's purchase of a sculpture by British artist Barbara Hepworth, *Torso II*, opining that it 'looks to me like the buttock of a dead cow washed up on a beach'. Yet this hyper-masculinist may have inadvertently given his daughter the tools with which to become a feminist. With no boys of his own, Pearce treated Sandra and her sister Helen as surrogate sons, encouraging them to swim, sail and surf, and not to blindly accept instructions or rules.

OBSCENE AND HEARD

Women's Liberation received a boost of publicity in early 1972 when New Zealand got a visit from Germaine Greer. Originally from Melbourne, the Australian writer, who had become an international star through the success of her book *The Female Eunuch*, had been part of a Sydney bohemian intellectual subculture known as the Sydney Push, which included at various times the writers and critics Lillian Roxon, Clive James and Robert Hughes. In Britain, where she had gone in 1964 to complete her doctorate, Greer contributed to *Oz* magazine, one of the pivotal publications of the underground press, edited by fellow Australian and countercultural character Richard Neville. She also helped found *Suck*—the 'first European sexpaper'—an experiment in 'radical pornography' in which, as American writer Chris Kraus puts it, 'sexuality and daily life were seen as the locus of politics' and 'the public exposure of traditionally private behavior … a means of disrupting the social order'.[14]

The Female Eunuch was published in 1970. Combining personal anecdote and historical scholarship in a vigorous intellectual prose, Greer looked at the ways society repressed women's sexuality to ensure that women served men. But she wasn't calling for equality in the existing system; she wanted liberty for all. 'The man who is expected to have a rigid penis at all times is not any freer than the woman whose vagina is supposed to explode with the first thrust of such a penis,' she wrote.[15]

The countercultural battle cry of freedom rang from the book's pages. A solution needed to go 'much further than equal pay for equal work … it ought to revolutionise the conditions of work completely'. Her prescription was 'a revolution in consciousness' that would include household co-operatives, macrobiotic food, marijuana in place of cigarettes and beer, the rejection of cosmetics except for fun, and women's reconnection to their own bodies and rejection of monogamy and male sexual control.[16]

Germaine Greer (left) in Auckland, with
Sharyn Cederman (centre) and Sue Kedgley.
John Miller photograph, private collection

Greer flew into New Zealand at the peak of her fame, on the Australasian leg of a world tour. Her trip was sponsored by local paper the *Sunday News* (largely owned by *Truth*) which had primed the public for her arrival with weeks of headlines focusing on the aspects of her persona most likely to cause disquiet — and sell newspapers — among conservative middle New Zealand. 'Kiwi male chauvinist pigs are in for trouble — nothing but trouble when sexual revolutionary Germaine Greer storms into New Zealand,' the paper announced. 'Fronting (bra-less) her first Sydney press conference, the freaky, spindly, six-foot-two academic showed how she could dominate — or intimidate — the opposite sex.'[17]

Sue Kedgley accompanied Greer as she spoke around the country. Men with high media profiles were eager to meet the celebrated author. Arts commentator Hamish Keith hosted her on his National Radio programme 'Guest of Honour', then opened his house up for a welcoming party. *Thursday* magazine took her out to dinner with half a dozen prominent media figures including Brian Edwards, and asked them to record their impressions. All those attending the dinner confessed to having found her intimidating. 'It was not merely that she was six feet one,' wrote Edwards, 'not merely that she was devastatingly brilliant, not merely that she could have demolished each and all of us with her intellect; it was quite simply that she was Germaine Greer, the chosen one of Women's Liberation ...' Surprised by his own reaction, he went on to confess that 'throughout the evening ... a tasty little fantasy was playing itself out in my subconscious, in which, on behalf of Men's Liberation, I mastered this feminist upstart intellectually, emotionally, or sexually. For any professed and practising liberal it is a little daunting to discover that there is within you a rabid male chauvinist waiting to get out.'[18]

At the Auckland Town Hall Greer gave a talk entitled 'Free Women, Free Society'. Though the audience was mostly made up of middle-class liberals and student politicos sympathetic to her message, a few evidently were not. After complaints were made to the police about Greer's use of the words 'fuck' and 'bullshit', she was arrested and charged with using indecent and obscene language.

The court case was scheduled for the day of her departure and became a cause célèbre. Coincidentally, the indecency trial over the musical *Hair* had ended only the day before. Hundreds of protesters who had rallied the previous year when Tim Shadbolt faced similar charges turned up for a rematch. Outside the court there were scuffles with police and vigorous chanting of 'Bullshit!' and 'Fuck!' Sue Kedgley, called on as a witness, had to climb a fire escape to get into the building. Twenty-seven arrests were made. Protests simultaneously broke out in Wellington, where Greer had spoken the night before, resulting in a further twenty arrests. A group of women tried to enter Wellington police headquarters, insisting that one of them had used an obscene word and demanding to be charged. Allen Ginsberg and Lawrence Ferlinghetti, visiting Adelaide for the annual arts festival, were motivated by news of the Greer case to send a telegram to New Zealand's Prime Minister Jack Marshall, accusing the country's police of 'mind rape'.[19]

Meantime, over the din from the protesters outside the courts, one of the complainants, Blanche Wynne of Māngere, said, 'I just understood it as a word that shouldn't be used and must be objectionable. I don't understand what it means.'[20] Greer herself argued that it would have been hypocritical to modify her language in speaking to what she presumed was the centre of the counterculture. She was found guilty of using obscene language, not guilty of indecent language, and fined $40 plus costs.

Craccum devoted several pages to Greer's visit and the ensuing debacle, including a transcript of most of the Town Hall talk. But it was evident that Tim Shadbolt, who with Heather McInnes was co-editor of *Craccum* that year, was not among her converts. 'Perhaps I'm a male chauvinist but I felt an instinctive dislike of her,' he wrote. 'A highly intelligent person who can brilliantly expose attitudes and prejudices, but who is somehow a cold academic. I felt sorry for all us naive kiwis. We turned out in our thousands to welcome our liberation, and all we got was an eccentric beatnik ... a selfish radical aristocrat — isolated from the people by fame, money and intellect ...' He also noted that when he had dropped off a copy of his own book *Bullshit and Jelly-*

CHANGING VALUES

Thirteen

The election of Norman Kirk as Prime Minister in November 1972 was not the dawning of the age of Aquarius, but after twelve years of National Party rule, it almost felt like it.

For the duration of the sixties the country had been governed by Keith Holyoake, an innate conservative with a plummy voice who seemed to represent the establishment in every way. When confronted with any aggregation of youth other than perhaps a meeting of the Young Nats, he gave the impression of being simply bewildered. Kirk, however, was working class, a big man with a strong conscience, who ate badly, spoke gently yet passionately, and acted on his morals.

Norman Kirk redecorates, Christchurch, 1971. Christchurch City Libraries. CCL Star-1971-0810-015-017N-01

Abortion march, Wellington, 1973. Keith Stewart photograph, private collection

Though Holyoake had announced in August 1971 that the New Zealand Army would be ending their combat role in Vietnam, New Zealand continued to train Cambodian troops and maintain a headquarters in Saigon right up until he left office.[1] Two hours after being sworn in, Kirk had confirmed 'the severance of New Zealand military involvement in Vietnam', and that it would be replaced with civil aid.[2]

In the brief time he would spend as Prime Minister, from his election until his sudden death twenty-one months later, Kirk gave the impression that he was interested in hearing what the country's younger citizens had to say. He responded to the back-to-the-land movement with the Ohu Scheme, ordered the Rugby Union to call off a New Zealand tour by the Springboks, dispatched a frigate with a Cabinet minister on board to sail to Mururoa Atoll to protest nuclear tests by the French, and halted National's plan to raise the level of Lake Manapōuri. In each of these acts he addressed one or more of the causes that had come to be associated with the counterculture, whether it was communalism, the environment, or calls for peace and equality.

Yet in other ways he was conservative. He was determined that his party would not get entangled in the agendas of protest groups.

Of the PYM he said that 'their behaviour is a fertile seed-bed for disorder and one that should be firmly controlled by the appropriate authorities'.[3] He opposed abortion, even if, as his secretary Margaret Hayward noted in her diaries, he was visibly disturbed by a letter from a twenty-year-old pregnant teacher trainee which began:

> By the male-made laws governing abortion, you have condoned the presence of another unwanted baby ... How can men decide what is best for women/girls when their whole future is at stake ...? It is a question of the right for a woman to be able to *choose* ... I do not think that the death of a foetus is murder. What I call murder is the death of a human being who has known life, love and earth, when his/her end does not come when it should have.

The letter went on to decry the barbarism of war and remind its male reader that her situation was 'something you will never experience'.[4]

Though Kirk's position on abortion didn't change, his government did make a significant contribution to the lives and wellbeing of unmarried mothers: in 1973 Labour introduced the Domestic Purposes Benefit, a social welfare payment given to single parents with dependent children. This acknowledgement that the nuclear family is not the only social unit and that childrearing is important work, and the handing of some degree of autonomy to young women, represented a major shift in social thinking.

A NEW CONSCIOUSNESS

Kirk's rise to the highest office of government coincided with the arrival of the first political party in the country—and one of the first in the world—to really represent a countercultural point of view. The Values Party was formed in Wellington in May 1972, and presented a utopian vision of an egalitarian, ecologically sustainable country.

Their first leader was Tony Brunt, at twenty-five a baby boomer and the youngest political leader the country had seen. Their founding document was *Blueprint for New Zealand: An Alternative Future*. It began with a grim pronouncement: 'New Zealand is in the grip of a new depression.' This would have been news to anyone used to judging such matters by falling GDP or rising unemployment. The economy seemed to be flourishing; there was plenty of work. But that wasn't what Values meant: 'It is a depression which arises not from a lack of affluence but almost from too much of it.'

Drawing on a range of fashionable texts, from Alvin Toffler's *Future Shock* to Tim Shadbolt's *Bullshit and Jellybeans*, the blueprint consolidated many of the counterculture's concerns into a political manifesto. It went on to denounce materialism, the 'obsession with the growth of the economy rather than with the growth of the human mind'. It noted 'a new current flowing in the country', seen in 'the movement

Values Party: Blueprint For New Zealand, 1972. Private collection

by young people to establish a warmer and more meaningful relationship with each other, with society, with nature and the land.'[5]

In its specific policies it proposed legalising abortion, restricting use of motor cars in cities, conservation of natural resources, legislation to require recycling, and the dismantling of the armed forces. While it advocated the legalisation of homosexuality, it stopped short of legalising marijuana, instead removing its listing as a narcotic and reducing the penalties for possession and supply. Perhaps its most radical proposal was to replace the existing model of continuous growth, in both economy and population, with one of zero-growth and sustainability. All of these policies were gathered under the broad banner of a 'new consciousness': an idea and slogan redolent of the counterculture's interest in Eastern spirituality and the psychedelic experience. Just six months after its formation, Values contested the 1972 general election in forty-two electorates, though failed to win any seats. But some of Values' policies, such as its opposition to nuclear testing, sporting relations with South Africa and the Vietnam War, were swiftly implemented by Kirk's incoming government.

To judge by their candidates and the regions in which they did well, Values' constituents came from the intellectual middle class. Some were the same people who had supported CND, and the anti-Vietnam and anti-South African tour movements in the sixties, and they were joined by baby boomers who had more recently reached voting age and grown up with these causes. But to call Values the party of the counterculture is not quite accurate. The counterculture, as we have seen, included people for whom Values' policies, even including the liberalisation of marijuana laws, did not go nearly far enough, and others for whom politics of any kind was anathema. Still, Values was the first attempt to formalise in a political framework the countercultural ideas that had been fomenting during the past decade, and a measure of how much those ideas had, by the early seventies, begun to take hold in the mainstream.

In 1975, Values stood candidates in eighty-seven seats, winning 5.19 percent of the total votes. Had the current MMP system been in place, this would have put half a dozen Values Party representatives into Parliament. Under the first-past-the-post system, they again failed to gain any seats. Though they went on to contest the next four elections, Values never managed to get into Parliament nor match the level of support they had at their 1975 peak. But they can be seen as an essential forerunner to the Green Party, which formed in 1990 around an environmental policy carried over from Values and involving a number of former Values Party members including Jeanette Fitzsimons and Rod Donald.

A ROOM FULL OF MIRRORS

Though Norman Kirk had to some degree mollified the protest movement, a decade of dissent left a restlessness that could not be assuaged by addressing single issues. The sense that America was meddling with impunity in the affairs of other nations now went far beyond Vietnam. There was emerging evidence of CIA involvement in the violent overthrow of popular socialist governments in Bolivia and Uruguay — a scenario which was being played out again in Chile by mid-1973. Meanwhile, the Cold War and ever-growing stockpile of nuclear weapons continued to put the whole world in peril.

Closer to home, the focus had turned to the secret station maintained by the American military within the New Zealand Air Force base at Woodbourne near Christchurch, and American observatories at Mount John and Harewood, also in Canterbury. In 1968, activist and peace campaigner Owen Wilkes had uncovered an American plan to build a submarine navigational transmitter at the foot of the Southern Alps that would have made New Zealand a prime nuclear target. A high-profile campaign, led by Wilkes, had brought the project to a halt, but existing installations increasingly became a target for protesters.[6]

Overseas, militant outlaw groups such as the German-based Red Army Faction (popularly known as the Baader-Meinhof Group), and the Weather Underground in the US, were rising up against what they saw as the foundations of the whole imperialist structure, mounting bomb attacks against military bases and police stations, and committing arsons and bank robberies in the name of the revolution. (Andreas Baader's favourite movie was reportedly *Bonnie and Clyde*.)

Protests at the Mount John and Harewood bases in 1972 and '73, respectively, saw violent clashes between protesters and police. But an incident in August 1973 might be as close as New Zealand came to a Baader-Meinhof/Weathermen-style act, which is not to say all that close. Nineteen-year-old Margaret Matheson and twenty-seven-year-old Neil Riethmuller, both studying at Canterbury University, had met earlier that year through the student political scene centred on the PYM. Riethmuller had come to New Zealand from Australia to study; Matheson was from Christchurch. They shared a loathing of American imperialism and a general sense of being part of a global resistance. Sometime before dawn on 15 August, they broke a kitchen window of the US Consulate—in fact, the unguarded offices of an accountancy firm in which Bill Quirk, a local accountant and Christchurch's honorary consular agent, was a partner. Matheson climbed inside, doused the place in petrol and, using either a makeshift fuse or Molotov cocktail, set it alight. Explosions woke the neighbours. A security officer arrived in time to see the bombers taking off in a stolen 1959 Austin A35, and gave chase. He was soon joined by half a dozen police cars. The pair were pursued for perhaps 30 kilometres through Sydenham, Spreydon, Hornby and out towards rural Templeton, Riethmuller running red lights, knocking wheels with a pursuing vehicle and, at one point, driving towards the oncoming traffic on the Sockburn overbridge. But the circular chase ended after forty or so minutes just 150 metres from the charred Consulate when the stolen car came to a crashing halt against an outside wall of Riethmuller's own flat.[7]

While their anti-American views were noted in court, the couple were not charged with terrorism offences—the Terrorism Suppression Act would not be introduced until 2002, in the wake of the 11 September 2001 attacks in the US—but with burglary, arson, car theft and dangerous driving, to which they pleaded guilty. Matheson was sentenced to three years in prison, Riethmuller to four.

Though acts such as Matheson and Riethmuller's were rare, they seemed to express a more widespread feeling among the counterculture that there was a war being fought against shadowy forces. 'Just because you're paranoid doesn't mean they aren't after you' was the famous maxim of John Yossarian, hero of *Catch-22,* Joseph Heller's widely read satire on the futility of war. For some it had become a rule of life. Everything from laws against abortion to the prohibition of drugs could be seen as part of a broader repression. Drugs, with their tendency to heighten the senses, may have contributed to the paranoia.[8]

A continued source of anxiety and suspicion was the government spy agency the Security Intelligence Service. The SIS essentially followed what had begun in post-war America as the Truman Doctrine, in which the chief danger to the United States was considered to be the spread of communism, and the goal of America and its allies was to contain it. The secrecy of the SIS activities led to much speculation as to what they were actually up to. But it was no fantasy that among its activities the organisation was keeping an eye on any New Zealand citizens perceived to be members or affiliates of communist organisations, or who might be seen as providing some sort of assistance to communists internationally. Those in their sights included trade unions, left-wing publishers, booksellers and protest groups.[9]

The New Zealand Communist Party at that time could hardly have posed much of a threat to national security. It had emerged in the 1920s out of the broader socialist movement, advocating world communism along Soviet lines. It sometimes put up candidates in the general election, though never polled very highly. Its popular peak had been in 1949, when sixteen Communist candidates drew a total of 3499 votes between them. When the Soviet Union invaded Hungary in 1956 to quell a student-led uprising, most of the New Zealand Communist Party's intellectuals, identifying with the Hungarian students, resigned in protest. Some of them went on to found or join other left-wing organisations such as Socialist Forum, CND and Committee on Vietnam.

In 1963 the party divided again, this time between support for Khrushchev's Soviet Union and for Mao Zedong's China. By now the party leadership had decided that Soviet-style communism was untenable and had thrown its weight behind Mao, though its criticism was confined to the current 'revisionist' Khrushchev administration and it would still speak no word against Stalin, even as the world learned of his brutal purges. Vic Wilcox, party secretary since 1951, now proudly led 'the only Communist party of a western country on ... an anti-Soviet anti-revisionist path' — in other words, the only one following China, not USSR — while the pro-Soviet faction regrouped in Auckland as the Socialist Unity Party. Later, after the death of Mao in 1976, the Communist Party of New Zealand would shift its allegiance yet again, this time to the Albanian regime.[10]

Despite the party's ever-dwindling membership and obscure alliances, the SIS expended plenty of time and energy infiltrating its meetings, planting undercover agents and keeping files on its members, as well as monitoring all its various offshoots. The SIS also turned its attention to what was being labelled internationally as the New Left. In America this term encompassed everything from the Free Speech movement to the Abbie Hoffman/Jerry Rubin-led Yippies to the militant Weather Underground. In Europe the term had originated with organisations like CND and was now being applied to student radicals involved in the various university uprisings. In New Zealand it included the PYM, some of the younger Communist Party breakaway groups such as the Socialist Action League, campus activists such as

Tim Shadbolt, radical organisations like the Resistance Bookshops, and underground publishers like Chris Wheeler.

In *Cock*, Wheeler acknowledged the SIS interest in the New Left, while challenging the idea that such a movement even existed:

> The New Left is a curious myth ... as all its members can be said to have in common is youth and a marked lack of sympathy for the established order. If you're under 90 and have ever stood in Albert Park on Sunday or joined a march to Parliament or Latimer Square, man, you're the New Left and chances are some conservatively-suited, short-back-and-sides screwball from Security has you down on his list.[11]

New Left or not, Wheeler saw the activities of those 'conservatively-suited, short-back-and-sides screwballs' as an invasion of privacy and infringement of civil rights, and made it his mission to monitor and mock their efforts. In the fifth issue of *Cock* he published what was purportedly a list of SIS agents. It had been passed on to Wheeler by Alister Taylor, who had obtained it from a woman he was having an affair with, whose husband had come by it during his work as a cleaner of government offices. It appears the original list included only surnames, to which *Cock* added initials, some incorrectly. The result was that a few individuals bearing distinctive names, such as the actor Peter Vere-Jones, were implicated as being SIS employees. *Cock* ran an apology to an indignant Vere-Jones in its next issue. Meanwhile, Wheeler received visits from the police, inquiring as to how the list was obtained and threatening criminal action. In the end, no charges were forthcoming. It was the first of several such incidents in which the magazine published apparently sensitive material and charges were threatened, only to evaporate. This led Wheeler to believe that the SIS considered the magazine 'too useful to close down'.

'Thinking back,' he said in 2019, 'I'd say that probably to some degree we were protected because *Cock* actually concentrated a lot of dissidents in one place and we were such a chaotic, gossipy and disorganised bunch of yahoos that the SIS and cops probably actively used us as a major source of information on the local dissident scene.'[12] He became convinced that at least one *Cock* insider was working for the SIS.

Alister Taylor, too, believed himself to be under surveillance. In the months leading up to the 1968 Peace, Power and Politics conference, he had hired rooms in an office block on Lambton Quay which became the base of operations not only for the upcoming conference but also for the organisation of the Vietnam mobilisations in which he was involved. After a few weeks a visitor noticed a cord running from the outside of one of the windows to a room on the floor above, and pointed it out to Taylor: 'You're being bugged.' To Taylor this explained why, when he had gone to inform police of plans for an upcoming mobilisation, as legally required, the police appeared already to know the plans in detail. The day after its discovery, the cord had gone.

Others in the movement, however, wondered if Taylor himself was working for the SIS. There had been his early history with the National Party, his world trip as a student leader at the behest of the CIA, his apparently insatiable interest in knowing everything about everybody. When I spoke to Taylor not long before his death in 2019, he still bridled at such suggestions. An associate from the protest days had recently demanded: 'Tell me the truth, Alister, you really were an SIS agent all along, weren't you?'

'Why would he think that?' Taylor asked rhetorically, fixing me with his gaze. 'Apparently because he'd been told by Wheeler. You can't win.' He sighed.[13]

Into this twilight world wandered a brash, bearded American with a curious past. New Yorker Harvey Matusow had come home from the Second World War and joined the American Communist Party. By 1950, with fear of communism being kindled by the likes of Senator Joseph McCarthy, he had begun working for the FBI as a paid informer. Among the names he supplied was that of folk singer Pete Seeger, who was duly summoned before McCarthy's House Un-American Activities Committee in 1955. The singer of 'We Shall Overcome' and 'Which Side Are You On?' refused to answer questions concerning his political beliefs and associations, and was given a prison sentence for contempt (later reversed) and a blacklisting that lasted well into the 1960s.

By the time Matusow turned up in New Zealand in 1967, he had himself served prison time, having been convicted for perjury after confessing the deception in a book, *False Witness* (1955). He was now presenting himself as an avant-garde musician, collaborating with his Christchurch-born fourth wife, the composer Annea Lockwood. Lockwood had studied in London and Darmstadt, and developed a unique instrumental palette involving lengths of glass tubing that were variously blown, struck and strummed. One of their first performances together had been at the London countercultural nightspot Middle Earth, where local hippies had given them an enthusiastic reception. At Downstage Theatre in Wellington, audiences were more reticent, although the chiming, droning and bubbling sounds intrigued filmmaker John O'Shea enough for him to feature part of a performance in his snapshot documentary *Wellington in the '60s: The Way It Seemed*.

Matusow also popped up as a self-proclaimed expert on LSD on national television in current affairs programme *Compass*. He announced that in the United States 'upwards of ten million students and people under the age of twenty-five have taken LSD in the past year' and predicted that the drug would 'change the whole concept of

America' within the next ten years. He said he opposed indiscriminate banning of LSD and advocated the setting up of a centre 'similar to a religious retreat' where it could be taken under controlled conditions.[14]

Matusow and Lockwood's visit lasted just a few months. On their return to Britain, Matusow took up managing an underground rock band and marketing a stringless yo-yo. He broke up with Lockwood and went to live on a Massachusetts commune, remarried, and remarried again, moved to Arizona where he performed as a clown, then to Utah where he became a Mormon. He died in New Hampshire in 2002, but for the short time he was in New Zealand his presence added to a general unease, especially among the folk-music contingent who regarded Pete Seeger as a martyr and a hero. Which side was Matusow really on?[15]

But if there was a mood of paranoia amongst the counterculture, the spies appeared to be gripped by their own fantasies of the 'reds under beds' variety. Keith Locke, son of communists Elsie and Jack Locke, discovered that the SIS had opened a file on him when he was eleven years old. In it had been noted such suspicious boyhood activities as attending a Christchurch performance of the Moscow Circus.

Stories abound of the spy agency's clumsy efforts to infiltrate the Left, only to leave themselves humiliated and exposed. In 1966 a part-time political studies student was caught trying to enlist the secretary of the Auckland Students' Association to spy on two visiting Russian students, as well as inquiring about students enrolling for an Association trip to China and Russia. A demonstration against this suspected infiltration of a university department brought traffic on Symonds Street to a halt. Elsewhere in Auckland, a group including John Bower and Alan Robson had fortuitously learned the location of an SIS office in St Georges Bay Road. Bower's brother Colin had picked up this information from a radio conversation overheard in the back of a police car while under arrest, so the group set up their own watch station in a parked van, from which they would take photographs of agents as they came and went. 'At 8.30 they would arrive and meet up at the gate and march in,' Bower remembers. 'They used to park in all sorts of different places, they'd never park outside, and then they'd approach. There was a laundromat across the road—and we'd observe them go in and do an exchange of a laundry bag in the laundromat. I don't know if they were just doing their laundry or what.'[16]

One night, some of Bower and Robson's group broke into the office and forced open a safe, in which they apparently found files on the Communist Party. But it seems their only real aim had been to freak out the agents—which seemed to work, as the office was vacated almost immediately afterwards. SIS premises, which were invariably housed in unidentified buildings, would continue to be the target of student-dominated protest groups, particularly after the introduction of the Security Intelligence Service Act in 1969 and amendments in 1977 which increased their powers and responsibilities.

In his 2006 memoir *Spy*, former SIS officer Kit Bennetts boasts that 'we really didn't much care what the students were up to on campus' and that 'threats to New Zealand's wellbeing came from agents of the KGB, not from enthusiastic protesters and part-time anarchists', though he mourns the fact that the agency was never able to step up its campus activity. 'After protests, students held the best parties,' he writes with a touch of jealousy.[17]

Picture the whole scene as a party, a real sixties happening. It is taking place in a mirror maze, the kind you might find at a travelling carnival. The Jimi Hendrix song 'Room Full of Mirrors' is blasting loudly over the speaker system. Everyone is there, the spies and the spied upon. But through the miasma of ideology and faint haze of pot smoke, it isn't always clear whether what you're seeing are real enemies, reflections or hallucinations.

MERCHANT ADVENTURERS AND RED RATS

While a fundamental principle of the counterculture seemed to be an opposition to big business, the counterculture generated a whole industry of its own.

David White was in his Sixth Form year boarding at Scots College, a private boys' school in Wellington, and considering a law degree when a geography teacher, who did some record reviewing on the side, brought a pile of unwanted LPs to school to sell off. David took a punt on a couple by a folk singer he'd heard people talking about, and went home with the first two Bob Dylan albums. 'And that changed my entire idea of everything. Literally.'[18]

For him, songs like 'A Hard Rain's A Gonna Fall', 'Masters of War' and 'Blowin' in the Wind' articulated a growing sense that it was his generation's right—responsibility, even—to question their elders and the world they had made. 'I listened to those records again and again and they had such a profound effect that the powers-that-be could just bugger off.' By the time he got to university—where friends, knowing his father was a doctor, began calling him Doc—he was listening to local folk singers such as Max Winnie at the Monde Marie and rock groups such as the Joyful Crye at the Psychedelic Id. Though nominally studying law, his mind was wandering.

In the fantasy novels of C. S. Lewis, Narnia is a parallel world that can be entered by a number of ways, including by falling into a painting, putting on a magic ring and climbing into a wardrobe. Doc got there via a party at a student flat in Glenmore Street. It was nearly the end of the year, exams were over, and someone he didn't know had asked him what he was planning for the summer holidays.

'I'll be tie-dyeing T-shirts,' he replied. He had recently seen the *Woodstock* movie, paid attention to the bright dye-splattered outfits worn by stars like Joe Cocker and John Sebastian, and could see how they had been made. 'I just got a pot and some dyes and screwed up

Raiments from the East in the original Narnia shop, Willis Street, early 1970s.
Keith Stewart photograph, private collection

these shirts, sometimes put rubber bands around them. All a bit slapdash but you get a feel for it.' For some months he had been selling his shirts to a poster shop in Cuba Street.

'I'm doing suede,' said the stranger. 'Fringed shoulder-bags, Sly and the Family Stone jerkins, that sort of stuff. Why don't we join forces?'

The stranger's name was David McLatchie, and like White he was a student at Vic. They spent that summer in McLatchie's flat, making a mess. Sometime in 1971 they began retailing their wares out of a two-storey villa in Willis Street, downstairs from the Resistance Bookshop. Casting themselves as romantic traders from some fantastical parallel universe, they called themselves the Merchant Adventurers of Narnia.

The next year, McLatchie made his first trip to Asia and came back with genuinely exotic goods: goatskin coats from Afghanistan, boots from Kathmandu, brass trays from India, a sitar. Among McLatchie's flatmates at the time were Zeke Alley and his soon-to-be wife Judy. Zeke had arrived in Wellington in 1970 after two years studying biochemistry at Massey University in Palmerston North. 'At Massey, student life revolved heavily around beer and not much else, to be frank,' he remembers. 'I think the uni might have had a dramatic troupe, I don't remember anything musical. No political life. I think we had one demonstration through town in all the time I was there.'[19]

While finishing his degree at Victoria, Zeke joined in the anti-war and apartheid demos, was introduced to marijuana, and turned on to Tamburlaine and Mammal in the Union Hall. In late 1973, Zeke and Judy set off on their year-long trek of the hippie trail [as described in Chapter 9]. But before they departed, the Narnians (as the Merchant Adventurers became known) asked if they would mind doing some shopping for them on the way. As promised, Zeke and Judy found instructions waiting for them *poste restante* in Kabul. McLatchie had compiled a detailed list of contacts, goods and expected prices, at the bottom of which Doc had scrawled 'and see if you can buy any Kuchi dresses'. The Kuchi are nomadic tribes, found mostly in southern and eastern Afghanistan; Doc had heard about their remarkable embroidered clothes from returning travellers. Zeke and Judy managed to track down a supplier, and Kuchi dresses were included along with other exotic raiments in the shipment they sent back from Kabul. When the wares reached Wellington, McLatchie and White were so pleased they asked Zeke to become a partner. That sounded better than being a biochemist in London, and within a week of the invitation, Zeke and Judy were back in Willis Street, working in the Narnia store.[20]

The local appetite for Eastern accoutrements was growing. Scarcity, due to New Zealand's policy of restricting imports to protect local manufacturing, only increased their allure. Narnia was the place you could walk in looking like a shopper from Woolworth's and exit ten minutes later smelling of patchouli oil, wearing a hand-embroidered muslin shirt and carrying a hash pipe.

Gradually the Narnians set about finding ways to work around the regulations. Though there were heavy restrictions on the importing of manufactured goods, no licence was needed to import materials for local manufacturing, so they would travel to India and buy fabrics —sometimes printed, sometimes tie-dyed, often woven by hill tribes— and bring them back as industrial raw materials, then employ local dressmakers to sew the finished garments. Tins of essential oils such as patchouli, which became the shop's dominant fragrance, were sourced from an Indian importer in Sydney by the vaguely implicative name of Mr Ezy. The Ezy oils would be decanted into small bottles and stamped with a Narnia label. Other essential countercultural accessories—candles, hookahs, cigarette rolling papers printed to resemble American dollar bills—were sourced either locally or from the US and Europe.

Eventually Narnia acquired a licence to trade with Nepal thanks to Edmund Hillary's special relationship with the country. Another was granted to bring in carpets from Bangladesh for an International Trade Fair. The coveted and hard-to-come-by licences, combined with the Narnians' street-level knowledge of the places and people they were buying from, gave them the edge in the local hippie marketplace. Narnia began supplying to other shops around the country, and eventually opened their own stores in Christchurch and Auckland as well.

'You learn from the establishment, then do it better.' Alister Taylor, 1972. Dominion Post Collection, Alexander Turnbull Library, 0882

In 1969, after the success of the Peace, Power and Politics conference, Alister Taylor rented an office in the historic nineteenth-century Plimmer House, named after one of Wellington's early settler entrepreneurs, and launched *Affairs*, a monthly magazine for secondary schools. With enough links to the school curriculum to win the support (and all-important subscriptions) of broad-minded teachers, it doubled as a countercultural primer for students. Along with sober features on topics like Britain's mineral resources and French regional and economic planning were cover stories on BLERTA and Baxter, demonstrations and drugs, introductions to Karl Marx and Confucius, reviews of rock albums, and backgrounders on Vietnam and apartheid. The inky reproduction, psychedelic graphics and provocative comic strips gave it the feel of an underground paper.

Affairs, May 1970. Student Publications Ltd, private collection

Affairs was also an amplifier for student voices. 'There's one thing I'd like to say now for the people who say I'm a fanatical revolutionary,' says seventeen-year-old self-described Wellington secondary school activist Clive Wilson in a double-page interview. 'Well it's quite true — I am.'

Nelson College student Scott Kennedy sent in some of his satirical comic strips, inspired by American cartoonists like Ron Cobb and Robert Crumb but with a scalpel wit of his own, and became a regular paid contributor. Poet Sam Hunt, not long out of Teachers' College, was the magazine's poetry editor, selecting student poems for publication and writing back to dozens of young poets with personal encouragement and advice. Sixteen-year-old Catherine Delahunty, a founder of the Secondary Schools Students' Association, whose portrait graced the cover of an early issue above the strapline 'How Revolutionary?', was employed by Taylor to review manuscripts for publication.

Though Taylor was credited as editor, much of the real work was done by his partner Gil McGregor, who oversaw the layout and design as well as wrangling much of the content. Taylor, meanwhile, juggled his usual array of projects, stepping nimbly between the counterculture and the establishment where most of the money and power still resided.

In 1970 he took a job with A. H. & A. W. Reed, one of New Zealand's oldest publishing firms. Founded in 1907 by Alexander Hamish Reed as a mail-order business supplying texts to Sunday schools, by the time Taylor joined it was under the direction of A. W. (Clif) Reed, A. H.'s Christian, teetotal nephew. Of Taylor's appointment, Clif wrote to his uncle: 'He and I would hold radically different views on many subjects but he's a fine chap, even though he has a scruffy beard & elastic-sided boots.'[21]

As the new head of Reed Education, Taylor was soon commissioning and overseeing the publishing of hundreds of titles, though he found himself in the awkward position of rejecting several collections penned by his employer, Clif Reed, which he later described as 'a strange melange of curbside homilies and Māori history'.[22] Taylor's commercial instincts were acute and some of the books he commissioned did very well for Reed's. A particular hit was *Probing Plant Structure*, an electron microscope study of anatomical features in plants, with a strikingly phallic cover image chosen by Taylor. On a trip to London he successfully sold the book to Chapman & Hall, the original publishers of Charles Dickens.

That week the buzz around Bloomsbury was about the arrest of Richard Handyside, the young proprietor of a small publishing house called Stage 1, who had been charged with publishing an obscene book. *The Little Red Schoolbook*, with a humorous nod to Chairman Mao's *Little Red Book*, was effectively a countercultural manual for students. First published in Denmark in 1969, and written by two Danish schoolteachers, it aimed to revolutionise children's attitudes to sex, drugs, adults and education by encouraging them to take charge of their own learning. 'Adults do have a lot of power over you,' authors Søren Hansen and Jesper Jensen wrote. 'But in the long run they can never control you completely: they are paper tigers.'[23] Handyside had secured rights for an English translation, and in early 1971 sent out copies for review. Almost immediately he was swooped on by the obscene publications squad who confiscated as many copies of the book as they could find, though by that time several thousand had already been distributed.

Hearing that Handyside was due to be released on bail, Taylor went directly to the publisher's office where he waited in ambush and, upon Handyside's return, demanded the Australasian rights for the *Schoolbook*. Taylor secured them, and now it was Clif Reed's turn to say no. There was no way the prudish Reed was going to give *The Little Red Schoolbook* his imprimatur, so Taylor decided to publish it himself. It would not be easy. Afraid of the possible legal repercussions of printing the *Schoolbook*, printer after printer turned Taylor down. Eventually he leased the Wellington printing plant of Service Print from its nervous owner for several weeks, taking responsibility for the operation himself. He and his brother-in-law Graeme Culliford then drove box after box of unbound copies to a pliable bookbinder in Palmerston North.

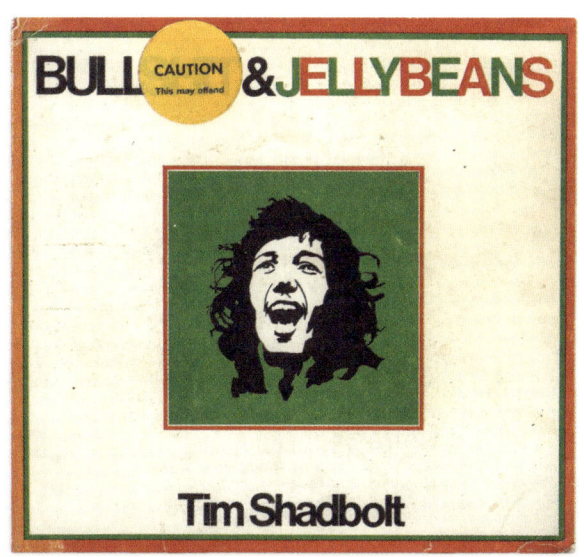

Bullshit and Jellybeans, 1971.
Alister Taylor Publishing Ltd

The First New Zealand Whole Earth Catalogue, 1972. Alister Taylor Publishing Ltd

The Little Red Schoolbook, 1972.
Alister Taylor Publishing Ltd

The Little Red Schoolbook caused a sensation in New Zealand. The word that it had already been banned in Britain was the best possible publicity, and the threat that it might soon be banned here as well was an instant spur to sales. Though morals campaigners referred it to the Indecent Publications Tribunal, it was classified unrestricted, with the qualification that 'decisions of the Tribunal do not abrogate parental responsibility; that remains, and parents are fully entitled to exercise control over their children's reading if they so wish'.[24]

I was in the Third Form at Onslow when the *Schoolbook* came out. I remember first seeing the red-jacketed, palm-sized publication being furtively passed between kids at the back of the maths room. Soon one of my friends acquired a copy and we all got to read about how LSD trips lasted for eight or nine hours, that masturbation is normal, and that schoolchildren have the right not to be bored by their teachers.

In Auckland, student teacher Sue Kedgley was inspired by the *Schoolbook* to ask questions about the job for which she was being trained. With another student she organised a talk under the banner 'Why Headmasters Should Be Abolished', which drew five hundred people to the college hall. Afterwards she was called before the principal and asked to leave the college on account of her 'negative influence'. She refused, so eventually an arrangement was negotiated whereby she would continue to carry out her teaching sections and receive her student bursary provided she stayed away from the college itself—a situation she found quite agreeable.

The Little Red Schoolbook sold like pop records, and did especially well in underground bookshops such as Resistance. The bookbinder struggled to keep up with the demand. 'With the huge runs his machines broke down,' Taylor remembered. 'I turned up there one night from Wellington and he was lying on his back underneath and feeding these things through manually. The poor bastard had a nervous breakdown. I exerted enormous pressure on him.'[25]

It did even greater numbers in Australia: Taylor once cited a figure of a quarter of a million copies, though his accounting was notoriously unreliable. But unlike in New Zealand, the book was quickly banned there, and although thousands of copies had already crossed the counter, Taylor claimed he never saw any of the Australian profits, citing the ban as the reason.

In the wake of the publication's success, Taylor launched his own shop Printed Matter, in Plimmer's Emporium, an adapted Edwardian hotel on Wellington's Plimmer Steps that housed a small enclave of alternative retailers. He imported stock from Straight Arrow, the San Francisco-based publishers of *Rolling Stone* magazine, who had branched into paperbacks: book-length interviews with rock heroes like Jerry Garcia and John Lennon, gonzo journalism by Hunter S. Thompson and the novels of hippie fabulist Richard Brautigan.

Taylor was also publishing more books. *The Muldoon Annual Joke Book* was whipped up over a couple of nights by Taylor and Jim Barr, the pair penning satiric captions to photographs of the Minister of Finance and prospective Prime Minister Robert Muldoon. Taylor, as a joke, sent the book's subject an invitation to the launch of the book at Plimmer's Emporium. To his surprise, Muldoon, a firm believer that all publicity is good publicity, turned up at the event and stuck around afterwards autographing copies of the book.

Taylor followed this with a similar quickie aimed at another of his nemeses. Patricia Bartlett was a very active proponent of censorship, particularly of nudity and portrayals of sex. A former nun, she had shocked some of the other sisters at St Mary's convent in Thorndon with the intensity of her interest in pornography and passion to stem what she saw as society's moral decline. By the late sixties she had left the convent to devote more time to her campaign, and in 1970 had been a founder of the Society for the Promotion of Community Standards. Naturally she had tried to have *The Little Red Schoolbook* banned. Taylor, by now based just a block away from the convent in Sydney Street West, retaliated with *The Patricia Bartlett Cookbook*. Lacking photographic proof of Bartlett's former calling, he paid a carpenter and his son to break into her flat, steal a photograph of her in her nun's habit, and copy and replace the original before she returned. The burglary was successful and the image was reproduced on the cover of the book. That Bartlett was disconcerted seems to have been the sole object of the elaborate and invasive exercise.

The Little Red Schoolbook was not quite the first achievement of Alister Taylor Publishing, nor the first to stir controversy. It had been narrowly preceded by *Bullshit and Jellybeans*, the memoir-cum-manifesto of Tim Shadbolt which, like the *Schoolbook*, had been offered to Reed's and, not surprisingly, turned down. Written mostly during a three-week prison stay for non-payment of fines, it had arrived in bookstores just before Christmas 1971 with an enticing sticker over the first word of the title that read 'Caution—This may offend'. Essentially it was an account of the recent years of the New Zealand protest movement, interspersed with anecdotes to illustrate the twenty-four-year-old author's journey from disaffected schoolboy to protest leader. Combining revolutionary rhetoric with blokey yarn-spinning, it offered a distinctly Kiwi take on the global movement: a cross between *Revolution for the Hell of It* and *A Good Keen Man*. In its final chapters Shadbolt looks ahead to a New Zealand utopia of communes, co-operatives, rock music, pot-smoking and underground media, the growth of biculturalism and 'the end of all war'.

Though broadly factual, Shadbolt had a habit of placing himself at the centre of the stories, in some of which he had played only a minor role. One of the first people Shadbolt showed a copy to was Roger Fowler, with whom he had liberated Albert Park, participated in countless protests and been arrested numerous times. 'Well, it's all very well Tim,' said Fowler, after appraising its contents, 'but where are the jellybeans?'[26]

Bullshit and Jellybeans was a bestseller, though like all of Taylor's publications it is hard to know how many were actually sold; Shadbolt believes around 25,000 copies, though he saw little of the profits. A policeman he had accused of violence took a defamation action against both Shadbolt and Taylor and won $8000, an amount that more than doubled with the addition of court costs.

Taylor was undaunted and his publications continued to come thick and fast, each one chronicling some further corner of an alternative New Zealand. Under the one-off Glenbervie Press imprint he had already produced *Bracken Country*, Sam Hunt's first collection of poems, when the wandering poet was staying in a Glenbervie Terrace cottage owned by Bill Sutch. Now Hunt was holed up in a boatshed on the Pāuatahanui estuary north of Wellington. An inveterate namer of things, he christened the neighbourhood Bottle Creek, perhaps in honour of the piles of empties left after his own binges. For Hunt's next volume, *From Bottle Creek*, Taylor went all out, producing an unconventional package that presented the poems on a series of coloured folded cards housed in a silver slipcase.

Hunt had been touring with the rock band Mammal, cultivating an audience among his longhaired, pot-smoking peers rather than just the established poetry circle. In 1972 Taylor released Sam Hunt/ Mammal's *Beware the Man,* a long-playing album of the poet/rock band collaboration, with its emblematic title song. Taylor called his record label — some would say appropriately — Red Rat.

When James K. Baxter died suddenly that October, Taylor rushed out a memorial volume, including tributes, photographs and some of Baxter's own writing. As in a lot of his publications, the binding was bad and the books fell apart at the slightest handling. But before too many people had had the chance to discover the defect, Taylor was served with a cease and desist order by Baxter's executor, his wife Jacqui, who had not given Taylor permission for the book, and it was withdrawn from sale. Just as timely, though in this case authorised, was *Sexist Society*, a collection of essays and interviews edited by Sue Kedgley and Sharyn Cederman, illuminating some of the issues behind the Women's Liberation movement, one of the first local publications to do so.

✱

A big seller across the underground bookshops for a number of years had been the *Whole Earth Catalogs*: A3-sized publications that operated as a kind of countercultural survival guide (or 'take home kit for the counter culture revolutionary').[27] They were full of do-it-yourself techniques, reviews of books and tools, and sections on shelter, learning, communications and other subjects of interest to the alternative lifestyler. The *Catalog* was the brainchild of Stewart Brand, a San Francisco-based former associate of Ken Kesey and his Merry Pranksters. First published in 1968 and updated several times a year, by 1971 editions had grown as fat as phone books. It was Taylor's idea to produce a *Whole Earth Catalogue* for the New Zealand market. Published in summer 1972, *The First New Zealand Whole Earth Catalogue* survives as arguably the most detailed time capsule of the Kiwi counterculture at the time, and the closest thing to a survey of the movement as it approached critical mass.

Taylor's *Catalogue* roughly follows Brand's template, though almost all the material is locally written and particular to New Zealand. Thirty pages under the heading 'Shelter' provide how-to guides on rammed-earth construction, unconventional uses of concrete, ferro-cement building, and twelve pages on geodesic domes. (Alister Taylor had his own dome constructed behind his home in Sydney Street West.) There are shorter entries on snow caves and igloos. There is a nuclear war survivors guide, and a section on alternative education which includes a piece my mother wrote about an alternative programme she was running within a Wellington state primary school. A section titled 'Ways Of Life' includes progress reports from some of the recently established communes, a dispatch from a BLERTA tour of the South Island, and an article headed 'Where is the Maori at today?' in which Bronwen Castle writes admiringly of 'the quiet hipness' of 'the kuias' and 'korouas' and of 'the Maori way of life as a source of inspiration'.[28] A piece on Nga Tamatoa, while showing support for the Māori liberation organisation, again views Māori through the lens of a Pākehā counter-culture: 'Think how the Pakeha has evolved to this state of ecological madness, militarism and freaked-out consumerism. Look at how he tries to make the Maori into a respectable tourist attraction. Walk a busy street and look at the grim faces. Then buy a pack of matches … we have many plastic tikis to burn.'[29]

Four pages are devoted to what it calls 'fringe medicine'. An introduction attempts to summarise the 'variety of healing systems or methods offering alternatives to conventional medicine' by generalising that 'they all prefer to treat ill-health by working with the patient's own "life force" and powers of recuperation rather than employing drugs to eradicate symptoms', and goes on to offer capsule entries on naturopathy, homeopathy, chiropractic, hypnotherapy, autosuggestion and radiesthesia. 'Radiesthesia is difficult to describe, since even its practitioners disagree as to how the method works …' begins the latter, with a vagueness typical of this section.[30] Under the title 'Clearing Your Head', psychologist and educator Jim Ritchie offers what reads like a preparatory exercise for entry to the counterculture. It begins: 'Clear away mind pollution … there is joy, peace, serenity, humane warmth, and other good things too … so get ready (if you aren't already on the way) by seeing that you get enough (not your "fair share", whatever that might be, but enough) of the good things: sleep, sex, wholesome food and good water', and concludes, several paragraphs later, with: 'A good regular sauna. Doodling.'[31]

Though gauche at times, the *Catalogue* also contained a lot of solid practical information; given that it is hard to find a copy today that hasn't fallen apart, it seems to have been used as the practical manual Taylor intended. He would go on to publish two more volumes over the next five years. When the filmmaker Dan Salmon went to visit a long-abandoned commune deep in the Coromandel bush in 2009, the sole remaining item in the derelict dwelling was a well-thumbed copy of the *Catalogue*.

Taylor's publishing successes helped fund his increasingly opulent lifestyle. He was a connoisseur of wine and food, and would host lavish parties. His art collection grew. He had a fine assemblage of furniture and fittings, poozled from properties around Thorndon that were awaiting demolition. But some began to view Taylor as an exploiter of the culture he had helped propagate.

CASHING IN

It is a mark of how seriously the counterculture took its music that, for a brief time in the early seventies, so many column inches of the local underground press were devoted to Robert Raymond. During this period the Australian music promoter, along with his Kiwi sidekick Barry Coburn, mounted the biggest rock shows New Zealand had seen: Led Zeppelin, Elton John, plus the Great Ngaruawahia Music Festival. Though ticket prices for these events seem ridiculously cheap today — to see Led Zeppelin in Auckland in 1972 cost $3.60, the equivalent of about $50 in 2021 — this was a time of considerable worldwide debate about whether there should be any charge for music at all. If rock groups were the marching bands of the revolution, then surely their music should be played for free? Bill Dwyer, the acid anarchist whose exploits are chronicled in Chapter 3, after his deportation from Australia, had attended the huge three-day 1970 Isle of Wight rock festival along with more than half a million others. There he had taken part in an anarchist incursion, pulling down fences and storming the site in defiance of the £3 ticket price.

Back in New Zealand, the counterculture wanted to know: who is Robert Raymond and whose side would he be on when the revolution came? Was he another 'pig promoter'? Robert 'Rip-off' Raymond, as some called him? In a profile commissioned by Alister Taylor in 1973 for his local *Rolling Stone*, Chris Wheeler got straight to the essentials:

> Robert Raymond is a 27-year-old Virgo born 16 September. He's got a wife and a new baby and, along with his partner Barry Coburn, owns a popular nightspot Levi's Saloon, which is supposed to have some promotional tie-up with the jean manufacturers; a $20,000 record company Down Under Records, a music publishing company and a management company … After meeting him I was struck straight away by the fact that in many respects he and

on a variety of charges including abusive language, intent to commit a breach of the peace, and damaging police-car windows. When he attempted to organise a fourth Windsor Free Festival the following year, he was found in contempt of a High Court injunction forbidding the event, and sent to prison.

By the mid-seventies, the Merchant Adventurers of Narnia were doing better than ever, selling much the same clothes and fabrics they had a few years earlier, though these now seemed less outlandish than they once had. Other shops had opened treading similarly exotic territory: Chaikhana, Balouchi, Memsahib. Hookahs, kaftans, beads and scented oils had become a staple of institutions such as Auckland's Cook Street Market, a hippie bazaar set up by Londoners Brian and Ronnie Jones.

As elements of hippie fashion found their way into the well-heeled suburbs, such items started to appear in the posh shops at higher prices. Only a few years earlier the most coveted item in a hippie's wardrobe was an Afghan jacket, handmade from goatskin, the fleece on the inside, the leather exterior finely embroidered with silk threads, each garment unique and seeming to tell its own story. A boyfriend of Rachel Stace's had returned wearing one from an adventure on the hippie trail with what appeared to be a bullet hole through the leather. Eventually the beautiful jackets (usually without bullet holes) began to appear in the menswear stores. But as Rosemary McLeod said wistfully, 'I feel the magic goes out when it's in Vance Vivian's, really.'[36]

As time went by, some of the Narnians became more businesslike, others more eccentric. David McLatchie had always been flamboyant. The first time Zeke Alley met his future business partner, at a Union Hall dance, McLatchie had tried to steal his girlfriend. Alley admits McLatchie's entrance that night had been impressive, arriving dressed in a top hat and cape via a second-storey window. He bought a turreted house on Brooklyn Hill which he named Dragon Lodge, and changed his name to Prince Rupert.

Meanwhile, Stewart Thwaites, a bootmaker-turned-property-buyer whose own hippie handcraft shop Sonora Leather had been just a few doors from Narnia, had bought into Narnia and, through a complicated deal of his devising, wound up with a controlling interest. Though they had started out as friends, the Narnians fell out with Thwaites and lost control of the business. But though their paths would ultimately diverge, the four original Adventurers—Doc, Prince Rupert, Zeke and the last to join the quest, Wayne Sampson—retained each other's respect and goodwill. Zeke credits this in part to an application of the Buddhist principles he had picked up along the hippie trail. 'You learn about the nature of karma. If you do something wrong you will be the person who suffers most, and when you understand this it helps you make the right decisions in life.'[37]

By this time Alister Taylor (whose first name, coincidentally, was Rupert) had established a princedom of his own. With the profits from his publications he had bought a crumbling colonial mansion in Martinborough—it was the original home of nineteenth-century wheeler-dealer John Martin, after whom the town was named—and set about doing it up in grand style.[38] Handcrafted plaster ceilings were restored; a tower which had been toppled by an earthquake was rebuilt and sheathed in copper. There were stables, a billiard room and a complex of outhouses. Taylor employed Max Wilkinson, an old communist and neighbour from Thorndon, as his Clerk of Works. Tim Shadbolt, now running a concreting business, was contracted to build a wine cellar. In the *Whole Earth Catalogue*-approved manner, Taylor grew his own vegetables. Chinese pheasants roamed the grounds. And he established one of the first vineyards in what would go on to become one of the country's major wine regions. His hospitality was legendary. Some of the writers he hosted were quicker than others to suspect that this extravagant lifestyle was paid for in part by money that was owed to them. As Deborah Coddington, who became Taylor's partner and mother of his children, would later recall: 'Authors would come over from Wellington saying, "This time I'm going to get my royalties", and Alister would get out a bottle of Chateau Mouton Rothschild or whatever and whip up a quiche and a persimmon steamed pudding with whipped cream and they would leave wined and dined and still with no money.'[39]

Among those queuing up to be paid were historians Michael King and Tony Simpson, whose first books, King's *Moko: Maori Tattooing in the 20th Century* (1972) and Simpson's *The Sugarbag Years: An Oral History of the 1930s Depression in New Zealand* (1974), were groundbreaking works and solid sellers. Taylor had shown foresight and daring in publishing these soon-to-be major non-fiction authors; both King and Simpson felt that in some ways they owed him their professional careers. But there was no question about what Taylor owed them, and it was not forthcoming.

By the mid-seventies Taylor was thoroughly established in Martinborough, a longhaired lord of the manor, and the change of lifestyle was reflected in the kind of books he was publishing. He was no longer the 'publisher of last resort', as he had referred to himself, for books too hot for the mainstream to handle, but was turning his attention instead to high-end publications for an elite market: a numbered-edition volume of reproductions of the portrait artist C. F. Goldie with a retail price of $295 (over $3000 in today's currency), and a similarly lavish and high-priced *Notable New Zealand Thoroughbreds*.

The wine kept flowing, the debts kept growing, and old friends grew disillusioned. The last time Sam Hunt would publish a collection of his poems with Taylor was in 1975. The title of the book was *Time to Ride*.

Sam Hunt gets ready to ride.
Max Oettli photograph, Alexander Turnbull Library, PAColl-1386-1

WHO KILLED THE COUNTERCULTURE?

Fourteen

In 1975 Alister Taylor stood poised between the counterculture and the life of a country squire, but he was not the only person in this story who, in that year, found themselves at a crossroads. Chris Wheeler, having given up publishing *Cock*, left for India to pursue his study of Sufi mysticism. Jenny McLeod, now a practising member of the Divine Light Mission, was preparing to move to the United States to work for the organisation, and would remain there for a number of years. Sue Kedgley had taken a job at the Women's Secretariat of the United Nations in New York after attending the first global Women's Liberation Convention at Harvard University. The commune that James K. Baxter had founded at Jerusalem finally disbanded.

A sea of Muldoons. *Earwig*, July 1972, collage by Jonathan Milne. Jonathan Milne private collection

BLERTA had returned after eighteen months in Australia and been funded to make a series for New Zealand television. At last their anarchic mix of jazz, psychedelic rock and drug-fuelled lampoons of straight society were going to be beamed into the living rooms of suburban New Zealand. But while Lawrence and Murphy would continue to work together and make their names in film, Lawrence as an actor and Murphy a director, this would turn out to be their final endeavour as a band, as though tacit acceptance had ultimately sapped their rebellious spirit.

Mammal also sputtered to a halt, despite the frantic appeals of Union Hall revellers such as Brian King (now Brian Potiki), who wrote in *Salient*: 'Let's try and get a Mammal motif emblazoned onto the Victoria University pendant, organise a "Save Mammal" campaign, support Mammal by buying their records and going to their concerts. After all, Mammal is kin, man ...'[1]

That year Mammal's Rick Bryant and their manager Graeme Nesbitt both went to prison for selling marijuana, an operation they had maintained to support their music, while John Bower, having served four years in Paremoremo, had just been released to find the world had moved on without him. 'Everything I knew was four years earlier. The Vietnam War—that had virtually stopped. The bombing had stopped. You can't talk to people 'cause they're all talking about recent things. That's quite hard, in that respect. I went back to university to do Stage Three mathematics but I couldn't hack it.'[2]

Rachel Stace was taking too many drugs. 'I became a postie in Wellington but I would throw up in people's gardens, became very, very ill. I was using [heroin] every other day and thinking, Oh this is bad, this is not good, I've got to get out of this scene. I got an invitation to go to a ten-year class reunion in Minnesota so I jumped on a plane, went there, completely cut all ties. I went overseas and quit the druggy scene and went, Right, I'm not coming back until I've found a career.'[3]

STRONGER THAN BUDDHA

In 1975, age sixteen, I left home, and went to live with a few friends in a four-bedroom flat just a few minutes' walk from Victoria University, though only one of us was studying there and he didn't seem to be taking it too seriously. Itinerants would crash on our couches and floors. I had left school at the end of the previous year and had no urge to get back into the education system. *System*. Just the word conjured the image of a machine geared to conformity.

Dropping out was easy. Our rent was $4 a week each. There was plenty of casual work in Wellington. We laboured on building sites, filled orders in warehouses, cleaned windows, washed dishes, waited tables, but none of us stayed in any job for very long. For a few months I was employed as a cellarman at the Commercial Travellers Club, an anachronistic institution with a dwindling membership that would not survive the decade. My duties entailed restocking the club's four lounge bars after the previous night's revelry, and began cruelly early at nine in the morning and nominally finished at midday, though I often sloped off before then. The bearish bar manager was persistently ill-tempered on account of a perpetual hangover, and told me when I started that he hoped I wasn't 'on the drugs' like the last cellarman.

In my leisured afternoons I listened to records and tried to make music of my own. I also read in a haphazard way, guided by the recommendations of friends or prompts from pop culture: *On the Road*, because it seemed to be mandatory; *Junky*, because I had come across an interview with the group Steely Dan in which they mentioned William Burroughs and said they had taken their name from one of his books. I was led to John Steinbeck by the line about *Cannery Row* in Bob Dylan's 'Sad Eyed Lady of the Lowlands'. In *Tortilla Flat*, Steinbeck's noble portrayal of a bunch of errant *paisanos* who wile away their nights drinking wine by the gallon and talking shit, I saw a romantic reflection of my own indolent existence.

In fact we didn't drink wine by the gallon. There was the occasional carafe of Blenheimer or bottle of Stone's Green Ginger, but mostly we smoked marijuana. Lots of it. There was a dairy between our flat and the university where the longhaired stoner in charge would sell you Buddha sticks from under the counter, if you asked. These looked a bit like fossilised kebabs, but were in fact bundles of dried marijuana buds wrapped around a bamboo skewer. (Local Buddhists grumbled about the name being appended to an unholy substance like cannabis.) Sometimes we had hash oil, which came in little capsules as a sticky black goo which you could paste on the inside paper of a hand-rolled cigarette or dissolve in a cup of tea, and which was even stronger than Buddha. Occasionally there was LSD and, on one occasion, datura, which a visitor boiled up on our stove and dispensed as a foul-smelling liquid in coffee mugs. I didn't partake, but I saw others completely lost trying to find their way from one side of the room to the other. There was also, briefly, Mandrax, the hypnotic sedative, which a friend brought back from Australia and administered liberally, turning us all into rubber monkeys until after a week it had all gone. There would no doubt have been other drugs too had I gone looking for them, but that seemed like the path to a scary William Burroughs world and I was far too risk-averse for that.

Unknown to me and my mates as we smoked ourselves into a pleasant delirium was the provenance of the Buddha sticks. We had vaguely heard that they came from somewhere in Asia. In fact, they were being imported from Thailand by a former Auckland menswear salesman and petty criminal called Marty Johnstone. People remember him as having a gentle manner, a lot of girlfriends and a penchant for sandals. With marijuana use spreading into mainstream New Zealand and demand growing fast, in 1975 the entrepreneurial Johnstone brought 450,000 Buddha sticks into the country on a yacht he had purchased with a group of investors. To distribute the haul he teamed up with a psychopath called Terry Clark. Clark, a safecracker, receiver and occasional police informer, was recently out of jail. During a three-year stretch in Wi Tako (now Rimutaka Prison) he had been married in the prison chapel to a heroin addict called Norma Fleet, who would die of an overdose a year or so later. While inside, he had also taken a lot of LSD, met a lot of drug dealers and read Dale Carnegie's *How to Win Friends and Influence People*.[4]

For a while, Buddha seemed to be everywhere. It is believed Johnstone and Clark each made $3 million out of that single haul. After that they branched into heroin. Not only were the profit margins higher but, as writer David Herkt says, 'its addictive nature and the increasing amounts needed as a user's tolerance developed ensured an ongoing and growing demand, making it the ideal product for a capitalist paradigm'.[5]

Basing himself in Singapore, Johnstone would source the drugs and arrange couriers, usually young New Zealand women, to deliver it to Clark in Sydney, who would on-sell it to wholesale buyers in Australia and New Zealand. Suddenly the counterculture was awash with heroin, and it was being offered as a supplement or alternative by many of the local dealers who had previously peddled only Buddha. One such dealer was Greg Ollard. His name meant nothing to me at the time, though I once visited a flat with a couple of friends where an immaculate pair of snakeskin boots had been left standing just inside the door. 'They're Greg's. He's staying here', we were told. We had no idea who Greg was, but we marvelled at his boots, handmade in either Mexico or Spain and obviously very expensive. We held them up for close inspection and took

A wedding in Wi Tako, 1973. Left to right: Terry Clark, Norma Fleet, Errol Hincksman, unidentified. Keith Stewart photograph, private collection

Embroidery and sandals at the wedding of Robert Muldoon's daughter Barbara, Wellington, 1972. Dominion Post Collection, Alexander Turnbull Library, EP/1972/2734/9-F

turns at trying them on. A year or so later Terry Clark murdered Greg Ollard in Sydney, one of maybe a dozen killings he would action as his megalomania spiralled out of control. The final one would be Johnstone's.

Opiates including heroin had always been used by a small number of New Zealanders. In the 1940s a cabal of intravenous opioid users comprising a European shopkeeper, a pair of nurses and a Chinese market gardener was identified in Hawke's Bay, and colorfully described by health officials as the 'Hastings Incubus'.[6] Prior to then, opium use had mostly been confined to a dwindling group within the New Zealand Chinese community, a hangover from when it was used recreationally by some of the nineteenth-century gold miners (opium having been previously introduced to China by the British). It appealed to those of a romantic bent, inspired by its association with poets such as Coleridge and Shelley, just as heroin gained some cachet from its use by great jazz musicians like Charlie Parker and Miles Davis.

Heroin was less common than marijuana or LSD, though by 1969 there were enough addicts in Auckland for James K. Baxter to acknowledge, if overestimate, the 'five thousand junkies in Auckland' in his poem 'The Ballad of the Junkies and the Fuzz'. Junk had been a slang name for heroin since the 1920s, but the term — and thus the distinction between heroin and other drugs — remained blurry in the minds of middle New Zealand well into the 1970s. It didn't help that politicians, magistrates and policemen drew on the same lurid vocabulary — 'debauchery', 'insanity', 'deadly', 'evil' — whether they were talking about heroin or marijuana, while headline-seeking journalists would use junkie (or junky, the spelling was variable) synonymously with 'drug taker', lumping together everyone from the weekend acid tripper or recreational pot-smoker to the long-term or even casual opiate user.

In fact, the authorities were alarmed at an epidemic of pharmacy burglaries as drug experimentation became popular with the young. On 26 June 1968, seventeen-year-old Boyle Crescent resident Phillip Sharples died from a drug overdose. The tragedy drew only muted headlines, but behind the scenes, health and law enforcement agencies were shocked. That month saw a high-profile team of officials and experts sitting down in Wellington to examine the growing illegal drug culture. The Drug Dependency and Drug Abuse Committee was asked to take a 'careful and dispassionate' look at the problem, but its early energies were diverted at the start of July. A telex marked 'urgent and confidential' flew between Auckland's CIB boss and committee member Detective Chief Superintendent Bob Walton at Police HQ in Wellington. It talked of an outbreak of abuse involving 'literally hundreds of people in Auckland'.[7]

The counterculture had its own views. 'THERE ARE NO SUCH THINGS AS JUNKIES' Chris Wheeler had declared in screaming capitals in a 1969 *Salient* article. 'Like fairies, Father Xmas and God, the Junky does not exist—not even at the bottom of the garden or up the chimney—not even in Mt Eden Jail.' The junkie, he argued, was an invention of the state, designed to frighten, control and strengthen its own power. 'God never existed but we still had the Inquisition. Witches never existed but we still had the Salem witch trials. Junkies never existed but we still have a Narcotics Squad.'

Not that Wheeler didn't believe in addicts. It was rather a question of who was qualified to identify and deal with issues of addiction:

> In New Zealand the Cop definition of the Junky is the definition which rules our drug legislation. No-one asks the only expert who matters—the scientist—what his opinion of the drug 'problem' is. One does not ask a blind man his opinion of a painting. One should not ask a Cop for his opinion of the drug addiction problem. Neither by training nor temperament is he capable of giving an informed answer. His training helps him to become an efficient man-hunter—it does not help him to understand men.
>
> A rational, well-ordered society does not need to traffic in dope, does not need a Junky myth. It does not deliberately generate an under-privileged class from which may come unhappy, neurotic people to be ignored until they turn to narcotic drugs for relief. It does not need anti-drug laws which provide a convenient veil for Police and State fascism; for the suppression of the unconventional and the unpopular.[8]

Like Wheeler, Rod Bicknell, writing in *Craccum*, blamed The Man, then went a step further. He called junk 'the Man's weapon against us disguised as part of our community … The police, the government and [head of the Auckland drug squad] Brian Stewart (the great high-priest) are all doing their best to encourage the spread of heroin among the "counter culture."'

Neither Wheeler nor Bicknell denied that heroin could be destructive. But Bicknell saw its greatest threat as being to the counter-culture itself: 'The biggest lie going about heroin is that it will kill you, that it will do you harm as an individual, that it is a risk. That's crap. It will kill our community, our life style, our revolution long before it kills many single people.'

Bicknell went on to recount a conversation he had with a police sergeant 'the last time I was busted and sitting in the back of the court room waiting to be called'. He claims the sergeant, a former head of the vice squad in the days when its primary concern was sly grogging, had confirmed that the CIB were involved in the selling of heroin. But the sergeant's testimony blurs into speculation as Bicknell goes on to suggest that 'the little pigs [distribute heroin] to obtain information, the chiefs … act under the orders of the government … The potential revolutionaries can be and are completely torn apart from within by heroin.'

Governmental sabotage of the counterculture with drugs, in other words. As tends to be the case with conspiracy theories, the details of how and why remain vague, while the tone suggests a broader paranoia. Did Bicknell mean that heroin's tendency to focus the user on individual need rather than the common good was antithetical to the movement's goals? If so, it is hinted at only in the most shadowy terms. 'This is partly the way in which Haight-Ashbury was changed from a happy hopeful society into a grey vicious ghetto ... There is no reason to try smack, and less reason to get strung out on it. It will keep us from freeing ourselves.'[9]

Nevertheless, towards the mid-1970s, as the idealistic glow of the counterculture receded, the number of young people using heroin steadily grew. This was due in large part to its increased availability, thanks to Johnstone, Clark and their numerous minions. A flatmate from this period recalls using heroin 'just a few times, when I couldn't get hold of any pot. I got it from the same people. It was like, "Sorry, we're out of Buddha, why don't you try this?"'

Unlike marijuana or LSD, heroin is physically addictive; if the regular user's supply is interrupted, they will become sick and desperate. In this way, the heroin user is more comparable to the alcoholic. But in a society where alcohol is legal, it is possible for the alcoholic to manage their addiction within the bounds of the law. The junkie, on the other hand, is an instant outlaw. Assuring a supply can become an all-consuming occupation. As David Herkt says, 'While I've known junkies who have held down demanding jobs for quite long periods — lawyers, accountants and so on — it is really hard to operate on a normal time-table as a dependent user. There is the work-schedule of everyday employment and there is the competing time-table of dependency. And there's always a lot of waiting ...'[10]

When supplies are scarce, some resort to crimes such as burglary, including of doctors' surgeries and chemist shops. Preoccupied with getting their fix, junkies are drawn to others with the same need. So while in some ways heroin could be considered the most countercultural of drugs, in that the user can appear to have completely rejected the cultural values of the mainstream society, it also created an isolated subculture within the counterculture — one which ultimately contributed to its disintegration. Though New Zealand's geographical insularity soon terminated supply lines like those of Mr Asia, the demand was now in place, and in time homegrown ingenuity generated the home-bake heroin phenomenon.

It would be convenient to say that heroin killed the counterculture — a fatal, if accidental, overdose. But the counterculture was already dying in other ways. Like the first whisperings of its arrival, the idea that it was coming to an end was being transmitted from overseas. As usual, there was a time lag between such reports and any material change to life in New Zealand. But in the last days of the sixties a couple of particularly grim stories, extensively covered by both mainstream and underground media, would plant the idea that the counterculture had failed in its mission; its ideals had been corrupted, proved unworkable or had been pie-in-the-sky all along.

Charles Manson had been released from prison in 1967 after spending more than half of his thirty-two years in correctional institutions, and come to Los Angeles via Haight-Ashbury. He looked like a hippie, spoke like a prophet and trailed a cult of admirers, some of whom would, on his instructions, commit a series of horrific murders, including that of Hollywood actress Sharon Tate. In December 1969, the month Manson was indicted on murder charges, the Rolling Stones concluded a North American tour with the free concert at the Altamont Speedway, just outside San Francisco, where they struggled to perform their music as an out-of-it crowd spilled over the low stage. Members of Hells Angels, who had been paid in beer to provide security, responded by meting out violence, in one case stabbing to death an audience member who had apparently produced a gun. The end of the sixties was just three weeks away, though some would say it ended that night.

In the months that followed, portents of a counterculture staggering to a self-destructive end came thick and fast. There were the acts of extreme violence by radical protesters the Weather Underground and Baader-Meinhof Group, and the violent ends of several of their leaders.

There were the drug-related deaths of leading rock figures Jimi Hendrix, Janis Joplin and Jim Morrison, while Brian Jones, founder member of the Stones, had perished six months before Altamont. Meanwhile, Mick Jagger would go on to disappoint anyone who might have mistaken him for the leader of the revolution by making a lot of money and getting into bed with the bourgeoisie. The conservative English journalist William Rees-Mogg, who surprised the counterculture when his 1967 *Times* editorial on the Rolling Stones' drug bust contributed to their convictions being quashed, would subsequently become friendly with Jagger and, in his 2011 memoir, reflect that the Stone 'took a libertarian view of ethical and social issues which turned out to be one of the constituents ... of Thatcherism ... Mick Jagger was a Thatcherite before Thatcherism had been invented.'[11]

Rolling Stone, the magazine that had traded on the name of Jagger's band and codified the counterculture for mass consumption, didn't just advance the idea that the movement had sold out; it provided a working model of how to do it. 'All this counterculture hippie stuff ... that's all ended,' founder and editor Jann Wenner would say as his magazine moved its headquarters from San Francisco to New York City and its cover stories shifted from underground icons like Captain Beefheart to middle-of-the road megastars like the Carpenters.[12]

Mickey Mouse and John Rowles join the counterculture. Max Oettli photograph, Alexander Turnbull Library, PAColl-1386-1

✱

In New Zealand things were changing too. Clark and Johnstone may have made their special contributions to the counterculture's demise, but as I look back on my own experiences I can see that it was already over.

I had been hovering on the edges of the counterculture since high school; growing my hair, going to anti-war demos and rock happenings, papering my walls with posters of John Lennon and *Easy Rider*, visiting the Resistance Bookshop, poring over Robert Crumb comics and *The Little Red Schoolbook*, all while living in the comfort of my family's Kelburn home and waiting until I was old enough to become a full-time member of a rebellion that had begun around the time I was born.

But by 1975 many of the things the rebels had laid themselves on the line for had been absorbed into the life of middle New Zealand. Now there were longhairs in suits, and moustachioed policemen. At parties I would run into some of the boozy rugby players I had given a wide berth at school. Now they were smoking pot and having sex with their girlfriends. Almost everyone listened to rock music.[13] The number of people going to church or identifying themselves as religious had declined steadily between 1960 and 1975. Christian morality was no longer much of a deterrent to drug-taking or pre-marital sex. Contraception was becoming easier to acquire. Society seemed to have adopted the trappings of the counterculture, while separating these from the ideals with which they had once been entwined.

Moreover, countercultural signifiers no longer automatically linked a person to a string of radical causes. The Vietnam War was over, at least as far as New Zealand was concerned, so having long hair and smoking dope no longer made you, by implication, a dirty protester. The fact that Norman Kirk had called off the proposed 1973 Springbok tour and opposed nuclear testing in the Pacific had put radical action on pause. Protest leaders like Trevor Richards had become, in his own words, 'energetic little bureaucrats working alongside the third Labour government'.[14] The Labour government had also acknowledged that solo motherhood was a fact of New Zealand life, and women and their children deserved a measure of state support.

All these things could perhaps be seen as signs that the counterculture had achieved its goals. Yet in another way they created a vacuum, which emergent forces would come to exploit.

In 1975, living in this post-countercultural space, I was still able to explore the things I was curious about: books and music, sex and drugs. It was a soft rebellion, with little risk or opposition. What I didn't know was that the space was about to close up.

There are many reasons why this happened. One is entirely personal. Out of the blue, in June that year, my father died. I had been lucky to come from a family in which everyone was loved and respected. My parents' priorities may not have been quite the same as mine; rock music was meaningless to them, they took their cultural sustenance mostly from the great art and literature of Europe, and didn't waste time sitting around in a stoned stupor. Yet our divergent passions caused more curiosity than conflict. For a while they had been involved with a group of parents and teachers trying to start an alternative secondary school. It never got off the ground, but they applied its principles of student-directed learning and freedom of choice in their parenting. Militant counterculturists might have described them derogatorily as liberals, but their liberality and that of others like them was, in part, what had enabled the counterculture to exist. Throughout the period covered in this book, in institutions such as teachers' colleges, universities, schools and government departments, there were individuals like my parents who dared to imagine a kinder, fairer country in which all people were valued and creativity was held in the highest regard. From the School Publications office to the Ohu Advisory Committee, there were idealists who had, in effect, been willing the counterculture into existence, using their power to enable others to explore their dreams.

Though I had left home at the earliest opportunity, preferring to conduct my personal experiments away from my parents' scrutiny, it was in the knowledge that they would be there should I need their counsel, shelter, food and love. Suddenly, all that had gone. While my mother moved to the Kāpiti coast to raise my youngest siblings, I went back to live in the old family home in Kelburn with my sister and a group of our friends. Though still buffered by what was left of our family's middle-class appurtenances, in reality I was in free-fall.

But if I had lost the personal support that had enabled me to free-range, more turbulent forces were being unleashed on the country as a whole. Globally, the sixties had been the perfect time to launch the countercultural experiment, and in New Zealand the conditions were ideal. Unemployment was almost non-existent and state-funded pensions, along with a range of other social welfare benefits introduced in 1938 under the Social Security Act, remained firmly in place. A boom in meat, wool and dairy exports—processed grass, to use Brian Easton's term—ended with a big drop in wool prices in 1966, but rapid diversification overseen by a hands-on government had seen the economy continue to prosper into the seventies.[15]

It was this affluence that had enabled an unprecedented number of young people to leave home, live cheaply and experience a life with few restrictions. With an A or B Bursary they could go to university without paying fees or incurring debt; some even managed to save money while studying.[16] By cramming before exams, they could spend much of the academic year engaged in extra-curricular activities of one kind or another. The campuses became loci for teach-ins and happenings, but there were other centres of countercultural activity in pubs, parks, crash pads and communes. Some people never went to university at all, but became students of life; casual work, cheap accommodation and a culture of sharing kept them from poverty. It wasn't even difficult to pull together enough money to travel. With the luxury of both time and resources, young people could explore the world, or the world of ideas, at their leisure. They could consider global injustices or appreciate the finer qualities of Afghani hash.

Germaine Greer was among the first counterculturists to recognise that this way of life was unsustainable. 'The hippie is the scion of surplus value. The drop-out can only claim sanctity in a society which offers something to be dropped out of,' she wrote just a few months after her New Zealand visit.[17] For others, the first hint that an era was coming to an end was the international oil shock of 1973. This, in combination with a gradual decline in export earnings, tipped the country into economic recession. Persuaded that a National government would be better equipped to manage the crisis than Labour, who had lost their leader Norman Kirk in 1974, the country elected National to power in 1975, and Robert Muldoon became Prime Minister. Inflation and unemployment slowly rose while incomes stagnated as Muldoon tried to soften the blow with overseas borrowing.[18]

But it wasn't his interventionist approach to the economy that had the biggest impact on the counterculture; ironically, that may have helped prolong its life. It was the way he went into combat against almost every political change the counterculture represented. He would say repeatedly that he stood for the 'ordinary bloke', so by implication anyone who fell outside this category—students, Māori and Pasifika activists, protesters, hippies and, by definition, women—were his enemy. When it came to sporting relations between New Zealand and South Africa, he favoured the view that a brutally racist system shouldn't get in the way of ordinary blokes enjoying a good game of rugby. He ramped up the harassment and deportation of Pacific Island overstayers that had begun under Labour with the implementation of Gestapo-style dawn raids on Pasifika households, workplaces and even schools. He introduced a 'get tough' policy on law and order, which included the stepping-up of drug raids.

There were certainly more drugs about. Not only were Clark and Johnstone peddling their wares but local cannabis-growing operations were also becoming professional, feeding into a creeping mood of self-destructiveness. Rose Beauchamp remembers: 'When certain people, who are now dead, were coming to visit I would decant vodka into a milk bottle and pour a whole lot of water into the vodka. My rationale was I didn't want them to die at my place! It was a culture of binge. Like, how much can you take before you fall over?'[19]

For some people LSD was still a source of creative inspiration or connection to the cosmos, the first step on a spiritual path. But others were beginning to be identified as 'acid casualties': individuals who had tripped too often and fallen too hard, whose psyches had been unduly vulnerable to the drug's effects and who now wandered about in a permanent psychedelic stupor. One formerly brilliant musician paced the Wellington streets looking dishevelled, disoriented, apparently homeless. Once I stopped to ask him how he was and what he was doing with his music. He stared at me for a long time, forlorn and confused. The only sentence he was able to utter was brief, yet seemed to say it all: 'I broke my sitar.'

THE WORLD RUSHES IN

Terry Clark, Rob Muldoon: such characters make natural folk devils, and in a fairytale rendition of this story they might be held solely responsible for the counterculture's demise. Yet you can also see a cycle coming to an inevitable conclusion. In their 1997 book *The Fourth Turning*, William Strauss and Neil Howe suggest that at the core of modern history is a pattern of cycles, each cycle lasting roughly as long as a human life. Each cycle consists, like seasons, of four *turnings*, each with its own identifiable mood. The second turning, which they refer to as an *Awakening*, is always 'a passionate era of spiritual upheaval, when the civic order comes under attack from a new values regime'. Tracing the beginning of the current cycle to around the end of the Second World War, they place the start of the second turning in the early sixties, just as the counterculture was hitting its stride, winding up around the end of the following decade.[20]

If you take 1945 as the start of the baby boom, then in 1975 the first boomers were turning thirty.[21] Having devoted their teens and twenties to challenging the rules of their parents, many were now parents themselves and trying to figure out what rules might actually be required for their own survival. They had enjoyed many privileges their parents never had: shelter, mobility, affordable education, work when they wanted it, leisure if they preferred. They had had the time and means to ask questions, and had seemingly questioned everything except their own good luck. Though their protest cries sometimes made them sound like victims of a totalitarian regime, they had actually enjoyed considerable freedoms. When these privileges were threatened by changes in the country's economic fortunes, some simply reverted to type; went back to university, completed their degrees, joined the family law firm or took up accountancy, and got on with their middle-class lives. They could still smoke dope on the weekends.

Men were the most privileged of all. Though some had lent support to Women's Liberation, in reality few were moved to make substantial changes to their own behaviours. Oblivious in the patriarchal roles they had inherited from their fathers, they were reluctant to shut up, listen, share or relinquish power. Some took their privileges into the counter-cultural communities, where in many cases women's liberation seemed hardly to have made a mark. A potent example was offered to Jane Tolerton by Miriam Cameron, who by the mid-seventies was living on a commune in Huia where it was expected that such tasks as cooking, washing and childrearing would not only be handled by the women, but also undertaken with the same primitive resources as the nineteenth-century pioneers:

> I used to go home to do the washing and the men would say, 'The pioneering women used to do it, why can't you?' My husband, or mate as I used to call him, accused me of being bourgeois. But Dad said, Listen Miriam, those pioneering women suffered. Throughout history the working class has fought for better conditions, they've suffered so you can have a washing machine and your kids don't get pushed down chimneys. You don't want to go back to that. He was against the whole idea of going back to the land.[22]

Cameron's 'mate' at the time was Tim Shadbolt.

Though the women's movement would itself fragment, for now female activists tended to turn away from alternative communities and focus on changing the existing establishment institutions.

✼

Not that the alternative communities ended there; far from it. In 1975 many communes were only just getting started. Yet as each one strived to define itself, the connection to a wider idea of counterculture was often lost. In her study of four intentional communities, Olive Jones notes that many would gradually break up into separate households; co-operative activity would become inconsistent; and 'initial utopian idealism' would be replaced by 'the desire for a comfortable lifestyle'.[23] Eventually some communes would seem little different from a friendly rural suburb, and as the founding populations grew older, the younger members of the community moved away.

As the seventies flowed into the eighties, some communes also began to experience the effects of a volatile social cocktail: rising unemployment, alcohol, the widespread availability of drugs, and a new generation coming of age without the hopes and opportunities the boomers had enjoyed. The Renaissance commune in Motueka, where Olive Jones had lived, saw an influx from this new social group, who were younger than the original residents and from lower socio-economic backgrounds:

> They also stood apart in a cultural sense, contrasting in both appearance and attitude from the others who were described by outsiders as hippies. Hippies wore colourful clothes, believed in healthy living, organic food production, environmental concerns and world peace. The new group dressed in black, drank heavily and often became aggressive when drunk. They listened to heavy metal or punk music rather than rock'n'roll and were, for the most part, uninterested in the ideology of self-sufficiency or creating community.[24]

In other parts of the countryside, artists and artisans would continue to pursue their work as practising outsiders, irrespective of any wider counterculture. At Driving Creek near Coromandel the potter Barry Brickell created a clayworks, wildlife sanctuary and even his own railway. It was Brickell's belief that, as far as the suburban norm was concerned, 'the best thing to do rather than fight it, is to quietly withdraw from it'.[25] Not far away in Coroglen, painter Michael Illingworth subsistence-farmed to feed his family. Poet and painter Christina Conrad went completely off the grid, first in the Wakamarina Valley in Marlborough, then in the Avoca Valley outside Dargaville where, by her own account, she went without clothes for fifteen years and, with neither electricity nor running water, was able to work only during daylight hours.

In the cities, while some settled into lives remarkably similar to those of their parents, others would continue to explore alternative living arrangements and build, in various ways, on the ideals they had formed during the previous years. Even after the People's Union disbanded in 1979—by which time its food co-operative encompassed six hundred households—Roger Fowler kept organising the weekly bus service to Paremoremo maximum security prison that he had initiated so families and friends could visit their loved ones. He eventually bought a bus of his own and added to the schedule a monthly trip to Waikeria borstal. When I interviewed him in 2019, the service was still operating, nearly fifty years after it had begun.

And there were countless others—activists and acid-heads, herbalists, healers and hippies-without-portfolio—unnamed in this account, and yet an essential part of the countercultural fabric, who would continue to weave their alternative visions, even if the fabric itself had begun to unravel into a mass of separate strands.

KEEPING THE ROMANCE ALIVE

Then there were those who were still out on the road, and for whom there would be no turning back.

After meeting up in Bali in 1973, Alan Brunton and Sally Rodwell decided they would form a troupe of players that would combine Alan's poetry with Sally's masks and mime. Red Mole would include puppets, politics, satire, songs. They would travel the world, and worlds within worlds. Martin Edmond, who was part of the group for several years, identifies an opium den behind a Shell service station in Laos as the location of Red Mole's 'originary moment'. He cites a manifesto in which Alan and Sally outlined five main principles, the first of which was: 'To keep the romance alive.'[26]

After returning to New Zealand in 1974, Red Mole began performing in various configurations that always included Brunton and Rodwell, and often the musician Jan Preston and fire-eating mime Deborah Hunt. For the remainder of the decade they maintained a prolific schedule, sometimes supporting themselves with a parallel venture, White Rabbit Puppet Theatre, which played in schools, hospitals and department stores.

Red Mole toured as opening act for Split Enz. They mounted their own extravaganzas in theatres and opera houses. For their 1978 theatre production *Ghost Rite*, Brunton had composed what Martin Edmond has described as 'both a ritual performed by ghosts and a play ghost-written by channelling the voices of the dead'.[27] Spanning the history of civilisation, from Ancient Egypt to pre-war Berlin, passing through Europe in the plague years on its way to some unsettling unspecified future, it was as much a poem of images as words. The eerie sight of a man spreadeagled inside a giant wheel rolling silently back and forth across the stage has stayed with me for more than forty years. 'Some day all theatre will be like this!' promised the programme, though it hasn't happened yet.

Their most manically sustained period involved performances of their Cabaret Capital Strut in Wellington at The Balcony, the nightclub of the city's most famous transvestite, Carmen. Those cabarets were a high point in terms of Red Mole's connection to a community, drawing a mixture of counterculture survivors and theatre luvvies, rock'n'roll fans (the Country Flyers, the Moles' backing band for the season, were the best in town) and Carmen's own demi-monde. The content was topical and under constant construction. Deborah Hunt's papier-mâché pig snout was instant shorthand for Muldoon. There was Neville Purvis, the alter-ego of poet and screenwriter Arthur Baysting: a petty crim from 'Taita College and Mt Crawford [prison] finishing school' with greasy hair, pencil moustache and tatty white suit, who as Master of Ceremonies would dispense laconic capsules of Hutt Valley wisdom. ('The Mark II Zephyr is the pinnacle of twentieth-century technology, you should see the size of the back seat, and that's Neville on the level.') And there was Brunton, for whom poetry and performance were inseparable, slightly malevolent in greasepaint, and punctuating the spectacle with dark soliloquies:

> welcome my friends to the cabaret
> the show that never ends though men go to war
> and stars collapse in vacant space
> come with me, children, let us walk the street of a thousand joys
> don't look left: look right—ahead
> child there are dangers on a street of contradictions
> here in the cabaret where the stars collapse and all the
> world rushes in and the night clings to your teeth[28]

Within six months the Moles went from a Sunday-evening slot at The Balcony to performing every night of the week. At one point they did thirty-seven nights straight. And then, right at the point when there were punters queuing around the block for every show, they pulled the plug. Martin Edmond recalls Brunton explaining that he was sick of

cleaning the toilets there, but you sense that wasn't the real reason. He never saw himself as a popular entertainer. Staying for any length of time in any one place, being part of an institution let alone becoming one, was anathema to Red Mole.

Soon Rodwell and Brunton had departed for America where real-life encounters with Israeli commandos, armed policemen and dodgy drug dealers provided fertile material for further fables. For the next few years they would base themselves in New York and London, making occasional forays back home, bringing ever-more apocalyptic

Sally Rodwell on Alan Brunton. Bryan
Staff photograph, private collection

productions that sometimes left audiences bewildered. Eventually the couple returned to live in Island Bay. Rodwell founded other theatre projects, in which she worked exclusively with women, while the pair continued to collaborate as Red Mole, keeping the romance alive. Brunton's writing became ever-more layered and allusive, though the crowds who had once queued outside Carmen's had dwindled to almost nothing. It didn't seem to bother them. Their work had always derived from the perspective of the outsider. Wellingtonians would sometimes ask, 'Whatever happened to Red Mole?', not realising Sally and Alan were at that moment in a hall not far away, rehearsing or performing another show, mapping new and uncharted places. In their own way they were always on the road, even in their hometown.

AFTERMATH

Towards the end of the seventies I spent a couple of years as bass guitarist in a rock band, Rough Justice, led by the former Mammal and BLERTA singer Rick Bryant. In January 1978, breaking from our usual itinerary of student union halls and provincial taverns, we went to play at the first Nambassa festival near Waihī. This was the brainchild of Peter Terry, a New Zealander who had spent a good chunk of his life in the New Hebrides. It was there, staying amongst a tribe known as the Big Nambas, he had his vision of the festival.

We pulled up in Rick's bus, a battered ex-Railways Bedford hand-painted with fallen angels. Other vehicles—cars, caravans, Kombis, house trucks, a horse and cart—were being herded in various directions. A shirtless hippie with a clipboard directed us to the performers' area. On the smaller of two stages a band was playing. They were called Mahana and were the musical flagship for a Coromandel commune that was in the early stages of establishing itself. Thousands of punters had arrived before us. Some were dancing in the dust where the dry grass had already been worn away. With hours to go until our performance, I wandered about the 200-acre site. In the open air, a group of thirty or forty people were being guided through a Tai Chi lesson. Elsewhere workshops were getting underway in clay therapy, weaving, home birth, palmistry, windmill building and Aboriginal emu-egg carving. Krishna Fast Foods were serving coleslaw and yoghurt shakes.

At Nambassa it might have been hard to support an argument that the counterculture era was over. On the contrary, the counter-culture seemed to be everywhere. Yet in many ways the Nambassa experience was, as Andrew Schmidt noted, 'more akin to a multi-day A&P (agricultural and pastoral) show': a New Zealand institution dating back to the nineteenth century, at which the general public as well as farmers would come to see displays of livestock, crops and farm machinery, domestic crafts, sideshows, and competitions such as wood chopping and sheep shearing.[29] At Nambassa a wide range of pedlars were promoting their products and practices, and just as not everyone who came to A&P shows was a farmer, not everyone at Nambassa was a hippie. Some came for the music. Others were window-shopping, trying and occasionally buying from the range of options on display. Did this add up to a culture, or just a whole lot of individuals seeking personal fulfilment?

Some commentators had already remarked on this strain of individualism. On the first page of *The First New Zealand Whole Earth Catalogue* the editors had posited that the book could have had any one

Band truck at Mahana commune, 1980s. Peter Aagaard photograph, private collection

of a number of alternative titles. These included *Everybody's Guide To Doing Their Own Thing*, *How To Drop Out*, *Possibilities Open To People*, *Make Your Life More Interesting* and *Means of Self-Fulfilment*. To Dick Scott, reviewing the *Catalogue* for the *Listener*, such titles betrayed a 'narcissistic preoccupation amply reinforced in the text … The whole earth, that slice of territory occupied by the liberated young, is a private world lived from within. Or so it would appear …' Scott, born in 1923, was a self-described 'radical historian' who had spent his life engaged in various movements for social change, including a spell in the Communist Party. To him, the countercultural manual was 'a grafting of pioneer New Zealand do-it-yourself on to back-to-nature Californian crankiness'. In the final paragraph of his review he conceded that the *Catalogue* did offer 'chunks of value', identifying Tim Shadbolt and James and Jane Ritchie as worthwhile contributors, but the tone and breadth of his criticisms implied a suspicion not just with the book but with the entire movement it represented.[30]

As a twenty-year-old musician arriving at Nambassa, I could not help but share a little of Scott's cynicism. There was much talk of 'self-realisation' and 'finding oneself'. But could all this pursuit of personal autonomy just as easily be seen as working against the desires of those looking to build a new society?

While weekend hippies and dedicated counterculturists alike were 'finding themselves', not far away a much more malevolent form of self-fulfilment was being pursued.

Sometime after Sandra Coney had declined Bert Potter's invitation to join one of his therapy groups, neighbours of Potter's mattress-filled Campbells Bay home where the live-in sessions were taking place grew increasingly alarmed, and took their complaints to police. A court injunction stopped the week-long therapy groups, and Potter briefly moved his activities to a location in Gillies Avenue in Epsom; then, inspired in part by a visit to Bhagwan Shree Rajneesh's ashram in western India, he set about establishing a full-time community on 70 acres of land at Albany. He called it Centrepoint, and declared himself its spiritual leader.

Visiting in 1980, three years after Centrepoint's establishment, Phil Gifford's initial impression was that:

> [I]f there was such a thing as a middle-class commune this is it … Among the more than 50 people living at Centrepoint the few who work outside the commune include doctors and teachers. The people who join Centrepoint bring, usually, a lot more than the traditional commune baggage of peace, love and good vibes. They are required to sell up house, car, and, in many cases, business, and put all the proceeds into the community.[31]

Gifford was there to write a story for the *Listener*, the country's highest-circulation magazine with a wide reach into middle New Zealand. None of the Centrepoint adults Gifford spoke to expressed any qualms about Potter's claims as a guru. Potter himself told Gifford he could remember 'fairly clearly' the first eighteen months of his life:

> [E]ven then I realised that I had a difference that some people would see and some couldn't. I was always the leader of the kids around, not necessarily the one up front making all the noise, but people did what I wanted them to do ... It is a special gift [I have] if you like. There is something special there, something very different. It is very like Christ, like Krishna, like all the great religious leaders ... I see a spiritual community as one in which each individual has to find their own place, their own body of truth, if you like. There's nothing they have to be, there's nothing they have to attain. Where they are right now is fine, and if they want to move from that place it's up to them. They make the moves.[32]

Reflecting on his encounter with Potter forty-odd years later, Gifford remembers 'the little smirk that would cross his face' when he made such pronouncements as, 'Some people read *Penthouse* letters. We *are* a *Penthouse* letter', which he knew were catnip to journalists. 'He was an evil genius at public relations. He was aware that the selling point, and what made the general public fascinated, was sex.'[33]

The community followed a principle of individual freedom, including total sexual freedom. 'When people come here there are no actual rules or laws or anybody telling them they must have sex with somebody else,' Potter told Gifford. 'But obviously if you were to come here with a wife and you've been totally monogamous, and all the rest of it, and you see everybody else having the goodies, you're going to look around and say "Why am I missing out? It's all here. Why don't I get into it?"'

There may have been no rules, but Potter as therapist-guru would sometimes set assignments. One woman was instructed to have sex with five different men a day for several days. And the children would sometimes watch adults having sex. There were no doors on the toilets or showers. 'There's nothing hidden from them,' Potter would boast. 'They'll grow up very sophisticated, but they have very few problems.'[34]

In fact, the children were not merely having a sophisticated exposure to adult sexuality but many were being sexually abused by adults, including by Potter. Adolescents were given LSD and MDMA (also known as ecstasy), which was being manufactured on site, and made to participate in naked 'self-discovery' sessions overseen by Potter. Sometimes they were required to perform sexual acts on him, and vice versa. Other adults, male and female, took teenage concubines or enabled in various ways the abuses their fellow communards were enacting on a regular basis.

Finally in 1990, Bert Potter was arrested in a police drug raid on Centrepoint. While serving his prison sentence he was further convicted on thirteen charges of indecently assaulting five girls, all minors, the youngest of whom was three. Six other Centrepoint males were also convicted on various charges, including sexual assault on a minor.

✳

That same year the country elected a National government which would continue the sweeping neoliberal reforms introduced by the previous Labour administration. It had all begun in 1984, the year in which George Orwell set the novel that would introduce terms like Newspeak, Big Brother and Thought Police: core vocabulary in the more distrustful corners of the counterculture. New Zealand had finally rid itself of Robert Muldoon, the man many held responsible for their sense of unease, and elected a Labour government for the first time since the Kirk victory of 1972.

Headed by David Lange, this would be the first Cabinet substantially made up of baby boomers. Some had been students in the late sixties and early seventies when the university quadrangles were ringing to the sounds of anti-war chants and psychedelic rock. Theirs was the generation that had challenged the restrictions on a whole catalogue of freedoms — restrictions their parents had accepted as a fact of life. They had campaigned for women's liberation, sexual liberation, environmental awareness and freedom from nuclear annihilation. Almost immediately the fourth Labour government enacted a number of reforms that acknowledged such campaigns. They established a Ministry of Women's Affairs to address issues raised by the women's liberation movement; they passed the Homosexual Law Reform Act, decriminalising sexual relations between men over sixteen. They set up a Department of Conservation charged with protecting the natural environment, and once more suspended sporting relations with apartheid South Africa.

Most flamboyantly, they turned down a request for a visit by an ageing missile-carrier, the USS *Buchanan*, after the US said it 'could neither confirm nor deny' that the ship would be carrying nuclear weapons. As a result, the US and Australia suspended New Zealand from the ANZUS alliance. David Lange, who in his own mythology had been haunted by 'a vision of a man-made apocalypse' since witnessing the glow from a nuclear test at age twenty, seized the moment. The month after the ship showdown, he debated right-wing American evangelist Jerry Falwell at the widely televised Oxford Union debate, arguing, with charisma and aplomb, the proposition that 'nuclear weapons are morally indefensible'. He won the debate, and the global anti-nuclear movement hailed New Zealand as an example to the world, with Lange their new poster boy.

Labour followed up in 1987 by passing the New Zealand Nuclear Free Zone, Disarmament, and Arms Control Act. In celebration, singer-songwriter Shona Laing wrote the upbeat anthem 'Neutral and Nuclear Free'. It seemed as though all the counterculture's calls for freedom were finally being heeded at the highest levels of power.

But for those boomers now in government, freedom came in many forms. And with their endorsement of a freer society came their insistence on a freer economy. 'I want to see central government off the backs of private enterprise,' David Caygill (born 1948) said prior to the election.[35] As a student Caygill had been a member of the National Party, but he had switched to Labour because of his opposition to the Vietnam War. Once in government, Lange appointed him Minister of Trade and Industry and Minister of National Development. Richard Prebble (also born in 1948) was assigned, among his many portfolios, Minister for State Owned Enterprises.

At the centre of this so-called 'Treasury Troika' was Minister of Finance Roger Douglas: not a boomer (he was born in 1937) but a man with a strong belief in freedom, at least when it came to capital. Between them they set about freeing the economy: removing subsidies, lifting import restrictions, and deregulating broadcasting, air transport, petrol, retail and the ports. 'Are government departments necessary?' Douglas had asked in his 1980 book *There's Got To Be A Better Way!* Prebble began preparing to corporatise or convert into state-owned enterprises as many government departments as possible, stripping them of their social objectives and turning them into profit-making businesses, some of which would subsequently be sold.

The prices of consumer goods fell quickly as protections were lifted from local industry. Suddenly there were imported second-hand Japanese cars everywhere—and the local car-assembly plants closed. Buildings went up, wages went down. A few people made a lot of money; a lot of people lost jobs and would never again have the security of regular work and income. By the end of the decade, 10 percent of the population, and a quarter of all Māori, were unemployed.

Other boomers, some of whom had been active in the counter-culture, took up new positions in this businessman's utopia. As a student radical in the early seventies, Rob Campbell had been a shareholder and member of the executive of the Wellington Resistance Bookshop. Now the government was appointing him to boards, including the BNZ and the newly corporatised NZ Post.[36]

Along with deregulating most other aspects of the economy, the fourth Labour government lifted the traditional ban on weekend trading, so that by the end of the eighties weekends were as desanctified and commercial as any other day of the week.

Is this what Jumping Sundays had come to mean?

EPILOGUE

Paradoxes were plentiful in the counterculture. There were visions of nuclear apocalypse and dreams of a utopian future; a belief that the world could be changed and a simultaneous retreat from society. Ideas of tolerance, diversity and acceptance were celebrated, yet white middle-class males predominated. There was an emphasis on large collective projects—festivals, happenings, protest marches, communal living experiments—yet a high value was placed on the individual experience.

The Love Machine, the morning after. Pekapeka Festival, Easter 1971. Ans Westra photograph, Alexander Turnbull Library, PA-Group-00941

To the previous generation, home improvement mattered more than self-improvement. They hadn't had time for health foods, marijuana, meditation or therapies; there were fences to paint and lawns to mow. Dick Scott spoke for them when he characterised the inwardly-directed activities of the counterculture as a lot of narcissistic navel-gazing. To the left-wing commentator Bruce Jesson, the political discourse during the countercultural era, even when it looked outward, was focused on the wrong things, dominated by debates about the Vietnam War and South Africa, when it should have been a time of questioning the direction of New Zealand society. 'It was as though the protest movement felt New Zealand didn't need changing as much as other countries.'[1] While young questing minds were preoccupied with the moral failings of other nations—not to mention their own acid trips, sexual revolutions and paths to spiritual enlightenment—their neoliberal contemporaries were left unchecked to develop radical economic strategies that would reshape New Zealand.

And yet there is an argument that self-awareness is a first step to social awareness, or that the two are, at least, not mutually exclusive. 'The personal is political' was the slogan taken up by second-wave feminists, who argued that the personal issues brought to light by consciousness-raising and therapy groups were the result of the way society is organised, and that identifying these is a necessary step towards social change. Or as eighty-year-old yoga instructor Lew Postlewaight put it to a symposium at Nambassa, through examining the self one might gain a deeper empathy for others. 'I see people through my own nature, as you see people through your nature. If we find fault we should find it within ourselves.'[2]

Such ideas may not have cut much ice with the Gordon Gekko 'greed is good' types for whom the Treasury Troika designed a rich boys' playground, but they didn't entirely go away.[3]

Though no successive government, whether Labour- or National-led, has truly reversed the neoliberal reforms, when Prime Minister Jacinda Ardern describes herself as 'a child of the eighties' she speaks as a witness to their devastating social consequences. When she brings a term like 'wellbeing' into the political discourse, or talks of kindness and 'the simple concept of looking outwardly and beyond ourselves', she sounds more like she has come via a Nambassa workshop than a round-table with Roger Douglas.[4]

Then there are the Greens, who emerged from the remnants of the Values Party after Labour's rupture during the second term of Rogernomics, and by 2017 had taken a role in government via an agreement with Ardern's Labour. Grounded in countercultural principles, early Green candidates included various former communards, environmental activists and people who might once have been described as hippies.

There are many other ways in which countercultural seeds have taken root in New Zealand life. Such widely embraced institutions as food co-operatives, community law centres, markets, street fairs, festivals and Pride parades all show how the counterculture has expanded our sense of community. These days one in ten New Zealanders follows a vegetarian diet.[5] As for the communes, a few that started in the seventies continue successfully to this day. Some of the original experiments foundered on the skill shortages of their members or fell back on old patriarchal paradigms. One or two were subverted by predators like Bert Potter. Nevertheless, these all provided object lessons in what and what not to do as others began to consider alternatives to a quarter-acre section in the suburbs. Co-housing projects and eco-neighbourhoods with names like Earthsong address ideas of socially and environmentally sustainable living. If you squint hard, you might even see the popularity of the 'lifestyle block' in today's real-estate market as a more bourgeois descendant of the back-to-the-land movement.

New Zealanders have continued to lose their religion. In the 2018 census, almost half of all respondents said they had no religious affiliation, while alternative paths to spiritual fulfilment such as meditation and yoga have become so widespread as to be considered mainstream.

Tolkien's *The Lord of the Rings* trilogy has gone from being a well-thumbed paperback on hippie bookshelves to a series of blockbuster films, directed by New Zealander Peter Jackson and shot in the same landscapes where communards, acid-heads and mystics-in-the-making once dreamed their utopias.

Though Jackson is more businessman than bohemian, the fact that New Zealand has a skilled filmmaking community for him to utilise is thanks in large part to the pioneering work of truly countercultural figures like Geoff Murphy, Pat Robins, Alun and Helen Bollinger, and Bruno and Veronica Lawrence.

In music, left-field promoters like Graeme Nesbitt, and bands from Chants R&B to BLERTA who dared to make their strange sounds, paved the way for a country that now celebrates its own songs. Reflecting on my own working life, I realise I have spent most of it working from home as a freelance rock critic—a job that, in a sense, the counterculture created.

The old guard of moralising doctors who decided who of their patients could and couldn't have the Pill has largely disappeared. By the time Helen Smyth was writing *Rocking the Cradle*, her book on contraception, sex and politics in New Zealand published in 2000, surveys were showing that nearly all New Zealand women used some form of contraception. Pre-marital sex and couples living together and having children out of wedlock have ceased to be a subject of moral panic. Homosexuality was decriminalised by the Labour government in 1986; the Human Rights Act passed in 1993 made it illegal to discriminate on the grounds of sexual orientation; and the Marriage Amendment Act in 2013 allowed same-sex couples to marry. Public discussion has now turned to issues around gender diversity. While the expression 'free love' is currently out of vogue, terms like 'polyamory' and 'open relationship' are part of the post-millennial vernacular, and could perhaps be seen as free love with more clearly defined boundaries and conditions.

Then there are the things that haven't changed. New Zealand still grapples with high rates of rape and sexual abuse. Recreational drug use continues, and attitudes remain conflicted. Alcohol is still legal, with a market size of $2 billion, though it is involved in hundreds of fatal car crashes every year and half of serious violent crimes, while at least two alcohol-related deaths and over three hundred alcohol-related offences occur every day. Though there has been a revived discussion about the therapeutic uses of hallucinogens, LSD is still categorised as a Class A drug, with penalties up to life imprisonment for supply or manufacture, as are heroin and psilocybin mushrooms. While surveys show a majority of New Zealanders have smoked cannabis, in a 2020 referendum on the question of legalisation, a majority voted against. New amendments to the law, however, direct police to alternatives to prosecution in cases of personal use. Meanwhile, the use of other more destructive drugs such as methamphetamine and synthetic cannabinoids has grown, in part because these are often easier to obtain than cannabis and are offered by dealers in place of cannabis when supplies are scarce.

While government has recognised and legislated for some of the freedoms the counterculture stood for, other movements have arisen in opposition to what they regard as new forms of oppression. The anti-vaccination ideology has seen a militant resurgence in the era of Covid-19. Its proponents share certain traits with the protest groups of the sixties and seventies: a belief that personal liberties, including freedom of speech, are under threat; a fear of state surveillance and government conspiracies. Some of their ideas can be linked to theories about bodily purity and alternative medicine introduced by the counterculture. They employ familiar protest techniques such as marches, pickets and acts of civil disobedience. Though the movement has sprung up in different parts of the country, it has a particular visibility in some of the places that attracted the original communards, such as Nelson and Coromandel. There is at least one intentional community in the Nelson region that espouses anti-vaccination as one of its fundamental tenets. The message is a highly individualistic one, placing personal freedoms above the safety of the wider community.

The user-pays model of tertiary education, introduced as part of the neoliberal reforms, has undoubtedly had an impact on student protest. It is little wonder that today's university students are less inclined to sacrifice their grades for sit-ins when you consider the giant debts they incur before graduating. When home ownership is beyond the reach of all but the most privileged, when rents are extortionate and thousands are sleeping in cars and streets, James K. Baxter's laments about suburbia's 'well-lit prisons' seem oddly beside the point. Stories of job surpluses and landlords who demanded less than half your income in rent now seem like fantasies. Meanwhile, the nuclear sword that still hangs over the planet has been joined by the inexorable threat of climate change. The cumulative effect of all this on the young has created what appears to be an epidemic of anxiety.

And yet currents of hope keep bubbling up. A renewal of youth activism can be seen in climate strikes and rallies against racism, sexual violence and all forms of inequality. If these protests don't have the carnival spirit of Jumping Sundays, that is only a measure of how much more urgent the issues have become. Sustainability, a utopian aspiration in the early days of communes and *Whole Earth Catalogues*, is recognised by today's youth as a necessity for the survival of the planet.

They are also discussing a vision of this country's future that was barely articulated in the conversations of the counterculture: decolonisation or, as Moana Jackson prefers, the ethic of restoration.[6] As my millennial daughters explain it to me, this doesn't mean Pākehā going back to wherever their ancestors came from. Rather it requires them to recognise that to live in this country is to exist in terms of their relationship with Māori under Te Tiriti o Waitangi. Not only does this acknowledge tino rangatiratanga, the traditions, independence and authority of tangata whenua, the people of the land; it also gives Pākehā a positive and realistic way of seeing themselves. My parents knew they were Pākehā New Zealanders rather than Europeans only when they went to London in 1959 and saw that their creative dreams and visions of a better society did not belong there but back where they had come from. If the anti-apartheid movement that culminated in the 1981 Springbok tour protests helped speed the end of South African apartheid, it also made it harder for Pākehā to ignore the systemic racism in the country they called their home.

Today it seems almost quaint to have ever thought in terms of a counterculture in New Zealand when, to Māori, the whole of Pākehā society can be seen as just that: as counter to their culture, a barbaric intrusion upon the culture that was already here, fully formed, with its stories, its obligations and intellectual traditions, long before the colonists came. Viewed from this perspective, what we call the counterculture just looks like part of the colonial baggage.

Then again, to help create a successful decolonised future we might draw on some of the things that characterised the counterculture at its best: imagination, empathy, courage, romance, a respect for the land, good songs, a sense of humour, a sense of justice.

A change of consciousness.

NOTES

PROLOGUE

1. Details of Jumping Sundays are drawn from a variety of accounts, both written and oral, notably Barrie Southam, 'Auckland Is a Happening City', *New Zealand Listener*, 14 November 1969; Shadbolt, *Bullshit and Jellybeans*; Diana Wichtel, 'Doing the Time Warp Again', *New Zealand Listener*, 17 October 2009; and author interviews with Alison McClean, Roger Fowler and Julian Rosenberg.
2. 'The Hippies', *Time*, 7 July 1967.
3. https://www.theguardian.com/music/2009/sep/06/plastic-people-velvet-revolution-1989
4. John Sinclair, 'White Panther Statement', *Fifth Estate*, 14–17 November 1968.
5. *The Second New Zealand Whole Earth Catalogue*, p. 112.
6. Zolov, *Refried Elvis*, p. 15.
7. Roszak, *The Making of a Counter Culture*, p. 42.
8. Ibid., p. xi.
9. Jan Van Bavel and David S. Reher, 'The Baby Boom and Its Causes: What We Know and What We Need to Know', *Population and Development Review*, vol. 39, no. 2 (2013), pp. 257–88, http://www.jstor.org/stable/41857595
10. Beat Poets at the Royal Albert Hall, https://www.youtube.com/watch?v=x1E_iGn9Whk
11. Hamilton, *Till Human Voices Wake Us*, pp. 110, 152.
12. *Counter Culture Free Press*, April 1973 (4 A.W.).

ONE

1. Conrad Bollinger, letter to Hector McNeill, 22 March 1959, private collection.
2. Ibid., 1 November 1959, private collection.
3. Conrad Bollinger, letter to John and Maria Dronke, 31 December 1959, private collection.
4. All 38,000 copies of *Washday at the Pa* were withdrawn from circulation by the Ministry of Education after the book was criticised by the Māori Women's Welfare League, who argued that the sub-standard living conditions portrayed in Westra's photographs would reinforce Pākehā stereotypes of Māori as poor, rural and happily primitive. There were also complaints that the photos showed breaches of tapu, such as a child standing on top of a stove. Westra, who had spent a number of months living among rural Māori, defended the booklet, saying that the photos were not posed and that 'it was never meant to portray a typical Maori family. It is just a story of a happy family living in the country. It shows the warmth of family relationships.' 'Booklet Decision Angers Author', *Dominion*, 4 August 1964.
5. New Zealand History: Nga korero a ipurangi o Aotearoa, Waitangi Day, https://nzhistory.govt.nz/politics/treaty/waitangi-day/waitangi-day-1960s
6. Coney, *Out of the Frying Pan*, p. 24.
7. Ibid., p. 25.
8. Boyd Klap, interviewed by Dinah Priestley, Cappuccino Oral History Project 1993–1994, Oral History Archive OHA 1823, Alexander Turnbull Library, Wellington.
9. Ausubel, *The Fern and the Tiki*, pp. 13, 14, 15, 34, 52, 53.
10. Sturm (ed.), *Anna Kavan's New Zealand*. Kavan, whose work blended realism, absurdism and science fiction, and who flouted such conventions as marriage and monogamy and was for many years addicted to heroin, spent time in New Zealand during the Second World War as a guest of Ian Hamilton, the intellectual, pacifist and conscientious objector. She lived at Torbay on Auckland's North Shore, where a group of intellectuals, centred on the writer Frank Sargeson, developed their brand of literary nationalism. Yet even in these circles there was an insularity, not to mention misogyny. Describing Kavan in a letter to friend and academic Eric McCormick, Sargeson reported that poet Denis Glover 'rather unkindly describes her as one of those blondes who get around the world with their knees behind their ears. It has some truth to it but she puts it to good purpose.' Ibid., p. 46.
11. Klap, interviewed by Dinah Priestley, 11 August 1994.
12. Susy Pointon with Arthur Baysting, 'Rebels & Ratbags: The Real Story of the New Zealand Film Industry', unpublished manuscript, 2011, p. 75.
13. Ausubel, *The Fern and the Tiki*, p. 55.
14. B. R. Hancock, 'The New Zealand Security Intelligence Service', *Auckland University Law Review*, vol. 2 (August 1973), p. 1.
15. *Report of the Special Committee on Moral Delinquency in Children and Adolescents*, New Zealand Government Printer, Wellington, 1954.
16. Ibid.
17. Gary F. Whitcher, 'More Than America: Some New Zealand Responses to American Culture in the Mid-Twentieth Century', PhD thesis, University of Canterbury, 2011, p. 20.
18. Ibid., p. 80.
19. Gordon Campbell, email to author, 16 May 2019.

20 Report of the Special Committee on Moral Delinquency in Children and Adolescents.
21 Manning, The Bodgie, p. 6.
22 'Our Life and Times', New Zealand Listener, 11 March 1960.
23 Ibid.
24 Louis Johnson, 'The Icy Dawn of the Sixties', in Johnson (ed.), New Zealand Poetry Yearbook: Volume 9.
25 Letter to Michele Leggott, 22 October 2000.
26 From memoir by Peggy Garland, in Beatson (eds), Dear Peggy, p. 88.
27 'The poet becomes a seer through a long, immense and systematic derangement of the senses', wrote Arthur Rimbaud in a letter to Paul Demeny, Charleville, 15 May 1871, https://my-blackout.com/2019/03/03/arthur-rimbaud-letters-1870-18719-sean-bonney-letter-on-poetics-after-rimbaud/
28 Irene Zohrab, author interview, 14 August 2019.
29 John Esam, letter to Margaret Garland, File 91-181-11, Alexander Turnbull Library, Wellington, with permission of Lara Esam.
30 Edmond and Roberts (eds), Steal Away Boy, p. 6.
31 Ibid., pp. 8–9.
32 Ibid.
33 Genevieve McClean, author interview, 17 July 2019.
34 Mary Seddon, interviewed by Dinah Priestley, Cappuccino Oral History Project 1993–1994, OHC 007320, Alexander Turnbull Library, Wellington.
35 Ibid.
36 Ibid.
37 New Zealand Artists Doing Dylan, database compiled by Bill Hester, private collection.
38 Sir Robert Jones, interviewed by Dinah Priestley, Cappuccino Oral History Project 1993–1994, OH Coll-0281, Alexander Turnbull Library, Wellington.
39 Bourke, Blue Smoke, p. 306.
40 Hoffmann, Tales of Anna Hoffmann, p. 115.
41 Ibid., p. 60.
42 'I Am an Existentialist', New Zealand Truth, 6 March 1956.
43 Murphy, A Life on Film, p. 39.
44 Ibid., p. 45.
45 Brunton, Years Ago Today, p. 20.
46 Murphy, A Life on Film, p. 48.
47 Conrad Bollinger, unpublished memoir, undated, private collection.
48 Conrad Bollinger, letter to his mother, 1 April 1958, private collection.
49 Bell, The Brian Bell Reader, p. 1.
50 Boraman, Rabble Rousers and Merry Pranksters, p. 9.

TWO

1 Nuttal, Bomb Culture, p. 19.
2 Ibid.
3 Ken James, email to author, 28 August 2020.
4 Film of Aldermaston March 1959, https://www.youtube.com/watch?v=Cp7qIDnYbxs
5 Matthew O'Meagher, 'The New Zealand Campaign for Nuclear Disarmament: Its Birth and Early Years', BA (Hons) thesis, University of Otago, 1985.
6 Birchfield, Looking for Answers, p. 341.
7 Boraman, Rabble Rousers and Merry Pranksters, p. 5.
8 'Protest March to Parliament Proceeded Quietly', Evening Post, 3 August 1961.
9 '"Aurora" Lights N.Z. Sky—U.S. Bomb Effect', New Zealand Herald, 10 July 1962.
10 Lange, Nuclear Free—The New Zealand Way, p. 11.
11 Hugh Young, author interview, 30 July 2019.
12 'Ban the Bomb Marchers Nearing the End of Their Journey', Evening Post, 3 April 1961.
13 Mark Young, email to author, 26 March 2019.
14 'Forced By Russia', Evening Post, 21 April 1962.
15 Rowbotham, Promise of a Dream, p. 71.
16 'Ban the Bombers Join Establishment', Salient, 16 April 1964.
17 Rachel Stace, author interview, 13 March 2019.
18 'Reception for Beatles Criticised by Councillors', New Zealand Herald, 22 June 1964.
19 A. J. W. Taylor, 'Beatlemania: A Study in Adolescent Enthusiasm', British Journal of Social and Clinical Psychology, vol. 5 (1966), pp. 161–70.
20 Bruce Mason, 'The Beatles—A Postscript', New Zealand Listener, 10 July 1964.
21 Letters, Dominion, 10 July 1964.
22 Ibid.
23 Richard Brody, 'How The Beatles Created Self-conscious Stardom', The New Yorker, 7 July 2014.
24 Phil Gifford, email to author, 12 November 2019.
25 Chamber Music New Zealand: Records, 1951–1991, Thelonious Monk Quartet (1965)—Artists' papers, MS-Group-0138, Alexander Turnbull Library, Wellington.
26 Gordon Campbell, 'Memories of Monk', New Zealand Listener, 12 February 1983.
27 Phil Dadson, author interview, 4 May 2019.
28 Andrew Schmidt, AudioCulture, 12 May 2013, https://www.audioculture.co.nz/people/chants-r-b

29 Ibid.

30 Chants R&B released only two singles—four songs in total, both in 1966—for Action, an independent label. By far the strangest of the cuts was the sole original, 'I Want Her': a giddy three minutes of asymmetric rhythm and ambiguous intonation with an unexpected solo played by guitarist Jim Tomlin on a snake charmer's flute. By the end of '66 the Chants had moved to Melbourne where they soon disbanded, their impact never really having registered much outside of Christchurch.

31 Richard Hill, author interview, 19 March 2019.

32 Deborah Yates, author interview, 19 July 2019.

33 Shackleton, *Operation Vietnam*, pp. 18–19.

34 Boraman, *Rabble Rousers and Merry Pranksters*, p. 13.

35 Rabel, *New Zealand and the Vietnam War*, p. 98.

36 *Otago Daily Times*, 29 May 1965.

37 Rabel, *New Zealand and the Vietnam War*, pp. 155–56.

38 Alister Taylor, author interview, 18 July 2019.

39 Alister Taylor, 'Peace, Power & Politics', *City*, Spring 1987, p. 55.

40 Alister Taylor, author interview, 18 July 2019.

41 Taylor, 'Peace, Power & Politics', p. 51.

42 'Police Remove Chained Pickets—Bolt Cutters Were Needed', *Evening Post*, 21 February 1966. The protesters were Jane McElwee, Nick Rosenberg, Paul Melser and Elemer Kuna.

43 P. R. H. Jackman, 'The Auckland Opposition to New Zealand's Involvement in the Vietnam War, 1965–1972: An Example of the Achievements and Limitations of Ideology', MA thesis, University of Auckland, 1979.

44 Ibid.

45 Clark Clifford, *Foreign Affairs*, vol. 47, no. 4 (July 1969), pp. 601–22.

THREE

1 'Man Convicted of Selling Drug Marijuana', *New Zealand Herald*, 13 February 1960.

2 Ibid.

3 Yska, *New Zealand Green*, p. 36.

4 Ibid., p. 38.

5 Bainbridge, *The Bassett Road Machine Gun Murders*, p. 21.

6 Ibid., p. 161.

7 'Marijuana Smoke Filled Room Says Constable', *New Zealand Herald*, 7 June 1963.

8 Borrowdale, *Weed: A New Zealand Story*, p. 78.

9 Author interview, 27 September 2018; name withheld by request.

10 Dix, *Stranded in Paradise*, p. 60.

11 Rick Bryant, unpublished memoir, private collection.

12 Ticket, *Awake*, liner notes, Nick Bollinger, 2013.

13 *Dominion*, 18 March 1971.

14 'Drugs on the Campus', *New Zealand Listener*, 8 November 1971.

15 Yska, *New Zealand Green*, p. 76.

16 Bryce Peterson to David Herkt in *Inside New Zealand: High Times*, 2005, https://www.youtube.com/watch?v=nIrb4h76NZk

17 Aldous Huxley, 'Wanted, A New Pleasure', in *Music at Night and Other Essays*, 1931, Faded Page eBook #20180506, p. 116.

18 Stevens, *Storming Heaven*, p. 259.

19 Ibid., p. 123.

20 Hofmann, *LSD: My Problem Child*, p. 15.

21 Leary, *High Priest*, p. 12.

22 Quoted in Stevens, *Storming Heaven*, p. 94.

23 Alpert/Dass, *The Only Dance There Is*, p. 114.

24 Stevens, *Storming Heaven*, p. 242.

25 Beatson (eds), *Dear Peggy*, p. 64.

26 Ibid.

27 Dan Richter, author interview, 9 August 2019.

28 Ibid.

29 Originally from Durham, Hollingshead had been born Michael Shinkfield. He assumed the new surname because, according to Joe Mellen, also on the scene at the time, 'the highest chakra in the tantric scale is a hole in the top of the head'. Hollingshead would symbolise this by wearing a red dot in the centre of his forehead. As for Mellen, 'I would rather have the state of mind than the symbol itself,' he remarked, and he was not being flippant. In 1970, seeking a higher level of consciousness, Mellen successfully drilled a hole in his own skull. MacLean, *Behind Open Doors*, p. 76.

30 Miles, *London Calling*, pp. 179–80.

31 Dan Richter, author interview, 9 August 2019.

32 Beatles John Lennon and George Harrison first took LSD in London in 1965 when they were slipped it by their host, a dentist, at a dinner gathering. Almost instantly, their music took on another dimension, both sonically and lyrically. As Harrison told *Rolling Stone*, 'I had such an overwhelming feeling of well-being, that there was a God, and I could see him in every blade of grass. It was like gaining hundreds of years of experience in 12 hours.' *Rolling Stone* (eds), *Harrison*, p. 145.

33 MacLean, *Behind Open Doors*, p. 229.

34 'Vision of Hell Drug Charges—Two Men in Court', *The Times*, 7 April 1966.

35 Three weeks after Esam's acquittal, two much more high-profile youth figures, Rolling Stones Mick Jagger and Keith Richards, were arrested in a drugs raid on Richards' home in Sussex. It seemed the British law was determined to clamp down on drug use through making a public example of them.

36 'Effects of New Drug—Back to Childhood Experiences', *Press*, 18 June 1954.

37 David Livingstone, 'Usefulness of Lysergic Acid in Psychiatry', *New Zealand Medical Journal*, no. 65 (October 1966), pp. 657–65.

38 Ibid.

39 Tauranga Memories: New Zealand Society of Authors, October 2016, archived at https://perma.cc/T66M-WYSF https://perma.cc/T66M-WYSF

40 Rex Benson, author interview, 9 January 2019.

41 Nicholas Pounder, author interview, 28 September 2019.

42 Rex Benson, author interview, 9 January 2019.

43 *Sunday Telegraph* (Sydney), 18 October 1968.

44 Deborah Yates, author interview, 19 July 2019.

45 Pat Hanly's journals, courtesy of Gil Hanly.

46 Ibid.

47 Haley, *Hanly*, p. 155.

48 Edmond, *Chemical Evolution*, p. 28.

49 The information on Arthur Pearce and 'Big Beat Ball' draws on an article I wrote that first appeared in the *Listener*, 17 January 1998, and includes information and quotes from interviews I conducted at the time with Gordon Campbell and Laurie Lewis. A revised version of the article can be found at AudioCulture, https://www.audioculture.co.nz/people/arthur-pearce

50 AudioCulture, https://www.audioculture.co.nz/scenes/radio-hauraki-the-pirate-days-the-good-guys

51 Murray Cammick, email to author, 15 January 2021.

52 'Deranging Drug', *Dominion*, 23 June 1967.

53 *Evening Post*, 12 July 1967.

54 Ibid.

55 Ken James, email to author, 28 August 2020.

56 '"A Spreading Scourge"—Six Weeks Gaol for Having LSD', *New Zealand Herald*, 22 July 1967.

57 Deborah Yates, author interview, 19 July 2019.

58 Michael Morrissey, 'The Psychedelic Explosion', *Craccum*, 31 July 1967.

59 *Dominion*, 8 November 1967.

60 A. J. W. Taylor, 'Subjective Aspects of Drug Dependence and Drug Abuse: The Marihuana Issue', paper presented to the inter-disciplinary seminars arranged by the Board of Health, Wellington and Auckland, November 1970, pp. 2–3.

61 Ray Henwood, 'Opinion: Drugs and the Question of Authority', *Comment*, December 1968, pp. 2–3.

62 'Teenage Drug Use Seen As Growing Problem', *Evening Post*, 19 March 1971.

63 'After LSD, Man Tries To Kill Nurse', *Sunday Times*, 31 May 1971.

FOUR

1 'The Commissioner for Enlightenment: Alan Brunton talks to Chris Bourke', September 2000, New Zealand Electronic Poetry Centre, http://www.nzepc.auckland.ac.nz

2 Tom White, author interview, 2 April 2021.

3 Roger Steele, author interview, 3 February 2019.

4 AudioCulture, https://www.audioculture.co.nz/scenes/searching-for-the-south-island-long-hairs

5 'Long Hair & Eccentrics', *Auckland Star*, 18 October 1969.

6 'Long Hair Can Be Lethal for Firemen', *Evening Post*, 17 May 1973.

7 Shadbolt, *Bullshit and Jellybeans*, p. 9.

8 Rosemary McLeod, author interview, 11 February 2021.

9 Ibid.

10 Tolerton, *60s Chicks Hit the Nineties*, p. 128.

11 'Handmade Sandals', *Playdate*, Dec / Jan 1967 / 68, p. 22.

12 Liz Ross, 'Sandals of Indian Leather', *Playdate*, November 1970, p. 54.

13 *Playdate*, April 1971, p. 30.

14 Rachel Stace, author interview, 13 March 2019.

15 Bilbrough, *In the Time of the Manaroans*, p. 92.

16 Hugh Young, author interview, 30 July 2019.

17 Author interview, 30 March 2021; name changed by request.

18 Ritchie, *Child Rearing Patterns in New Zealand*, p. 62.

19 *Report of the Special Committee on Moral Delinquency in Children and Adolescents*, New Zealand Government Printer, Wellington, 1954.

20 Ibid.

21 '"To Know the Facts": The New Zealand Health Department's Sex Education Pamphlets, 1955–1983', *New Zealand Journal of History*, vol. 50, no. 1 (2016), p. 114.

22 Smyth, *Rocking the Cradle*, pp. 38–41.

23 Ibid., p. 82.

24 Barbara Brookes, Claire Gooder and Nancy De Castro, '"Feminine as Her Handbag,

Modern as Her Hairstyle": The Uptake of the Contraceptive Pill in New Zealand', *New Zealand Journal of History*, vol. 47, no. 2 (2013), p. 217.

25 Alan F. Guttmacher, 'The Pill Around the World', *IPPF Medical Bulletin*, vol. 1, no. 1 (October 1966), pp. 1–2.

26 Sandra Coney, 'Uncertain Times for Pill Users', *Dominion Sunday Times*, 6 August 1989.

27 'Three Youths on Drug Charges and Girl "Part of Hippie Cult"', *New Zealand Herald*, 23 November 1967.

28 *The Spinoff*, https://thespinoff.co.nz/society/24-06-2017/the-pill-women-contraception-and-the-myth-of-sexual-freedom-in-1960s-new-zealand/

29 Brookes, Gooder and De Castro, '"Feminine as Her Handbag, Modern as Her Hairstyle"', pp. 222–23.

30 Cook, *The Long Sexual Revolution*, p. 297.

31 Ibid., quoting M. Ingham, *Now We Are Thirty: Women of the Breakthrough Generation* (1981). Mary Ingham, a teenager in the first half of the 1960s, met up again in the late 1970s with her class year of 11-plus grammar school girls to discuss the era they had grown up in.

32 Rachel Stace, author interview, 13 March 2019.

33 *The Kama Sutra of Vatsyayana*, translated from the Sanscrit in Seven Parts With Preface, Introduction and Concluding Remarks, https://www.gutenberg.org/files/27827/27827-h/27827-h.htm

34 'I'm just like a turtle, hidin' underneath its horny shell, You know I'm very well protected, I know this goddamn life too well.' Janis Joplin, from the album *Cheap Thrills* by Big Brother and the Holding Company, Columbia, 1968.

35 Rachel Stace, author interview, 13 March 2019.

36 Rick Bryant, unpublished memoir, private collection.

37 Sue Belt, author interview, 19 February 2019.

38 Tolerton, *60s Chicks Hit the Nineties*, p. 130.

39 Rosemary McLeod, author interview, 11 February 2021.

40 Roszak, *The Making of a Counter Culture*, p. 14.

41 Debbie Jones, 'The Erotic Revolution', in Bunkle, Levine and Wainwright (eds), *Learning About Sexism in New Zealand*, pp. 30–32.

42 *Itch*, no. 3 (1973), p. 12.

43 *The Little Red Schoolbook*, pp. 107–9. For more on *The Little Red Schoolbook*, see Chapter 13.

44 Chris Brickell, 'Sex Education, Homosexuality, and Social Contestation in 1970s New Zealand', *Sex Education*, vol. 7, no. 4 (November 2007), pp. 387–406.

45 Alison J. Laurie, 'Sexism or Sanity? Gay Lib Climbs from the Closet', *Rolling Stone* (NZ), 26 April 1973, pp. 16–17.

46 Rebecca Jennings and Liz Millward, '"A Fully Formed Blast from Abroad?" Australasian Lesbian Circuits of Mobility and the Transnational Exchange of Ideas in the 1960s and 1970s', *Journal of the History of Sexuality*, vol. 25, no. 3 (September 2016), pp. 463–88.

47 Alison J. Laurie, 'From Kamp Girls to Political Dykes: A Personal View of 30 Years as a New Zealand Lesbian, Pt. 2', *Broadsheet*, December 1985, pp. 28–31.

48 Ngahuia Te Awekotuku, 'Dykes and Queers', *Broadsheet* 168, May 1989, p. 18.

49 John Bower, author interview, 3 May 2019.

FIVE

1 'Hippies Taking Over From the Beatniks', *Otago Daily Times*, 1 April 1967.

2 Escarpit, *The Revolution in Books*, pp. 4–10.

3 Barrowman, *A Popular Vision*, pp. 90–91.

4 Pat Bolster, *Resistance Shop Manual and Report of the Retiring Secretary*, Pat Bolster collection, Auckland, 1972.

5 Ibid.

6 Chris Wheeler, email to author, 31 March 2019.

7 Ibid.

8 Andrew Delahunty, author interview, 30 September 2020.

9 Elworthy, *Ritual Song of Defiance*, pp. 103–6.

10 *The First New Zealand Whole Earth Catalogue*, pp. 23–24.

11 Jonathan Milne, author interview, 21 February 2019.

12 Ibid.

13 Chris Wheeler, email to author, 31 March / 1 April 2019.

14 *Cock*, no. 17 (August 1973).

15 Ibid.

16 *Uncool*, vol. 1, no. 1, Uncool Publications, Christchurch, 1970.

17 Boraman, *Rabble Rousers and Merry Pranksters*, pp. 70–72.

18 *Counter Culture Free Press*, vol. 5, Dunedin, 4 A.W. (i.e. 1973).

19 Bill Gruar, author interview, 4 September 2020.

20 *Salient*, 8 July 1970, p. 1.

21 Tim Bollinger, '"Working my way back to bourgeois"—The Evolution of Barry Linton', unpublished article, private collection.

22 Ibid.

23 Alan Brunton, '1960–1969: Restoring the Commune', Introduction to Brunton, Edmond and Leggott (eds), *Big Smoke: New Zealand Poems 1960–75*, p. 2.

24 'The Commissioner for Enlightenment: Alan Brunton talks to Chris Bourke', September 2000, New Zealand Electronic Poetry Centre, http://www.nzepc.auckland.ac.nz
25 Ibid.
26 Shadbolt, *Bullshit and Jellybeans*, p. 97.
27 'There was a mix up of American and European ideas. From Europe was coming a very masked, costumed surrealistic revolution that urged performance whereas the revolution coming from the USA had a music background ...', from 'The Commissioner for Enlightenment: Alan Brunton talks to Chris Bourke'.
28 Alan Brunton, 'Restoring the Commune', in Brunton, Edmond and Leggott (eds), *Big Smoke*, p. 13.
29 Bollinger, 'Working my way back to bourgeois'.
30 Leggott and Edmond (eds), *Beyond the Ohlala Mountains*, p. 9.
31 'Editor Chan Dismissed, Staff Walk Out', *Craccum*, 5 August 1971.
32 Stephen Chan, 'Publishing Pipe Dreams in Ponsonby', http://www.nzepc.auckland.ac.nz/authors/mitchell/chan.asp
33 Ibid.
34 'Songs of Light', *New Zealand Listener*, 4 December 1972.
35 Record information, Archives New Zealand: *Easy Rider* R23964289; *Woodstock* R23962326; *Bonnie and Clyde* R23951722; *Butch Cassidy and the Sundance Kid* R23951101.
36 Susy Pointon with Arthur Baysting, 'Rebels and Ratbags: The Real Story of the New Zealand Film Industry', unpublished manuscript, 2011, Susy Pointon collection.
37 Ibid.
38 'Boost for the Peace Talks', *New Zealand Truth*, 19 March 1968.
39 Tony Larsen, author interview, 27 September 2018.
40 Pointon and Baysting, 'Rebels and Ratbags', p. 10.
41 *50 Years of New Zealand Television*, https://www.nzonscreen.com/title/50-years-of-nz-tv-episode-two-protest-2010
42 Rabel, *New Zealand and the Vietnam War*, p. 310.
43 *50 Years of New Zealand Television*.
44 Chamberlain, *Constant Radical*, p. 85.
45 John Bower, author interview, 3 May 2019.
46 Jonathan Milne, author interview, 21 February 2019.
47 Barry Southam, 'Auckland Is a Happening City', *New Zealand Listener*, 14 November 1969.
48 'Times Man Looks At ... A Happening', *Times* (Hamilton), 22 October 1969.
49 Edwards, *The Public Eye*, pp. 257–58.
50 Ibid., pp. 260–61.
51 Marcia Russell, 'Alister Taylor: Thursday Profile', *Thursday*, 14 September 1972.

SIX

1 Memo released under Official Information Act 1982, DMS42-6-3381.
2 Paul Jackman, 'The Auckland Opposition to New Zealand's Involvement in the Vietnam War 1965–72: An Example of the Achievements and Limitations of Ideology', MA thesis, University of Auckland, 1979, pp. 76–77.
3 Ibid.
4 Ibid.
5 Chamberlain, *Constant Radical*, p. 109.
6 Jackman, 'The Auckland Opposition to New Zealand's Involvement in the Vietnam War', p. 77.
7 'On Revolutionary Dedication', *PYM Organiser*, August 1969.
8 Ibid.
9 Ibid.
10 Barry Lee, 'Struggling to Make the World a Better Place: Exploring Some Experiences of Activists in the Auckland Progressive Youth Movement (1965–1977)', PhD thesis, University of Auckland, 2019, p. 3.
11 Ibid.
12 Deborah Yates, author interview, 19 July 2019.
13 Smith, *Working Class Son*, p. 147.
14 Ibid., p. 149.
15 From an unpublished memoir; author's name withheld by request.
16 Boraman, *Rabble Rousers and Merry Pranksters*, p. 38.
17 Winton Cassels, 'A State of Mind', *Dominion*, 5 March 1971.
18 'PYM Owes Government $350', PYM flyer, 1971, private collection.
19 'Demonstrators Strike Back', *Press*, 11 August 1969.
20 *The PYM Colouring Book*, publisher and location uncredited, c. 1970.
21 Memo released under Official Information Act. Declassified 23 March 2017, 26/8/113.
22 Jackman, 'The Auckland Opposition to New Zealand's Involvement in the Vietnam War', p. 105.
23 Ibid.
24 John Bower, author interview, 3 May 2019.
25 Ibid.
26 Police records obtained under Official Information Act 1982. Report of Detective Sergeant J. Russell, C.I.B. Office, Kaikohe, 6 May 1969. Whangerei P.N. 1969/54/13.
27 John Parkyn, 'Lyall Eric (Lemming) Carlisle 1943–1970', *Cock*, no. 11 (April 1970).

28 Public Inquiry Committee, '11.45 p.m, 16 January 1970: Incidents Relating to the Auckland Demonstrations, and the Case for a Public Inquiry', 1970, p. 3.
29 Ibid., p. 4.
30 John Bower, author interview, 3 May 2019.
31 Public Inquiry Committee, '11.45 p.m. 16 January 1970', p. 4.
32 'The Commissioner For Enlightenment: Alan Brunton talks to Chris Bourke', September 2000, www.nzepc.auckland.ac.nz/authors/brunton/brief/bourke.asp
33 'Found Guilty of Blast at Parnell', *New Zealand Herald*, 4 July 1970.
34 'South African Rugby Tour—Exclusion of Maoris—Sir Howard Kippenberger Protests', *Press*, 2 September 1948.
35 CABTA (Citizens' All Black Tour Association), 'No Maoris, No Tour: The Case For CABTA', 1960, p. 14.
36 'Sudden Move at Whenuapai—Demonstrators Rush All Blacks' Electra', *Evening Post*, 10 May 1960.
37 Thompson, *Retreat from Apartheid*, p. 30.
38 *Evening Post*, 5 May 1965.
39 Richards, *Dancing on Our Bones*, p. 41.
40 Ibid., p. 50.
41 Ibid., p. 119.
42 Ibid.
43 Ibid., p. 51.
44 Taylor, Brooke-White and Wheeler (eds), *The Whole World Watches*, p. 14.
45 Ibid., p. 30.
46 Richards, *Dancing on Our Bones*, p. 52.

SEVEN

1 McDermott's 'African Waltz' had been recorded by Cannonball Adderley, and he would go on to be a mentor to the great Canadian songwriter Kate McGarrigle.
2 'Aquarius / Let the Sunshine In', Gerome Ragni / James Rado / Galt MacDermot, lyrics © Sony / ATV Music Publishing LLC.
3 'Hair There and Home Again', *Playdate*, July 1971, p. 20.
4 Neil Illingworth (ed.), *The Hair Controversy! Full Transcript of the Trial, Plus Explanatory Comment by Iain Macdonald*, Comill Publications, Auckland, 1972, p. 24.
5 Ibid., p. 31.
6 Ibid., p. 27.
7 Jenny McLeod, author interview, 24 April 2019. All quotes from Jenny McLeod are from this source, unless otherwise identified.
8 Billy Williams, email to author, 10 August 2016.
9 Ibid.
10 Harvey Mann, email to author, 1 August 2016.
11 Billy Williams, email to author, 10 August 2016.
12 Sometime in 1968 Mann, seeking freer forms of expression, left the Underdogs to join the Brew, a fluid mix of rock and jazz musicians led by American expat Bob Gillette. This band also included Doug Jerebine and drummer Trix Willoughby, and played at the Tabla nightclub, opened that year in a former bank cafeteria in Lorne Street, Auckland. After the Brew dissolved, Mann briefly re-formed the Underdogs, which begat the Australasian Rock Squad before reaching its ultimate evolution in the early seventies as Space Farm.
13 Sam Gosson, author interview, 10 September 2020.
14 *Craccum*, 13 August 1970, p. 11.
15 Fa'amoana John Luafutu, 'A Boy Called Broke: Part B—Journey to the Cells', in Anae, Iuli and Tamu (eds), *Polynesian Panthers*, p. 39.
16 'It Was Like Balling for the First Time', *Rolling Stone*, 20 September 1969.
17 Anderson, *Imagined Communities*, pp. 6–7.
18 Some local media, unsure of the jargon, would continue to use the term 'folk', even when reporting on what were obviously rock festivals.
19 Glen Moffat, AudioCulture, https://www.audioculture.co.nz/scenes/the-national-banjo-pickers-convention
20 Bollinger, *Goneville*, p. 88.
21 As Jarrod Gilbert writes in *Patched: The History of Gangs in New Zealand*, gangs around that time would use the swastika 'not to demonstrate any racist attitudes, but in symbolic defiance of social norms'.
22 'There's Never Been Anything Like It', *Auckland Star*, 2 February 1970.
23 Much of the description of Redwood 70 is drawn from the NZBC documentary of the same name, which can be seen at NZ On Screen, https://www.nzonscreen.com/title/redwood-doco
24 Phil Dadson, author interview, 4 May 2019.
25 Tony Backhouse, author interview, 23 January 2019.
26 Cathy Wylie, 'Amamus—Alternative Theatre', *Salient*, 11 April 1972.
27 Ibid.
28 'Out of the Ruins', *Playdate*, July 1971, pp. 45–49.
29 'Nonstop Music At Two-Day Rock Festival', *New Zealand Herald*, 5 July 1971.
30 Screenprinted poster, Archie Bowie, c. July 1970.
31 Andrew Delahunty, author interview, 30 September 2020.
32 'Arts Festival as a Way of Life', *Craccum*, 17 September 1970.

33 Wendy Yee, 'Chris Knox', *Kahoutek*, no. 2 (c. 1992) p. 22.

34 'Pekapeka', *Salient*, April 1971.

35 Sue McCauley, 'And now for ...', *Thursday*, 3 February 1972.

36 Ibid.

37 Hamish Horsley, author interview, 3 May 2021. Also, Hamish's scrapbook of the Serenity Festival which is in the collection of the Sarjeant Gallery Te Whare o Rehua, Whanganui, and includes a wealth of photographs, letters and ephemera relating to the festival. Accession Number: 2021/2/1.

38 Ron Garbutt, 'Aquarius and Beyond: Thinking through the Counterculture', *M/C Journal*, 2014, http://journal.media-culture.org.au/index.php/mcjournal/article/view/911

39 'Travel', *New Zealand Herald*, 30 August 2016.

40 Dick Nicholls, 'On the Road with Muddy Waters', *Rolling Stone* (NZ), 9 June 1973.

41 'Live-In Music Festival Security Heavily Enforced', *Dominion*, 6 January 1973.

42 Ibid.

43 'The Great Ngaruawahia Music Festival—Freak-Out or Flop?', *Thursday*, 1 February 1973.

44 'Barry Coburn', *Southland Times*, 10 January 2013.

45 Billy Williams, Facebook post, 2019.

46 *New Zealand Sunday Times*, 7 January 1973. The headline alludes to *Oh! Calcutta*, the musical revue created by British critic and scenemaker Kenneth Tynan, with contributions from the likes of Samuel Beckett and John Lennon, which was stirring controversy for its extended nudity. Though *Hair* had by this time been performed in New Zealand, no production of *Oh! Calcutta* was ever mounted in this country.

47 'Pot Spread on Paddocks', *New Zealand Sunday Times*, 14 January 1973.

48 'Pop Goes the Festival', *Dominion*, 10 January 1973.

49 *The Great Ngaruawahia Music Festival*, trailer for short film by Cushla Donaldson, 2017, https://luxton.camera/portfolio/ngaruawahia-sabbath

50 Jonathan Milne, author interview, 21 February 2019.

51 Robert Raymond, email to author, 24 February 2021.

52 Hepworth, *A Fabulous Creation*, p. 3.

53 Though the Beatles had already recorded 'Let It Be' in early 1969, and the Stones evidently knew about it, the song would not be released until March 1970, the Stones pre-empting them by three months, possibly lessening the impact of the joke.

54 Rachel Stace, author interview, 13 March 2019.

55 Bill Payne, 'Best Intentions', in *Poor Behaviour*, Secker & Warburg, Auckland, 1994, pp. 26–48.

EIGHT

1 'A Small Ode To Mixed Flatting', in Paul Millar (ed.), *Selected Poems of James K. Baxter*, Auckland University Press, Auckland, 2013.

2 Letters, *Otago Daily Times*, 15 July 1967.

3 Ibid., 19 July 1967.

4 Sue Belt, author interview, 19 February 2019.

5 Rachel Stace, author interview, 13 March 2019.

6 Nicholas Pounder, author interview, 28 September 2019.

7 Deborah Yates, author interview, 19 July 2019.

8 Alison McClean, author interview, 20 July 2019.

9 Jones and Baker, *A Hard-Won Freedom*, p. 88.

10 Nicholas Pounder, author interview, 28 September 2019.

11 Letter to Louis Johnson, 8 October 1968, in Weir (ed.), *James K. Baxter: Letters of a Poet*, p. 358.

12 Brunton, *Years Ago Today*, p. 32.

13 *Wellington in the '60s: The Way It Seemed*, 1967, https://www.ngataonga.org.nz/collections/catalogue/catalogue-item?record_id=68216

14 Ibid.

15 'Commune Just Wants To Be Friends With Locals', *Evening Post*, 1 December 1971.

16 Kirsten Lawson, 'Waitati—Still Crazy After All These Years?', *New Zealand Geographic*, July–September 1989, pp. 48–61.

17 Treefoot, author interview, 3 September 2020.

18 Alison McClean, author interview, 20 July 2019.

19 *The Second New Zealand Whole Earth Catalogue*, p. 30.

20 Hayward, *Diary of the Kirk Years*, p. 173.

21 *Ohu: Alternative Lifestyle Communities*, published for the Ohu Advisory Committee by the Department of Lands and Survey, Wellington, 1975.

22 Pete Pharazyn, author interview, 31 March 2021.

23 Hayward, *Diary of the Kirk Years*, p. 173.

24 Lyman Tower Sargent, 'The Ohu Movement', *New Zealand Studies*, vol. 6, no. 3 (November 1996), p. 18.

25 Ibid.

26 Pete Pharazyn, author interview, 31 March 2021.

27 'Minister Doubts Social Value of Ohu Scheme', *Auckland Star*, 23 December 1975.
28 'Ohu Residents Called "Bludgers"', *Otago Daily Times*, 13 July 1975.
29 Julian Rosenberg, author interview, 10 March 2019.
30 Billy Te Kahika, author interview, 16 May 2011.
31 Alun Bollinger, author interview, 17 January 2019.
32 Gill Shadbolt, 'The End of Michael's Rainbow', *More*, February 2002, pp. 201–7.
33 David Mitchell, 'Out of the Ruins', *Playdate*, July 1971, pp. 45–48.
34 *Counter Culture Free Press*, no. 1 (c. 1972).
35 Olive Jones, 'Keeping It Together: A Comparative Analysis of Four Long-established Intentional Communities in New Zealand', PhD thesis, University of Waikato, 2011, p. 83.
36 Ibid.
37 *The Second New Zealand Whole Earth Catalogue*, p. 32.
38 Letter to Rod Finlayson, 11 April 1968, in Weir (ed.), *James K. Baxter: Letters of a Poet*, p. 346.
39 Letter to John Weir, 12 August 1967, in ibid., p. 302.
40 Letter to Rod Finlayson, 11 April 1968, in ibid., p. 347.
41 Ibid.
42 Newton, *The Double Rainbow*, p. 43.
43 Ibid., p. 38.
44 Letter to Rod Finlayson, 11 April 1968, in Weir (ed.), *James K. Baxter: Letters of a Poet*, p. 347.
45 James K. Baxter, 'Smoke Signals', *New Zealand Listener*, 3 May 1963.
46 Baxter, *Jerusalem Daybook*, p. 10.
47 Don Franks, author interview, 27 May 2019.
48 Ibid.
49 Oliver, *James K. Baxter: A Portrait*, p. 125; McKay, *The Life of James K. Baxter*, p. 248.
50 'Your Weekend', *Dominion Post*, 20 April 2019.
51 Merata Mita, 'The Soul and the Image', in Bieringa and Dennis (eds), *Film in Aotearoa New Zealand*, p. 45.

NINE

1 Ian Wedde, *Dick Seddon's Great Dive*, *Islands*, vol. 5., no. 2 (1976), p. 162.
2 Alison McClean, author interview, 20 July 2019.
3 Zeke Alley, author interview, 3 December 2020.
4 Much of the detail in this section is derived from Zeke's diaries, as well as from subsequent email correspondence.
5 Zeke Alley, author interview, 3 December 2020.
6 Wilson, *Flying Kiwis*, p. 55.
7 Zeke Alley, author interview, 3 December 2020.
8 Ibid.
9 John A. Saliba, 'The Earth is a Dangerous Place: The World View of the Aetherius Society', *Marburg Journal of Religion*, vol. 4, no. 2 (December 1999).
10 Wilderness, https://www.wildernessmag.co.nz/aorakis-holy-mountain/
11 'His Holiness Maharishi Mahesh Yogi and a Method of Meditation—My Impressions', *Salient*, 26 March 1962.
12 Robert Keyser, 'Krishna's Road', *New Zealand Listener*, 27 November 1972.
13 Ibid.
14 Harvey Mann, email to author, 27 September 2018.
15 'Dennis Flies With Guru', *Sunday Times*, 4 November 1973.
16 'Cooney and the Cosmic Constable', *Earwig*, no. 8½ (c. 1974).
17 'God In New Zealand: Divine Light and the Vision of the Third Eye', *Thursday*, August 1974.
18 'I Am Always With You', http://www.prem-rawat-bio.org/dlm_pubs/goldenage/52/gmj_iamalwayswithu.html
19 Elizabeth Kerr, Jenny McLeod interview, *Music in New Zealand*, Spring 1988, pp. 12–13.
20 Ibid., p. 12.
21 Ibid.
22 'Professor McLeod Rocks On', *New Zealand Listener*, 21 June 1975.
23 Terry Bell, 'From Earth and Sky to Divine Light—Jenny Has Found Peace', *New Zealand Woman's Weekly*, 31 July 1978.
24 Treefoot, author interview, 3 September 2020.
25 Dada Nabhaniilananda, author interview, 20 October 2020. All quotes and recollections from Danny / Dada Nabhaniilananda are from this source.
26 Lewis F. Carter, 'The "New Renunciates" of the Bhagwan Shree Rajneesh: Observations and Identification of Problems of Interpreting New Religious Movements', *Journal for the Scientific Study of Religion*, vol. 26, no. 2 (June 1987), pp. 148–72.
27 Robert Jenkin, 'Endless Connections: New Zealand Secular Intentional Communities Founded in the 1970s', MA thesis, Massey University, 2012, p. 52.
28 David Farrier, *Stuff*, 'My Secret Life as a Scientologist', https://www.stuff.co.nz/national/88487644/david-farrier-my-secret-life-as-a-scientologist
29 Berkeley Rice, 'The Pull of Sun Moon', *New York Times*, 30 May 1976.

30 Michael Grant Butler, 'Moonies Under Fire', unpublished manuscript, 1984, MS-Papers-3909-1, Alexander Turnbull Library, Wellington.
31 Rob Keyzer, 'A Christian Revolutionary', *New Zealand Listener*, 13 November 1972.
32 Newton, *The Double Rainbow*, p. 76.
33 Ibid.
34 Laing, *The Divided Self*, p. 12.
35 https://forum.culteducation.com/read.php?4,29124,page=2
36 Ibid.
37 Author interview, 23 March 2020; name changed by request. All quotes from Joanna are from this interview.
38 *Broadsheet*, November 1973, pp. 12–13.
39 Sandra Coney, author interview, 3 July 2020.

TEN

1 *Ko Aotearoa Tēnei: A Report into Claims Concerning New Zealand Law and Policy Affecting Māori Culture and Identity*, Legislation Direct, Wellington, 2011, p. 5.
2 Neil Challenger, 'A Comparison of Maori and Pakeha Attitudes To Land', Diploma of Landscape Architecture dissertation, Lincoln College, Christchurch, 1985, p. 34.
3 *Stuff*, 13 March 2017, https://www.stuff.co.nz/life-style/food-wine/89841124/meat-and-three-veg-the-history-of-new-zealands-diet
4 Belich, *Replenishing the Earth: The Settler Revolution and the Rise of the Angloworld*, p. 437.
5 Sanitarium, https://www.sanitarium.co.nz/about/sanitarium-story/history
6 Jones and Baker, *A Hard-Won Freedom*, p. 23.
7 Ibid., p. 76.
8 Rain, *Community: The Story of Riverside*, pp. 126–37.
9 Ibid.
10 Jim Kebbell and Marion Wood, author interview, 10 June 2019. All of the quotes and many details in this passage are drawn from this source.
11 Wilson, *From Manapouri to Aramoana*, is the source of much of the information in this section.
12 Roszak, *The Making of a Counter Culture*, p. 226.
13 Reich, *The Greening of America*, p. 132.
14 Bensemann, *Fight for the Forests*, p. 60.
15 *Focus On Youth: A Study Towards Understanding in Adult–Youth Relationships*, University of Auckland Library, 1971.
16 Bensemann, *Fight for the Forests*, p. 60.
17 Ibid., p. 71.
18 Murphy, *A Life on Film*, p. 75.
19 Dick Nicholls, 'Strangers from a Strange Land: Muddy Waters in New Zealand', *Rolling Stone* (NZ), 7 June 1973.
20 Robilliard, *Hard Country*, pp. 247–48.
21 Barry Thomas, letter to author, 31 May 2021.

ELEVEN

1 Rawiri Paratene, author interview, 5 September 2020.
2 *Nga Tamatoa, 40 Years On*, 2012, https://www.nzonscreen.com/title/nga-tamatoa-2012
3 Tame Iti, 'Mana: The Power In Knowing Who You Are', TEDx, 2015, https://tedxauckland.com/people/tame-iti/
4 Awatere, *Maori Sovereignty*, p. 8; Harris, *Hīkoi: Forty Years of Māori Protest*, p. 19.
5 Hill, *Maori and the State*, pp. 91, 95.
6 Harris, *Hīkoi: Forty Years of Māori Protest*, p. 48.
7 Bruce Wallace, 'Beating Their Heads Against White Marshmallows', *New Zealand Listener*, 21 February 1972.
8 James Mitchell, 'Immigration and National Identity in 1970s New Zealand', PhD thesis, University of Otago, 2003.
9 Luafutu, 'A Boy Called Broke: Part B—Journey To The Cells', in Anae, Lautofa and Tamu (eds), *Polynesian Panthers*, p. 44.
10 Tigilau Ness, author interview, August 2011.
11 Roger Fowler, author interview, 5 May 2019. This is the source of some quotes and much of the information in this section.
12 Terry Hogan, 'Two-Way Trip to "Parry"', *Thursday*, 12 October 1972.
13 *The People's Union for Survival and Freedom. Information Service*, no. 2 (October 1972).
14 Ibid.
15 Author interview, 27 September 2018; name withheld by request.
16 Roger Steele, author interview, 13 February 2019; Keith Stewart, author interview, 16 June 2021.
17 For more on Richard Holden, see Bollinger, *Goneville*, pp. 145–57.
18 Harris, *Hīkoi: Forty Years of Māori Protest*, pp. 68–77.
19 Awatere, *Maori Sovereignty*, p. 50.
20 Ibid., p. 35.

TWELVE

1 *Whicker's World*, 1973, recording in private collection.
2 'Teleview: Sue Kedgley's World and Whicker's (Home Was Never Like This!)', *Auckland Star*, 5 June 1973. Len Fairclough was a character in the British television series *Coronation Street*. Played by actor

Peter Adamson, he was portrayed on screen as rugged but loveable.
3 Sue Kedgley, author interview, 29 April 2019.
4 Therese O'Connell, author interview, 1 July 2021.
5 The name Women's Liberation Front was appropriated in 2013 by an American organisation calling themselves radical feminists and, among other things, opposing transgender rights and gender identity legislation, but there is no connection between this group and the one founded in Wellington in 1970.
6 'Women For Equality', *Broadsheet*, July 1972.
7 Ngahuia Te Awekotuku, 'Mana Wahine: Seeking Meanings from Ourselves', in Cahill and Dann (eds), *Changing Our Lives*, pp. 25–28.
8 Coney, *Standing in the Sunshine*, p. 142.
9 Chamberlain, *Constant Radical*, p. 92.
10 Sue Kedgley, author interview, 29 April 2019.
11 Rose Beauchamp, author interview, 28 March 2019.
12 Sandra Coney, author interview, 3 July 2020.
13 Sandra Coney, '"Another Bloody Girl": Daughter of a Kiwi Sporting Hero', in Coney, *Out of the Frying Pan*, pp. 25–26.
14 Chris Kraus, 'May 68: Suck', *Artforum*, May 2008, https://www.artforum.com/print/200805/suck-19854
15 Greer, *The Female Eunuch*, p. 305.
16 Ibid., p. 328.
17 'Germaine's Out To Make Big Trouble!', *Sunday News*, 27 February 1972.
18 Brian Edwards, 'Like Dummies at the Feet of a Guru', *Thursday*, 30 March 1972.
19 'Dr Greer "Mind Raped"', *Dominion*, 17 March 1972.
20 '"Good Old Anglo-Saxon Word"— Germaine Greer Fined $40 for Using Obscene Language', *New Zealand Herald*, 11 March 1972.
21 'Greer', *Craccum*, 16 March 1972.
22 'Never Seen So Much', *Evening Post*, 11 March 1972.
23 Jill Brasell, 'Women's Liberation Conference', *Salient*, 11 April 1972.
24 'Letters', *Broadsheet*, April 1973.
25 'The Case for Communes', *Broadsheet*, November 1972.
26 Helen Bollinger, author interview, 17 January 2019.
27 'Back to the Land: Women in Rural Communes', *Broadsheet*, June 1976.
28 'Talking To Polynesian Women Part II', *Broadsheet*, September 1973.
29 Ibid.
30 Coney, *Out of the Frying Pan*, p. 81.

THIRTEEN

1 Rabel, *New Zealand and the Vietnam War*, p. 281.
2 Hayward, *Diary of the Kirk Years*, p. 106.
3 Norman Kirk in Parliament, 21 April 1970, quoted in *PYM Rabble*, no. 2 (June 1970).
4 Hayward, *Diary of the Kirk Years*, p. 53.
5 *Blueprint for New Zealand: An Alternative Future*, New Zealand Values Party, Wellington, 1972.
6 Murray Horton, 'Owen Wilkes: Obituary', *Peace Researcher*, 31 October 2005.
7 Steven Walton, 'The Student Firebombers Who Targeted Christchurch's American Outpost', *Press*, 23 January 2021.
8 In 1982 arguably the most extreme act against a target representing political oppression took place when 21-year-old anarchist punk Neil Roberts carried out a suicide bombing mission on the Whanganui Police Computer. On a nearby wall he had spraypainted the graffiti: 'We have maintained a silence closely resembling stupidity'. While the punks tended to express a cynical attitude towards the counterculture, Roberts' act and the rhetoric surrounding it seemed to share an impetus with the bombers of the seventies chronicled in these pages.
9 B. R. Hancock, 'The New Zealand Security Intelligence Service', *New Zealand Law Review*, vol. 2 (August 1973), pp. 1–34.
10 Smith, *Working Class Son*, p. 138.
11 *Cock*, no. 5 (August 1968).
12 Chris Wheeler, email to author, 31 March / 1 April 2019.
13 Alister Taylor, author interview, 18 July 2019.
14 'Who Was Mystery American?', *Sunday Times*, 9 July 1967.
15 Charles Alverson, 'Harvey Matusow: I Led Twelve Lives', *Rolling Stone*, 17 August 1972; The Third Page, https://www.emptymirrorbooks.com/thirdpage/leteramort.html
16 John Bower, author interview, 3 May 2019.
17 Bennetts, *Spy*, p. 139.
18 David White, author interview, 29 January 2019. All quotes and information from David White are from this source.
19 Zeke Alley, author interview, 3 December 2020.
20 Ibid.
21 Bohan, *The House of Reed*, p. 173.
22 Alister Taylor, author interview, 18 July 2019.
23 Hansen and Jensen, *The Little Red Schoolbook*, p. 9.
24 Classification in New Zealand, 'History of Censorship', https://www.censor.org.nz/resources/history/1950s-1960s-and-1970s/1970/

25 Alister Taylor, author interview, 18 July 2019.
26 Roger Fowler, author interview, 5 May 2019.
27 'How To Be A Civilised Drop Out', *Thursday*, 1 February 1973.
28 *The First New Zealand Whole Earth Catalogue*, Summer 1972, p. 177.
29 Ibid., p. 246.
30 Ibid., pp. 19–22.
31 Ibid., p. 5.
32 Chris Wheeler, 'Robert Raymond Presents Himself', *Rolling Stone* (NZ), 29 March 1973.
33 Ibid.
34 Ibid.
35 http://www.ukrockfestivals.com/UBI-DWYER.html
36 Rosemary McLeod, author interview, 11 February 2021.
37 Zeke Alley, author interview, 3 December 2020.
38 In fact, Martin seems to have had a few traits in common with Taylor. He too could be a generous host. According to *Te Ara — The Encyclopedia of New Zealand*, 'At the Otaraia station woolshed in 1873 he held a ball to celebrate the opening of the Waihenga bridge. Festivities continued until daybreak: "it was a great shivoo." In early 1875, when he had a drinking fountain erected on Lambton Quay, the water at the opening ceremony was liberally mixed with whisky.' https://teara.govt.nz/en/biographies/2m35/martin-john
39 *Stuff*, https://www.stuff.co.nz/entertainment/books/115952190/farsighted-publisher-with-a-disregard-for-his-financial-obligations

FOURTEEN

1 'Mammal Last Thursday', *Salient*, 17 April 1974.
2 John Bower, author interview, 3 May 2019.
3 Rachel Stace, author interview, 13 March 2019.
4 Hall, *Greed: The Mr Asia Connection*, p. 29.
5 David Herkt, email to author, 4 March 2021.
6 Redmer Yska, 'Revenge of the Hastings Incubus', https://www.drugfoundation.org.nz/matters-of-substance/archive/october-2017/revenge-of-the-hastings-incubus/
7 Redmer Yska, 'James K. Baxter: Poetry and Political Influence', *Matters of Substance*, vol. 27, no. 2 (May 2016), www.drugfoundation.org.nz
8 Chris Wheeler, 'The Inseparable Duo—Fuzz Junkies', *Salient*, 28 May 1969.
9 Rod Bicknell, 'Shit Is Junk Is Shit', *Craccum*, 30 June 1972.
10 David Herkt, email to author, 4 March 2021.
11 Rees-Mogg, *Memoirs*, pp. 158–59.
12 Hagan, *Sticky Fingers*, p. 377.
13 However, substance had largely given way to spectacle. The biggest New Zealand concerts of 1975 were Rick Wakeman in a silly silver wizard's cape performing his bombastic *Journey to the Centre of the Earth* at Western Springs Stadium, and Eric Clapton, at the same venue, playing a desultory set that made it clear that a) he didn't want to be there, and b) he was not God, if there had ever been any doubt.
14 Richards, *Dancing on Our Bones*, p. 106.
15 Brian Easton, in *Te Ara — The Encyclopedia of New Zealand*, https://teara.govt.nz/en/economic-history/
16 Sarah Robson, 'A Short History of Tertiary Education Funding in New Zealand', *Salient*, April 2009.
17 Germaine Greer, 'The Arrogance of the Free-loading Hippie', *Sunday Times* (London), 27 August 1972.
18 Peter Brosnan and Moira Wilson, 'How Does New Zealand Compare Now? International Comparisons of Disaggregated Unemployment Data', *New Zealand Journal of Industrial Relations*, vol. 14. no. 3 (1989), pp. 242–43.
19 Rose Beauchamp, author interview, 28 March 2019.
20 Strauss and Howe, *The Fourth Turning*, p. 3.
21 'Never trust anyone over thirty' had been a hippie catch-cry. That same year, in London and New York, the first stirrings of what would become known as punk were taking place. One of their catch-cries would be 'Never trust a hippie'.
22 Tolerton, *60s Chicks Hit the Nineties*, p. 41.
23 Olive Jones, 'Keeping It Together: A Comparative Analysis of Four Long-established Intentional Communities in New Zealand', PhD thesis, University of Waikato, 2011.
24 Ibid.
25 'Interview with Barry Brickell', *The First New Zealand Whole Earth Catalogue*, pp. 200–1.
26 Edmond, *Bus Stops on the Moon*, pp. 37–38.
27 Ibid., p. 123.
28 Alan Brunton, 'Showman's First Speech' in Red Mole archives, University of Auckland; quoted in introduction to Leggott and Edmond (eds), *Beneath the Ohlala Mountains*, pp. 11–12.
29 Audioculture, https://www.audioculture.co.nz/scenes/the-nambassa-festivals-and-the-counterculture-movement
30 Dick Scott, 'How To Do Your Own Thing', *New Zealand Listener*, 18 December 1972.
31 Phil Gifford, 'The Good Life?', *New Zealand Listener*, 11 October 1980.

32 Ibid.
33 Phil Gifford, author interview, 6 March 2021.
34 Gifford, 'The Good Life?'.
35 'When the Cord Breaks: The Fourth Labour Government', Colin James talk to Christchurch Labour, May 2016, http://www.colinjames.co.nz/2016/05/20/when-the-cord-breaks-colin-james-on-the-fourth-labour-government/
36 National Business Review, https://www.nbr.co.nz/article/lunch-boardroom-rob-campbell-gb-123023

EPILOGUE

1 Jesson, *To Build a Nation*, p. 87.
2 Broadley and Jones (eds), *Nambassa*, p. 61.
3 Gordon Gekko is a character played by Michael Douglas in Oliver Stone's 1987 film *Wall Street*, a financier whose memorable line 'Greed, for lack of a better word, is good' became shorthand for unrestrained capitalism.
4 https://www.beehive.govt.nz/speech/wellbeing-cure-inequality
5 *Stuff*, https://www.stuff.co.nz/life-style/food-wine/100735629/the-average-kiwi-eats-20kg-less-meat-amid-concerns-over-sustainability-of-agriculture
6 Elkington, et al., *Imagining Decolonisation*, p. 149.

SOURCES

In addition to the sources cited below, many publications have been useful in providing information and context. Daily newspapers, notably the *Evening Post*, *Dominion*, *New Zealand Herald*, *Auckland Star*, *Truth*, *Otago Daily Times*, *Christchurch Star* and *Press*; student papers including *Craccum*, *Canta*, *Salient* and *Critic*; underground magazines from *Cock* to the *Counter Culture Free Press*, and over-ground ones such as the *Listener*, *Thursday* and *Playdate*—from the headlines to the display ads and all the ink in between, these and many others contributed to my overall sense of the period. Statistics are usually from *The New Zealand Official Yearbook*, www.stats.govt.nz/indicators-and-snapshots/digitised-collections/yearbook-collection-18932012/

READING

Alpert, Richard / Ram Dass, *The Only Dance There Is*, Anchor, New York, 1974.

Amey, Catherine, *The Compassionate Contrarians: A History of Vegetarians in Aotearoa New Zealand*, Rebel Press, Te Whanganui-A-Tara Wellington, 2014.

Anae, Melani, with Lautofa (Ta) Iuli and Leilasni Tamu (eds), *Polynesian Panthers: Pacific Protest and Affirmative Action in Aotearoa New Zealand 1971–1981*, Huia, Wellington, 2015.

Anderson, Benedict, *Imagined Communities*, Verso, New York, 1983.

Ausubel, David P., *The Fern and the Tiki: An American View of New Zealand National Character, Social Attitudes and Race Relations*, Angus & Robertson, London, 1960 / Holt Rinehart & Winston Inc., New York, 1965.

Awatere, Donna, *Maori Sovereignty*, Broadsheet, Auckland, 1975.

Baigent, Gary, *The Unseen City: 123 Photographs of Auckland*, Blackwood & Janet Paul, Auckland / Tri Ocean Books, San Francisco, 1967.

Bainbridge, Scott, *The Bassett Road Machine Gun Murders*, Allen & Unwin, Auckland, 2013.

Barrowman, Rachel, *A Popular Vision: The Arts and the Left in New Zealand 1930–1950*, Victoria University Press, Wellington, 1991.

Baxter, James K., *Jerusalem Daybook*, Price Milburn, Wellington, 1971.

Beatson, Peter and Dianne (eds), *Dear Peggy: Letters to Margaret Garland from her New Zealand Friends*, Massey University, Palmerston North, 1997.

Belich, James, *Paradise Reforged: A History of the New Zealanders*, Allen Lane / Penguin, Auckland, 2001.

Belich, James, *Replenishing the Earth: The Settler Revolution and the Rise of the Angloworld*, Oxford University Press, Oxford, 2011.

Bell, Brian, *The Brian Bell Reader*, Bumper Books, Wellington, 2001.
Bell, Leonard, *Strangers Arrive: Emigrés and the Arts in New Zealand, 1930–1980*, Auckland University Press, Auckland, 2017.
Bennetts, C. H. (Kit), *Spy*, Random House, Auckland, 2006.
Bensemann, Paul, *Fight for the Forests: The Pivotal Campaigns That Saved New Zealand's Native Forests*, Potton & Burton, Nelson, 2018.
Bieringa, Jan and Jonathan Dennis (eds), *Film in Aotearoa New Zealand*, Victoria University Press, Wellington, 1992.
Bilborough, Miro, *In the Time of the Manaroans*, Victoria University Press, Wellington, 2020.
Birchfield, Maureen, *Looking for Answers: A Life of Elsie Locke*, Canterbury University Press, Christchurch, 1998.
Bohan, Edmund, *The House of Reed*, Canterbury University Press, Christchurch, 2005.
Bollinger, Conrad, *Grog's Own Country*, Minerva, Auckland, 1967.
Bollinger, Nick, *Goneville*, Awa Press, Wellington, 2015.
Boraman, Toby, *Rabble Rousers and Merry Pranksters: A History of Anarchism in Aotearoa New Zealand from the Mid-1950s to the Early 1980s*, Katipo Books, Christchurch / Irrecuperable Press, Wellington, 2007.
Borrowdale, James, *Weed: A New Zealand Story*, Penguin, Auckland, 2020.
Bourke, Chris, *Blue Smoke: The Lost Dawn of New Zealand Popular Music 1918–1964*, Auckland University Press, Auckland, 2010.
Boyd, Joe, *White Bicycles: Making Music in the 1960s*, Serpent's Tail, London, 2005.
Brickell, Chris, *Teenagers: The Rise of Youth Culture in New Zealand*, Auckland University Press, Auckland, 2017.
Broadley, Colin and Judith Jones (eds), *Nambassa: A New Direction*, A. H. & A. W. Reed, Wellington, 1979.
Brunton, Alan, *Years Ago Today: Language and Performance 1969*, Bumper Books, Wellington, 1997.
Brunton, Alan, Murray Edmond and Michele Leggott (eds), *Big Smoke: New Zealand Poems 1960–75*, Auckland University Press, Auckland, 2000.
Bunkle, Phillida and Beryl Hughes (eds), *Women in New Zealand Society*, Allen & Unwin, Auckland, 1980.
Bunkle, Phillida, Steven Levine and Christopher Wainwright (eds), *Learning about Sexism in New Zealand*, Learmonth Publications, Wellington, 1976.
Burroughs, William, *Junky*, Penguin, Harmondsworth, 1977.
Cahill, Maud and Christine Dann (eds), *Changing Our Lives: Women Working in the Women's Liberation Movement, 1970–1990*, Bridget Williams Books, Wellington, 1991.
Chamberlain, Jenny, *Constant Radical: The Life and Times of Sue Bradford*, Fraser Books, Masterton, 2017.

Chapman, Rob, *Psychedelia and Other Colours*, Faber & Faber, London, 2017.
Coney, Sandra, *Out of the Frying Pan: Inflammatory Writings 1972–89*, Penguin, Auckland, 1990.
Coney, Sandra, *Standing in the Sunshine: A History of New Zealand Women Since They Won the Vote*, Viking, Auckland, 1993.
Cook, Hera, *The Long Sexual Revolution: English Women, Sex, and Contraception: 1800–1975*, Oxford University Press, Oxford, 2004.
Dann, Christine, *Up From Under: Women and Liberation in New Zealand, 1970–1985*, Bridget Williams Books, Wellington, 2015.
Davis, Mike and Jon Wiener, *Set the Night on Fire: L.A. in the Sixties*, Verso, London/New York, 2020.
DeGroot, Gerald J., *The Sixties Unplugged: A Kaleidoscopic History of a Disorderly Decade*, Harvard University Press, Cambridge MA, 2009.
Diski, Jenni, *The Sixties*, Profile Books, London, 2009.
Dix, John, *Stranded in Paradise: New Zealand Rock'n'Roll, 1955–1988*, Paradise Publications, Wellington, 1988.
Edmond, Martin, *Chemical Evolution: Drugs and Art Production 1970–80*, Bumper Books, Wellington, 1997.
Edmond, Martin, *The Resurrection of Philip Clairmont*, Auckland University Press, Auckland, 1999.
Edmond, Martin, *Bus Stops on the Moon*, Otago University Press, Dunedin, 2020.
Edmond, Martin and Nigel Roberts (eds), *Steal Away Boy: Selected Poems of David Mitchell*, Auckland University Press, Auckland, 2010.
Edmond, Murray, *Time to Make a Song and Dance: Cultural Revolt in Auckland in the 1960s*, Atuanui, Pōkeno, 2021.
Edwards, Brian, *The Public Eye*, A. H. & A. W. Reed, Wellington, 1971.
Elkington, Bianca, Rebecca Kiddle, Moana Jackson, Ocean Mercier, Mike Ross, Jennie Smeaton and Amanda Thomas, *Imagining Decolonisation*, Bridget Williams Books, Wellington, 2020.
Elworthy, Sam, *Ritual Song of Defiance: A Social History of Students at the University of Otago*, Otago University Students Association, Dunedin, 1991.
Escarpit, Robert, *The Book Revolution*, Harrap, London, 1966.
Felton, David, Robin Green and David Dalton, *Mindfuckers: A Source Book on the Rise of Acid Fascism in America*, Straight Arrow Books, San Francisco, 1972.
Fischer, David Hackett, *Fairness and Freedom: A History of Two Open Societies, New Zealand and the United States*, Oxford University Press, New York, 2012.
Fountain, Nigel, *Underground: The London Alternative Press, 1966–74*, Routledge, London/New York, 1988.
Gilbert, Jarrod, *Patched: The History of Gangs in New Zealand*, Auckland University Press, Auckland, 2013.

Gitlin, Todd, *The Sixties: Years of Hope, Days of Rage*, Bantam, New York, 1987.
Goldstein, Richard, *Another Little Piece of My Heart: My Life of Rock and Revolution in the '60s*, Bloomsbury Circus, London, 2015.
Green, Jonathan, *Days in the Life: Voices from the English Underground, 1961–1971*, Minerva, London, 1988.
Greer, Germaine, *The Female Eunuch*, MacGibbon & Kee, London, 1970.
Gruar, Bill, *Snakes of New Zealand*, Valid Press, Auckland, 2006.
Hagan, Joe, *Sticky Fingers: The Life and Times of Jann Wenner and Rolling Stone Magazine*, Viking, New York, 2017.
Haley, Russell, *Hanly*, Hodder & Stoughton, Auckland, 1989.
Hall, Richard, *Greed: The Mr Asia Connection*, Pan, Sydney, 1981.
Hamilton, Ian, *Till Human Voices Wake Us*, Auckland University Press/Oxford University Press, Auckland, 1984.
Hansen, Søren and Jesper Jensen, *The Little Red Schoolbook*, translated from Danish by Berit Thornberry, Alister Taylor Publishing, Wellington, 1972.
Harris, Aroha, *Hīkoi: Forty Years of Māori Protest*, Huia, Wellington, 2004.
Hayward, Margaret, *Diary of the Kirk Years*, A. H. & A. W. Reed, Wellington, 1981.
Heath, Joseph and Andrew Potter, *The Rebel Sell: How the Counterculture Became Consumer Culture*, Capstone, Mankato, 2005.
Hepworth, David, *A Fabulous Creation: How the LP Saved Our Lives*, Penguin, London, 2019.
Hill, Richard S., *Maori and the State: Crown–Maori Relations in New Zealand / Aotearoa, 1950–2000*, Victoria University Press, Wellington, 2009.
Hillman, Betty Luther, *Dressing for the Culture Wars: Style and the Politics of Self-presentation in the 1960s and 1970s*, University of Nebraska Press, Lincoln, 2015.
Hoffman, Abbie (as 'Free'), *Revolution for the Hell of It*, Dial, New York, 1968.
Hoffman, Abbie, *Woodstock Nation*, Vintage, New York, 1969.
Hoffmann, Anna, *Tales of Anna Hoffmann, Volume 1*, Anna Hoffmann, Auckland, 2009.
Hofmann, Albert, *LSD: My Problem Child*, McGraw Hill, New York, 1979.
Holiday, Billie, with William Duffy, *Lady Sings the Blues*, Doubleday, New York, 1956.
Horrocks, Roger, *Re-Inventing New Zealand: Essays on the Arts and the Media*, Atuanui Press, Pōkeno, 2016.
Hunt, Sam, *Bracken Country*, Glenbervie Press, Wellington, 1971.
Hunt, Sam, *From Bottle Creek*, Alister Taylor Publishing, Wellington, 1972.
Hunt, Sam, *Time to Ride*, Alister Taylor Publishing, Wellington, 1975.

Jesson, Bruce, *Behind the Mirror Glass: The Growth of Wealth and Power in New Zealand in the Eighties*, Penguin, Auckland, 1987.
Jesson, Bruce, *To Build a Nation: Collected Writings, 1975–1999*, Penguin, Auckland, 2005.
Johnson, Louis (ed.), *New Zealand Poetry Yearbook: Volume 9*, Pegasus Press, Christchurch, 1960.
Jones, Alison, *This Pākehā Life: An Unsettled Memoir*, Bridget Williams Books, Wellington, 2020.
Jones, Tim and Ian Baker, *A Hard-Won Freedom: Alternative Communities in New Zealand*, Hodder & Stoughton, Auckland, 1975.
Kedgley, Sue and Sharyn Cederman (eds), *Sexist Society*, Alister Taylor Publishing, Wellington, 1972.
Kedgley, Sue and Mary Varnham (eds), *Heading Nowhere in a Navy Blue Suit and Other Tales from the Feminist Revolution*, Daphne Brasell Associates, Wellington, 1993.
Keith, Hamish, *Native Wit*, Penguin, Auckland, 2008.
Kerouac, Jack, *On the Road*, Viking, New York, 1957.
King, Michael, *The Penguin History of New Zealand*, Penguin, Auckland, 2003.
Kurlansky, Mark, *1968: The Year That Rocked the World*, Random House, New York, 2005.
Laing, R. D., *The Divided Self*, Penguin, London, 1965.
Lange, David, *Nuclear Free—The New Zealand Way*, Penguin, Auckland, 1990.
Leary, Timothy, *High Priest*, New American Library, New York, 1968.
Leggott, Michele and Martin Edmond (eds), *Beyond the Ohlala Mountains: Alan Brunton Poems 1968–2002*, Titus Books, Pōkeno, 2013.
Lemke-Santangelo, Gretchen, *Daughters of Aquarius: Women of the Counterculture*, University Press of Kansas, Lawrence, 2009.
Lewis, Peter, *The Fifties*, Heinemann, London, 1978.
Luafutu, Fa'amoana John, *A Boy Called Broke: My Story So Far*, Macmillan Brown Centre for Pacific Studies, University of Canterbury, Christchurch, 1994.
MacDonald, Ian, *Revolution in the Head: The Beatles' Records and the Sixties*, Pimlico Press, London, 1994.
McKay, Frank, *The Life of James K. Baxter*, Oxford University Press, Auckland, 1990.
MacLean, Ingrid, *Behind Open Doors*, Resonance BookWorks, London, 2018.
McLeod, Rosemary, *A Girl Like I*, John McIndoe, Dunedin, 1976.
McMillan, John, *Smoking Typewriters: The Sixties Underground Press and the Rise of Alternative Media in America*, Oxford University Press, Oxford, 2011.
Manning, A. E., *The Bodgie: A Study in Abnormal Psychology*, A. H. & A. W. Reed, Wellington, 1958.

Mezzrow, Mezz and Bernard Wolfe, *Really the Blues* (1946), NYRB Classics, New York, 2009.
Miles, Barry, *In the Sixties*, Pimlico Press, London, 2003.
Miles, Barry, *London Calling: A Countercultural History of London Since 1945*, Atlantic, London, 2011.
Miller, Craig, *Coffee Houses of Wellington 1939 to 1979: Coffee in Pre-espresso New Zealand*, Miller, Auckland, 2015.
Minehan, Mike, *O Jerusalem*, Hazard Press, Christchurch, 2002.
Murphy, Geoff, *A Life on Film*, HarperCollins, Auckland, 2015.
Nelson, Elizabeth, *The British Counter-Culture, 1966–73: A Study of the Underground Press*, Palgrave/Macmillan, London, 1989.
Neville, Richard, *Playpower*, Jonathan Cape, London, 1970.
Newton, John, *The Double Rainbow: James K. Baxter, Ngāti Hau and the Jerusalem Commune*, Victoria University Press, Wellington, 2009.
Nuttall, Jeff, *Bomb Culture*, Paladin, London, 1970.
Oliver, W. H., *James K. Baxter: A Portrait*, Port Nicholson Press, Wellington, 1983.
Parkin, Frank, *Middle Class Radicalism*, Melbourne University Press, Melbourne, 1968.
Penelope, Julia and Sarah Valentine (eds), *Finding the Lesbians*, Crossing Press, Berkeley, 1988.
Priestley, Rebecca, *Mad on Radium: New Zealand in the Atomic Age*, Auckland University Press, Auckland, 2012.
Rabel, Roberto, *New Zealand and the Vietnam War: Politics and Diplomacy*, Auckland University Press, Auckland, 2005.
Rain, Lynn, *Community: The Story of Riverside, 1941–1991*, Riverside Community Trust Board, Upper Moutere, 1991.
Rees-Mogg, William, *Memoirs*, Harper Press, New York, 2011.
Reich, Charles A., *The Greening of America*, Random House, New York, 1970.
Richards, Trevor, *Dancing on Our Bones: New Zealand, South Africa, Rugby and Racism*, Bridget Williams Books, Wellington, 1999.
Riley, Murdoch, *Maori Healing and Herbal*, Viking/Seven Seas Publishing, Auckland, 1994.
Ritchie, Jane and James, *Child Rearing Patterns in New Zealand*, A. H. & A. W. Reed, Wellington, 1970.
Robilliard, Robyn, *Hard Country: A Golden Bay Life*, Random House, Auckland, 2014.
Rolling Stone (eds), *Harrison*, Simon & Schuster, New York, 2002.
Roszak, Theodore, *The Making of a Counter Culture*, Faber & Faber, London, 1970.
Rowbotham, Sheila, *Promise of a Dream: Remembering the Sixties*, Penguin, London, 2000.
Sandbrook, Dominic, *White Heat: A History of Britain in the Swinging Sixties*, Abacus, London, 2006.

Shackleton, Michael, *Operation Vietnam: A New Zealand Surgical First*, Otago University Press, Dunedin, 2004.
Shadbolt, Tim, *Bullshit and Jellybeans*, Alister Taylor Publishing, Wellington, 1971.
Shadbolt, Tim, *A Mayor of Two Cities*, Hodder Moa, Manukau, 2008.
Sinclair, Keith, *A History of New Zealand*, Penguin, Auckland, 1969.
Smith, Ron, *Working Class Son: My Fight Against Capitalism and War*, Ron Smith, Wellington, 1994.
Smyth, Helen, *Rocking the Cradle: Contraception, Sex and Politics in New Zealand*, Steele Roberts, Wellington, 2000.
Spittle, Gordon, *Beat Groups and Courtyard Parties*, GWS Publications, Wellington, 1996.
Stax, Mike, Andy Neill and John Baker, *Don't Bring Me Down ... Under: The Pretty Things in New Zealand 1965*, Ugly Things Publications, San Diego, 2006.
Stevens, Jay, *Storming Heaven: LSD and the American Dream*, Paladin, London, 1988.
Strauss, William and Neil Howe, *The Fourth Turning: An American Prophesy*, Crown, New York, 1997.
Sturm, Jennifer (ed.), *Anna Kavan's New Zealand: A Pacific Interlude in a Turbulent Life*, Vintage, Auckland, 2009.
Taylor, Alister (ed.), *Peace, Power & Politics in Asia*, The Organising Committee of the Peace, Power & Politics in Asia Conference, Wellington, 1969.
Taylor, Alister, Lyn Brooke-White and Chris Wheeler, *The Whole World Watches*, Cockerel Print, Wellington, 1970.
Taylor, Derek, *It Was Twenty Years Ago Today*, Penguin, London, 1987.
Te Awekotuku, Ngahuia, *Mana Wahine Maori: Selected Writings on Maori Women's Art, Culture and Politics*, New Women's Press, Auckland, 1991.
Thompson, Richard, *Retreat from Apartheid: New Zealand's Sporting Contacts with South Africa*, Oxford University Press, Wellington, 1975.
Tolerton, Jane, *60s Chicks Hit the Nineties*, Penguin, Auckland, 1997.
Weir, John (ed.), *James K. Baxter: Collected Poems*, Oxford University Press, Oxford, 1979.
Weir, John (ed.), *James K. Baxter: Letters of a Poet*, Victoria University Press, Wellington, 2015.
Westra, Ans, *Washday at the Pa*, School Publications Branch, Department of Education, Wellington, 1964.
Wilson, Jude, *Flying Kiwis: A History of the OE*, Otago University Press, Dunedin, 2014.
Wilson, Roger, *From Manapouri to Aramoana: The Battle for New Zealand's Environment*, Earthworks, Auckland, 1982.
Wolfe, Tom, *The Electric Kool-Aid Acid Test*, Bantam, New York, 1968.
Yska, Redmer, *New Zealand Green: The Story of Marijuana in New Zealand*, Bateman, Auckland, 1990.

Yska, Redmer, *All Shook Up: The Flash Bodgie and the Rise of the New Zealand Teenager in the Fifties*, Penguin, Auckland, 1993.
Zolov, Eric, *Refried Elvis: The Rise of the Mexican Counterculture*, University of California Press, Berkeley, 1999.

The First New Zealand Whole Earth Catalogue, Alister Taylor Publishing, Wellington, 1972.
The Second New Zealand Whole Earth Catalogue, Alister Taylor Publishing, Martinborough, 1975.
The Third New Zealand Whole Earth Catalogue, Alister Taylor Publishing, Martinborough, 1977.
Splash Five: From Scratch Special Issue, Small Bore Books, Auckland, 1987.

VIEWING

50 Years of New Zealand Television, TVNZ, 2010, www.nzonscreen.com/title/50-years-of-nz-tv-episode-two-protest-2010
Dirty Bloody Hippies, directed by Dan Salmon, 2009, www.nzonscreen.com/title/dirty-bloody-hippies-2009
Inside New Zealand: High Times, directed by David Herkt, 2005, www.youtube.com/watch?v=nIrb4h76NZk
Landfall—A Film about Ourselves, directed by Paul Maunder, 1975, www.nzonscreen.com/title/landfall-1975
Nambassa Festival, directed by Philip Howe, 1979, www.nzonscreen.com/title/nambassa-festival-1979
Nga Tamatoa: 40 Years On, directed by Kim Webby, Māori TV, 2012, www.nzonscreen.com/title/nga-tamatoa-2012
Polynesian Panthers, directed by Dan Salmon, 2012, www.nzonscreen.com/title/polynesian-panthers-2010
Redwood 70, produced by NZBC, 1970, www.nzonscreen.com/title/redwood-doco
The Shadow of Vietnam, directed by Bryce Campbell and Grant Campbell, 1995, www.nzonscreen.com/title/the-shadow-of-vietnam-1995
Start Again, directed by Roger Donaldson, 1972, www.nzonscreen.com/title/start-again-1972
Wellington in the '60s: The Way It Seemed, directed by John O'Shea, Pacific Films, NZBC, 1967, www.ngataonga.org.nz/collections/catalogue/catalogue-item?record_id=68216
Where Have All The Wowsers Gone?, presented by Michael Dean, produced by Michael Scott-Smith, 1972, www.nzonscreen.com/title/survey-where-wowsers-gone-1972

LISTENING

A soundtrack to the period covered in this book could go on and on. This discography does not pretend to be complete but includes most of the music mentioned in the text, along with a few other significant examples. Artists and recordings are listed more or less in the order in which they appear in the book.

Bob Dylan, *The Freewheelin'* (1963); *Highway 61 Revisited* (1965). The former consolidated Dylan's reputation as a writer of folk anthems with songs like 'Masters of War' and 'Blowin' in the Wind'; the latter redefined rock'n'roll songwriting in such lyrical explosions as 'Like a Rolling Stone' and 'Desolation Row'.

Various, *Folk Concert Down Under* (1965). A snapshot of the Monde Marie scene, circa mid-1960s. Whaling songs, West Coast ballads, old English folk songs, and Dylan and Seeger covers, performed by coffee-bar regulars Rod McKinnon, Val Murphy, Don Toms and others.

Ravi Shankar, *Portrait of Genius* (1964). Released around the time of Shankar's 1965 visit, this was many listeners' introduction to the classical rāga form, the virtuosic playing of Shankar, and the intricate interplay between his multi-stringed sitar and the hand-drums known as tabla.

Thelonious Monk, *Criss-Cross* (1963), *It's Monk's Time* (1964), *Monk* (1964). Though his greatest recordings date from more than a decade earlier, these early 1960s albums all saw local releases around the time of Monk's 1965 tour. While hardly a classic, *Monk* is perhaps most representative of what New Zealand audiences heard, featuring the group that accompanied him here. Bass player Larry Gales would return to New Zealand a quarter-century later to perform with a group of local musicians which included Bruno Lawrence.

The Beatles, *With The Beatles* (1963). Their current album at the time of their New Zealand visit in 1964 captures all the exhilaration of their early quartet sound. *Sgt. Pepper's Lonely Hearts Club Band* (1967) may not have aged as well as some of their other work, but the impact of its vaudevillian psychedelia cannot be overstated.

The Rolling Stones, *Out of Our Heads* (1965). This includes the epochal '(I Can't Get No) Satisfaction' plus a representative swag of the rhythm and blues covers which dominated the Stones' early repertoire. *Let It Bleed* (1969) and *Sticky Fingers* (1971) confront the counterculture's dissolution, with irony and revelry in equal measure.

The Pretty Things, *The Pretty Things* (1965). The London quintet's self-titled debut album represents their primal blues-based music which, along with their unrestrainable drummer and generally bohemian demeanour, kept them in New Zealand's headlines for a fortnight in 1965.

Chants R&B, Christchurch band, notable for their independent spirit and uncompromising rawness. Though they released just two singles, both in 1966, a compilation album *Stage Door Witchdoctors* (1995) brings together all of their studio recordings plus some live performances.

Bob Dylan's 'Rainy Day Women #12 & 35', the Byrds' 'Eight Miles High' and Jimi Hendrix Experience's 'Purple Haze' were a few singles that slipped past local censors with their veiled references to chemically altered states. Likewise, Thunderclap Newman's 'Something in the Air' was a revolutionary call-to-arms that somehow passed the public broadcaster's scrutiny.

Pink Floyd, *The Piper at the Gates of Dawn*; Jimi Hendrix Experience, *Are You Experienced?*; The Doors, *The Doors*; Jefferson Airplane, *Surrealistic Pillow*; Country Joe and the Fish, *Electric Music for the Mind and Body* (all 1967); Big Brother and the Holding Company, *Cheap Thrills*; The Mothers of Invention, *We're Only In It For The Money* (both 1968); Grateful Dead, *Live Dead* (1969); Jimi Hendrix, *Band of Gypsies* (1970). All were released in New Zealand, each relaying its own report from the countercultural frontlines.

Captain Beefheart and the Magic Band, *Trout Mask Replica*, The Velvet Underground, *The Velvet Underground* and the Flying Burrito Brothers, *The Gilded Palace of Sin* (all 1969) are just some of the significant albums *not* released in New Zealand at the time and which, as a consequence, acquired a near-mythic status. Listen and decide whether their reputations were justified.

Hair, Original Broadway Cast Recording (1968). 'Aquarius/Let the Sunshine In', 'Good Morning Starshine', 'Hashish', 'Sodomy' and other family favourites.

Jenny McLeod, *Earth and Sky*, Original Auckland Festival Cast (1970); *Under The Sun*, Palmerston North Centennial Cast (1971). McLeod's magnum opuses. The former is the more coherent, the latter the more ambitious, with a cast of a thousand, including four orchestras, a five-member rock group, two adult choirs, 440 children and a rock band.

The House of Nimrod, 'Slightly-Delic' (1967); Lew Pryme, 'Gracious Lady Alice Dee' (1968). Twee, LSD-inspired folk-rock from the pen of Auckland songwriter Bryce Peterson.

Many local bands active during the period never made commercial recordings. Performances of the Original Sun Blues Band, Killing Floor, Joyful Crye, Original Sin, Pussyfoot, Noah, Stash, Arkastra, Mandrake, Storm and many others survive only in the fading memories of those who witnessed them. Of the records that were made, a few of the best are:

The Underdogs (Pig, Mann and Edwards), *Wasting Our Time* (1970); Space Farm, *Space Farm* (1971); *Space Farm Live* (recorded

1971, released 2000). Harvey Mann and Glen Absolum take flight, with moments of psychic synchronicity, in spite of the bad singing.

The Human Instinct, S*toned Guitar* (1970). The Māori Hendrix in full effect.

Ticket, *Awake* (1971). More Hendrix-inspired sonic expeditionaries, with high-geared rhythm section and fully torqued guitar.

Highway, *Highway* (1971). Though their legendary improvisations are necessarily truncated for disc, there's still thrilling instrumental interplay in these seven tightly structured tracks.

BLERTA, 'Dance All Around The World'/'Freedom St. Mary's' (1971). BLERTA's vision summed up in their first single. The A-side is the children's show, the B-side is the full psychedelic-jazz-rock extravaganza.

Mammal/Sam Hunt, *Beware the Man* (1972). The collaboration with poet Sam Hunt was an experimental project rather than a representation of the group's customary psych-rock-funk. Still, the powerful title track remained a staple of Mammal's live sets.

Tamburlaine, *Say No More* (1972). Psychedelically tinged folk-rock from campus regulars.

Corben Simpson, *Get Up With the Sun* (1973). After his arrest for onstage nudity at Ngaruawahia, the sometime BLERTA singer captures the mood of the times in both nature-worshipping reveries such as the title track and paranoiac outbursts like 'No Trespassing'.

ACKNOWLEDGEMENTS

This book would not have existed without the enthusiasm of Sam Elworthy at Auckland University Press or the encouragement of Chris Bourke who sent me to Sam in the first place. Nor would it be the book it is without Jane Parkin's scrupulous and sensitive editing, Katharina Bauer who skilfully managed its production, Alan Deare who brought his empathetic eye to the design, Dave McDonald who typeset and corrected the images, Mike Wagg, Lauren Donald and Sophia Broom who assisted in checking the text, or Susan Brookes who produced the index.

The John David Stout Fellowship in New Zealand Studies for 2021 made it possible to complete the research and writing, a process that had already been helped significantly by Creative New Zealand, Friends of the Turnbull Library, the 2020 CLNZ/NZSA Writers' Award from Copyright Licensing New Zealand, and the New Zealand History Research Trust.

I am grateful to everyone who spoke or wrote to me, giving their time and sharing their memories: Zeke Alley, Tony Backhouse, Ricky Ball, George Barris, Karen Barris, Rose Beauchamp, Sue Belt, Rex Benson, Trudi Benham, Alun Bollinger, Helen Bollinger, Tim Bollinger, Pat Bolster, John Bower, Rick Bryant, Murray Cammick, Gordon Campbell, Stephen Chan, Sandra Coney, Phil Dadson, Andrew Delahunty, Catherine Delahunty, Martin Edmond, Lara Esam, Roger Fowler, Don Franks, Phil Gifford, Sam Gosson, Bill Gruar, Sir Bob Harvey, Kevin Hayward, Gerard Hill, Richard Hill, Hamish Horsley, Colin James, Ken James, Olive Jones, Jim Kebbell, Sue Kedgley, Bill Lake, Tony Larsen, Jeremy Love, Harvey Mann, Alison McClean, Stephanie McKee, Jenny McLeod, Rosemary McLeod, Tom McWilliams, Brent Morrissey, Derek Morton, Jeremy Mouat, Dada Nabhaniilananda, John Newton, Dennis O'Brien, Therese O'Connell, Rawiri Paratene, Gilbert Peterson, Peter Pharazyn, Nicholas Pounder, Dan Richter, Julian Rosenberg, Dan Salmon, Fiona Samuel, Graeme Scott, Megan Simpson, Tony Simpson, Ross Somerville, Rachel Stace, Roger Steele, Jim Stevenson, Ian Stewart, Richard Suggate, Bob Tait, Alister Taylor, Barry Thomas, Linus Treefoot, Patricia Watson, Chris Wheeler, Graeme Whimp, David White, Tom White, Marion Wood, Harry Wong, Joe Wylie, Deborah Yates, Hugh Young, Mark Young, Irene Zohrab.

Thanks to the photographers who shared their images and the stories behind them: Ian Baker, Gil Hanly, John Miller, Max Oettli, Bryan Staff, Keith Stewart, Geoff Studd and Ans Westra; to Patricia Fields and Judy Cope-Williams for sharing the work of their late husbands John Fields and Gordon Cope-Williams; to Sally Griffin for the photographs of the late Angela Middleton; John B. Turner and David Langman for their help with contacts; and to the estate of John 'Hoppy' Hopkins for the use of his iconic photographs. To all the librarians at the National Library of New Zealand and Alexander Turnbull Library, Archives New Zealand, Museum of New Zealand Te Papa Tongarewa, Auckland War Memorial Museum, Wellington City Libraries, Christchurch City Libraries Ngā Kete Wānanga o Ōtautahi and Auckland Libraries. Special thanks to Yvonne Boland and Yumi Nagafuchi at Infofind (Radio New Zealand Te Reo Irirangi o Aotearoa), Sue Hirst (Special Collections Librarian, J. C. Beaglehole Room at Victoria University of Wellington Te Herenga Waka) and Jennifer Taylor Moore and Michael McKeagg at the Sarjeant Gallery Te Whare o Rehua, Whanganui. To those who opened their personal archives: Anita Arlov, Archie Bowie, Chris and Margaret Cochran, Adam Gifford, David Herkt, Paul Jackman, Chargn Keenan, Bruce King, Jonathan Milne, Simon Ogston, Jackson Payne, Dinah Priestley, Ian Pryor, Craig Robertson, Jeff Smith, Jane Tolerton, Hugh Young and Redmer Yska.

To the staff and associates of the Stout Research Centre for New Zealand Studies — particularly Professor Anna Green, Professor Richard Hill, Professor Jim McAloon, Debbie Levy, Brad and Kathryn Patterson, Selwyn Katene, David Grant and Steven Loveridge — for conversation and comradeship. To John Newton, Redmer Yska and Piripi Walker for their invaluable feedback on the work in progress. And to Kathy McRae, my first reader and best friend.

INDEX

Illustrations have their page numbers in bold

A

A. H. & A. W. Reed 328
Aagaard, Peter, photos by 2, **236, 272, 275, 361**
abortion 109, 304, **314**, 315
Absolum, Glen 186, 256
Acid Tests 90, 185, 264, 303
Adam and Eve 237
Admore, Alan 223, 226–27
adoption 109
Aetherius Society 252, **253**
Affairs 127, 326–27, **327**
Agnew, Spiro, protest 169–73, **172**
Ahu Ahu Ohu commune 234
alcohol 17, 29–30, 44, 72–73, 75, 343, 370
Alexander, Dave 297
Alister Taylor Publishing 330–32
Allen, Keith 234
Allen, Percy 91, 93, 94
Allenby Terrace community 278
Alley, Judy 247–51, 324–25
Alley, Zeke 247–51, **250**, 324–25, 337
Alpers, Philip 281–82
Alpert, Richard 79–80, 304
Altamont Speedway event 214, 349
Amamus Theatre Group 195, **198**, 207
America, military installations 317–18
Ananda Marga 260, 261–62
Anarchist Association 45
Anderson, Benedict 190
Anderson, Lindsay 146
Antonioni, Michelangelo 145
ANZUS Treaty 64
apartheid protests 29, 173–79
Apirana, Steve 188
Aquarius Festival 207
Ardern, Jacinda 368
Ardern, Marcus 264–65
Are You Experienced? 85
Armstrong, Louis 72
The Art of Sensual Massage 113, 264
Arusha Declaration 282
Ashenden, Tony 67
The Association of Orientally Flavoured Syndics 145
Auckland **224**
 Albert Park **4–5, 10,** 13–15, 18–19, 23, 100, **152,** 166–67
  Bassett Road machine-gun murders 73–74, 78
 Domain, Peace Rally, 1973 **264–65**
 Freemans Bay, 1976 **226**
 Grafton, c. 1970 **228–29**
 Herne Bay, 1970s 71, **76–77, 110**
 Jam Factory **198**, 199
 Jeff Scholes' pottery **236**
 Mt Eden 181, **194**, 195
 Myers Park 12
 No.1 Port Depot Incident, 1970 173, **174**
 Queen Street **97**
 Town Hall protest, c. 1971 **162–63**
 Vulcan Lane 12, **41**, 160
 Waterloo Quadrant protest, 1970 **172**
 Wellesley St, 1972 **244**
 Western Springs Stadium 208, 214–17, **216–17**
Auckland Council on Vietnam 160
Auckland Police Task Force 295
Auckland Push 222
Auckland Star 99, 193, 302
Auckland Students' Association 322
AUSAPOCPAH 142, 153, 154
Australasian Architecture Student Association Congress **196–97**, 198
Australasian Rock Squad 199
Ausubel, David 30, 32
Avoca Valley 357
Awatere, Donna 289, 299

B

Baader-Meinhof Group 317–18, 349
baby boom 22–24
baby boomers 31, 64, 276, 315, 316, 355, 364
Backhouse, Tony 195, 203
Baez, Joan 39, 170
Bahá'í 255
Bailey, Rona 303
Baker, Ian, photos by **191, 219, 236**
Ball, Ricky 75
Band of Hope Jug Band 137
Barber, Bruce 195
Barr, Jim 330–31
Barr, Mani 230
Barrett, Syd 82–83
Barrington, Archibald 227
Barry Lett Galleries 138, 142, 199
Bartlett, Patricia 331
Bassett Road machine-gun murders 73–74, 78
Bauxhau **204–5**, 207
Baxter, James K. 20, 220, 224–25, 264–67, 276–78, 332, 346

Jerusalem & commune 238–43, **241,** 264, 266–67, 276–77, 341
Baysting, Arthur 358
Beaglehole, John 123
beards *see* hair styles & beards
The Beatles 19, 54–59, **55**, 88, 93, 147, 254
Beattie, Justice 173
Beauchamp, Rose 305, 354
Beck, Jeff 145
Beech Forest Action Committee 280–82
Beeville commune 24, 227, **275,** 276
Belich, James 101, 274
Bell, Brian 44–45
Bell, Norman 274
Belt, Sue 116, 221
Bennett, Henry 289
Bennetts, Kit 323
Benning, Terri 106, 109
Benson, Rex 84–85
Best Intentions 215–16
Beware the Man (album) 332
'Beware the Man' (poem) 203
Bhagwan Shree Rajneesh 235, 262
Bicknell, Rod 347–48
Big Brother and the Holding Company 90, 114
Bilbrough, Miro 105
Billy TK and the Powerhouse 237
Bischoff, Max **209,** 227, 230, 259–60
Black Panthers 292
Black Power 296–97, 298
Black Sabbath 208, 210–11
Blake, William 105, 287–88
Bleakley, Patrick 237
BLERTA 195, 203, **206,** 206–7, 310
 tours 207, 212, 237, 296, 342, 369
Blow-Up 145
Blueprint for New Zealand: An Alternative Future 315–17, **316**
The Bodgie: A Study in Abnormal Psychology 34
Body, Jack 195, 207
Bollinger, Alun 237, 310
Bollinger, Conrad & Marei 27–28, 35, 44–45, 48–49, **49,** 126, 169–70, 352–53
Bollinger, Helen 310
Bollinger, Nick, & photo by **241,** 246–47, 330, 342–44, 352–53, 360–62
Bollinger family 27–28, 32, 35, 43–45, 48, **49,** 53
Bomb Culture 47–48
Bone, Bill 168–69
Bonnevie, Anna 225–26
books & book shops 122–23
 see also specific books & shops

Booth, Pat 182
Boswijk, Eelco 31
Boulez, Pierre 185
Bourke, Chris 138
Bower, Colin 167–68, 322
Bower, John 119, 153, 154, 166–69, 171–73, 322, 342
Bowie, Archie, & album cover by 185, **186**
A Boy Called Broke 188–89, 292
Bracken Country 332
Bradford, Sue 123, 153, 158, 304
Bradwell, Cyril 100
Braithwaite, Martin 132
Brand, Stewart 332–33
Brash, Alan 50
Brash, Don 50
Brazier, Graham 192, 222–23
Brickell, Barry 357
Brickell, Chris 117–18
Broadley, Colin 146–47
Broadsheet 271, 299, 309–11
Brock, Warwick 137
Brody, Richard 57
Bromhead 309
Broughton, David 288–89, **289**, 298
Brunton, Alan 20, 98, 138, 142–44, **143**, 172–73, 192, 223–24, **359**
  writings & performances 43, 45, 137, 357–60
Brunton, David 99
Bryant, Rick 89, 114–16, 192, 203, 221, 360
  & drugs 75, 203, 342
Buddhism 251, 255, 260, 337, 343
Bullshit and Jellybeans 101, 308–9, **329**, 331–32
Butler, Michael 263
The Byrds 88, 146

C

Cabaret Capital Strut 358
Cameron, Miriam 310–11, 355–56
Cammick, Murray, & photo by 89, **152**
Campaign Against Foreign Control of Aotearoa 282
Campaign for Nuclear Disarmament *see* nuclear protests
Campbell, Gordon 33, 61
Campbell, Rob 365
Canta 136, 282
Captain Kiwi Battles the Dope Fiends 138, **139–41**
Cardew, Cornelius 195
CARE (Citizens Association for Racial Equality) 293
Carew, Paul 199
Carlisle, Lyle Eric 'Lemming' 169–71, 222
Carmen 119, 358, 360
Carter, Peter 'Jimmi' 188
Carter, Shayne 188
Castle, Bronwen 333
Catch-22 318
Catholicism 36, 239–40, 259, 277, 302
Cavell, Bruce 188, 201

Caygill, David 365
Cederman, Sharyn 302–4, **307**, 332
Centrepeace 257
Centrepoint commune 235, 362–64
Cerebral Vortex 281
Cernan, Eugene 169
Chain, Ernst 83
Challenge 75
Chalmers, Greg 243
Chamber Music Society 60
Chamberlain, Neville 'Cham The Man' 88
Chan, Stephen 144–45, 302, 304
Chants R&B 62, **63**, 137, 369
Chappaqua 83
Chappell, Geoff 195
Charles, John 42–43
Checkpoint 149
Cheltenham commune 237
Chermayeff, Serge 198, 237–38
Chippenham commune 226
Christchurch 126, 202
  apartheid protests 177
  PYM 164–65
  Stage Door **63**
  Uncool 133
  Viv Prince **58**
Christianity 252, 264–65
Christmas On Earth Continued 83
CIA 317
Citizens Association for Racial Equality (CARE) 293
Clairmont, Philip 87, 133
Clapton, Eric 187
Clark, Terry **344**, 344–46, 354–55
Clarke, Arthur C. 83
Clifford, Clark 68–69
clothes & costumes 97–98, 101–5, **103**, **104**, 208, 323–25, **324**, 337
Clothier, Barry, photo by **42**
C'mon 74–75, 192
CND march, London, 1959 **49**
Coburn, Barry 208, 210, 212, 213, 334–36
Cock 123–30, **124**, **125**, 129, **130**, 132–33, 135, 166, 170, 178, 320, 341
Cockerel Print 127
Coddington, Deborah 338
CoEnCo (New Zealand Conference on Environment and Conservation) 281
Cold War 32, 48, 50, 64, 317
Colville **218**
Colville Bay Point commune 235, 238
Comfort, Alex 113
Commercial Travellers Club 342–43
Committee on Vietnam 65–66, 126
Common Property farm 278
Commonsense Organics stores 278
communes 225–43, 355–56 *see also* specific communes

communism 32–33, 44–45, 50, 64, 161
Communist Party of New Zealand 319–20, 322
Coney, Sandra 29, 271, 305–6, 309–11
Conrad, Christina 357
consciousness raising 304
conscription 64–65
conservation 273–85
contraceptives 106–9, 369
Cook, Hera 109
Cook Street Market 337
Cooke, Don 168–69
Cooney, Dennis 259
Cooper, Rex 276
Cooper, Whina 299
Cope-Williams, Gordon, photos by **63**
Corbett, E. B. 175
Coroglen commune 237
Coromandel **92**, 235, 334 *see also* specific communes & places
Colville **218**
Corso, Gregory 80–81
costumes & clothes *see* clothes & costumes
The Counter Culture Free Press 25, 133–35, **134**, 238
counterculture, definitions 15–16, 20–21
Country Flyers 358
Covid-19 370
Craccum 93, 138, 143–44, **144**, 347
  on music 188, 201, 215
  on women's liberation 302, 308
crash pads 223–25, 296–97
Cream 187
cricket 175
Crimes Act 182
Crisp, Peter 145
Critic 135
Croixilles Ohu commune 234
Crumb, Robert 20
Crump, Barry 146–47
Cullen, Fred 'Cul', poster by **150**
Culliford, Graeme 328
culteducation.com 268
Cultural Liberation Front 142–43, 223

D

Dada Nabhaniilananda 260–62, 264
Dadson, Phil 62, 195
Daley, John, photos by **264–65**
'Damn the Dam' 279
Dancing on Our Bones 177
Dangerous Drugs Act 74
Danny 260–62, 264
Davies, Sonja 150–51
Davis, Gwenny 281
Dawson, Dr 108
Dayshur, Aysha 267–69
Delahunty, Andrew 199
Delahunty, Catherine 238, 327
Delahunty, Jim 44
Department of Maori Affairs 290

Dick Seddon's Great Dive 246
diet & food 32, 93, 208, 274,
  293–95, 356–57, 369
  organic 135, 276, 278,
    283–85
Divine Light Mission 257–60,
  341
Dobbie, Mary 107
Domestic Purposes Benefit 315
Dominion 55, 57, 91, 93, 164,
  208, 212, 303
Donaldson, Cushla 212–13
Don't Let It Get You 147
The Doors 85
The Doors of Perception 79
The Double Rainbow 239
Douglas, Roger 365
Downstage Theatre 321
Dragon 202, 212
Driving Creek 357
Drug Dependency and Drug
  Abuse Committee 346
drugs & drug taking 17, **70**,
  71–95, **76–77, 86**, 266–69,
  296, 342–44, 352, 354–55,
  363, 370 *see also* specific
  drugs
  & music 90–91, 181–82,
    190–92, 214–16
Duffy, Sean 151
Dunedin
  The Counter Culture Free
    Press 133
  Falus 127
  Highway 202
  music 199
  nuclear protests 50
Dutschke, Rudi 16
Dwyer, Bill 45, 84–85, 334,
  336, 336–37
Dyce, Tim 277
Dylan, Bob 38, 39, 81, 235, 245,
  265, 323
Dynamic Meditation 262

E

Earth and Sky 183, 185
Earwig **128–29**, 128–32, **131**,
  135, **340**
Earwig Collective 208, 213
Easy Rider 146, 245
Ecologic Foundation 282
Eden Security 212–13
Edmond, Martin 87, 144,
  357–58
Edwards, Brian 155, 307–8
Einhorn, Helmut, photo by **52**
Eisenhower, Dwight 64
Electric Picnic 192
Else, Anne 309
Embryo 195
encounter groups 269–70
environment 273–85
Eric Burdon and the Animals
  90
Esalen Institute 269
Esam, Gordon 73
Esam, John 24, **36**, 36–38, 39,
  80–83, **81**
Escarpit, Robert 122
European Economic
  Community 280
Evening Post 187
  apartheid protests 179

community living 225–26
drugs 78, 91
nuclear tests & weapons
  35, 50, 53
Vietnam War protests 68
exports 280, 353
Eyewitness News 268
Ezy, Mr & Ezy oils 325

F

Fairport Convention 208
False Witness 321
Falus 127
Falwell, Jerry 364
farming 273–85
Farnell, Billy 42
FBI 321
Federated Farmers 231, 279
The Female Eunuch 123, 306
feminism 105, 116, 135, **300**,
  301–11, **304, 307** *see also*
  Women's Liberation
Ferlinghetti, Lawrence 81,
  308
Ferret 132
festivals 190–99 *see also*
  specific festivals
Fields, John, photo by **172**
Fifth Dimension 181
First Human Be-In 15, 24
*The First New Zealand Whole
  Earth Catalogue* 309, **329**,
  333–34, 361–62 *see also*
  *The New Zealand Whole
  Earth Catalogue*
flatting 219–25
Flaws, Fane 237
Fleet, Norma 344, **344**
Focus 136
Focus On Youth 281
Folkestone Three 39
Fomison, Tony 87
food *see* diet & food
Food Reform and
  Humanitarian Society
  274
Forest Service 280, 282
forestry 280–82, 283
Foster, Frederick 40
Four Seasons Theatre 207
The Fourth Turning 355
Fowler, Roger 123, 293–95,
  294, 331, 357
France, Ross 297–98
Frank E. Evans Lunchtime
  Entertainment Band 154,
  293
Franklin, Aretha 114
Franks, Don 'Guitar Don' 242
Frater, Peter 199, **200–201**,
  202, 203
Free Speech movement 67
Freeman, Elsie 33, 50, 107
Fresh Air 199
Friends of Brutus 154
From Bottle Creek 332
From Scratch 62, 195

G

Gabolinsky, John 160
gangs 296–97 *see also*
  specific gangs
Gapes, David 89, 281

gardening 273–85
Garland, Peggy 36–37
Gay Liberation Front 118–19
  see also homosexuality;
  lesbianism
geodesic dome, Grafton
  228–29
Ghost Rite 358
Gibb, Robin 192–93
Gidlow, Bob 78
Gifford, Phil 59, 362–63
Gilbert, William 157, 165
Gillies, John 73–74, 78
Gilmore, Robert 302
Ginsberg, Allen 15, 80–81, **81**,
  83, 117, 240, 308
Glenbervie Press 332
Glover, Denis 31
Gluepot 144
Goldie, C. F. 338
Goodbye Pork Pie 127
Gooder, Claire 107
Gossen, Sam 197
Grace, Michael 191
graffiti **118**
Graham, James L. 178
Gramaphone, Malcolm
  133–35, 226–27, 238
Grant, Andy 127
Grateful Dead 15, 146
Greasy Handful 192
Great Ngaruawahia Music
  Festival **8–9, 206**, 208–13,
  209, 210–11, 334–35
*The Great Ngaruawahia Music
  Festival* (film) 212–13
Great Northern Hotel protest
  303
Green Party 317, 368
Greene, Felix 149
The Greening of America 280
Greer, Germaine 306–9, **307**,
  354
Greer, Maurice 188
Gricklegrass commune 226
Griffin, Sally, photo by **226**
Griffith, Robyn 310–11
Grimsdale, Murray 85–86,
  92–93
Grog's Own Country 44
Grosz, Chris, & cartoon by
  137, **137**
The Group 137
Gruar, Bill 136, 282
Guru Mahara Ji 235, 257–59
Gutbucket 192

H

Hagmann, Stuart 146
Haigh, Frank 91–92, 93
Hair 181–83
hair styles & beards 16–17, 20,
  22, 24, 35, 62, 98–101
Haley, Russell 87, 142
Hall, Roger 44
hallucinogens 79 *see also*
  specific drugs
Halt All Racist Tours (HART)
  175–79, 293, 298
Hamilton, National Banjo
  Pickers' Convention **191**
Hamilton County Bluegrass
  Band 75
Hamlin, Francis Rex 182

Hammond, Bill 137
Handyside, Richard 328
Hanlon, John 279
Hanly, Gil, & photo by 48, **49**, 87
Hanly, Pat 87, 145
Hans Ji Maharaj 257
Hansen, Eddie 197
Hansen, Ray 24, 227
Hansen, Søren 328
Hansen family 276
A Hard Day's Night 147
Hare Krishna movement 255–56, **256**, 276
Harewood 317–18
Harris, Aroha 290
Harris, Rex 31
HART (Halt All Racist Tours) 175–79, 293, 298
Hayward, John Roy 71–72
Hayward, Margaret 231
Hayward, Rudall 146
Health Department 107, 108, 113
Heathen Grace **189**
Heinegg, Christian, photo by **286**
Heller, Joseph 318
Hells Angels Motorcycle Club 245, 296, 349
Hendrix, Jimi 19, 85, 146, 190, 197
Henwood, Ray 94
Hepworth, David 213–14
Herald 160, 190, 207, 208
Herbs 298
Herkt, David 344, 348
heroin 225, 249, 342, 344–46, 346–48
Hesse, Hermann 122, 123
Highway **198**, 200–202, 237
Hill, Morrie, photo by **65**
Hill, Richard 62, 290
Hillary, Edmund 24, 325
Hincksman, Errol **344**
hippie trails 247–52, **250**
hitch-hiking **244**, 246–47
Ho Chi Minh 64
Hobbs, Marian 226
Hoffman, Abbie 190
Hoffmann, Anna Karina 40–42, **41**
Hofmann, Albert 79, 83
Holden, Richard 298
Holiday, Billie 72
Hollingshead, Michael 82
Holy Modal Rounders 146
Holyoake, Keith 44, 124, 313–14
& protests 53, 64–67, 69, 154, 157, 165, 171
homosexuality 31, 117–19, **118**, 135, 303, 316, 364, 369
Hopkins, John 'Hoppy', photos by **36, 81**
Hopper, Dennis 146
Horsley, Hamish **204**–5, 207
Horton, Murray 282
housing 219–25, 369, 371
Howe, Neil 355
Howze, Hamilton 64
Hubbard, L. Ron 263
Hudson, Margot Jacqueline 182
Human Instinct 188

Human Rights Act 369
Humanitarian and Anti-Vivisection Society 274
Humphrey, Hubert, & protests 68
Humphrey, Kevin 255
Hunn, J. K. 290
Hunt, Deborah 357, 358
Hunt, Gary & Paul 258
Hunt, Sam 203, 207, 327, 332, **339**
Huxley, Aldous 79–80

I

If 146
Illingworth, Michael 40, **41**, 237, 357
'Ilolahia, Will 292
Indecent Publications Tribunal 125, 330
'Inside' the Garden 87
International Poetry Incarnation 24, 80–82
International Times 24
Islands 246
Israelite House of David 24
Itch 117, 127
Iti, Tame 132, 288–89, **289**, **291**

J

Jackman, Paul 158, 160, 165
Jackson, Hana 289, 311
Jackson, Henry 142
Jackson, Moana 371
Jackson, Peter 369
Jackson, Syd 290
Jagger, Mick 36, 59, 114, 214, 349
Jam Factory **198**
James, Ken 48, 91
James, Malcolm 133–35
James, William 261
Jamieson, Lachie 40
Jenks, Lorna 40–42, **41**
Jensen, Jesper 328
Jerebine, Doug 197
Jerusalem & commune 238–43, **241**, 264, 266–67, 276–77, 341
Jesson, Bruce 368
Jesus Freaks 264
jipitecas 16
John, Elton 208, 334–35
John Mayall & the Bluesbreakers 187
Johnson, Louis 34, 224–25
Johnson, Lyndon, & protests 64–65, 68
Johnstone, Marty 343–46, 354
Jones, Brian & Ronnie 337
Jones, Debbie 117
Jones, Olive 238, 356
Jones, Selwyn 192
Jones, Tim 223, 276
Joplin, Janis 114
Jorgensen, Ronald 73–74
The Joy of Sex 113
The Joyful Crye 187–88, 323
Jumping Sundays, Albert Park **4**–5, **10**, 11–14, **13–15**, **18–19**, **23**, 154
Jung, Carl 267–68

K

Kaa, Wi Kuki 127
kaitiakitanga 273
The Kama Sutra 112–13, **113**
Kavan, Anna 30
Kebbell, Jim 277–78
Kedgley, Sue 20, 144, 301–4, **307**, 307–8, 330, 332, 341
Keen, Justin, photo by **284**
Keith, Hamish 307
Kelsey, Peter 231
Kennedy, Peter 221
Kennedy, Scott 327
Kerouac, Jack 38, 40, 43, 72, 112, 122, 240, 245
Kerr, Joan 60–61
Kesey, Ken 90, 185
King, Brian 342
King, Bruce, photo by **58**
King, Chris 17
King, George 252, **253**, 262
King, Michael 338
Kingsley Hall 267
Kinsey, Alfred 107
Kippenberger, Howard 175
Kirk, Norman 155, 169, 231, 234, 279, **312**, 313–17
Kirkland, Bruce 202
Kiwi Hotel 137, 142
Klap, Boyd 30–31
Knox, Chris 202
Kosmic Krumbia 132
Kraus, Chris 306
Kuhaupt, Siegrun 263
Ky, Air Vice-Marshal, & protest 68, **156**, 160

L

The La De Da's 208, 210
Lady Chatterley's Lover 122
Lady Sings the Blues 72
Laing, R. D. **266**, 267
Laing, Shona 365
Laking, George 65
Lands and Survey Department 231, 283
Lange, David 50–51, 293, 364
Larsen, Tony 151
Laurie, Alison 118
Lawrence, David 'Bruno' **42**
& movies 127, 148, 282, 342, 369
& music 42–43, 195, 203, **206**, 206–7, 237
Lawrence, D. H. 122
Lawrence, Veronica 203, 369
Lawrie, Jim 200–202
Leary, Timothy 79–80, 82, 185, 304
Led Lettuce **139**–41
Led Zeppelin 208, 334–35
Lee, Barry 161
Lee, Bill 160–61
Leggott, Michele 144
lesbianism 117–19, 303, 311
Lesmoir-Gordon, Nigel & Jenny 82
Lesnie, Leon, photo by **41**
Let It Bleed 214
Lett, Barry 138, 142
Lewis, C. S. 323
Lewis, Ros 243
Librettos 62

Limbidis, George 200–202
Linton, Barry, & comic by 137–38, 142–43, **144**
Lion Breweries 75, 298
Listener 34, 57, 145, 255, 264, 290, 362, 363
The Little Red Schoolbook 117, 328–31, **329**
Littlejohn 206
Living Force 256
Living Theatre Troupe 195
Livingstone, David 84
Locke, Elsie 33, 50, 107
Locke, Keith 322
Lockwood, Annea 321–22
Lodge, Henry Cabot 65
Logeman, Marian 226
London **49, 81, 336**
London School of Economics 16
Long Louis commune 227, 230
The Long Sexual Revolution 109
Lord, Richard Greville 24
The Love Machine **366**
Love Shop 264–65
Lowry, Bob 31
LSD 78–87, 90–95, 122, 138, 202, 212, 221, 231, 258
  & the law 75, 91–95, 222
  trip experiences 136, 185–86, 192, 247, 259–61, 305
  in USA 321–22
Luafutu, Fa'amoana John 188–89, 292
Lynn, Hugh 212–13
Lyons, Al, photo by **336**

M

MacDermot, Galt 181
Macdonald, Iain 182
MacGregor, Evan **189**
Mad Men 269
magazines *see* newspapers
Mahana commune 2, **236**, **272, 275, 360, 361**
Mahara Ji *see* Guru Mahara Ji
Maharishi Mahesh Yogi 254
Mahauriki, Horace 188, 297
Mahauriki, Phil 297
Mailer, Norman 178
mainstream society 28–35
Makamaka, Danny 297
The Making of a Counter Culture 21, 116, 279–80, 287
Mammal 200, **200–201**, 203, 211, 332, 342
Manapōuri dam 153, 278–81
Mandrax 114–16, 343
Mandrax Mansion, Herne Bay 114
Mann, Harvey 148, 186–87, 199, 256, **256**
Manning, A. E. 34
Manson, Charles 349
Māori 28–29, 238–43, 273, 311
  & music 188–89, 192–93
  & protests 168, 173–79, 288–99
Maori Affairs Amendment Act 168
Māori Land March **286**, 299

Maori Sovereignty 299
Māori Women's Welfare League 175, 290, 299
Marchbanks, Jim 127
marijuana 11, 17, 179, 202, 212, 234, 242, 246–47, 251, 258
  & music 81, 114, 203
  & the law 40, 71, 91, 173, 258
  effects of 37, 135–36, 214, 222, 261
Mark Young Quartet 43
Marley, Bob 190
marriage 105, 107, 112, 170, 214, 219–21, 256, 263, 270
Marriage Amendment Act 369
Marshall, Jack 308
Martin, John 338
Martin, Wally 197
Maruia Declaration 282
Maruia Society 282
Mason, Bruce 57, 182
Matheson, Margaret 318
Matthews, Sue 123, 153, 158, 304
Matusow, Harvey 321–22
Maunder, Paul 195, 198
Mayall, John 187
Mazengarb, Oswald Chettle 32, 145
Mazengarb Report 32–33, 106–7
McCartney, Paul 24
McCauley, Sue 206
McClean, Alison 222–23, 230
McDonald, Ian 195
McFarlane Street community 277–78, 296
McGowan, Elizabeth 123
McGrath, Tom 82
McGregor, Gil 327
McInnes, Heather **128–29**, 129–32, 308
McIntosh, Alister 65
McKay, Frank 242–43
McKenzie, Scott 90
McKenzie, Thomas 99
McKinnon, Walter 151
McLatchie, David 324–25, 337
McLean, Ron 279, 282
McLeod, Donald **204**, 207
McLeod, Helen **184**
McLeod, Jenny 20, 182–85, 257–58, 341
McLeod, Rosemary 101, 116, 337
McMullin, Duncan, Justice 182
McNeish, James 258
meditation & Transcendental Meditation 17, 251–52, 254, 259, 260–62
Menon, V. K. Krishna 122, 149
mental illness treatments 267–71, 278
The Merchant Adventurers of Narnia 208, 323–25, **324**, 337
Merry Pranksters 90
mescaline 186
Messiaen, Olivier 185
Metzner, Richard 80
Mexicali 39, 42
Mezzrow, Mezz 72
Mickey Mouse **350–51**
Mickey Mouse Motors 127

Middleton, Angela, photos by 104, **232–33, 247, 304**
Miles, Barry 24, 82
Miller, John, photos by **6–7, 128–29, 176, 206, 291, 294, 307**
Milne, Jonathan, & collage by 128–32, 135, 153, 213, **340**
Milnthorpe Park Scenic Reserve 283
Ministry of Maori and Island Affairs 297
Mirams, Anna 38
Mirams, Gordon 33
Mirams, Roger 31
Miss New Zealand Contest 303
Mita, Merata 243
Mitchell, Adrian 82
Mitchell, David, & photo by 37–38, 144, **196–97**
Mitchum, Robert 72
Modern Books 123
Moko: Maori Tattooing in the 20th Century 338
Monde Marie 38–39, 44, 126, 323
Mongrel Mob 202, 296
Monk, Chip 191
Monk, Thelonious 60–62, **61**, 195
The Monk Dude 260–62, 264
Moon, Sun Myung 263
Moonies 263
Morgan, Robin 302
Morris, Larry 75
Morrison, Howard 147
Morrissey, Brent 222
Morrissey, Michael 84, 93
motorbikes 245–46, **247**
Mount John 317–18
movies 31, 33, 145–48, 280, 369
Muhammad Subuh Sumohadiwidjojo 255
Muldoon, Barbara **345**
Muldoon, Robert 149–50, 155, 174, 330–31, **340, 345**, 354–55, 364
The Muldoon Annual Joke Book 330–31
Murphy, Geoff 74, 136
  & movies 127, 147–48, **148**, 237
  & music 31–32, **42**, 42–43, 282
  BLERTA 195, 206, 342
Murphy, Michael 269
Murphy, William 93
Mushroom 223
music 31, 33, 113–14, 181–217 *see also* specific musicians & bands
  albums 213–14
  blues 187
  classical 16, 38, 60
  folk 38–39, 191, 199
  jazz 39–43, 60–62, 72–74
  pop 35–36, 38, 74–75, 89
  psychedelic 87–91
  punk 202
  rock 6, 8, 9, 20–21, 33–34, 36, 62, 75, 81, 88, 185–86, 199–203
Mystic 199
mysticism 21–22, 181, 185, 246, 262, 268, 341, 369

N

Nambassa festival 360–62
Narcotics Act 74
Narnia shop 323–25, **324**
    see also The Merchant Adventurers of Narnia
Nash, Walter 28
National Banjo Pickers' Convention 191, **191**
National Blues Conventions 192
National Club 67
National Film Unit 146
National Observer 68
National Radio 78
National Student Arts Festival 199–202
National Teach-In on Vietnam 66
Native Forest Action Council 282
Needham, Julie 221
Nelson 51, 370 *see also* specific communes & places
Nelson, Elizabeth 25
Nepal **250**
Nesbitt, Graeme 199–203, 221, 342, 369
Ness, Tigilau 292
Neumegen, Dave 293
Neville, Janet 171
Neville, Richard 306
New Left 319–20
New Zealand Army 151, 154, 164, 168, 173, 314
New Zealand Broadcasting Corporation 33, 59, 60, 88–90, 114, 148, 149 *see also* radio; television
New Zealand Communist Party 319–20, 322
New Zealand Conference on Environment and Conservation (CoEnCo) 281
New Zealand Council for Nuclear Disarmament 50 *see also* nuclear protests
New Zealand Family Planning Association 107
New Zealand Herald see Herald
New Zealand Listener see Listener
New Zealand Māori Council 175, 290
New Zealand Medical Journal 84
New Zealand Nuclear Free Zone, Disarmament, and Arms Control Act 365
New Zealand Rugby Football Union 173–79
New Zealand Security Service 32
New Zealand Truth 42
New Zealand Vegetarian Society 274
The New Zealand Whole Earth Catalogue 17 *see also The First New Zealand Whole Earth Catalogue*
New Zealand Woman's Weekly 107, 259

newspapers & magazines 121–45 *see also* specific publications
Newton, John 239, 266–67
Ngā Mōkai 240, 242–43
Nga Tamatoa 132, 289, **289**, 290, **291**, 298, 333
Ngaruawahia (The Great Ngaruawahia Music Festival) 8–9, **206**, 208–13, **209**, **210**–11, 334–35
The Ngaruawahia Chronicle 208
Ngāti Hau 240–43
Nicholls, Dick 208, 282–83
Nicol, Gray 195
Nielson, Elsebeth 38
No.1 Port Depot Incident, 1970 **174**
Nock, Mike 40
Notable New Zealand Thoroughbreds 338
nuclear protests 21, 47–54, 364
    CND march, London, 1959 48, **49**
    in New Zealand 49–54, **51**, **52**
nuclear tests **46**, 50, 53
Nuttall, Jeff 47–48
Nyerere, Julius 282

O

O'Brien, Conor Cruise 149
O'Connell, Therese 151–53, 302–3
Oettli, Max, photos by **4–5**, **23**, **70**, **76–77**, **110–11**, **143**, **162–63**, **180**, **194**, **198**, **215**, **228–29**, **339**, 350–51
Ohu Scheme 231–34, **232–33**, 238
Oliver, W. H. 242–43
Ollard, Greg 344–46
Olympic Games, Mexico 16
On the Beach 51, **51**
On the Road 38, 40, 43, 72, 112, 122, 240, 245
O'Reilly, Denis 296–98
organic gardening & growing 135, 238, **275**, 276, 278, 283, 356
Original Sin 147, 199, 200
Original Sun Blues Band 192
Orpheus, Eurydice 37
O'Shea, John 31, 146–47, 321
Osmond, Humphrey 79
Otago Daily Times 122, 190, 220–21
Oz 306

P

Pacific Films 146
Page, Frederick & Evelyn 183–85
Pakistan **250**
Papesch, Claude 74
Paratene, Rawiri 288–89, **289**, 298
Parkinson, Jenny 182
Parkyn, John 170–71
Parliament, protests at **65**
Parsons, Roy 31
Parsons Bookshop 31, 122

Pasifika 190, 290, 293–99, 311, 354
The Patricia Bartlett Cookbook 331
Patterson, Hew 129
Payne, Bill 215–16
Peace, Power and Politics in Asia conference, 1968 122, 149–51, **150**, 320–21
Peace News 21
Peace Rally, Auckland Domain, 1973 **264–65**
Pearce, Arthur 'Cotton-Eyed Joe' 37–38, 88–89
Pearce, Tom 55, 59, 306
Pekapeka Festival 202, **366**, 367
Penguin Books 122
People's Park, California 15
The People's Union for Survival and Freedom 293–95, 298, 309, 357
The People's Voice 161
Perry, E. G. 182
Peterson, Bryce 73, 78, 90
Pharazyn, Pete 231, 234
Phillips, John 90
PIG (Police Investigation Group) 295
Pilcher, John 186
the Pill 107–9
Pink Floyd 146
Pipe Dreams in Ponsonby 144–45
Pipi 227, 230
Pirsig, Robert 245
Pischoff, Larry **209**, 227, 230, 259–60
Pitney, Gene 89
Plastic People of the Universe 16
Playdate 54, 102–3
Plischke, Ernst 31
Poata, Tama 175
poetry 36–38
police, NZ **41**, 119, 132–33, 243, 246, 308, 320–21, 332, 362, 364
    alcohol 73, 303
    anti-Vietnam protests 64, **65**, 68, **156**, 158, 160–61, 166–73, **167**, **172**
    apartheid protests 177–79, 318
    Auckland Police Task Force 295
    bands & concerts 54–55, **56**, 193, 201, 203
    drugs 71, 78, 85, 90–94, 108, 346–47
    industrial action 32
    Jumping Sundays 12, 14
    Māori & Pasifika 288, **294**, 295
    perception of 147, 165
    PIG (Police Investigation Group) 295
    undercover 40, 71, 74, 138
Polices Offences Amendment Act 1954 106
politics & political parties 313–21, 354, 364–65, 368–69 *see also* specific parties & politicians

INDEX 403

Pollard, Walter 166
Polson, Ron 37
Polynesian Panthers 188–89, 290–93, **291**, **294**, 295
Ponsonby Club Hotel 144
Porirua **26**
Postlewaight, Lew 368
Potiki, Brian 342
Potter, Herbert 'Bert' 269–71, 362–64
Potter, Tony 193
Pounder, Nicholas 84–85, 222, 223
Poutini, Toro 242–43
Powerhouse 211, 237
Prabhat Ranjan Sarkar 260
Prebble, Richard 365
Press 99, 258
Preston, Jan 357
The Pretty Things **58**, 59–60
Price, Hugh 44
Price, Richard 269
Prichard, Phil 200–202
Prince, Viv **58**, 59–60
Printed Matter 330
Probing Plant Structure 328
Progressive Books 123
Progressive Youth Movement 68, 157–66, 315, 318
Pryme, Lew 90, 147
The Psychedelic Experience 80
Psychedelic Id 187, 323
public bars **300**
Public Service Association 126
publications *see* newspapers & magazines; specific publications
Pūtiki, Serenity festival **204–5**, 206–7
PYM 68, 157–66, 315, 318
The PYM Colouring Book 165
PYM Organiser 158, **159**
PYM Rabble 164
PYM Rebel 164

Q

Quaalude 114–16
Quirk, Bill 318

R

Rabel, Roberto 64
radio 33, 59, 60, 88–89 *see also* New Zealand Broadcasting Corporation
Radio Hauraki 89
Rado, James 181
Rae, Ken 195
Ragni, Gerome 181
Rajneeshpuram 262
rangatiratanga 290, 299
Rata, Matiu 175, 230–31, 238
Rauhihi, Miriama 292
Ray Columbus & the Invaders 62
Raymond, Robert 208, 211, 213, 334–36
Red Army Faction 317–18, 349
Red Mole 119, 357–60
Red Rat 332
Redding, Otis 114
Redwood 70: The First National Music Convention 192–94

Reed, A. W. 'Clif' 328
Reed Education 328
Reefer Madness 71
Rees, Grynwyd 160, 161
Rees-Mogg, William 349
Reich, Charles A. 280
religions 251–71, 263–66, 352, 369 *see also* specific faiths
Renaissance commune 356
Renata, Tama 188
The Report of the Special Committee on Moral Delinquency in Children and Adolescents 32–33, 106–7
Report on the Department of Maori Affairs 290
Reserve Bank 149–50
Resistance Bookshop **120**, 123, 132, 154, 164, 257, 303, 304
Reynolds, Dick 123
Richards, Trevor 175–79, **176**, 352
Richter, Dan 80–83, **81**
Richter, Jill 81
Riddell, Alistair 142, 192
Riethmuller, Neil 318
Riley, David 78
Rique 102
Ritchie, Jane and James 'Jim' 106, 333
Riverside commune 227, 276
RNZAF, No.1 Port Depot Incident, 1970 173, **174**
road side petrol pumps **247**
Robinson, Dove-Myer 55, 154, 282
Robson, Alan 123, 166, 322
Rocking the Cradle 369
Rodwell, Sally 20, 144, 172, 357–60, **359**
Rogers, Patricia Ann 108
Rogers, William P. 157–58
Rolling Stone 190, 349
Rolling Stone, NZ edition 118, 208, 283, 334
The Rolling Stones 19, **56**, 59, 114, 172, 214–17, **215**, 349
Rollins, Sonny 40
Ronald, Rosemary 309
Rook, Conrad 83
Rose, Micky 53
Rosenberg, Gerhard 31
Rosenberg, Julian 98, 235, 238
Roszak, Theodore 21–22, 116, 279–80, 287
Rotary Club 265
Rough Justice 360
Rouse, Charlie 62
Rowbotham, Sheila 53
Rowlands, Murray 53–54
Rowles, John 181, **350–51**
Roxon, Lillian 122
Royal Forest and Bird Protection Society 279, 281–82
Rubbishers 44
Rubin, Barbara 81
Rudd, Mike 62
rugby 29, 173–79
Ruka, Reggie 210
Runaway 146–47
Russell, Marcia 155, 182
Rutherford, Philip 227, 230

S

Sache, David, photo by **55**
Salient 53–54, **134**, 135, 202, 254, 297, 342
Salmon, Dan 334
Salmon, Guy 281–82
Salmon, John 281–82
Sampson, Wayne 337
San Francisco 8, 16, 90–91, 122
Sandals of Indian Leather 102
Sanderson, Martyn 237
Sandoz Pharmaceuticals 79
Sanitarium company 274
Santa's Liquid Dream 195
sanyasi 262
Satan's Slaves 202, 207
Savage, P. P. E. 94
Save Manapouri Campaign 278–80
Sayle, Tony 20
the Scene 80–81
Scenery Preservation Society 279
Schindler, George 83
Schmidt, Andrew 360
Scholes, Jeff **236**
The School of Radiant Living 24
Scientology 262–63
Scott, Dick 362
Scratch Orchestra (NZ) **180**, **194**, 195
Seamen's Union 165
Security Intelligence Service 32, 64, 126, 157, 173, 318–21, 322–23
Seddon, Mary 39
Seeger, Pete 321
Senators 67
Serenity festival **204–5**, 206–7
Serenity Letter 207
Seresin, Chris 206, 237
Seresin, Harry 31
Seresin, Michael 147
Service Print 328
sex 105–19, **110–11**, **113**, 219–21, 301–2, 306, 352, 363, 369
 & consent 106, 116–17
 & teenagers 32–34
sexism 135, 332
Sexist Society 332
Shadbolt, Gill 48, **49**, 225
Shadbolt, Maurice 48, **49**
Shadbolt, Tim 20, 132, 142, **152**, 153–55, 166, 179, 201–2, 281, 292, 293, 304, 320, **329**, 356, 362
 Bullshit and Jellybeans 101, 308, 315, 331–32
 employment 281, 338
Shand, Tom 60
Shankar, Ravi 39, 60, 83
Shard 138
Sharples, Philip 225, 346
Shaw, Artie 72
Shelton, Gilbert 135
Sherlock, Les 62
Siddhartha 122
Simpson, Corben 206, **210–11**, 212, 213
Simpson, Tony 338
Sinclair, John 17

Sinclair, Pete 88, 192–93
Sisterhood Is Powerful 302
Skiffington, Sharon 40
Smisek, Mirek 31
Smith, Ron 161
Smith's bookshop 122
Smyth, Helen 369
Snail 230
Snoring Waters commune 237
Social Security Act 353
Socialist Forum 166
Socialist Unity Party 319
Society for Krishna Consciousness 207
Society for the Promotion of Community Standards 331
Solar Plexus 195
Somervell's Milk Bar 40
Somerville, Ross 16
Sonic Circus 195
Sonora Leather 337
Soul Talk 258
Sounds Unlimited 197
South Africa 173–79
South East Asia Treaty Organisation 149
Space Farm 185–87, **186**, 256, **256**
Sparrow, Margaret 109
Spiers, Jim 282
Spiritual Regeneration Movement 254
spiritualism & spirituality 17, 57, 82, 87, 227, 252–66, 273, 316, 354–55, 362–63
Split Enz (previously Split Ends) 202, 211–12, 358
sport 29
Spy 323
Stace, Rachel 54–55, 57, 87, 101, 103, 112, 114, 214–15, **216–17**, 221, 342
Staff, Bryan, photo by **359**
Stafford, Danny *see* Dada Nabhaniilananda
Stage Door 62, **63**, 137
Standard Press 126
Steed, John 136
Steele, Robert 31
Steele, Roger 98, **134**, 297
Stevens, Jay 80
Stevenson, Jim 142, 223–24
Stewart, Brian 347
Stewart, Keith, photos by **115**, **118**, **120**, **134**, **200–201**, **259**, **266**, **314**, **324**, **344**
Stockhausen, Karlheinz 185
Stone, David, photos by **209**, **210–11**
Stoned Guitar 188
Storm **297**, 297–98
Strauss, William 355
Strawberry Fields commune 266–67
The Strawberry Statement 146
Strewe, Odo 31
Stringer, Gilbert 149
Studd, Geoff, photos by **10**, **13–15**, **18–19**, **96**, **100**
Student and Staff Nursery Society 305
Student Congress in Curious Cove 277
Studio Jazz Club 43

Sturm, Jacqui 225, 239, 332
Subud 255
Suck 306
The Sugarbag Years: An Oral History of the 1930s Depression in New Zealand 338
Sunburst commune 231, 235
Sunday Creek commune 262
Sunday News 307
Sunday Telegraph 85
Sunday Times 136, 212
Superbag 137, **137**, 138
Sutch, Bill 123
Sutch, Helen 66
Sutcliffe, Herbert 24
Sydney Push 306

T

Tahuna Farm commune 238
Tai Tapu commune 225–26
Tamburlaine 202, 210
Tank Busters 147–48, 282
Taylor, Alister 20, 66–67, 122, 149–51, 155, 178–79, 341
as publisher 283, 320–21, **326**, 326–34, 338, 341
Taylor, Greg 237
Taylor, Maxwell 68–69
Taylor, Robert 203
Taylor, Tom 55–56
Taylor, Tony 93–94
Te Awekotuku, Ngahuia 119, 303, 311
Te Awhitu, Wiremu Hakopa Toa 240
Te Kahika, Billy 197–98, 211, 237, 257, **259**
Te Kanawa, Kiri 146–47
Te Tiriti o Waitangi 28, 166, 289, 299
Tehei, Reno 197
television 35, 122, 151–53, 155, 160, 192 *see also* New Zealand Broadcasting Corporation
Television New Zealand 268
Terrorism Suppression Act 318
Terry, Peter 360
theatre 195, 198 *see also* specific productions & groups
Theatre Action 207
Thelonious Monk Quartet, programme 61
Theosophists 274
There's Got To Be A Better Way! 365
Thomas, Barry 283, **284**, 285
Thompson, Lynda & Leo **226**
Thompson, Robin 125
Thomson, David 151
Thursday 307–8
Thwaites, Stewart 337
Tibetan Book of the Dead 80, 82
Ticket 75, 186, 202, 210–11
Time 15–16, 60, 122, 227, 264
Times 349
Tirikatene, Eruera 175
TK, Billy 197–98, 211, 237, 257, **259**
Tolepuddle 210
Tolerton, Jane 355–56

Toliafua, Wayne **294**
Tong, Marlene 74
Toogood, Selwyn 33
Traffic 199, 235
Transcendental Meditation *see* meditation & Transcendental Meditation
transgender 119
travels 247–52
Treaty of Waitangi 28, 166, 289, 299
Treefoot **209**, 227, 230, 259–60
Trocchi, Alexander 82
Troggs 114
Truman doctrine 319
Trussell, Denys 281
Truth 75
Tuirirangi, Kemp 188, 206, 237
Turnbull, Frank 263
Tuwhare, Hone 207

U

Uncool 133
Under the Sun 257–58
Underdogs 74–75, 148, 187
Underground Press 135
Unification Church 263
University Arts Festival 199
University of Otago 219–21
Usmani, Arif 293
USS *Buchanan* 364
USS *Frank E. Evans* 293

V

vaccinations & anti-vaccinations 370
Values Party 315–17
Van der Ryn, Sim 198
van Ruyssevelt, Bob 168–69
The Varieties of Religious Experience: A Study in Human Nature 261
Veart, Dave 274
vegetarianism 274–75, 369
Vere-Jones, Peter 320–21
Verschaffelt, Peter 179
Victoria University Jazz Club 43
Vietnam Quote & Comment 126
Vietnam War & protests 12, 16, 21, 62–69, 149–50, 157–66, 166–73, 203, 226–27, 298, 309, 314, 320–21
Villard, Nick 39
Vipassana 260
Volkerling, Keir 199
Volkerling, Ngahuia 119, 303, 311
Vulcan Lane, Auckland 12, 41, 160

W

Waikato Times 154
Waimarama Beach commune 237, 310
Waitangi & Waitangi Day 28, 168

INDEX   405

Waitati commune 226–27
Waitati Militia 226–27
Walton, Bob 74, 94, 346
Ward, Clare **8–9**
Wareham, J. A. 310
Wark, Betty 311
Warkworth, Australasian Architecture Student Association Congress, 1971 **196–97**, 198
Warren, Phil 192, 194
Washday at the Pa 28
Waters, Muddy 283
Watkin, Ian 237
Watts, Alan 255
The Way of Zen 255
Weather Underground 317–18, 349
Webster, Lenore 20
Wedde, Ian 246, 305
Wein, George 60
Wellington **115**
   1962 nuclear protest march **52**
   abortion march **314**
   The Beatles tour **55**
   cabbage garden 283, **284**
   Civic Square **86**
   Māori Land March **286**
   Narnia shop 324
   Parliament **289**
   Resistance Bookshop, Willis St **120**
   Town Hall **167**
   Town Hall, Rolling Stones concert **56**
   Victoria University **118**, **200–201**
Wellington in the '60s: The Way It Seemed 321
Wenner, Jann 349
Westra, Ans, & photos by 28, 86, **125**, **244**, **256**, **275**, **366**
Wheeler, Christopher Robin 'Chris' **125**, 125–27, 155, 334–36, 341, 346–47
   Cock 129, 130–33, 166, 178, 320–21
Whicker, Alan 301–2
Whitcher, Gary 33
White, David 323–25
White, Patrick 80
White, Tom 98
White Rabbit Puppet Theatre 358
Whiteford, Helen 127
Whole Earth Catalogs 332–33
The Whole World Watches 178–79
Wichtel, Diana 281
Wickliffe, Dean 278
Wilcox, Andy 161–62
Wilcox, Vic 161, 164, 319
Wilderland community 276
Wilkes, Owen 317
Wilkinson, Max 338
Williams, Billy 186–87, 210–11
Williams, Rangi 192
Williams, Robin 219–21
Williams, Tony 147
Willoughby, Trix 223–24
Wilson, Clive 327
Wilson, Jude 251
Wilson, Peter 207
Wilson, René **70**

Winchester commune 225–26
Winder, Duncan, photo by **26**
Windsor Free Festival 336–37
Winnie, Max 39
Wishart, Kitty 309
Witten-Hannah, Kubi 129, 132
Wollstonecraft, Mary 105
Woman Today 50
Woman's Weekly see New Zealand Woman's Weekly
Women for Equality 303
Women's Liberation *see also* feminism
   Women's Liberation Front 303
   Women's Liberation movement 301–11, 332, 355
Wood, Marion 277–78
Woodbourne 317–18
Woodley, Bruce 335
Woodstock 17, 190–92
Woodstock (film) 146, 191
Woodstock Nation 190
Woodward, Mary 50
Wootton, Wendy 267–69
The Word Is Freed 142–43
World Psychedelic Centre 82
Wright, Gridley Lorimer 266–67
Wylie, Gerald 'Joe', & comic by 138, **139–41**
Wynne, Blanche 308

Y

Yardbirds 145–46
Yates, Deborah 62, 85–86, 92–93, 161, 222
Yelash, John 73
yoga 252–53, 369
Young, Garth 181
Young, Hugh 51, 105–6
Young, Mark 36, 43, 53, 91–92
Young, Venn 234
Youth CND 51, **51**, 62, 65, 160–61
Yska, Redmer 78

Z

Zabriskie Point 145–46
Zen and the Art of Motorcycle Maintenance 245
Zen Buddhism 255 *see also* Buddhism
Zolov, Eric 18

Photo by Robert Cross

Nick Bollinger is a Wellington-based writer, broadcaster and critic. He was a music columnist for the *Listener* for more than twenty years, a writer for *Mojo* and the voice of Radio New Zealand's music review programme *The Sampler*. He is the author of *How to Listen to Pop Music* (2004), *100 Essential New Zealand Albums* (2009) and *Goneville: A Memoir* (2016), all published by Awa Press. Originally a thesis written for the creative non-fiction programme at the International Institute of Modern Letters, the manuscript of *Goneville* won the 2015 Adam Foundation Prize in Creative Writing and was longlisted for the New Zealand Book Awards.

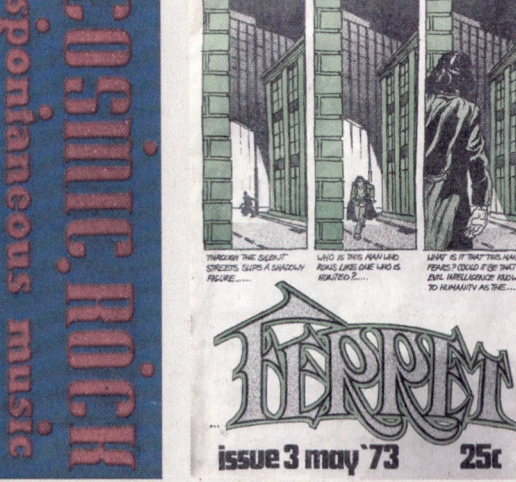

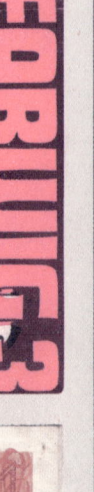